CHIP ZDARSKY ERICA HENDERSON

Jughead®

VOLUME ONE

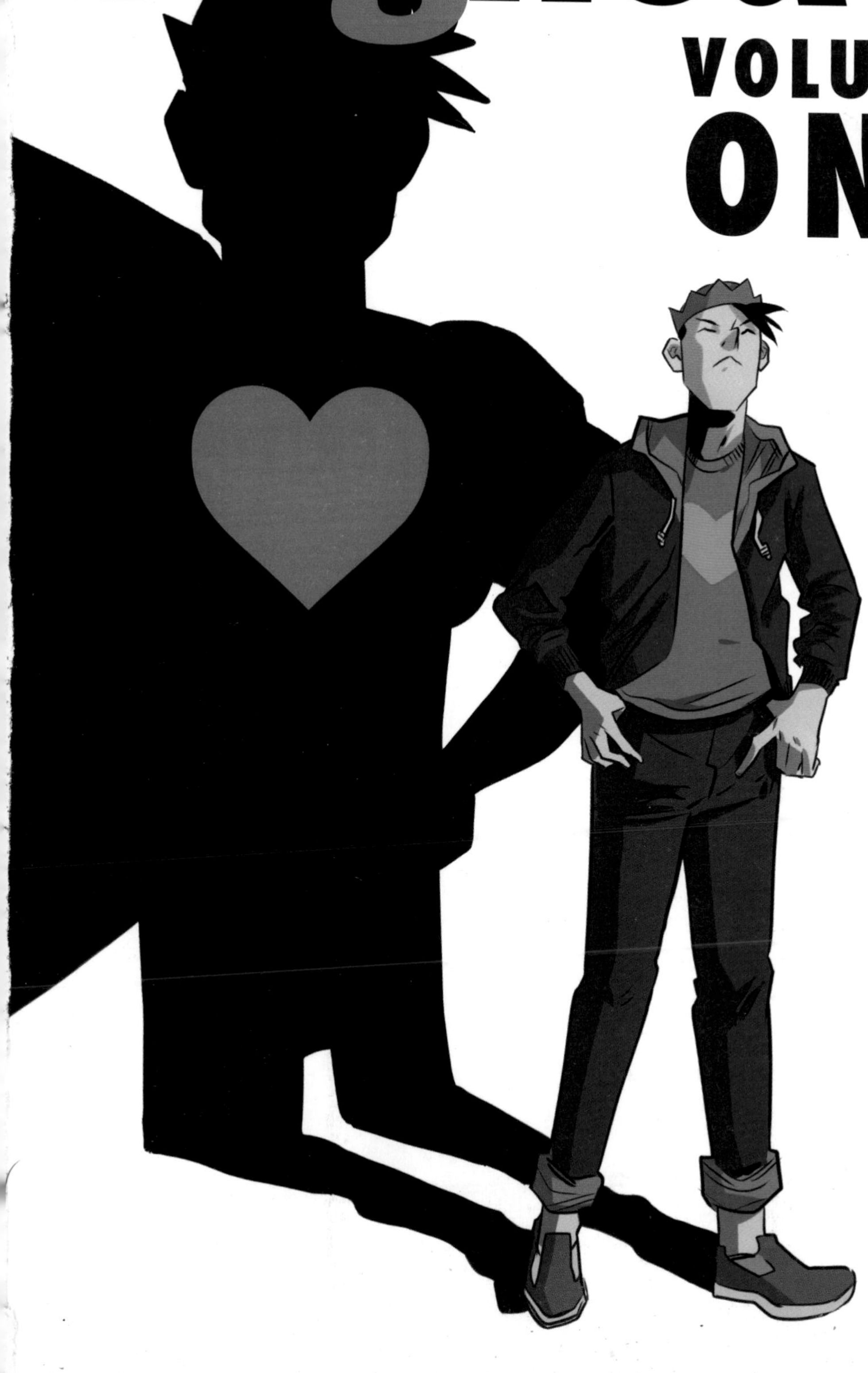

STORY BY:
CHIP ZDARSKY

ART BY:
ERICA HENDERSON

COLORING BY:
ANDRE SZYMANOWICZ
(ISSUES 5-6)

LETTERING BY:
JACK MORELLI

PUBLISHER:
JON GOLDWATER

EDITOR:
MIKE PELLERITO

THE LEGEND HIMSELF

Jughead®

HEY EVERYBODY, JUGHEAD JONES HERE. First off, I want to thank you all for picking up my book! I know what you're thinking: how could anyone resist purchasing a graphic novel featuring an ALL NEW REIMAGINING of a CLASSIC ICON starring yours truly? I don't know, but I'd hate to meet any of those people. They're probably weirdoes who don't enjoy video games and don't have great taste in food and literature and comics and ART.

But you, my friends, have great taste in all those things I'm sure. That's why you're here— but enough about you, more about me.

Sometime in the summer of 2015, my best pal Archie Andrews took a little break from the tough rigmarole that is high school life and came back a changed man. What I mean is that he came back "hot," as you kids would say. That was due in large part to two very important friends he met: MARK WAID and FIONA STAPLES (you should really check him out, I hear he has a book kind of like mine in finer book stores now. I'll give you a moment to run out and buy it or download it on your fancy smart phone if you haven't yet. Go ahead. I'll wait.)

Ok good, you're back. ANYWAY, I still haven't gotten to the part where I come in. MARK and FIONA also had some pals 'n' gals named CHIP ZDARSKY and ERICA HENDERSON who were eagerly awaiting the chance to make another transformation on another important person in Riverdale (this is the part where I come in). LO AND BEHOLD an all-new *Jughead* series was born! Personally, I'm not one for change (you'll notice that in the stories you're about to read), but CHIP and ERICA were an unstoppable force that changed my life for the best.

I'm excited to see what the future of Riverdale brings.

But mostly I'm excited to see how many burgers I can buy once the sweet, sweet $$$ from this graphic novel comes rolling in. So thanks especially for that, friends.

Yours truly,

JUGHEAD

Forsythe Pendleton Jones III

ISSUE ONE

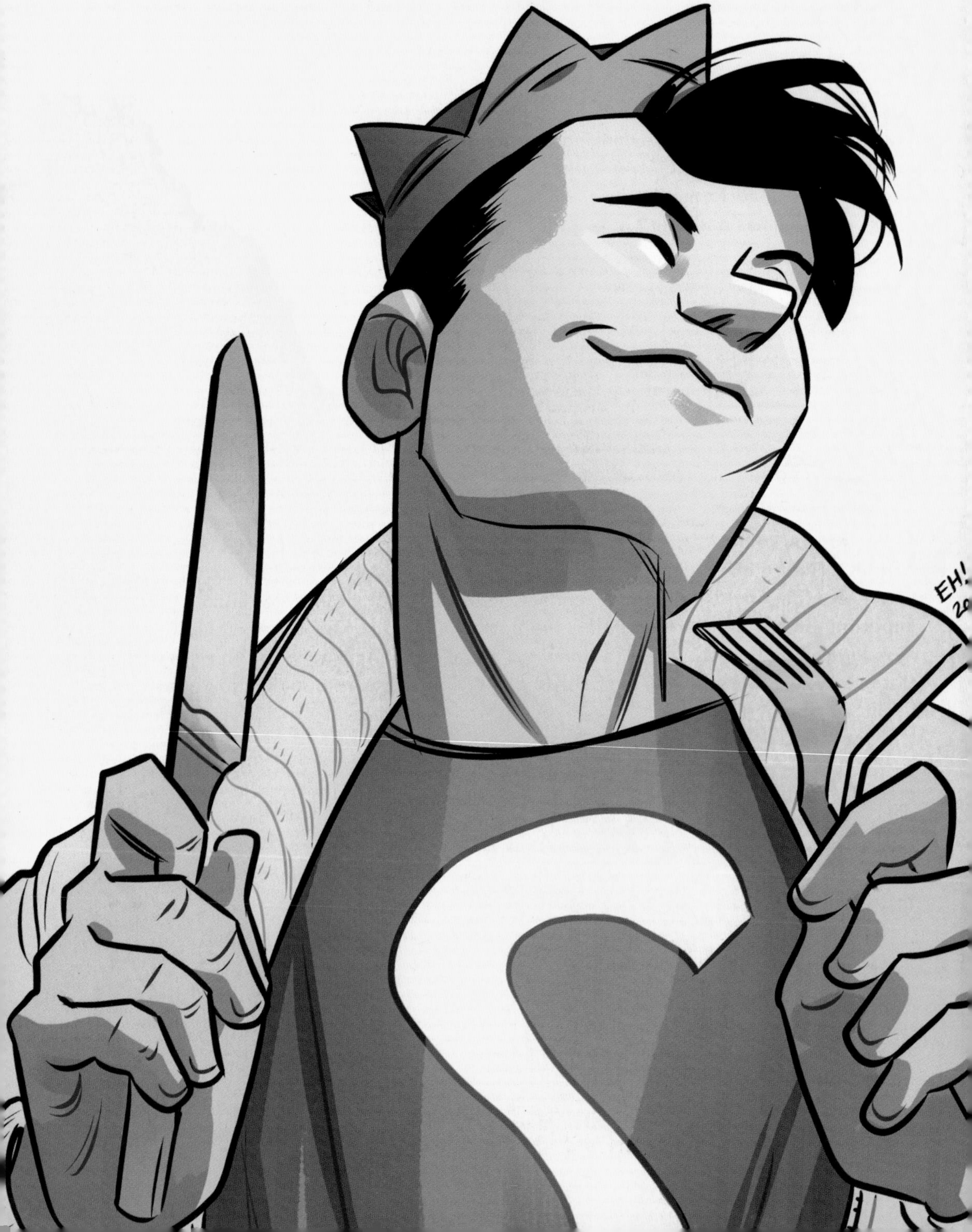

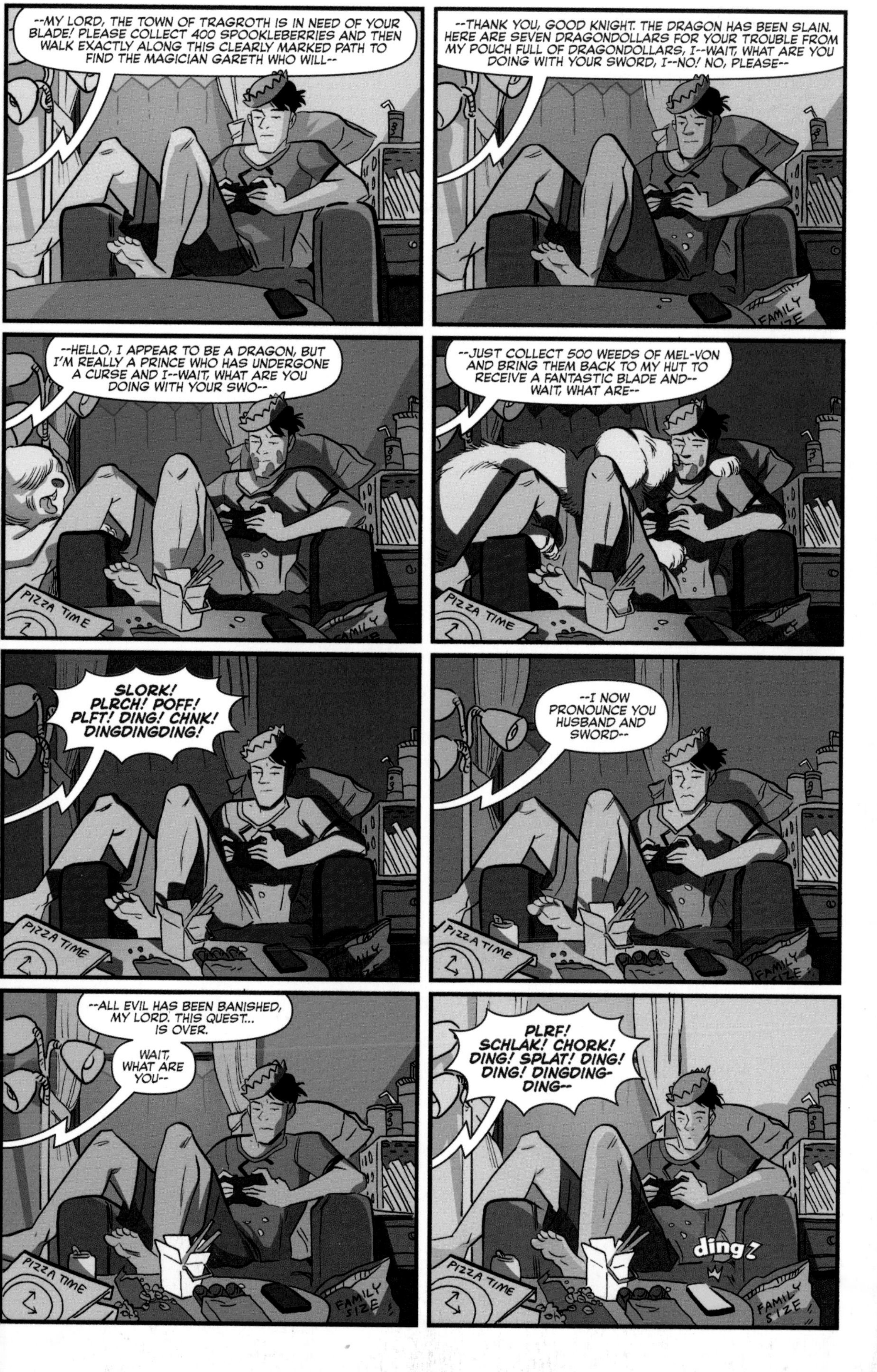
--MY LORD, THE TOWN OF TRAGROTH IS IN NEED OF YOUR BLADE! PLEASE COLLECT 400 SPOOKLEBERRIES AND THEN WALK EXACTLY ALONG THIS CLEARLY MARKED PATH TO FIND THE MAGICIAN GARETH WHO WILL--
--THANK YOU, GOOD KNIGHT. THE DRAGON HAS BEEN SLAIN. HERE ARE SEVEN DRAGONDOLLARS FOR YOUR TROUBLE FROM MY POUCH FULL OF DRAGONDOLLARS, I--WAIT, WHAT ARE YOU DOING WITH YOUR SWORD, I--NO! NO, PLEASE--
--HELLO, I APPEAR TO BE A DRAGON, BUT I'M REALLY A PRINCE WHO HAS UNDERGONE A CURSE AND I--WAIT, WHAT ARE YOU DOING WITH YOUR SWO--
--JUST COLLECT 500 WEEDS OF MEL-VON AND BRING THEM BACK TO MY HUT TO RECEIVE A FANTASTIC BLADE AND--WAIT, WHAT ARE--
SLORK! PLRCH! POFF! PLFT! DING! CHNK! DINGDINGDING!
--I NOW PRONOUNCE YOU HUSBAND AND SWORD--
--ALL EVIL HAS BEEN BANISHED, MY LORD. THIS QUEST... IS OVER.
WAIT, WHAT ARE YOU--
PLRF! SCHLAK! CHORK! DING! SPLAT! DING! DING! DINGDING-DING--
dingZ

ARCHIE COMICS PROUDLY PRESENTS

JUGHEAD

LOVINGLY BROUGHT TO YOU BY

CHIP & ERICA

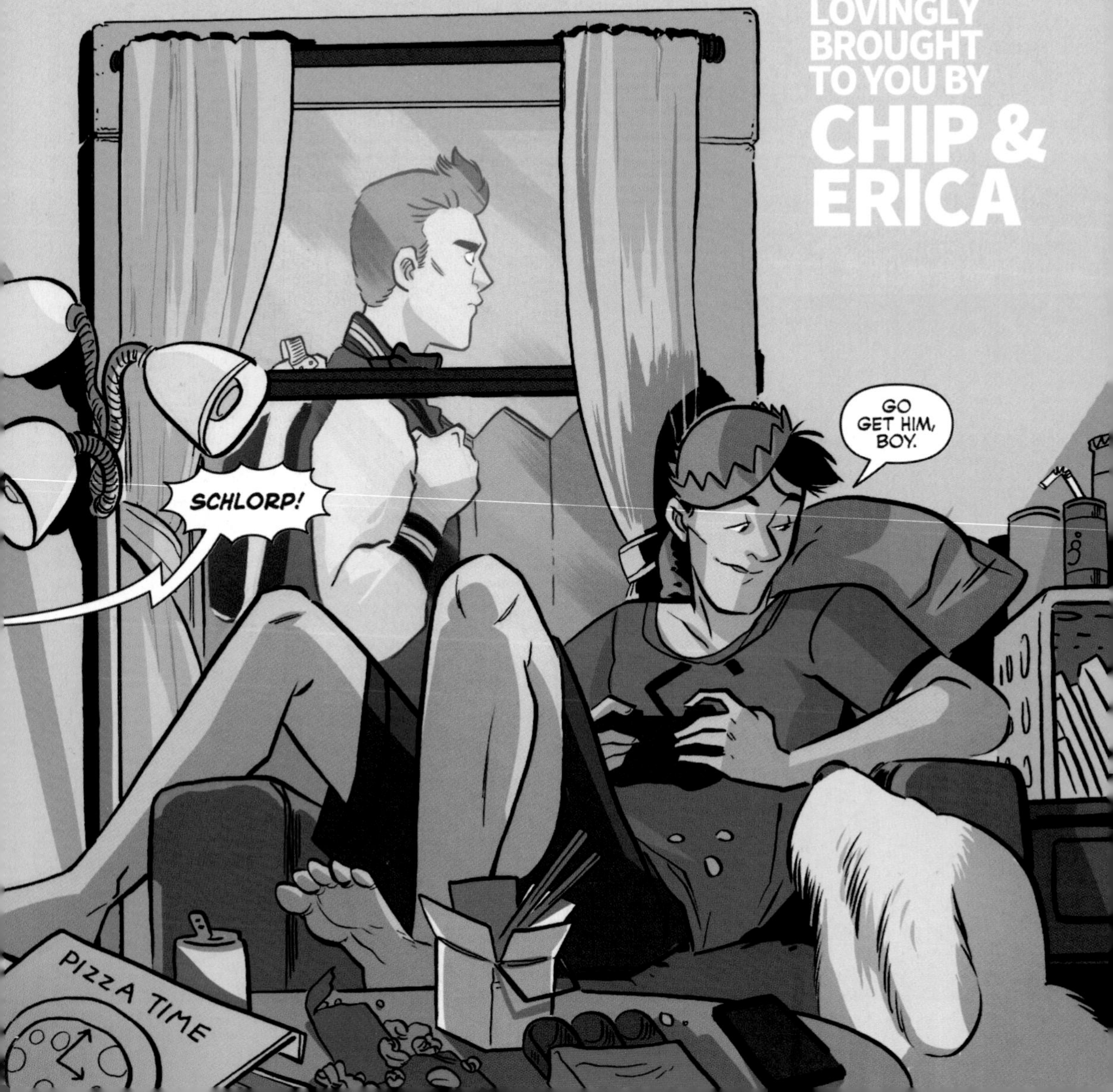
GO GET HIM, BOY.
SCHLORP!
PIZZA TIME

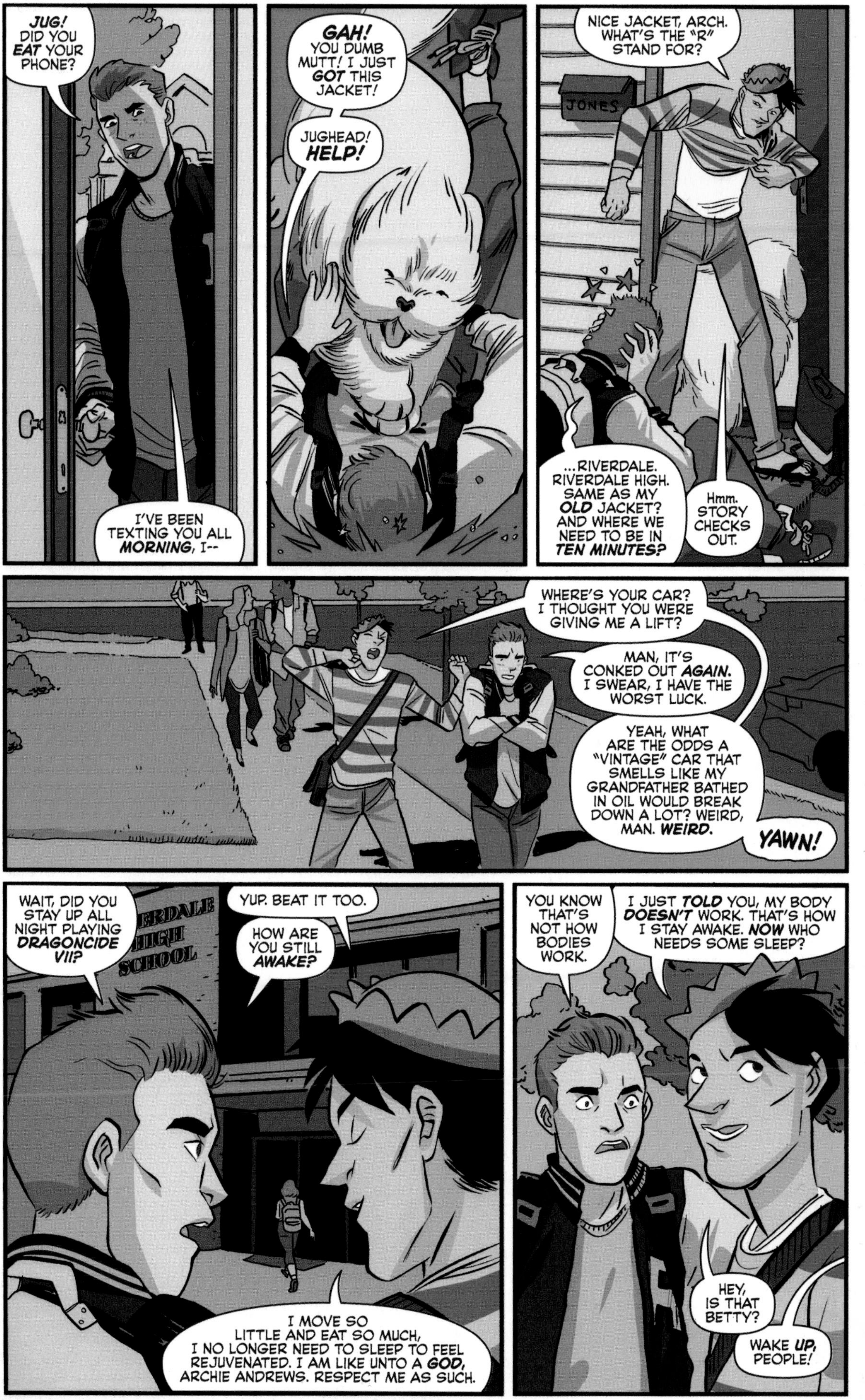
JUG! DID YOU EAT YOUR PHONE?
I'VE BEEN TEXTING YOU ALL MORNING, I--
GAH! YOU DUMB MUTT! I JUST GOT THIS JACKET!
JUGHEAD! HELP!
NICE JACKET, ARCH. WHAT'S THE "R" STAND FOR?
JONES
...RIVERDALE. RIVERDALE HIGH. SAME AS MY OLD JACKET? AND WHERE WE NEED TO BE IN TEN MINUTES?
Hmm. STORY CHECKS OUT.
WHERE'S YOUR CAR? I THOUGHT YOU WERE GIVING ME A LIFT?
MAN, IT'S CONKED OUT AGAIN. I SWEAR, I HAVE THE WORST LUCK.
YEAH, WHAT ARE THE ODDS A "VINTAGE" CAR THAT SMELLS LIKE MY GRANDFATHER BATHED IN OIL WOULD BREAK DOWN A LOT? WEIRD, MAN. WEIRD.
YAWN!
WAIT, DID YOU STAY UP ALL NIGHT PLAYING DRAGONCIDE VII?
YUP. BEAT IT TOO.
HOW ARE YOU STILL AWAKE?
I MOVE SO LITTLE AND EAT SO MUCH, I NO LONGER NEED TO SLEEP TO FEEL REJUVENATED. I AM LIKE UNTO A GOD, ARCHIE ANDREWS. RESPECT ME AS SUCH.
YOU KNOW THAT'S NOT HOW BODIES WORK.
I JUST TOLD YOU, MY BODY DOESN'T WORK. THAT'S HOW I STAY AWAKE. NOW WHO NEEDS SOME SLEEP?
HEY, IS THAT BETTY?
WAKE UP, PEOPLE!

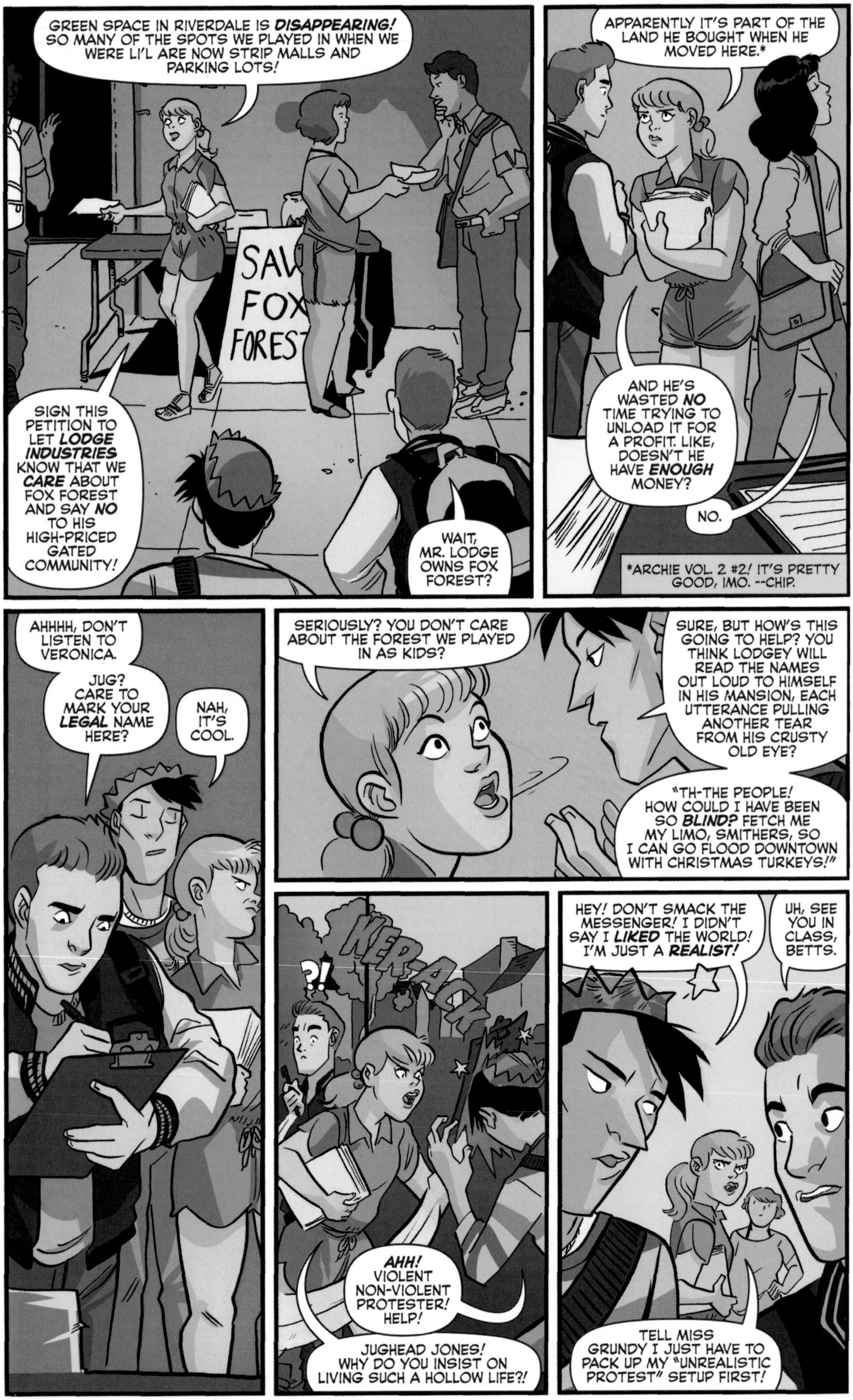
GREEN SPACE IN RIVERDALE IS DISAPPEARING! SO MANY OF THE SPOTS WE PLAYED IN WHEN WE WERE LI'L ARE NOW STRIP MALLS AND PARKING LOTS!
SAVE FOX FOREST
SIGN THIS PETITION TO LET LODGE INDUSTRIES KNOW THAT WE CARE ABOUT FOX FOREST AND SAY NO TO HIS HIGH-PRICED GATED COMMUNITY!
WAIT, MR. LODGE OWNS FOX FOREST?
APPARENTLY IT'S PART OF THE LAND HE BOUGHT WHEN HE MOVED HERE.*
AND HE'S WASTED NO TIME TRYING TO UNLOAD IT FOR A PROFIT. LIKE, DOESN'T HE HAVE ENOUGH MONEY?
NO.
*ARCHIE VOL. 2 #2! IT'S PRETTY GOOD, IMO. --CHIP.
AHHHH, DON'T LISTEN TO VERONICA.
JUG? CARE TO MARK YOUR LEGAL NAME HERE?
NAH, IT'S COOL.
SERIOUSLY? YOU DON'T CARE ABOUT THE FOREST WE PLAYED IN AS KIDS?
SURE, BUT HOW'S THIS GOING TO HELP? YOU THINK LODGEY WILL READ THE NAMES OUT LOUD TO HIMSELF IN HIS MANSION, EACH UTTERANCE PULLING ANOTHER TEAR FROM HIS CRUSTY OLD EYE?
"TH-THE PEOPLE! HOW COULD I HAVE BEEN SO BLIND? FETCH ME MY LIMO, SMITHERS, SO I CAN GO FLOOD DOWNTOWN WITH CHRISTMAS TURKEYS!"
KER-ACK
?!
AHH! VIOLENT NON-VIOLENT PROTESTER! HELP!
JUGHEAD JONES! WHY DO YOU INSIST ON LIVING SUCH A HOLLOW LIFE?!
HEY! DON'T SMACK THE MESSENGER! I DIDN'T SAY I LIKED THE WORLD! I'M JUST A REALIST!
UH, SEE YOU IN CLASS, BETTS.
TELL MISS GRUNDY I JUST HAVE TO PACK UP MY "UNREALISTIC PROTEST" SETUP FIRST!

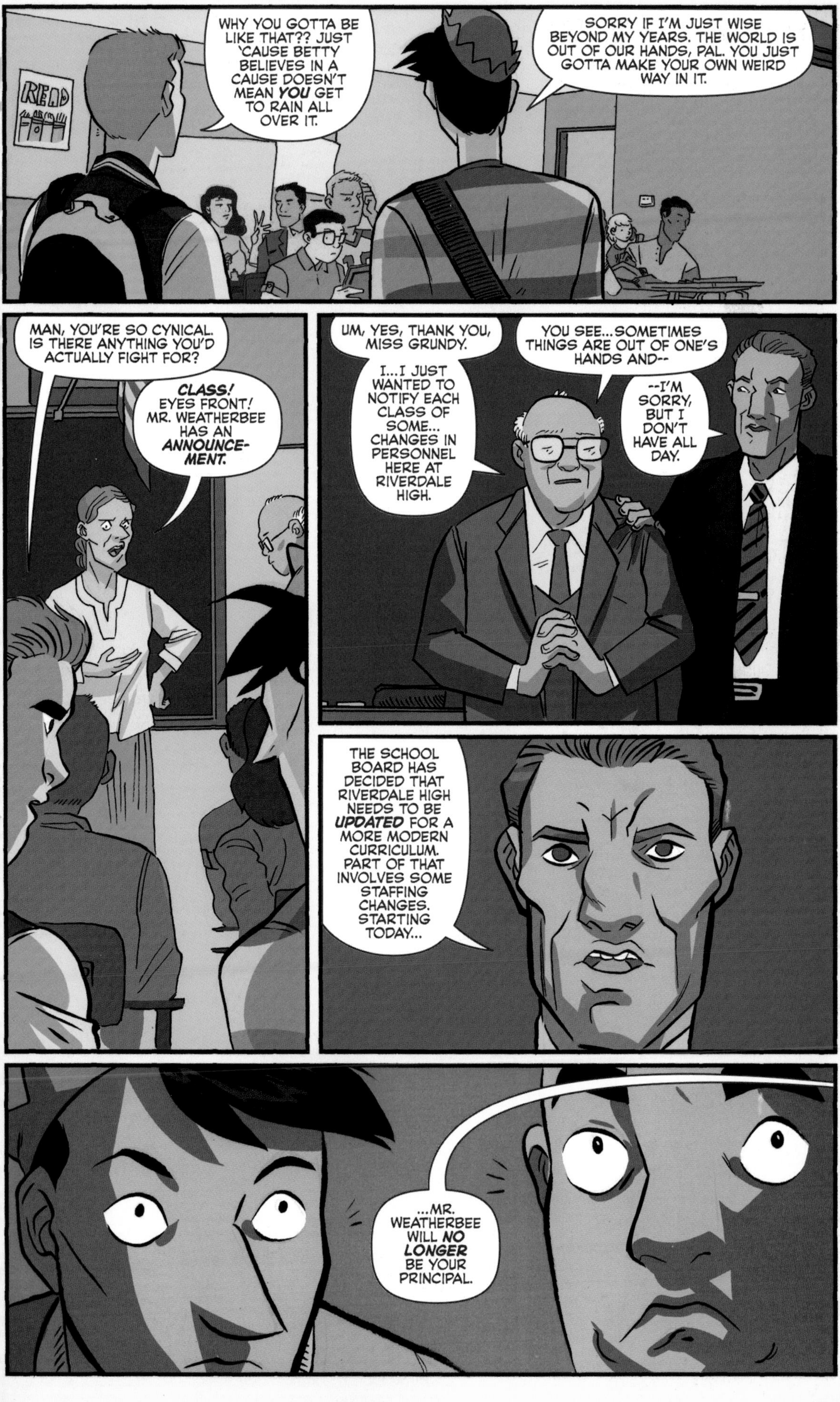
WHY YOU GOTTA BE LIKE THAT?? JUST 'CAUSE BETTY BELIEVES IN A CAUSE DOESN'T MEAN ***YOU*** GET TO RAIN ALL OVER IT.
SORRY IF I'M JUST WISE BEYOND MY YEARS. THE WORLD IS OUT OF OUR HANDS, PAL. YOU JUST GOTTA MAKE YOUR OWN WEIRD WAY IN IT.
READ
MAN, YOU'RE SO CYNICAL. IS THERE ANYTHING YOU'D ACTUALLY FIGHT FOR?
CLASS! EYES FRONT! MR. WEATHERBEE HAS AN ***ANNOUNCEMENT.***
UM, YES, THANK YOU, MISS GRUNDY.
I...I JUST WANTED TO NOTIFY EACH CLASS OF SOME... CHANGES IN PERSONNEL HERE AT RIVERDALE HIGH.
YOU SEE...SOMETIMES THINGS ARE OUT OF ONE'S HANDS AND--
--I'M SORRY, BUT I DON'T HAVE ALL DAY.
THE SCHOOL BOARD HAS DECIDED THAT RIVERDALE HIGH NEEDS TO BE ***UPDATED*** FOR A MORE MODERN CURRICULUM. PART OF THAT INVOLVES SOME STAFFING CHANGES. STARTING TODAY...
...MR. WEATHERBEE WILL ***NO LONGER*** BE YOUR PRINCIPAL.

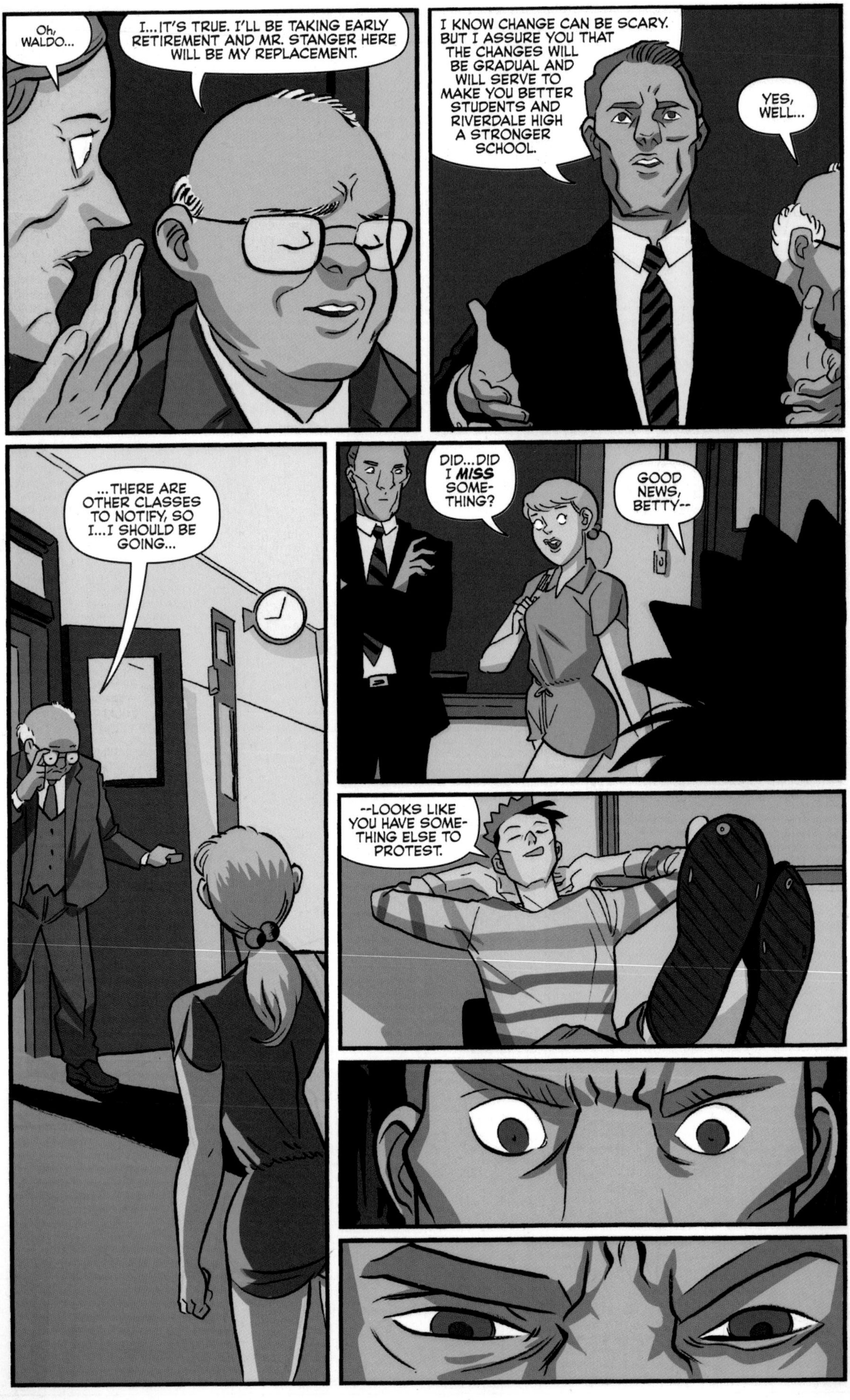
Oh, WALDO...
I...IT'S TRUE. I'LL BE TAKING EARLY RETIREMENT AND MR. STANGER HERE WILL BE MY REPLACEMENT.
I KNOW CHANGE CAN BE SCARY. BUT I ASSURE YOU THAT THE CHANGES WILL BE GRADUAL AND WILL SERVE TO MAKE YOU BETTER STUDENTS AND RIVERDALE HIGH A STRONGER SCHOOL.
YES, WELL...
...THERE ARE OTHER CLASSES TO NOTIFY, SO I...I SHOULD BE GOING...
DID...DID I MISS SOME-THING?
GOOD NEWS, BETTY--
--LOOKS LIKE YOU HAVE SOME-THING ELSE TO PROTEST.

Jughead *in*

GAME OF JONES

THE WILD ONE IS GONE, JUGHEAD JONES. MY HEART... IS NOW AS COLD AS CREAMED ICE.

UGH. YOU KNOW NOTHING, ARCHIE ANDREWS. SHE JUST TRANSFERRED TO VALORIUS TECH. BIG WHOOP.

YOU KNOW NOTHING OF LOVE! CHERYL AND I WERE *FOREVER!* NOW SHE LIVES THIRTY MILES AWAY AND MY HORSE IS CONSTANTLY AT THE VET!

HEY, SERVES YOU RIGHT FOR FALLING IN LOVE WITH A PERSON. IT'S A GAME YOU CAN NEVER WIN, OLD FRIEND, WHICH IS WHY MY HEART ONLY BELONGS TO...

...*FOOD??*

DOWN-GRADED TO GREYMEAL FER THE FORESEEABLE FUTURE, KIDS. CUTBACKS.

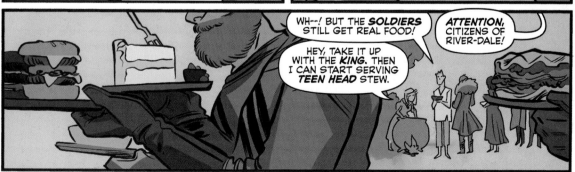

WH--! BUT THE *SOLDIERS* STILL GET REAL FOOD!

HEY, TAKE IT UP WITH THE *KING.* THEN I CAN START SERVING *TEEN HEAD* STEW.

ATTENTION, CITIZENS OF RIVER-DALE!

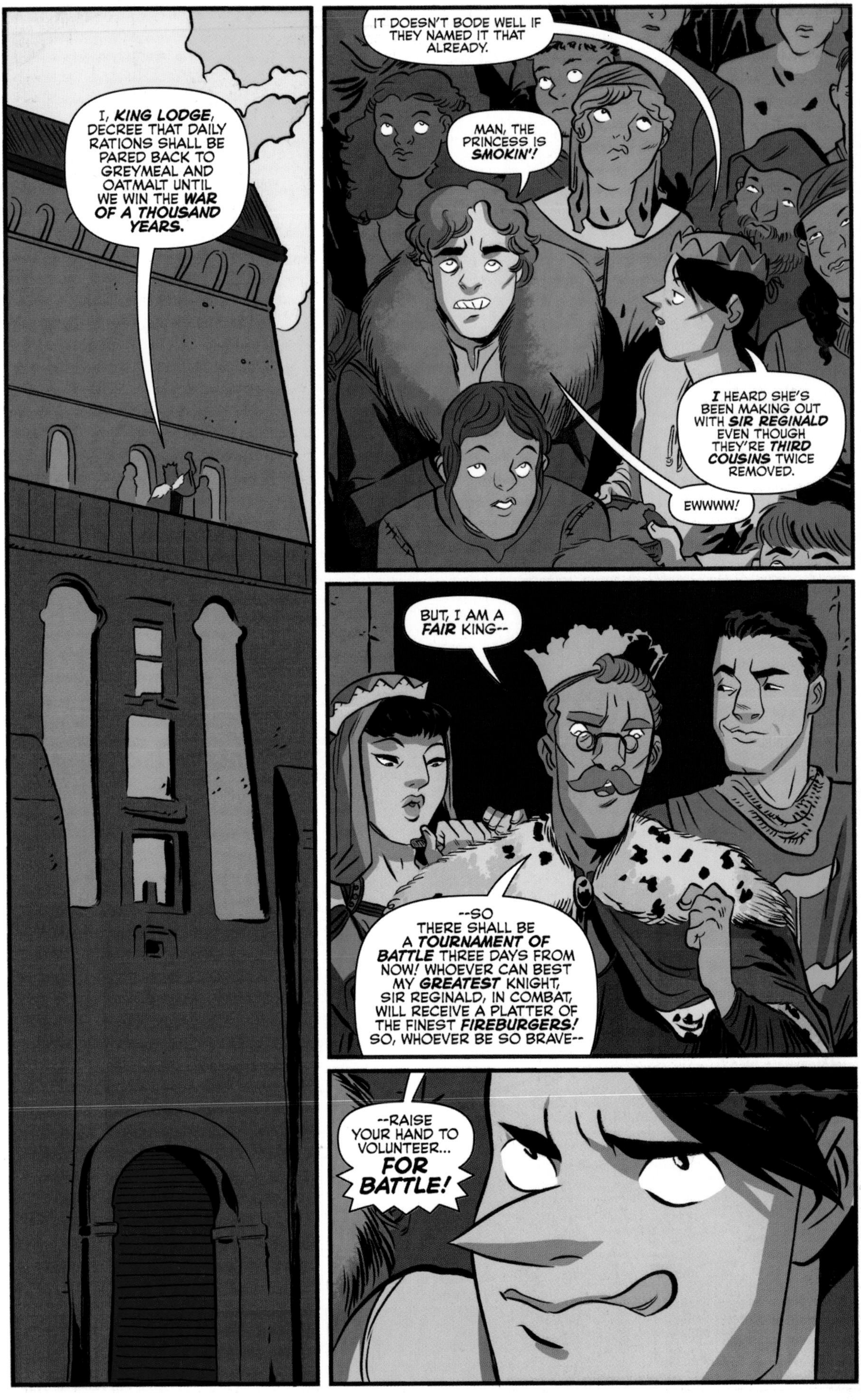
I, KING LODGE, DECREE THAT DAILY RATIONS SHALL BE PARED BACK TO GREYMEAL AND OATMALT UNTIL WE WIN THE WAR OF A THOUSAND YEARS.
IT DOESN'T BODE WELL IF THEY NAMED IT THAT ALREADY.
MAN, THE PRINCESS IS SMOKIN'!
I HEARD SHE'S BEEN MAKING OUT WITH SIR REGINALD EVEN THOUGH THEY'RE THIRD COUSINS TWICE REMOVED.
EWWWW!
BUT, I AM A FAIR KING--
--SO THERE SHALL BE A TOURNAMENT OF BATTLE THREE DAYS FROM NOW! WHOEVER CAN BEST MY GREATEST KNIGHT, SIR REGINALD, IN COMBAT, WILL RECEIVE A PLATTER OF THE FINEST FIREBURGERS! SO, WHOEVER BE SO BRAVE--
--RAISE YOUR HAND TO VOLUNTEER... FOR BATTLE!

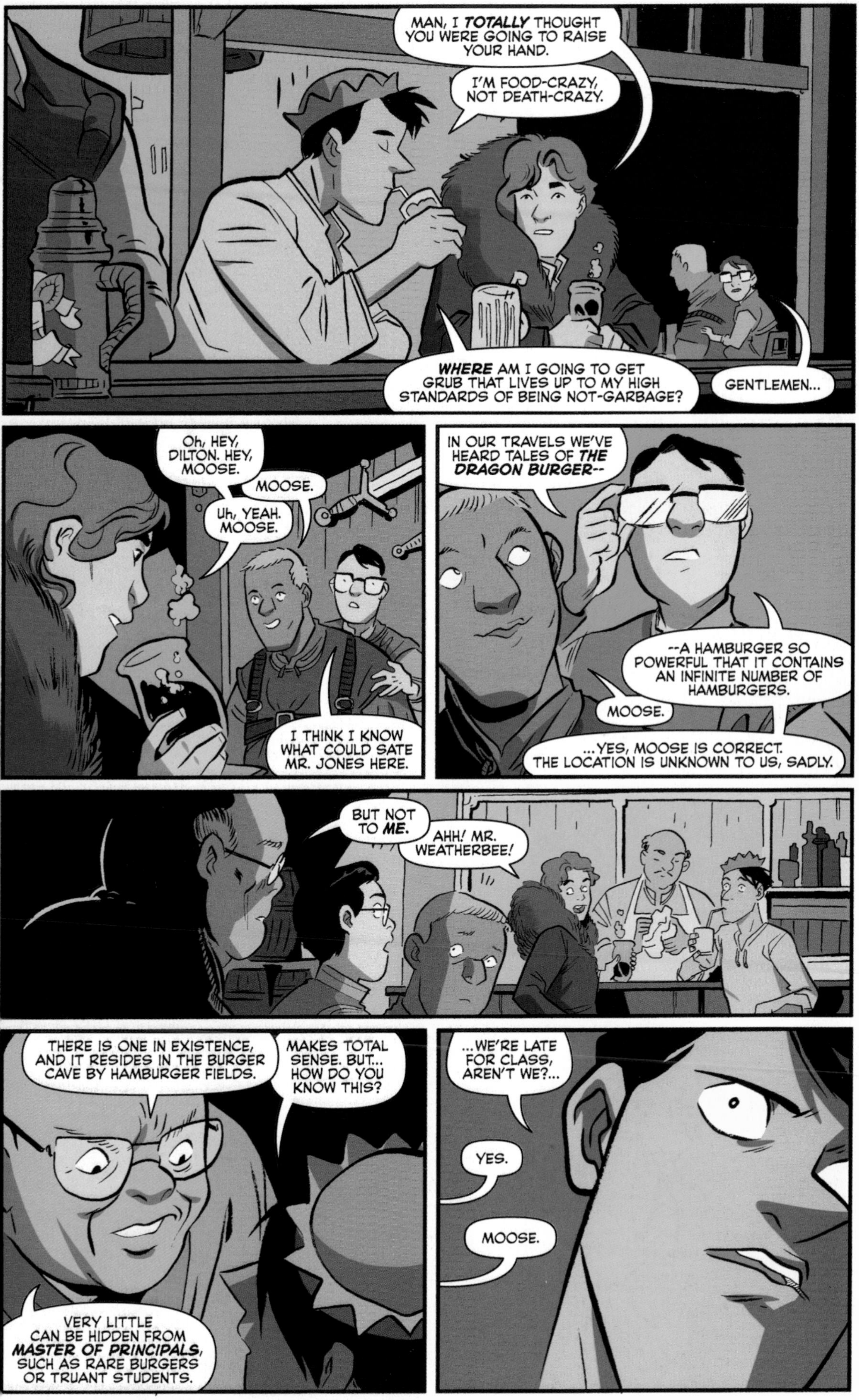
MAN, I TOTALLY THOUGHT YOU WERE GOING TO RAISE YOUR HAND.
I'M FOOD-CRAZY, NOT DEATH-CRAZY.
WHERE AM I GOING TO GET GRUB THAT LIVES UP TO MY HIGH STANDARDS OF BEING NOT-GARBAGE?
GENTLEMEN...
Oh, HEY, DILTON. HEY, MOOSE.
MOOSE.
Uh, YEAH. MOOSE.
I THINK I KNOW WHAT COULD SATE MR. JONES HERE.
IN OUR TRAVELS WE'VE HEARD TALES OF THE DRAGON BURGER--
--A HAMBURGER SO POWERFUL THAT IT CONTAINS AN INFINITE NUMBER OF HAMBURGERS.
MOOSE.
...YES, MOOSE IS CORRECT. THE LOCATION IS UNKNOWN TO US, SADLY.
BUT NOT TO ME.
AHH! MR. WEATHERBEE!
THERE IS ONE IN EXISTENCE, AND IT RESIDES IN THE BURGER CAVE BY HAMBURGER FIELDS.
MAKES TOTAL SENSE. BUT... HOW DO YOU KNOW THIS?
VERY LITTLE CAN BE HIDDEN FROM MASTER OF PRINCIPALS, SUCH AS RARE BURGERS OR TRUANT STUDENTS.
...WE'RE LATE FOR CLASS, AREN'T WE?...
YES.
MOOSE.

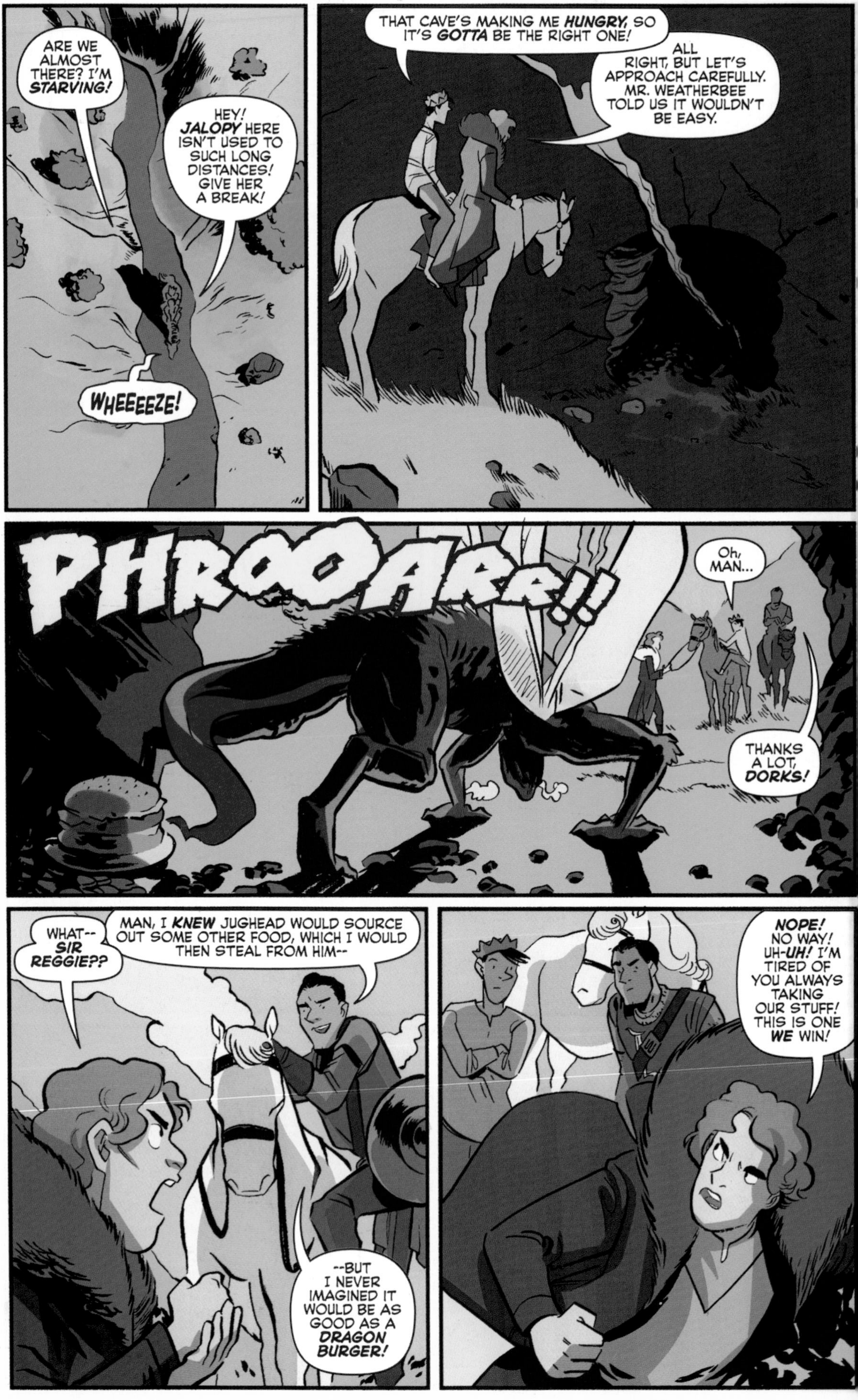
ARE WE ALMOST THERE? I'M STARVING!
HEY! JALOPY HERE ISN'T USED TO SUCH LONG DISTANCES! GIVE HER A BREAK!
WHEEEEZE!
THAT CAVE'S MAKING ME HUNGRY, SO IT'S GOTTA BE THE RIGHT ONE!
ALL RIGHT, BUT LET'S APPROACH CAREFULLY. MR. WEATHERBEE TOLD US IT WOULDN'T BE EASY.
PHROOARR!!
Oh, MAN...
THANKS A LOT, DORKS!
WHAT-- SIR REGGIE??
MAN, I KNEW JUGHEAD WOULD SOURCE OUT SOME OTHER FOOD, WHICH I WOULD THEN STEAL FROM HIM--
--BUT I NEVER IMAGINED IT WOULD BE AS GOOD AS A DRAGON BURGER!
NOPE! NO WAY! UH-UH! I'M TIRED OF YOU ALWAYS TAKING OUR STUFF! THIS IS ONE WE WIN!

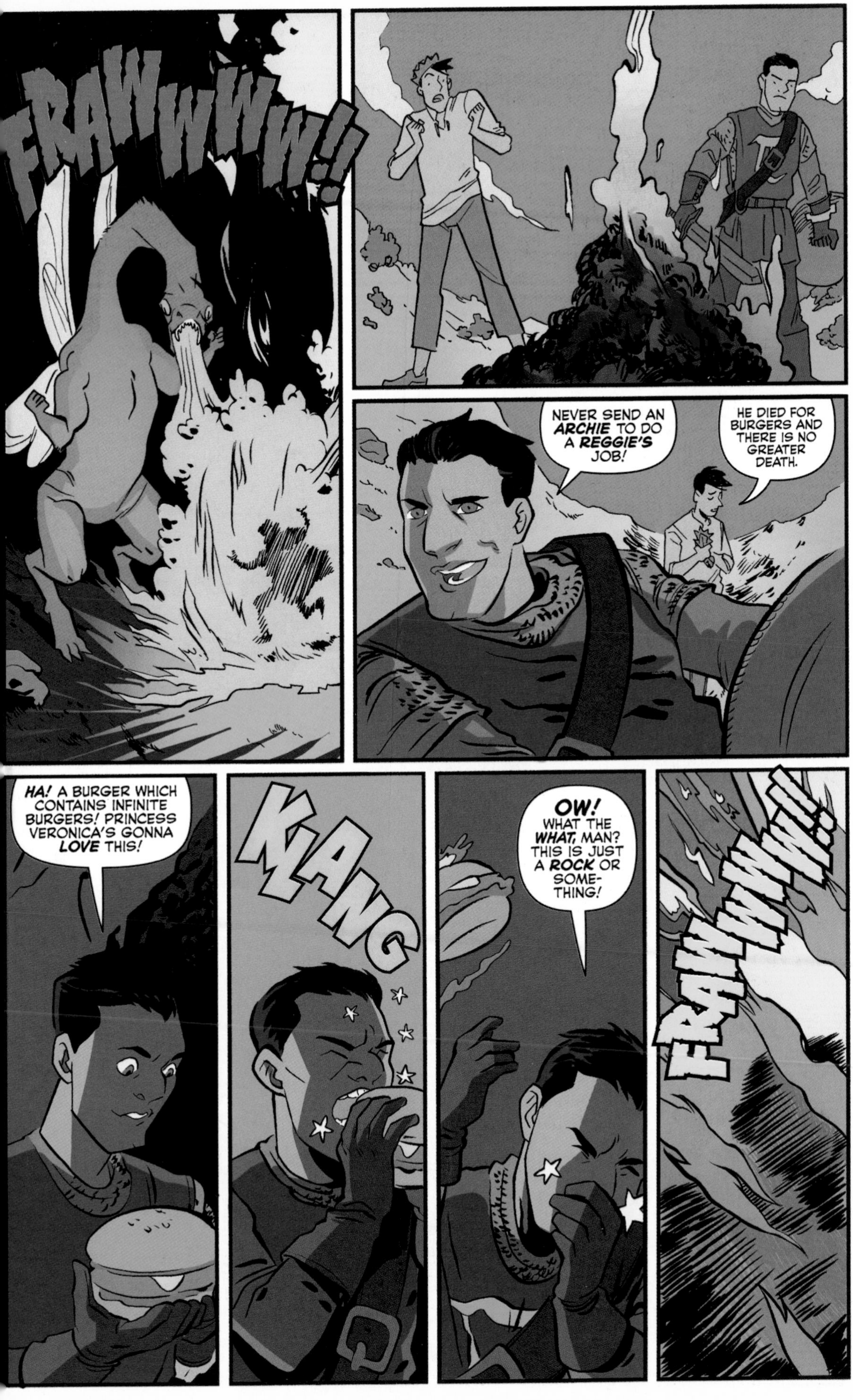
FRAWWWW!!
NEVER SEND AN ARCHIE TO DO A REGGIE'S JOB!
HE DIED FOR BURGERS AND THERE IS NO GREATER DEATH.
HA! A BURGER WHICH CONTAINS INFINITE BURGERS! PRINCESS VERONICA'S GONNA LOVE THIS!
KLANG
OW! WHAT THE WHAT, MAN? THIS IS JUST A ROCK OR SOME-THING!
FRAWWWW!!

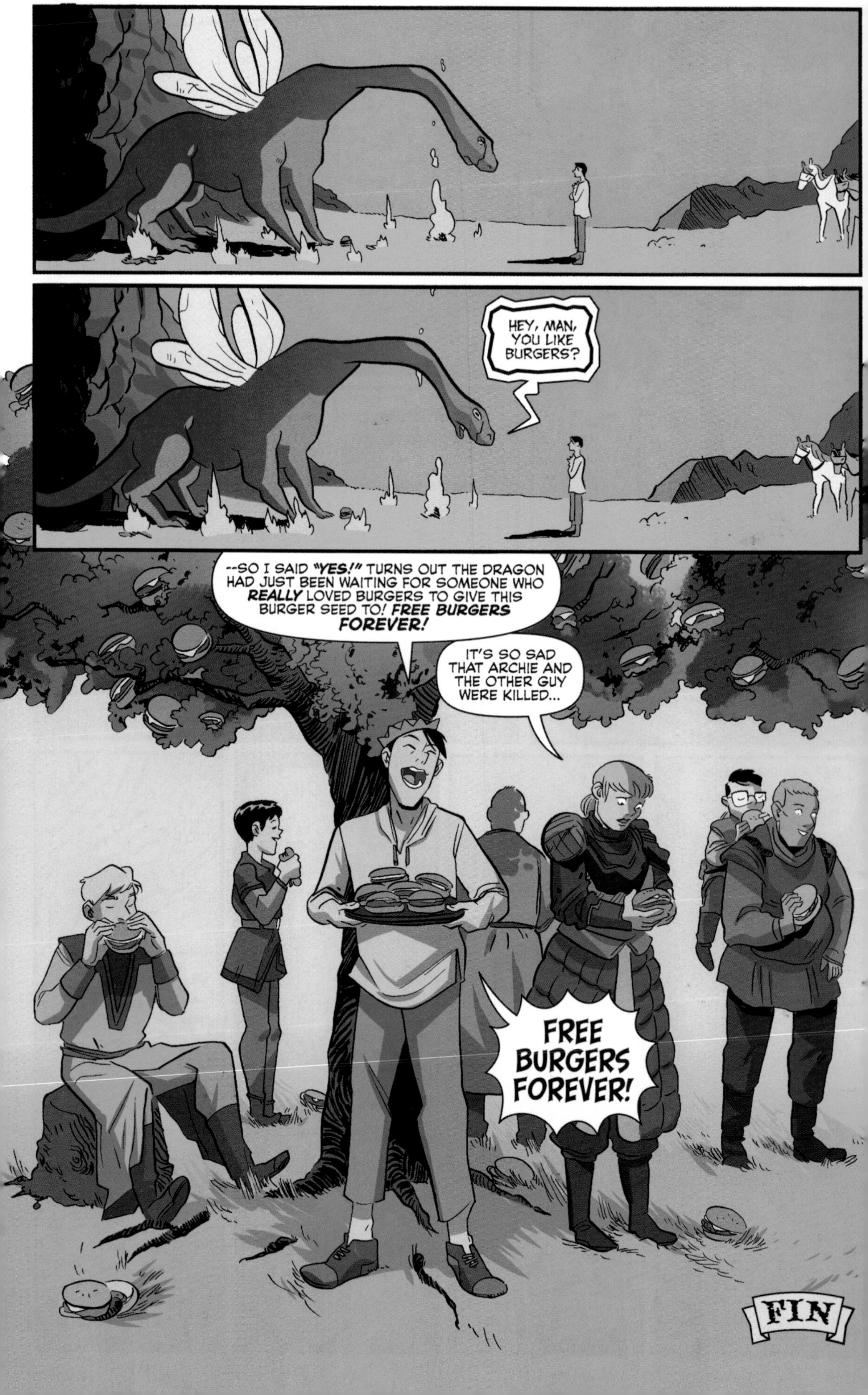
HEY, MAN, YOU LIKE BURGERS?
--SO I SAID "YES!" TURNS OUT THE DRAGON HAD JUST BEEN WAITING FOR SOMEONE WHO REALLY LOVED BURGERS TO GIVE THIS BURGER SEED TO! FREE BURGERS FOREVER!
IT'S SO SAD THAT ARCHIE AND THE OTHER GUY WERE KILLED...
FREE BURGERS FOREVER!
FIN

--GIVE HIM SOME ROOM! I THINK HE'S COMING TO!

Ohhh, what *HAPPENED?*

YOU FOUND OUT THE CAFETERIA NO LONGER SERVED GOOD FOOD AND--

--AHHHHH--

--LOOK, I'VE GOT SOMEPLACE TO BE, SO--

--JUGGIE! *DON'T* FREAK OUT THIS TIME, OKAY?

IT'S COOL, I'M--I'M FINE. WE JUST...NEED TO WORK ON GETTING FOOD BACK TO THE CAF...

DOESN'T MATTER TO *ME.* ALL OF *MY* LUNCHES ARE CATERED BY *LA CHOUETTE BALLONNÉ.*

YEAH, I'M NOT *VERONICA*-RICH OR ANYTHING, BUT I JUST BUY MY LUNCHES AT THE MALL.

MOM AND DAD USUALLY PACK *MY* LUNCH...

I USUALLY JUST MAKE FOOD AT HOME AND BRING IT IN...

WAIT, *WHAT?*

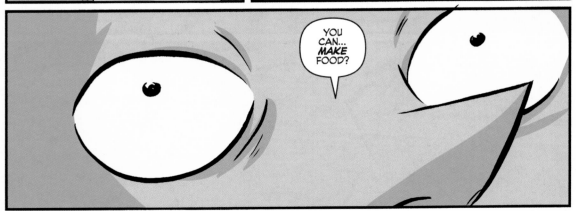

YOU CAN... *MAKE* FOOD?

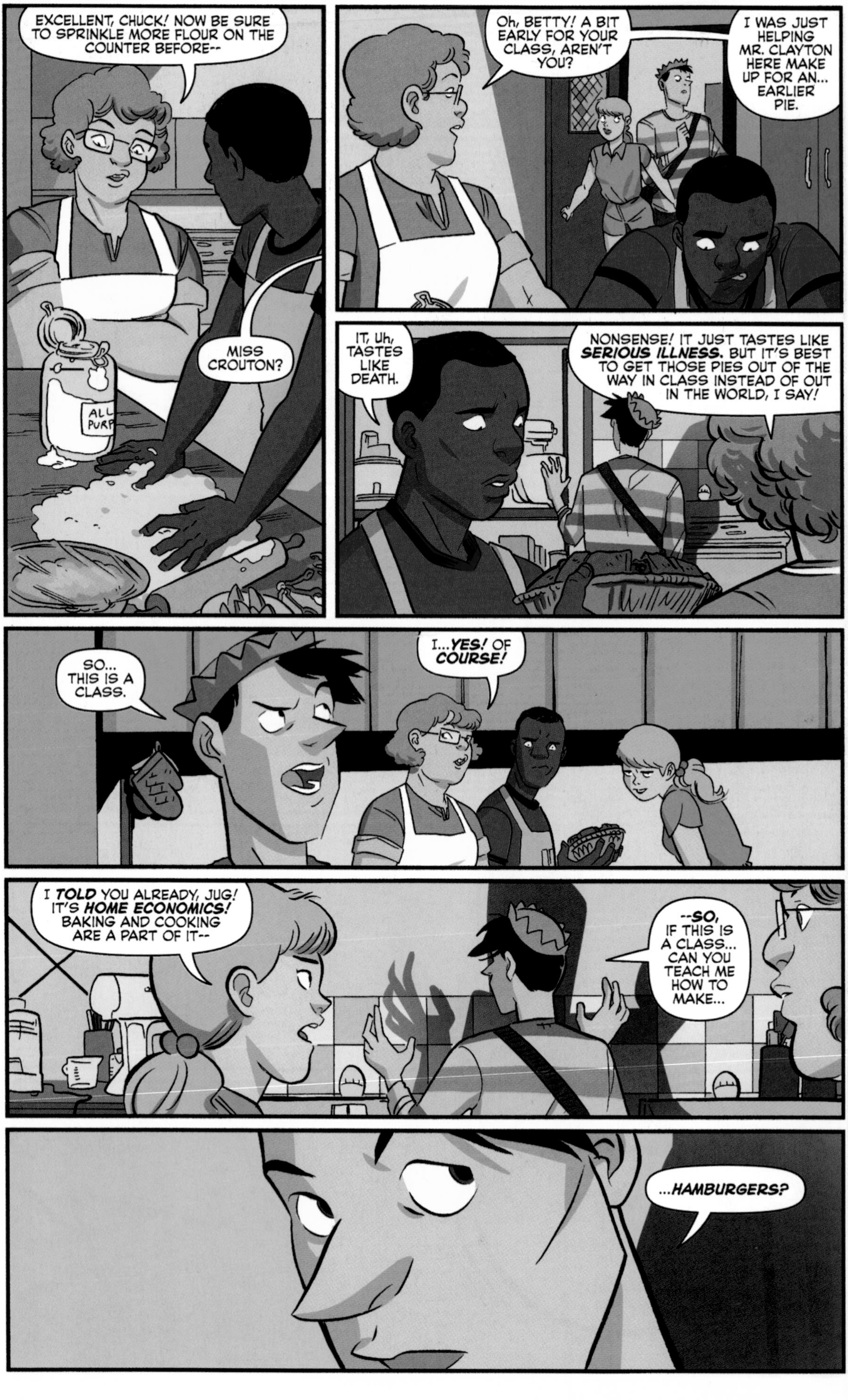
EXCELLENT, CHUCK! NOW BE SURE TO SPRINKLE MORE FLOUR ON THE COUNTER BEFORE--
MISS CROUTON?
ALL PURP
Oh, BETTY! A BIT EARLY FOR YOUR CLASS, AREN'T YOU?
I WAS JUST HELPING MR. CLAYTON HERE MAKE UP FOR AN... EARLIER PIE.
IT, Uh, TASTES LIKE DEATH.
NONSENSE! IT JUST TASTES LIKE SERIOUS ILLNESS. BUT IT'S BEST TO GET THOSE PIES OUT OF THE WAY IN CLASS INSTEAD OF OUT IN THE WORLD, I SAY!
SO... THIS IS A CLASS.
I...YES! OF COURSE!
I TOLD YOU ALREADY, JUG! IT'S HOME ECONOMICS! BAKING AND COOKING ARE A PART OF IT--
--SO, IF THIS IS A CLASS... CAN YOU TEACH ME HOW TO MAKE...
...HAMBURGERS?

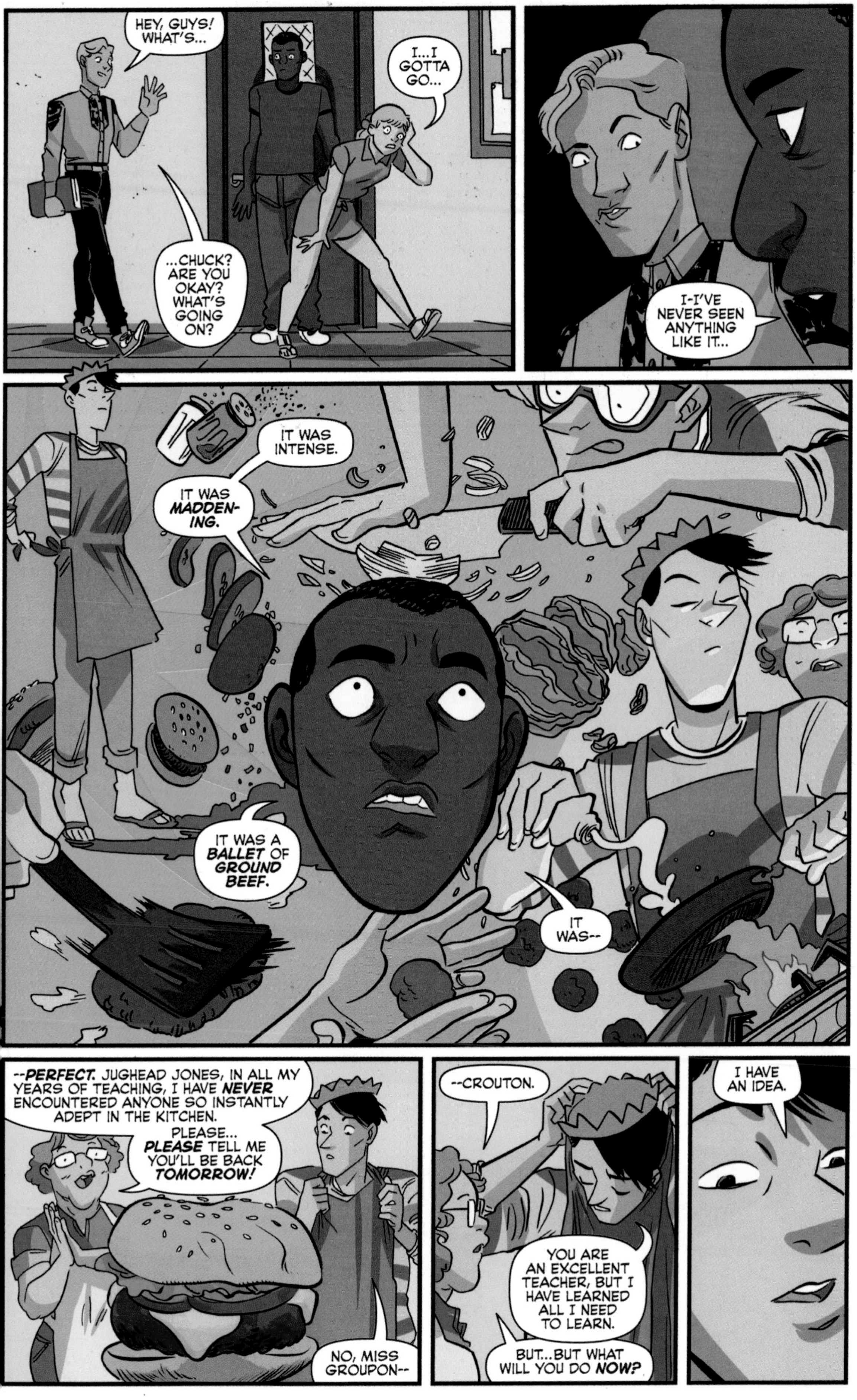
HEY, GUYS! WHAT'S...
I...I GOTTA GO...
...CHUCK? ARE YOU OKAY? WHAT'S GOING ON?
I-I'VE NEVER SEEN ANYTHING LIKE IT...
IT WAS INTENSE.
IT WAS *MADDEN-ING.*
IT WAS A *BALLET* OF *GROUND BEEF.*
IT WAS--
--*PERFECT.* JUGHEAD JONES, IN ALL MY YEARS OF TEACHING, I HAVE *NEVER* ENCOUNTERED ANYONE SO INSTANTLY ADEPT IN THE KITCHEN.
PLEASE... *PLEASE* TELL ME YOU'LL BE BACK *TOMORROW!*
NO, MISS GROUPON--
--CROUTON.
YOU ARE AN EXCELLENT TEACHER, BUT I HAVE LEARNED ALL I NEED TO LEARN.
BUT...BUT WHAT WILL YOU DO *NOW?*
I HAVE AN IDEA.

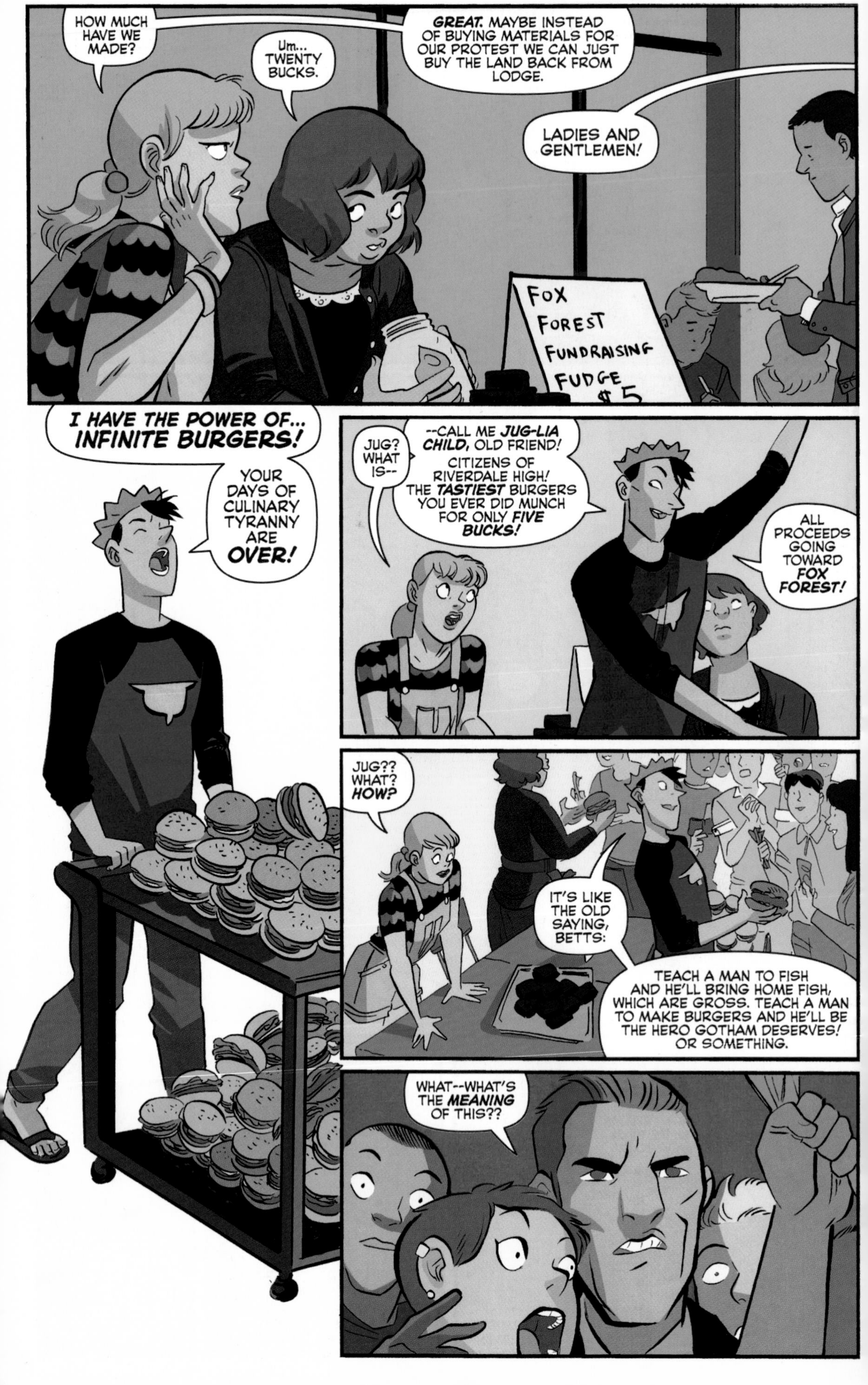
HOW MUCH HAVE WE MADE?
Um... TWENTY BUCKS.
GREAT. MAYBE INSTEAD OF BUYING MATERIALS FOR OUR PROTEST WE CAN JUST BUY THE LAND BACK FROM LODGE.
LADIES AND GENTLEMEN!
FOX FOREST FUNDRAISING FUDGE $5
I HAVE THE POWER OF... INFINITE BURGERS!
YOUR DAYS OF CULINARY TYRANNY ARE OVER!
JUG? WHAT IS--
--CALL ME JUG-LIA CHILD, OLD FRIEND!
CITIZENS OF RIVERDALE HIGH! THE TASTIEST BURGERS YOU EVER DID MUNCH FOR ONLY FIVE BUCKS!
ALL PROCEEDS GOING TOWARD FOX FOREST!
JUG?? WHAT? HOW?
IT'S LIKE THE OLD SAYING, BETTS:
TEACH A MAN TO FISH AND HE'LL BRING HOME FISH, WHICH ARE GROSS. TEACH A MAN TO MAKE BURGERS AND HE'LL BE THE HERO GOTHAM DESERVES! OR SOMETHING.
WHAT--WHAT'S THE MEANING OF THIS??

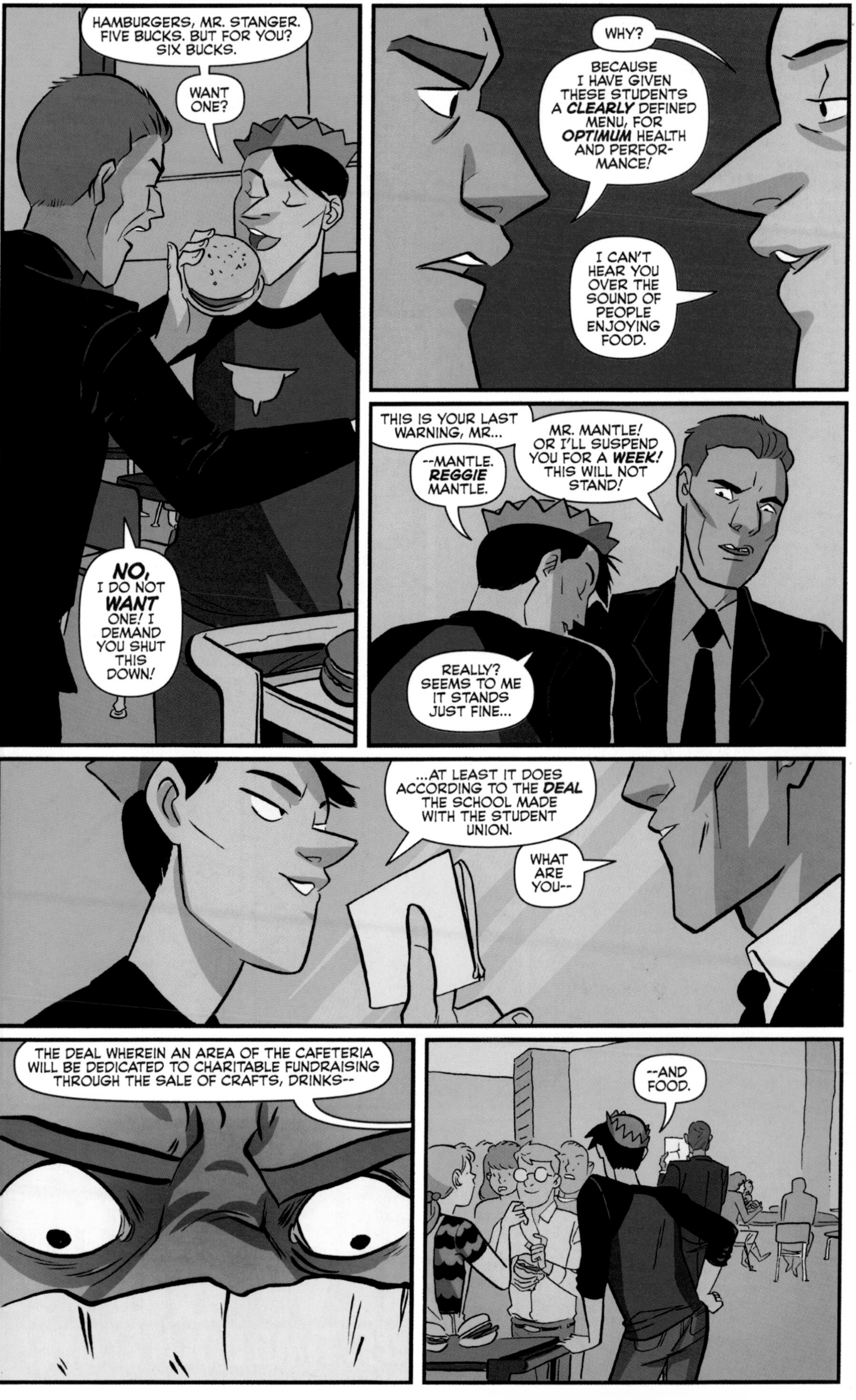
HAMBURGERS, MR. STANGER. FIVE BUCKS. BUT FOR YOU? SIX BUCKS.
WANT ONE?
NO, I DO NOT WANT ONE! I DEMAND YOU SHUT THIS DOWN!
WHY?
BECAUSE I HAVE GIVEN THESE STUDENTS A CLEARLY DEFINED MENU, FOR OPTIMUM HEALTH AND PERFORMANCE!
I CAN'T HEAR YOU OVER THE SOUND OF PEOPLE ENJOYING FOOD.
THIS IS YOUR LAST WARNING, MR...
--MANTLE. REGGIE MANTLE.
MR. MANTLE! OR I'LL SUSPEND YOU FOR A WEEK! THIS WILL NOT STAND!
REALLY? SEEMS TO ME IT STANDS JUST FINE...
...AT LEAST IT DOES ACCORDING TO THE DEAL THE SCHOOL MADE WITH THE STUDENT UNION.
WHAT ARE YOU--
THE DEAL WHEREIN AN AREA OF THE CAFETERIA WILL BE DEDICATED TO CHARITABLE FUNDRAISING THROUGH THE SALE OF CRAFTS, DRINKS--
--AND FOOD.

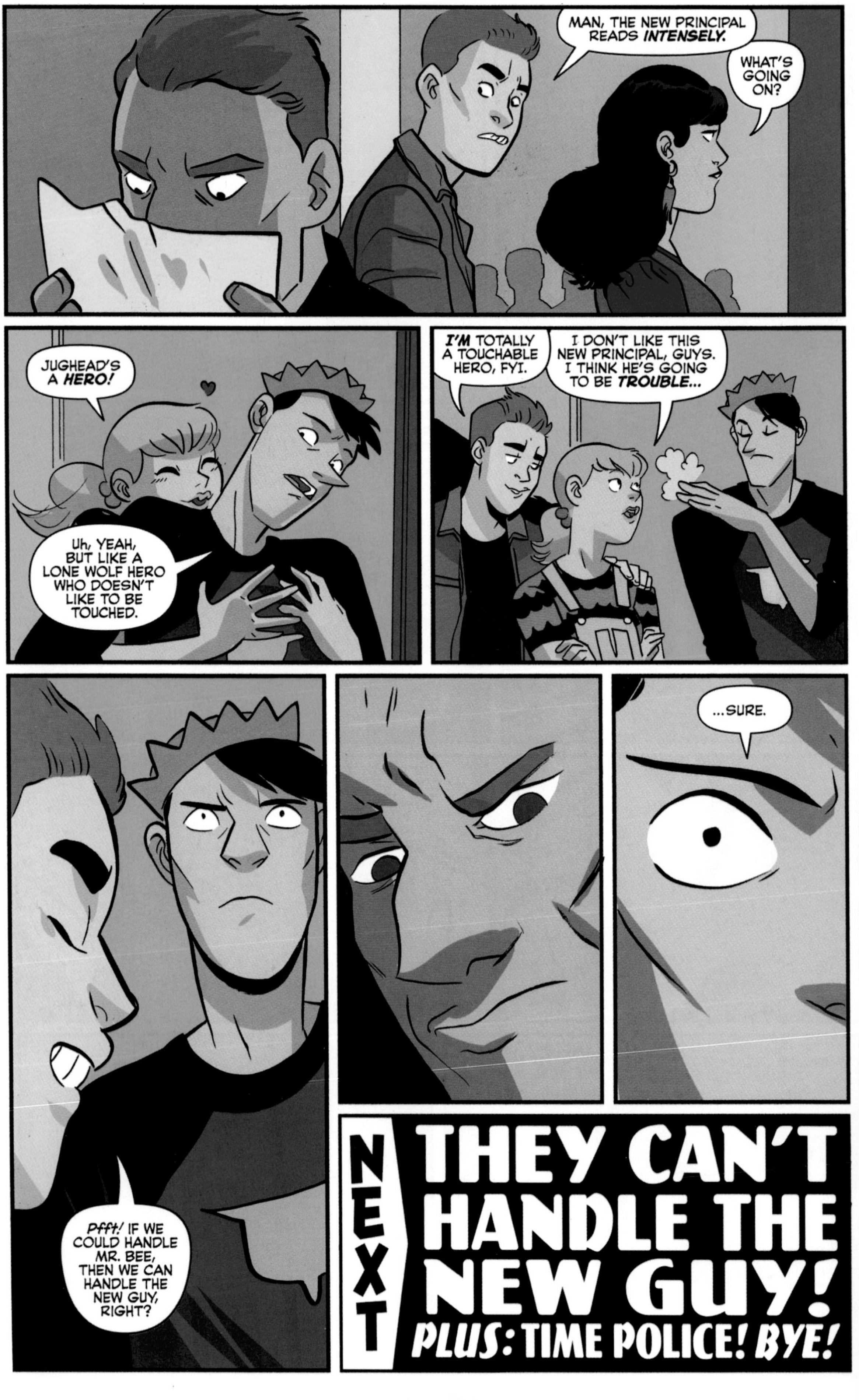
MAN, THE NEW PRINCIPAL READS INTENSELY.
WHAT'S GOING ON?
JUGHEAD'S A HERO!
Uh, YEAH, BUT LIKE A LONE WOLF HERO WHO DOESN'T LIKE TO BE TOUCHED.
I'M TOTALLY A TOUCHABLE HERO, FYI.
I DON'T LIKE THIS NEW PRINCIPAL, GUYS. I THINK HE'S GOING TO BE TROUBLE...
Pfft! IF WE COULD HANDLE MR. BEE, THEN WE CAN HANDLE THE NEW GUY, RIGHT?
...SURE.
NEXT
THEY CAN'T HANDLE THE NEW GUY!
PLUS: TIME POLICE! BYE!

TO BE
CONTINUED...

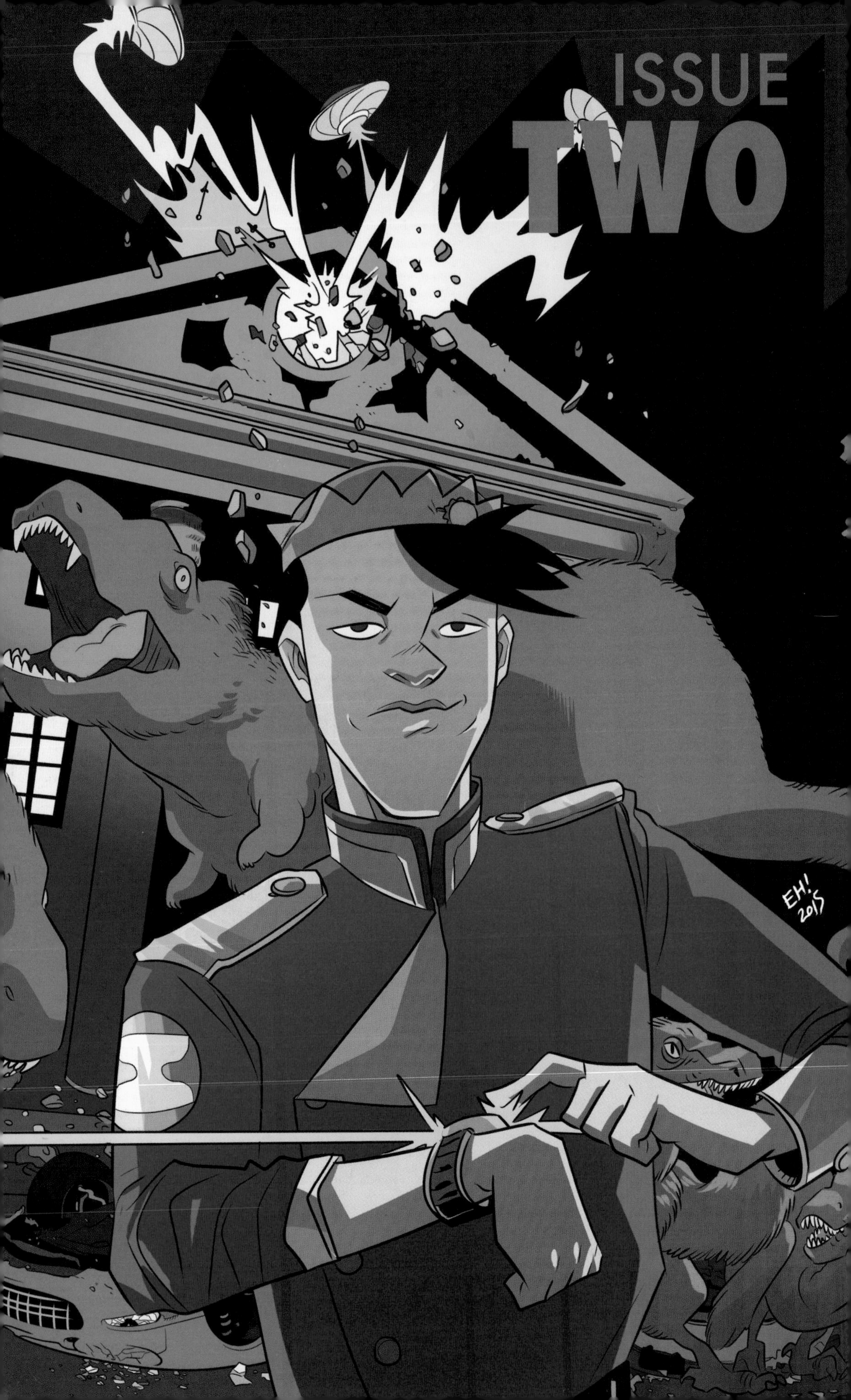
ISSUE
TWO
EH!
2015

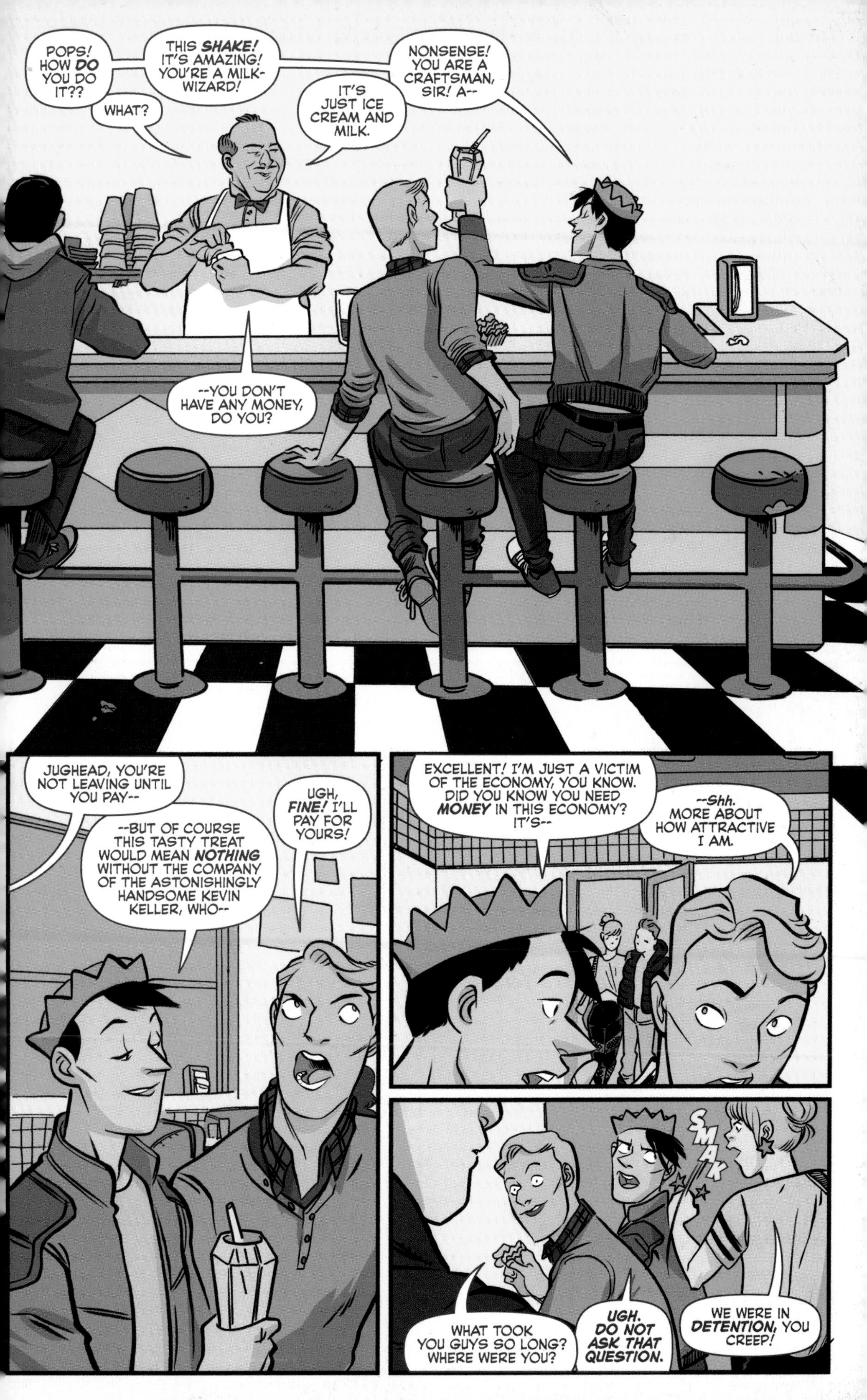
POPS! HOW DO YOU DO IT??
THIS SHAKE! IT'S AMAZING! YOU'RE A MILK-WIZARD!
WHAT?
IT'S JUST ICE CREAM AND MILK.
NONSENSE! YOU ARE A CRAFTSMAN, SIR! A--
--YOU DON'T HAVE ANY MONEY, DO YOU?
JUGHEAD, YOU'RE NOT LEAVING UNTIL YOU PAY--
--BUT OF COURSE THIS TASTY TREAT WOULD MEAN NOTHING WITHOUT THE COMPANY OF THE ASTONISHINGLY HANDSOME KEVIN KELLER, WHO--
UGH, FINE! I'LL PAY FOR YOURS!
EXCELLENT! I'M JUST A VICTIM OF THE ECONOMY, YOU KNOW. DID YOU KNOW YOU NEED MONEY IN THIS ECONOMY? IT'S--
--Shh. MORE ABOUT HOW ATTRACTIVE I AM.
SMAK
WHAT TOOK YOU GUYS SO LONG? WHERE WERE YOU?
UGH. DO NOT ASK THAT QUESTION.
WE WERE IN DETENTION, YOU CREEP!

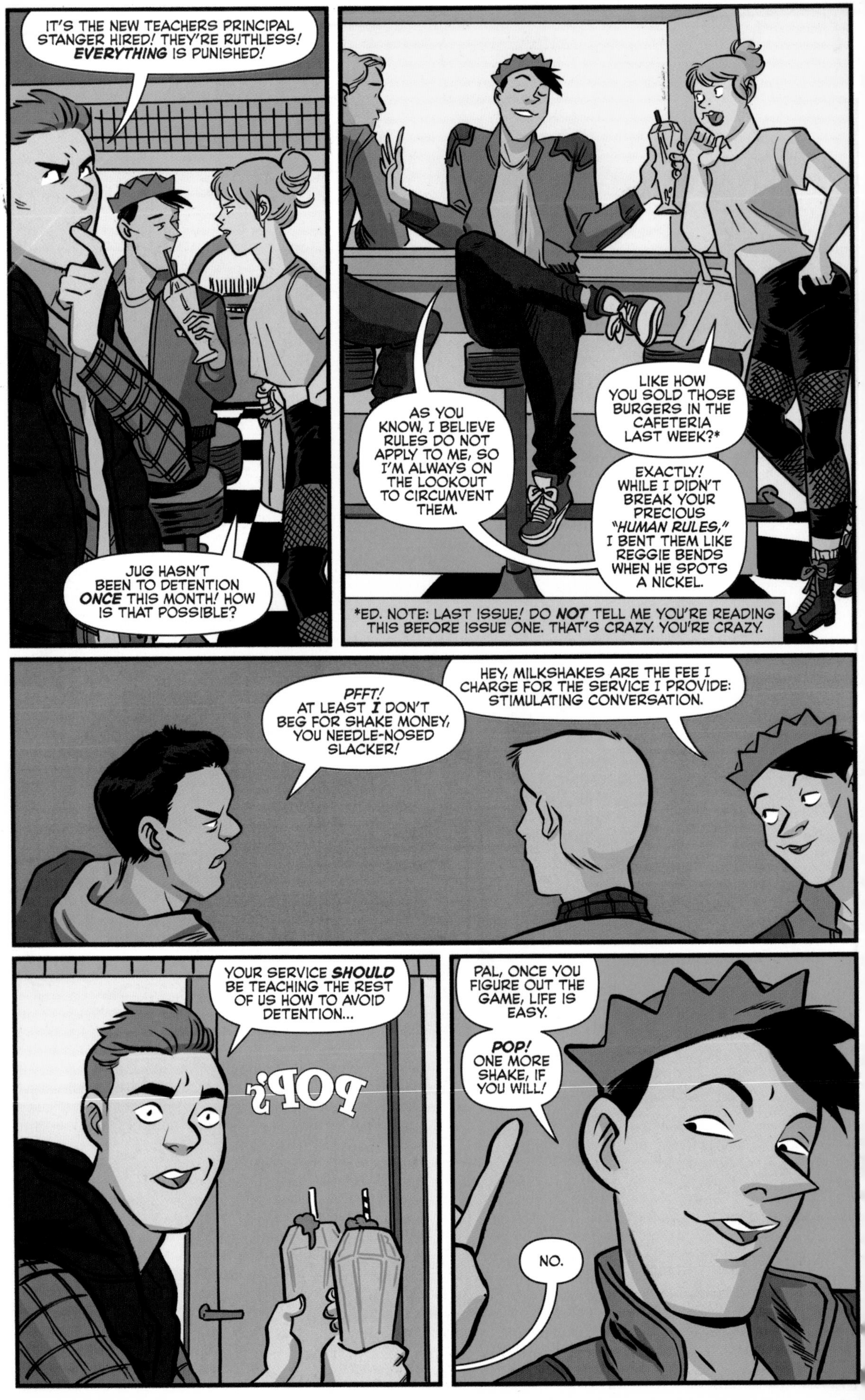
IT'S THE NEW TEACHERS PRINCIPAL STANGER HIRED! THEY'RE RUTHLESS! EVERYTHING IS PUNISHED!
JUG HASN'T BEEN TO DETENTION ONCE THIS MONTH! HOW IS THAT POSSIBLE?
AS YOU KNOW, I BELIEVE RULES DO NOT APPLY TO ME, SO I'M ALWAYS ON THE LOOKOUT TO CIRCUMVENT THEM.
LIKE HOW YOU SOLD THOSE BURGERS IN THE CAFETERIA LAST WEEK?*
EXACTLY! WHILE I DIDN'T BREAK YOUR PRECIOUS "HUMAN RULES," I BENT THEM LIKE REGGIE BENDS WHEN HE SPOTS A NICKEL.
*ED. NOTE: LAST ISSUE! DO NOT TELL ME YOU'RE READING THIS BEFORE ISSUE ONE. THAT'S CRAZY. YOU'RE CRAZY.
HEY, MILKSHAKES ARE THE FEE I CHARGE FOR THE SERVICE I PROVIDE: STIMULATING CONVERSATION.
PFFT! AT LEAST I DON'T BEG FOR SHAKE MONEY, YOU NEEDLE-NOSED SLACKER!
YOUR SERVICE SHOULD BE TEACHING THE REST OF US HOW TO AVOID DETENTION...
POP'S
PAL, ONCE YOU FIGURE OUT THE GAME, LIFE IS EASY.
POP! ONE MORE SHAKE, IF YOU WILL!
NO.

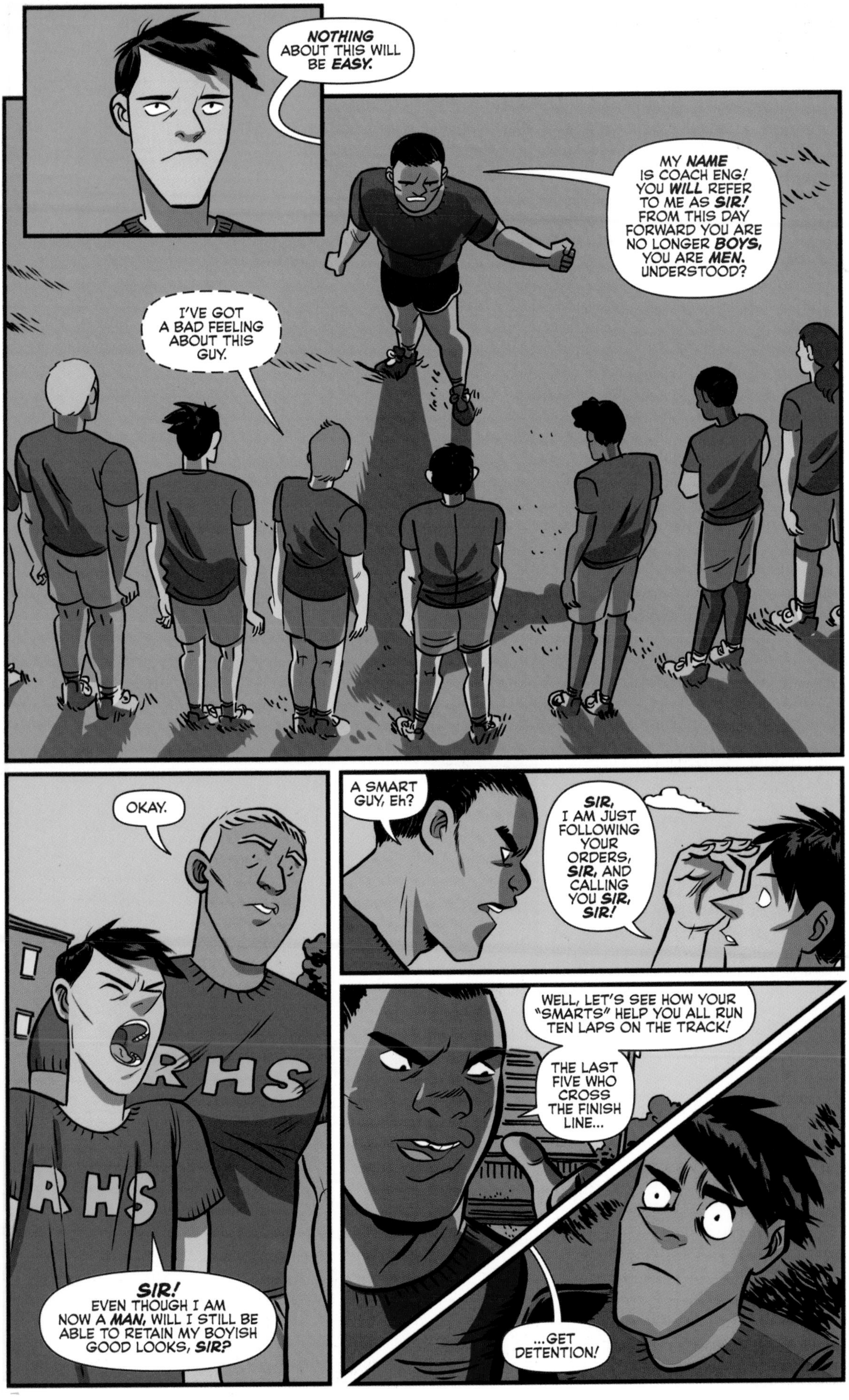
NOTHING ABOUT THIS WILL BE EASY.
MY NAME IS COACH ENG! YOU WILL REFER TO ME AS SIR! FROM THIS DAY FORWARD YOU ARE NO LONGER BOYS, YOU ARE MEN. UNDERSTOOD?
I'VE GOT A BAD FEELING ABOUT THIS GUY.
OKAY.
SIR! EVEN THOUGH I AM NOW A MAN, WILL I STILL BE ABLE TO RETAIN MY BOYISH GOOD LOOKS, SIR?
RHS
A SMART GUY, Eh?
SIR, I AM JUST FOLLOWING YOUR ORDERS, SIR, AND CALLING YOU SIR, SIR!
WELL, LET'S SEE HOW YOUR "SMARTS" HELP YOU ALL RUN TEN LAPS ON THE TRACK!
THE LAST FIVE WHO CROSS THE FINISH LINE...
...GET DETENTION!

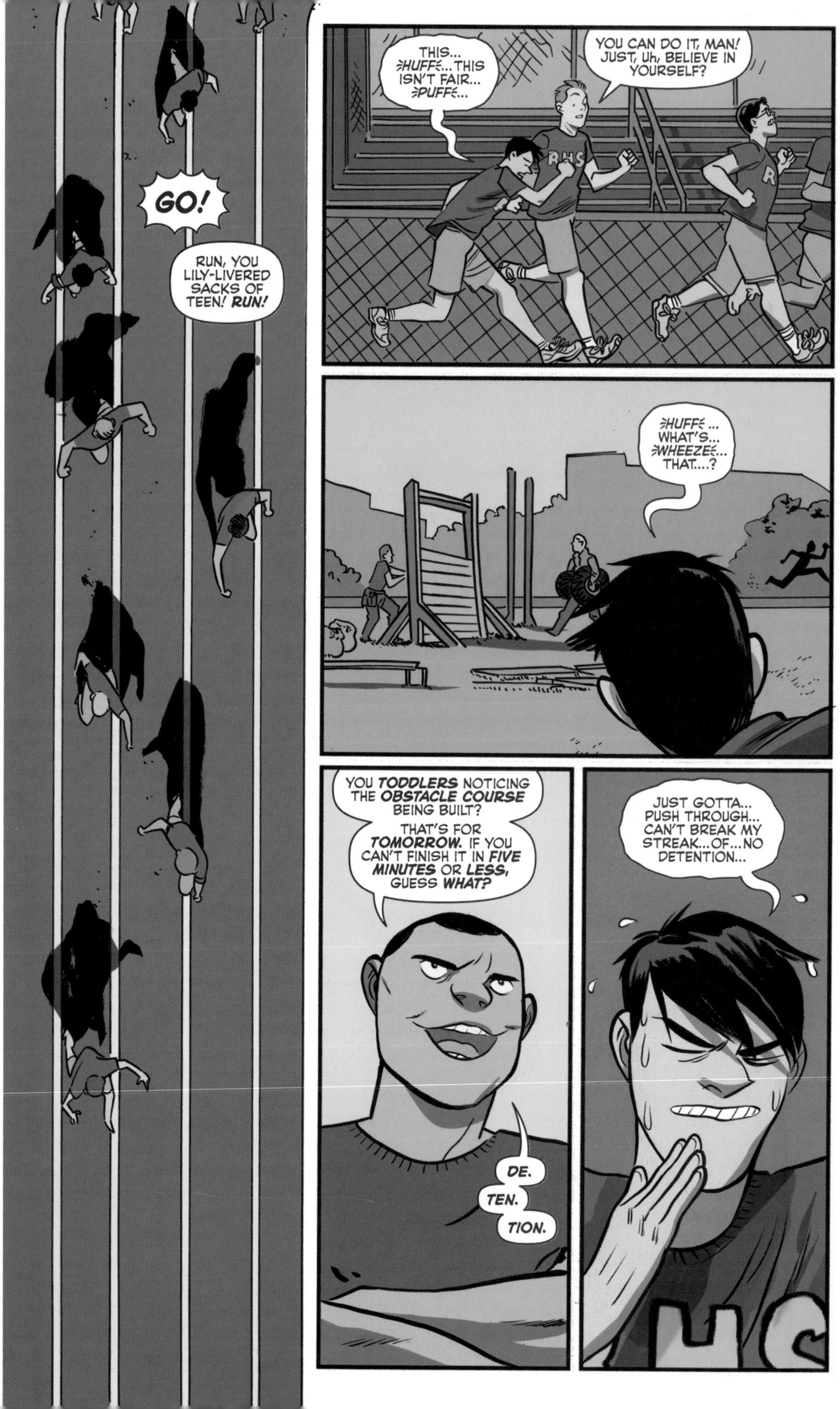
GO!
RUN, YOU LILY-LIVERED SACKS OF TEEN! RUN!
THIS... HUFF... THIS ISN'T FAIR... PUFF...
YOU CAN DO IT, MAN! JUST, UH, BELIEVE IN YOURSELF?
RHS
R
HUFF... WHAT'S... WHEEZE... THAT...?
YOU TODDLERS NOTICING THE OBSTACLE COURSE BEING BUILT?
THAT'S FOR TOMORROW. IF YOU CAN'T FINISH IT IN FIVE MINUTES OR LESS, GUESS WHAT?
DE.
TEN.
TION.
JUST GOTTA... PUSH THROUGH... CAN'T BREAK MY STREAK...OF...NO DETENTION...

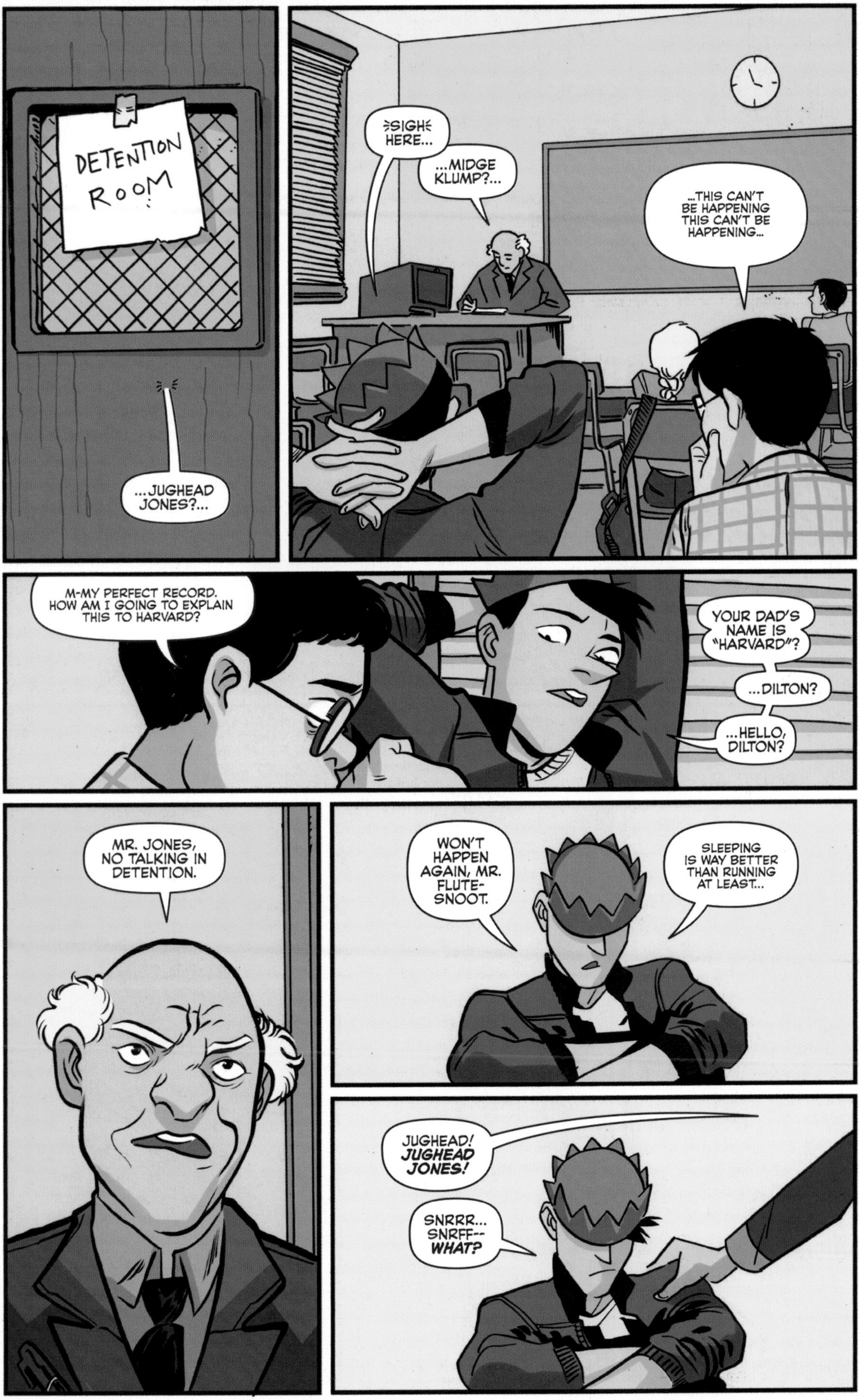
DETENTION ROOM
...JUGHEAD JONES?...
≷SIGH≶ HERE...
...MIDGE KLUMP?...
...THIS CAN'T BE HAPPENING THIS CAN'T BE HAPPENING...
M-MY PERFECT RECORD. HOW AM I GOING TO EXPLAIN THIS TO HARVARD?
YOUR DAD'S NAME IS "HARVARD"?
...DILTON?
...HELLO, DILTON?
MR. JONES, NO TALKING IN DETENTION.
WON'T HAPPEN AGAIN, MR. FLUTE-SNOOT.
SLEEPING IS WAY BETTER THAN RUNNING AT LEAST...
JUGHEAD! *JUGHEAD JONES!*
SNRRR... SNRFF-- *WHAT?*

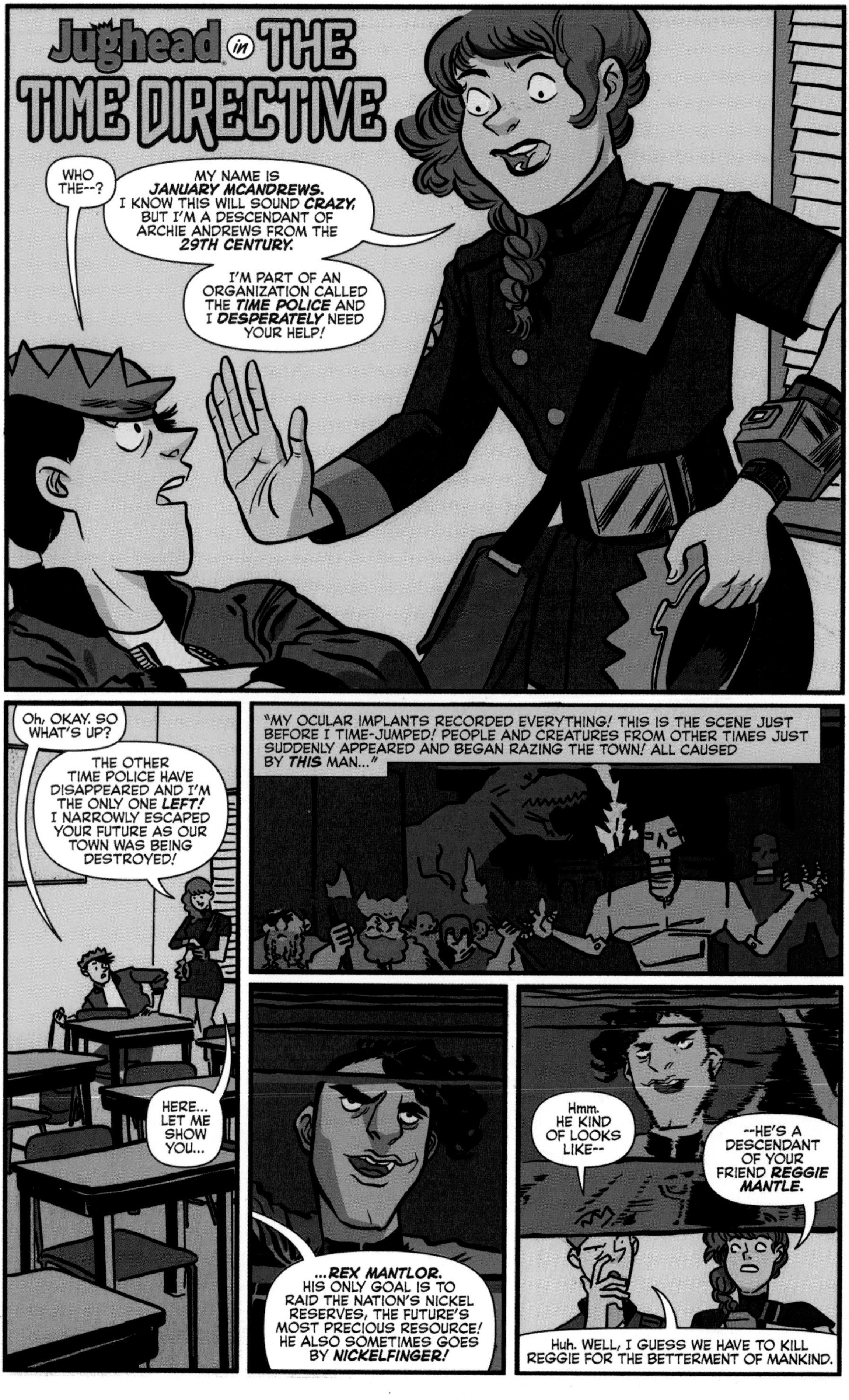
Jughead in THE TIME DIRECTIVE
WHO THE--?
MY NAME IS JANUARY MCANDREWS. I KNOW THIS WILL SOUND CRAZY, BUT I'M A DESCENDANT OF ARCHIE ANDREWS FROM THE 29TH CENTURY.
I'M PART OF AN ORGANIZATION CALLED THE TIME POLICE AND I DESPERATELY NEED YOUR HELP!
Oh, OKAY. SO WHAT'S UP?
THE OTHER TIME POLICE HAVE DISAPPEARED AND I'M THE ONLY ONE LEFT! I NARROWLY ESCAPED YOUR FUTURE AS OUR TOWN WAS BEING DESTROYED!
HERE... LET ME SHOW YOU...
"MY OCULAR IMPLANTS RECORDED EVERYTHING! THIS IS THE SCENE JUST BEFORE I TIME-JUMPED! PEOPLE AND CREATURES FROM OTHER TIMES JUST SUDDENLY APPEARED AND BEGAN RAZING THE TOWN! ALL CAUSED BY THIS MAN..."
...REX MANTLOR. HIS ONLY GOAL IS TO RAID THE NATION'S NICKEL RESERVES, THE FUTURE'S MOST PRECIOUS RESOURCE! HE ALSO SOMETIMES GOES BY NICKELFINGER!
Hmm. HE KIND OF LOOKS LIKE--
--HE'S A DESCENDANT OF YOUR FRIEND REGGIE MANTLE.
Huh. WELL, I GUESS WE HAVE TO KILL REGGIE FOR THE BETTERMENT OF MANKIND.

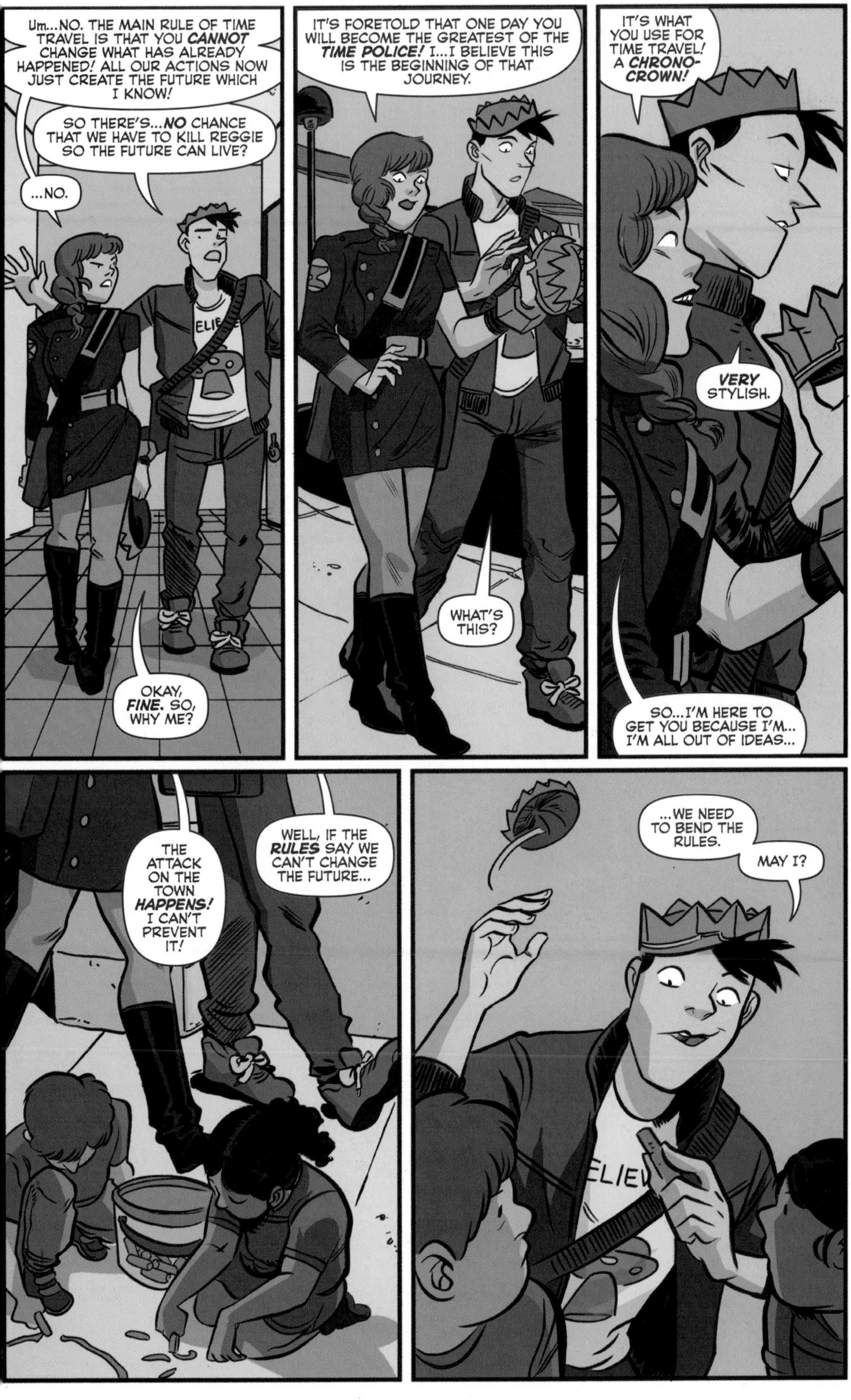

Um...NO. THE MAIN RULE OF TIME TRAVEL IS THAT YOU CANNOT CHANGE WHAT HAS ALREADY HAPPENED! ALL OUR ACTIONS NOW JUST CREATE THE FUTURE WHICH I KNOW!
SO THERE'S...NO CHANCE THAT WE HAVE TO KILL REGGIE SO THE FUTURE CAN LIVE?
...NO.
OKAY, FINE. SO, WHY ME?
IT'S FORETOLD THAT ONE DAY YOU WILL BECOME THE GREATEST OF THE TIME POLICE! I...I BELIEVE THIS IS THE BEGINNING OF THAT JOURNEY.
WHAT'S THIS?
IT'S WHAT YOU USE FOR TIME TRAVEL! A CHRONO-CROWN!
VERY STYLISH.
SO...I'M HERE TO GET YOU BECAUSE I'M... I'M ALL OUT OF IDEAS...
THE ATTACK ON THE TOWN HAPPENS! I CAN'T PREVENT IT!
WELL, IF THE RULES SAY WE CAN'T CHANGE THE FUTURE...
...WE NEED TO BEND THE RULES.
MAY I?

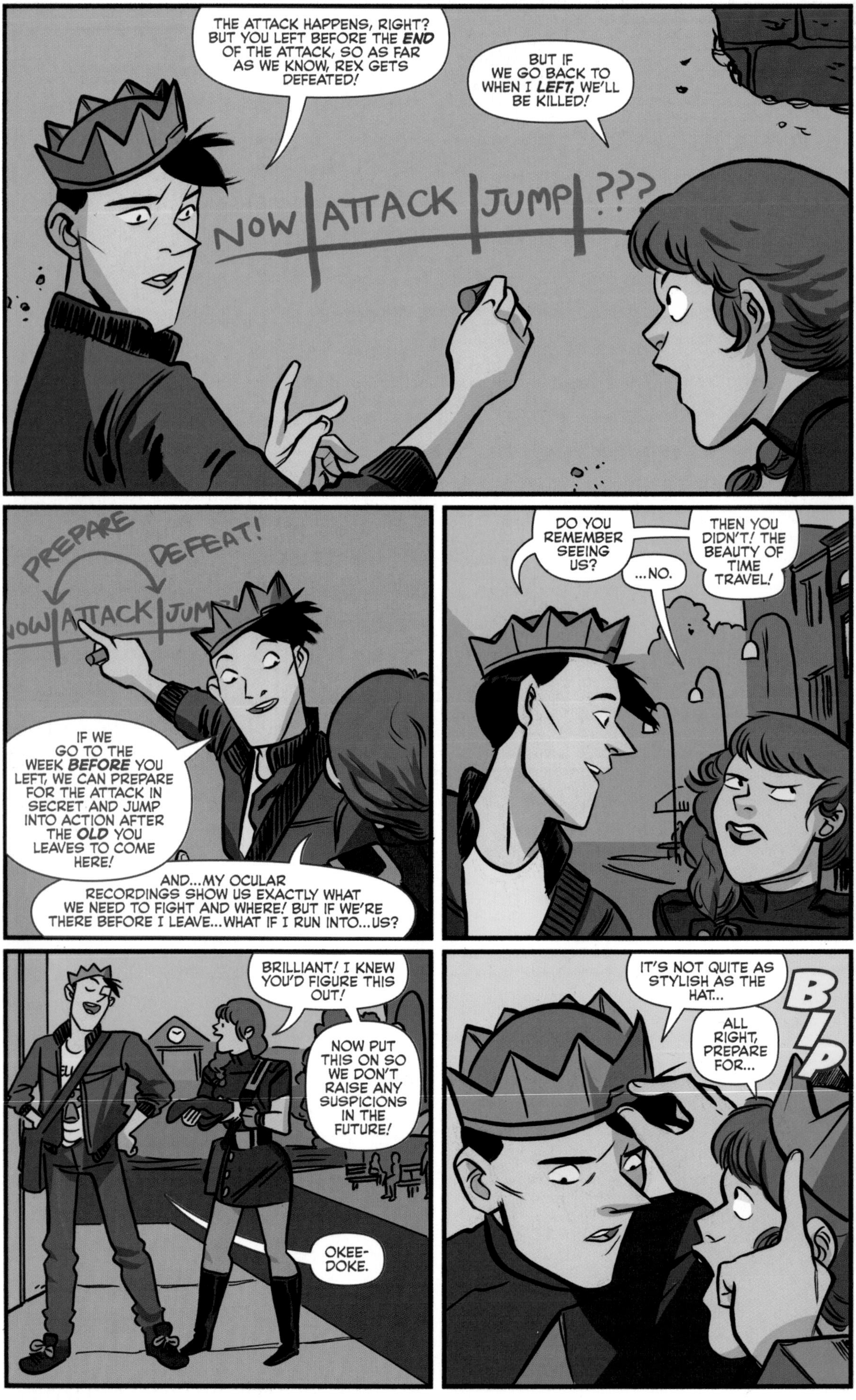
THE ATTACK HAPPENS, RIGHT? BUT YOU LEFT BEFORE THE END OF THE ATTACK, SO AS FAR AS WE KNOW, REX GETS DEFEATED!
BUT IF WE GO BACK TO WHEN I LEFT, WE'LL BE KILLED!
NOW ATTACK JUMP ???
PREPARE DEFEAT!
IF WE GO TO THE WEEK BEFORE YOU LEFT, WE CAN PREPARE FOR THE ATTACK IN SECRET AND JUMP INTO ACTION AFTER THE OLD YOU LEAVES TO COME HERE!
AND...MY OCULAR RECORDINGS SHOW US EXACTLY WHAT WE NEED TO FIGHT AND WHERE! BUT IF WE'RE THERE BEFORE I LEAVE...WHAT IF I RUN INTO...US?
DO YOU REMEMBER SEEING US?
...NO.
THEN YOU DIDN'T! THE BEAUTY OF TIME TRAVEL!
BRILLIANT! I KNEW YOU'D FIGURE THIS OUT!
NOW PUT THIS ON SO WE DON'T RAISE ANY SUSPICIONS IN THE FUTURE!
OKEE-DOKE.
IT'S NOT QUITE AS STYLISH AS THE HAT...
ALL RIGHT, PREPARE FOR...
BIP

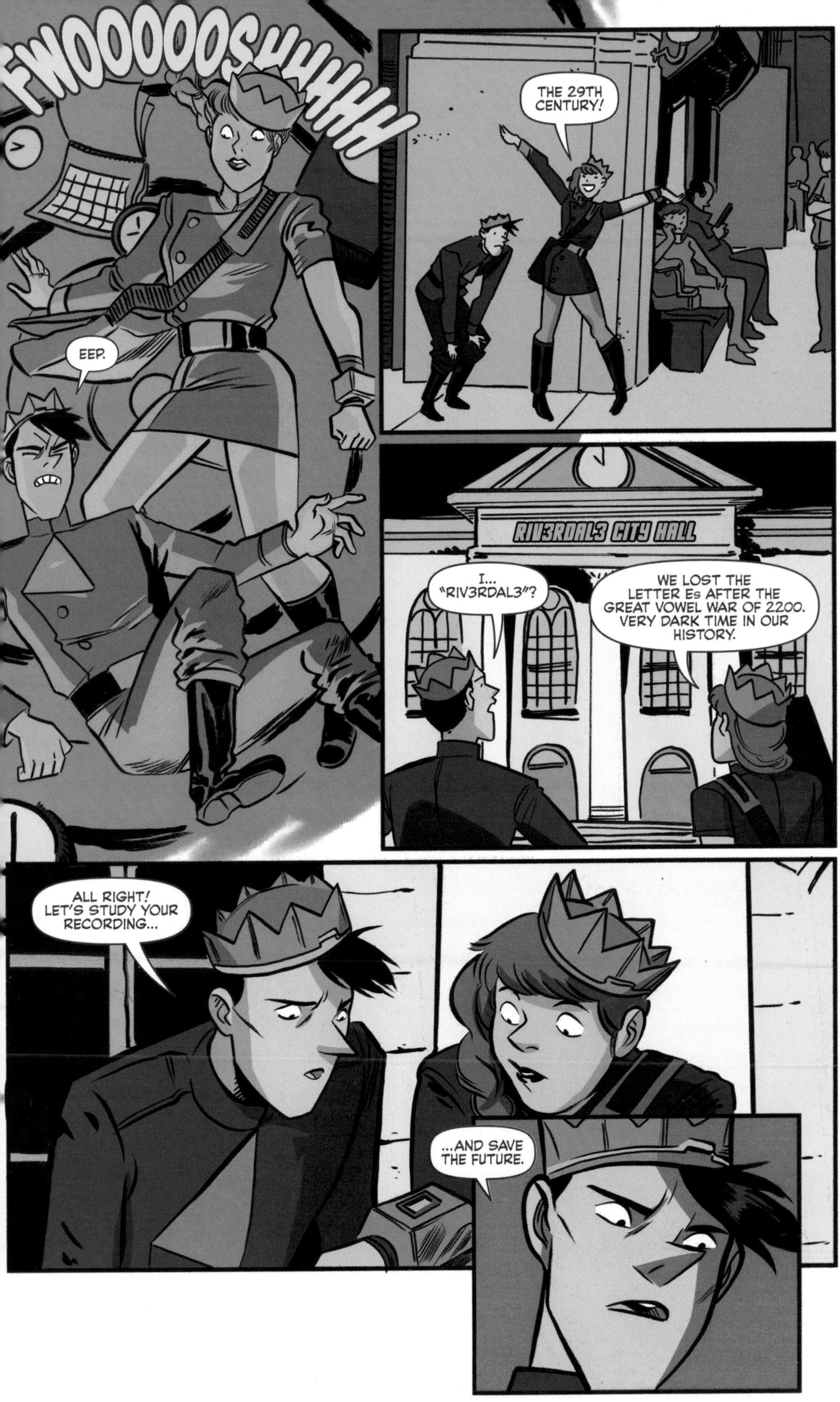
FWOOOOSHHHH
EEP.
THE 29TH CENTURY!
RIV3RDAL3 CITY HALL
I... "RIV3RDAL3"?
WE LOST THE LETTER Es AFTER THE GREAT VOWEL WAR OF 2200. VERY DARK TIME IN OUR HISTORY.
ALL RIGHT! LET'S STUDY YOUR RECORDING...
...AND SAVE THE FUTURE.

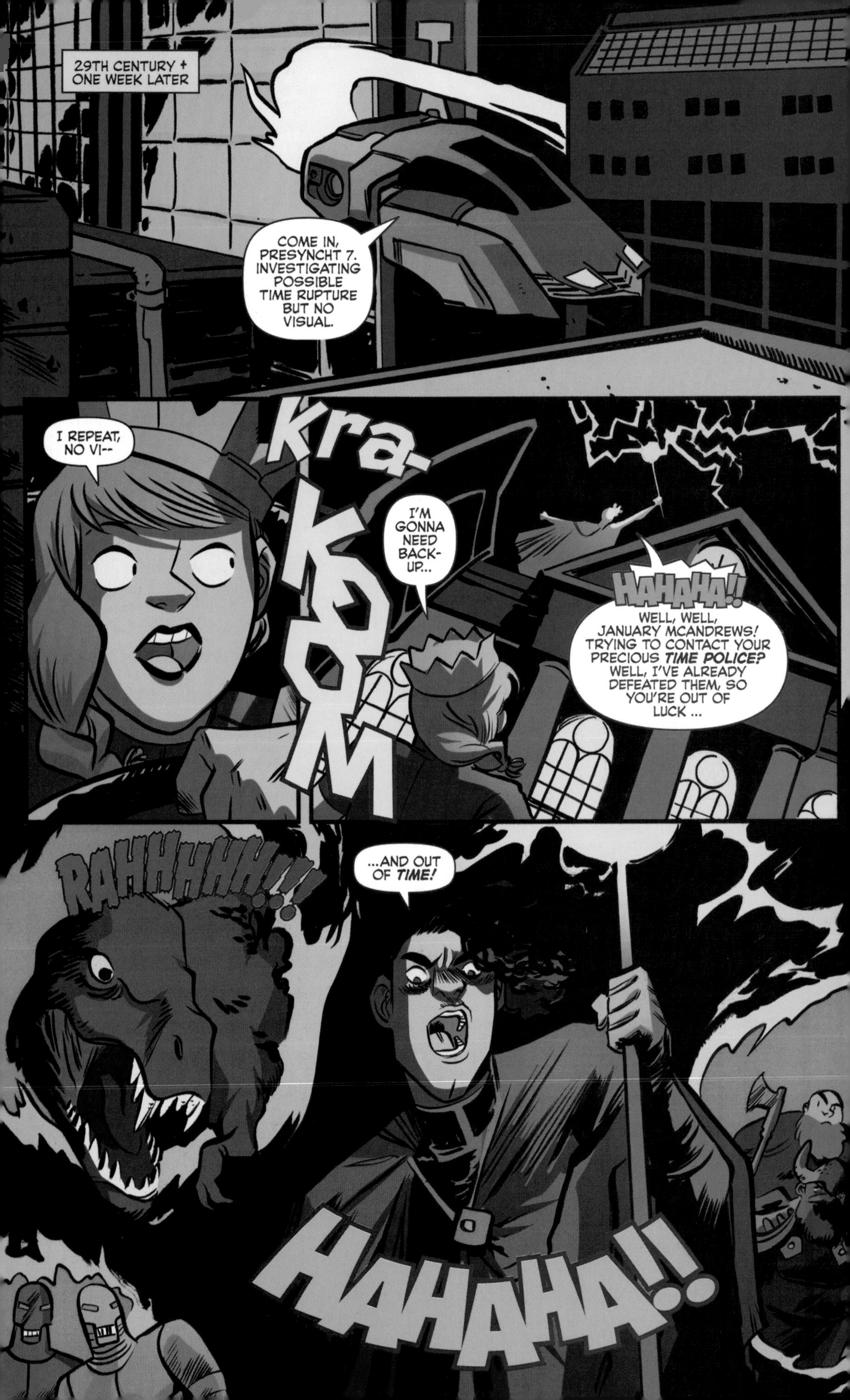

29TH CENTURY + ONE WEEK LATER
COME IN, PRESYNCHT 7. INVESTIGATING POSSIBLE TIME RUPTURE BUT NO VISUAL.
I REPEAT, NO VI--
kra-KOOM
I'M GONNA NEED BACK-UP...
HAHAHA!!
WELL, WELL, JANUARY MCANDREWS! TRYING TO CONTACT YOUR PRECIOUS *TIME POLICE?* WELL, I'VE ALREADY DEFEATED THEM, SO YOU'RE OUT OF LUCK ...
RAHHHHHH!!!
...AND OUT OF *TIME!*
HAHAHA!!

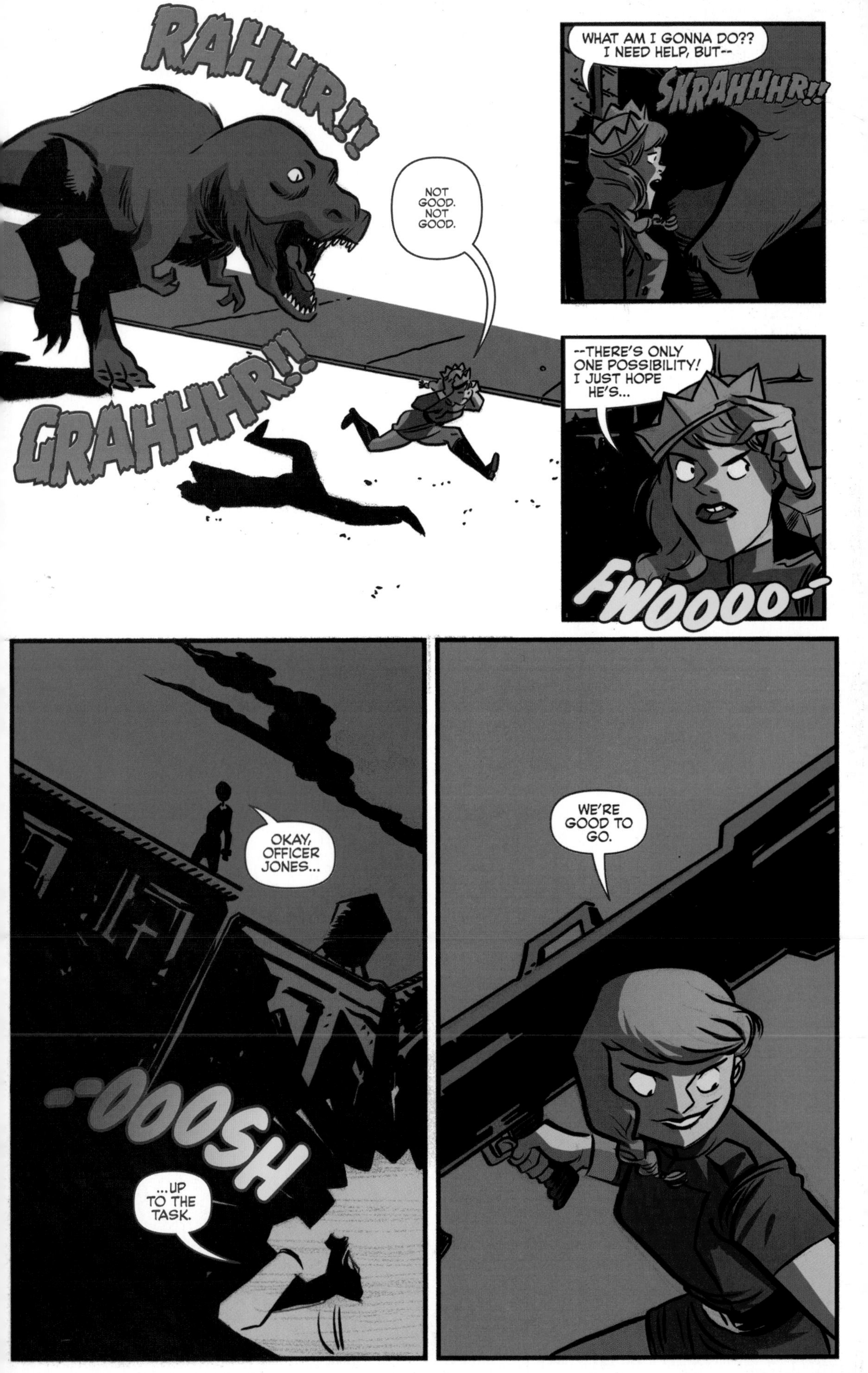
RAHHR!!
NOT GOOD. NOT GOOD.
GRAHHHR!!
WHAT AM I GONNA DO?? I NEED HELP, BUT--
SKRAHHHR!!
--THERE'S ONLY ONE POSSIBILITY! I JUST HOPE HE'S...
FWOOOO-
OKAY, OFFICER JONES...
-OOOSH
...UP TO THE TASK.
WE'RE GOOD TO GO.

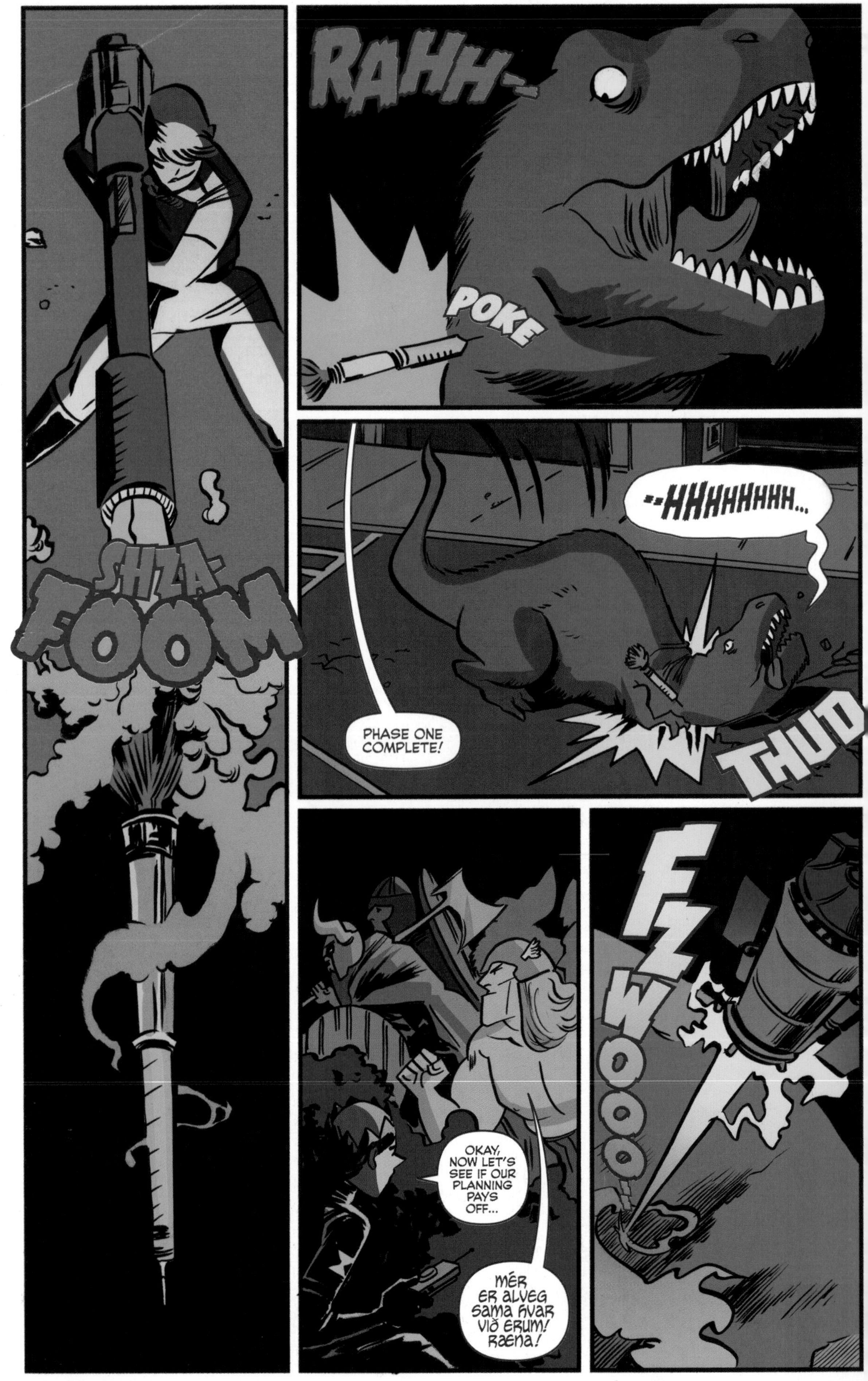
SHZA-FOOM
RAHH-
POKE
--HHHHHHHH...
PHASE ONE COMPLETE!
THUD
OKAY, NOW LET'S SEE IF OUR PLANNING PAYS OFF...
MÉR ER ALVEG SAMA HVAR VIÐ ERUM! RÆNA!
FZWOOOO

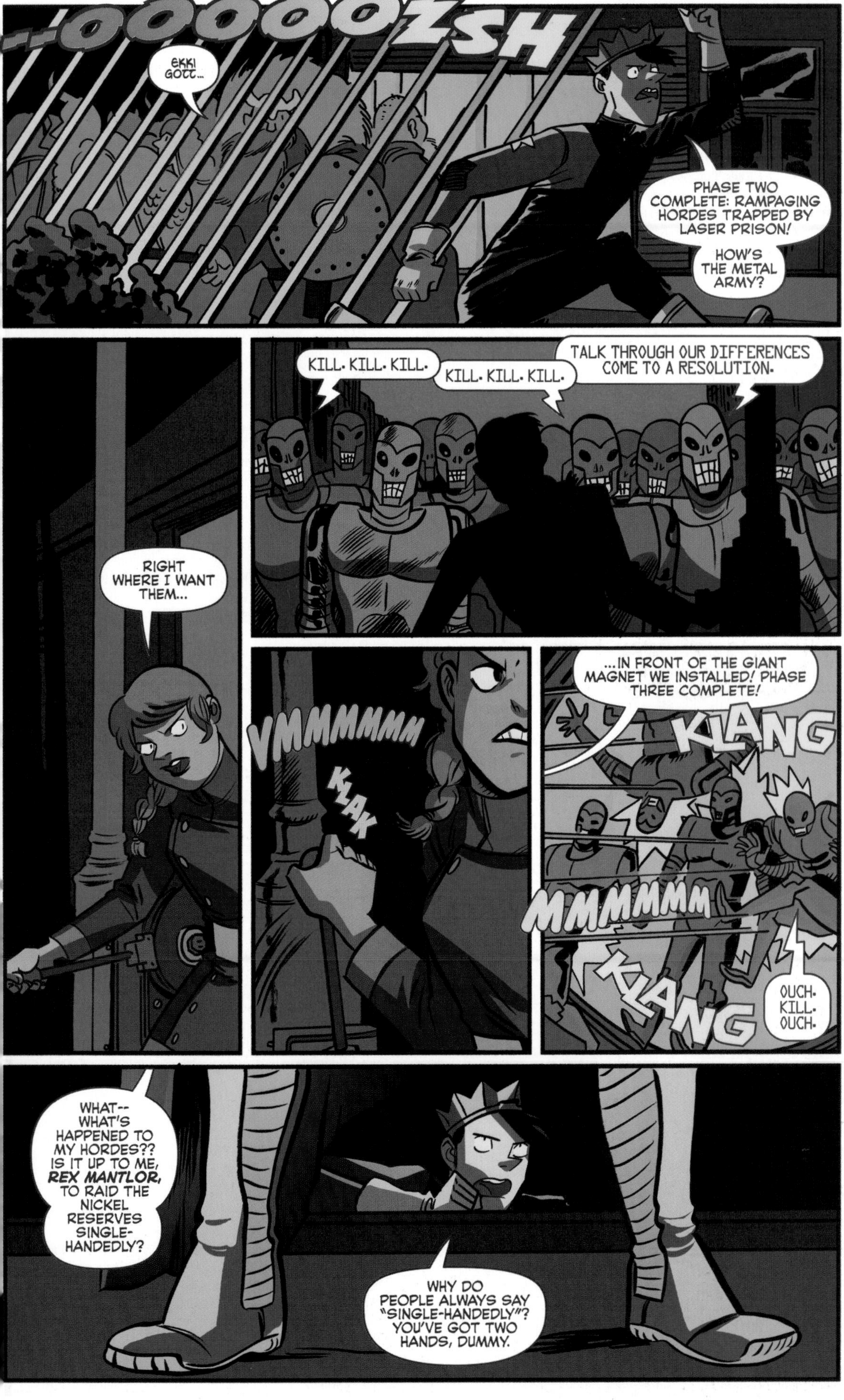
--OOOOOOZSH
EKKI GOTT...
PHASE TWO COMPLETE: RAMPAGING HORDES TRAPPED BY LASER PRISON!
HOW'S THE METAL ARMY?
RIGHT WHERE I WANT THEM...
KILL. KILL. KILL.
KILL. KILL. KILL.
TALK THROUGH OUR DIFFERENCES COME TO A RESOLUTION.
VMMMMMM
KLAK
...IN FRONT OF THE GIANT MAGNET WE INSTALLED! PHASE THREE COMPLETE!
KLANG
MMMMMM
KLANG
OUCH. KILL. OUCH.
WHAT-- WHAT'S HAPPENED TO MY HORDES?? IS IT UP TO ME, REX MANTLOR, TO RAID THE NICKEL RESERVES SINGLE-HANDEDLY?
WHY DO PEOPLE ALWAYS SAY "SINGLE-HANDEDLY"? YOU'VE GOT TWO HANDS, DUMMY.

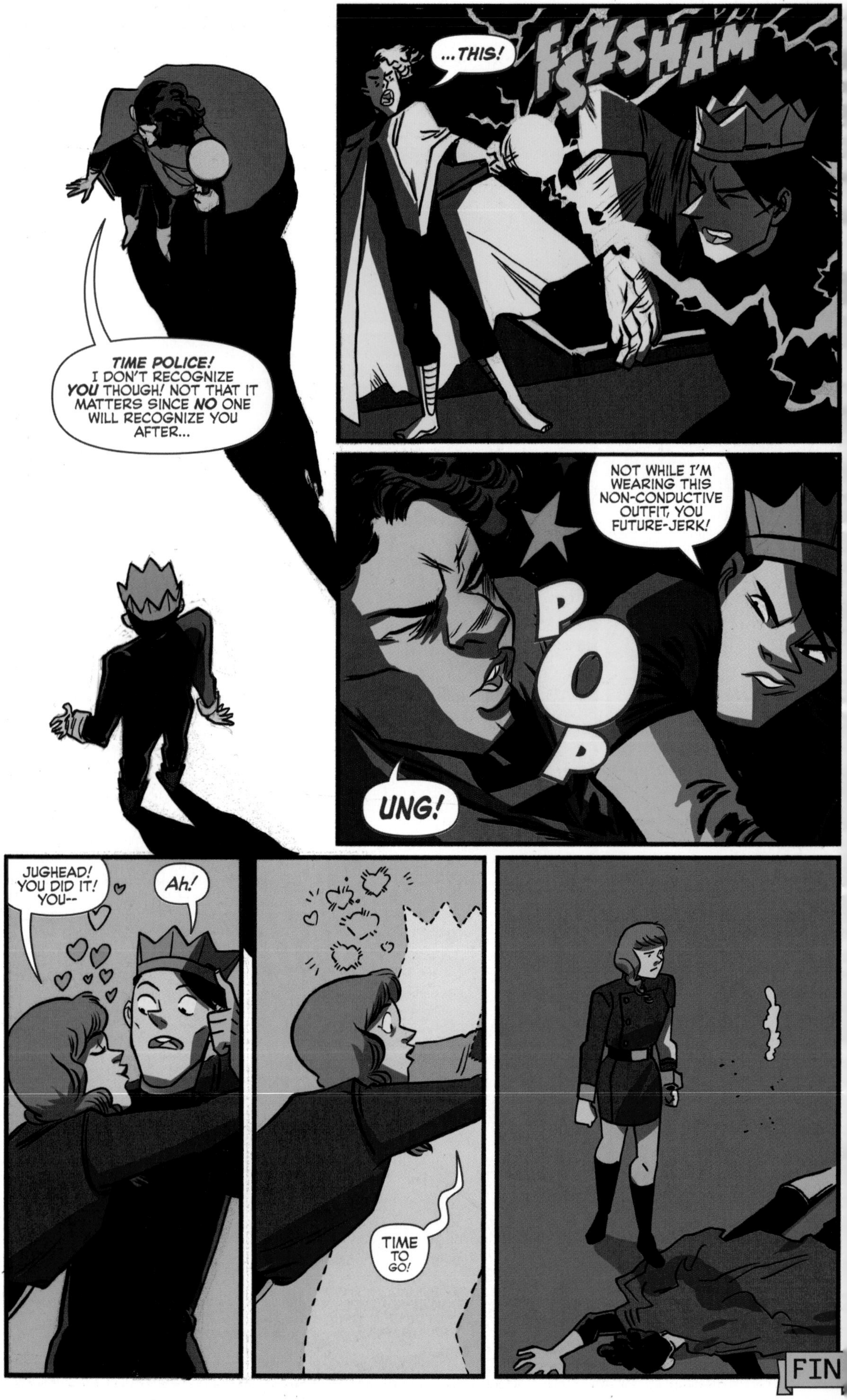

TIME POLICE! I DON'T RECOGNIZE YOU THOUGH! NOT THAT IT MATTERS SINCE NO ONE WILL RECOGNIZE YOU AFTER...
...THIS!
FSZSHAM
NOT WHILE I'M WEARING THIS NON-CONDUCTIVE OUTFIT, YOU FUTURE-JERK!
POP
UNG!
JUGHEAD! YOU DID IT! YOU--
Ah!
TIME TO GO!
FIN

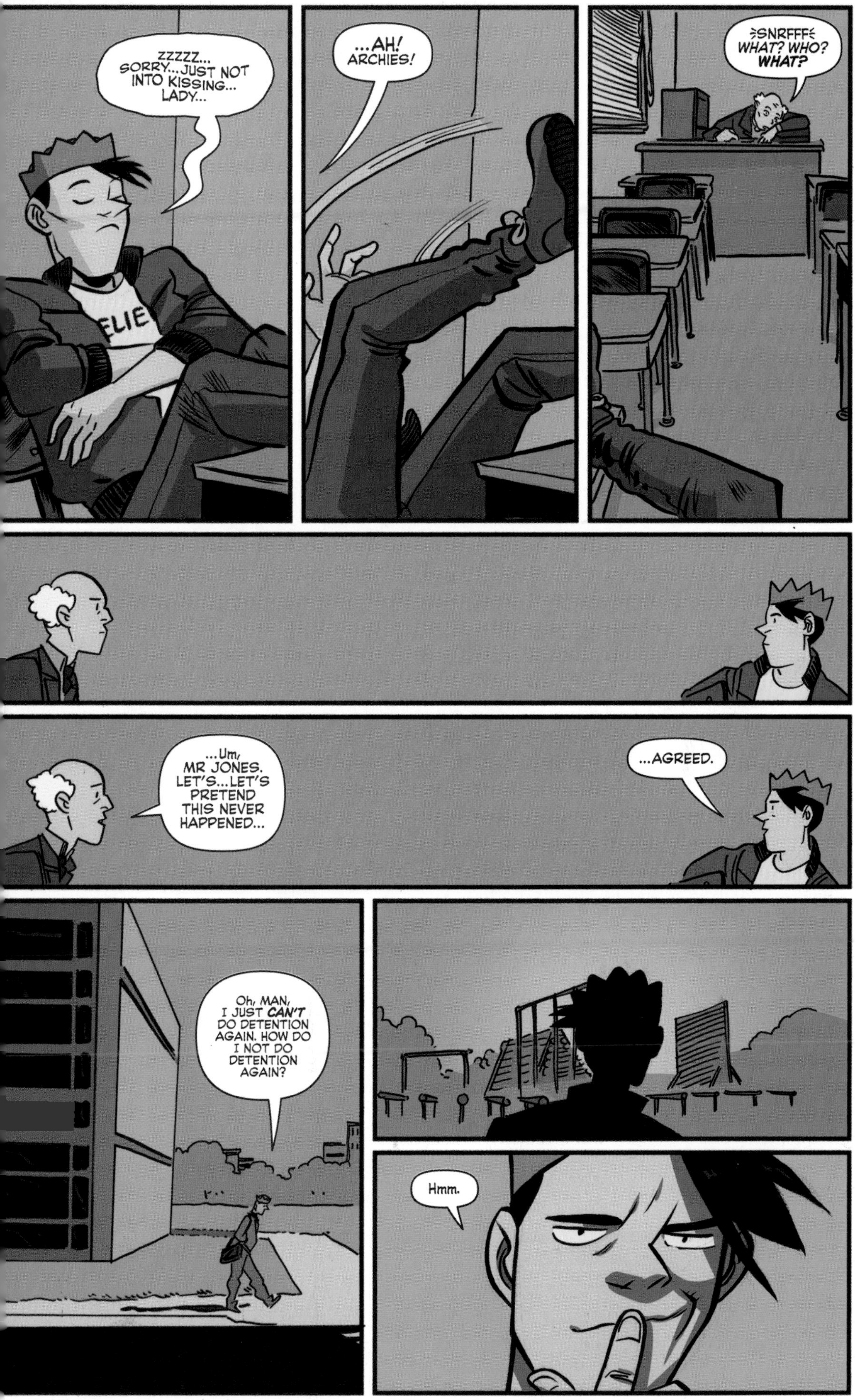

ZZZZZ... SORRY...JUST NOT INTO KISSING... LADY...
...AH! ARCHIES!
SNRFFF WHAT? WHO? **WHAT?**
...Um, MR JONES. LET'S...LET'S PRETEND THIS NEVER HAPPENED...
...AGREED.
Oh, MAN, I JUST **CAN'T** DO DETENTION AGAIN. HOW DO I NOT DO DETENTION AGAIN?
Hmm.

ALL RIGHT, YOU *MAGGOTS!* HERE ARE THE RULES!

IT'S *OBSTACLE COURSE* DAY! IF YOU DO NOT FINISH IT IN LESS THAN FIVE MINUTES, YOU *WILL* HAVE DETENTION! DOES THAT SOUND *HARSH* TO YOUR *BABY EARS?* WELL, I'M A *FAIR MAN,* SO....

...IF YOU FINISH IN UNDER *THREE* MINUTES, I'LL LET YOU SIT OUT THE NEXT *THREE* GYM CLASSES! DO I HAVE ANY *VOLUN--*

I'LL DO IT.

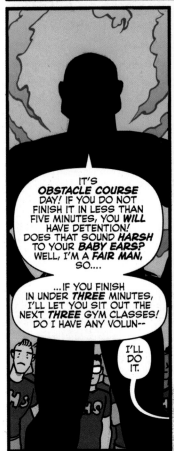

JUG? WHAT'S GOTTEN INTO YOU? THERE'S NO WAY--

START THE TIMER, COACH.

Heh. I LIKE THE INITIATIVE. ALL RIGHT, SLIM. READY, SET...

...GO!

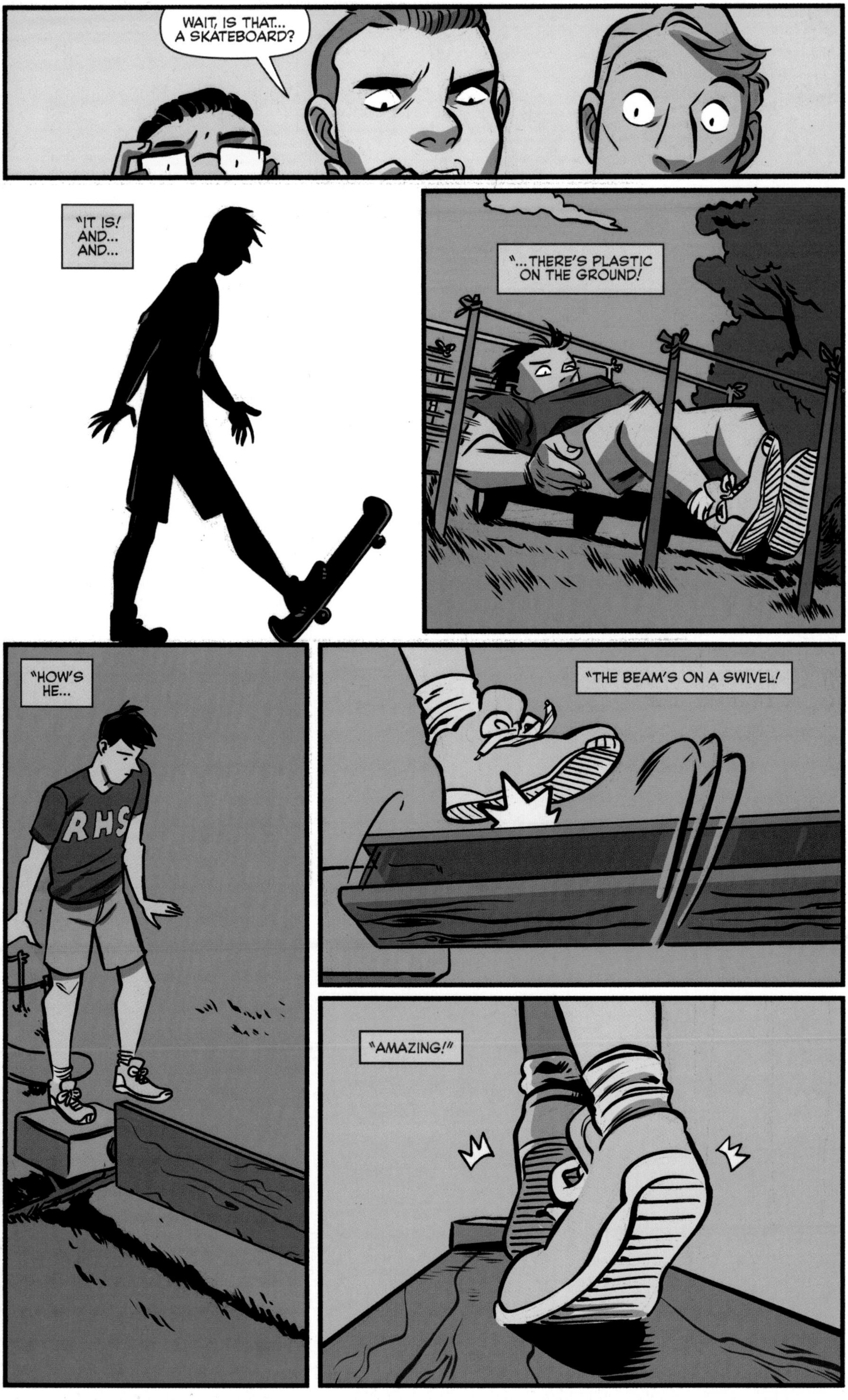
WAIT, IS THAT... A SKATEBOARD?
"IT IS! AND... AND...
"...THERE'S PLASTIC ON THE GROUND!
"HOW'S HE...
"THE BEAM'S ON A SWIVEL!
"AMAZING!"

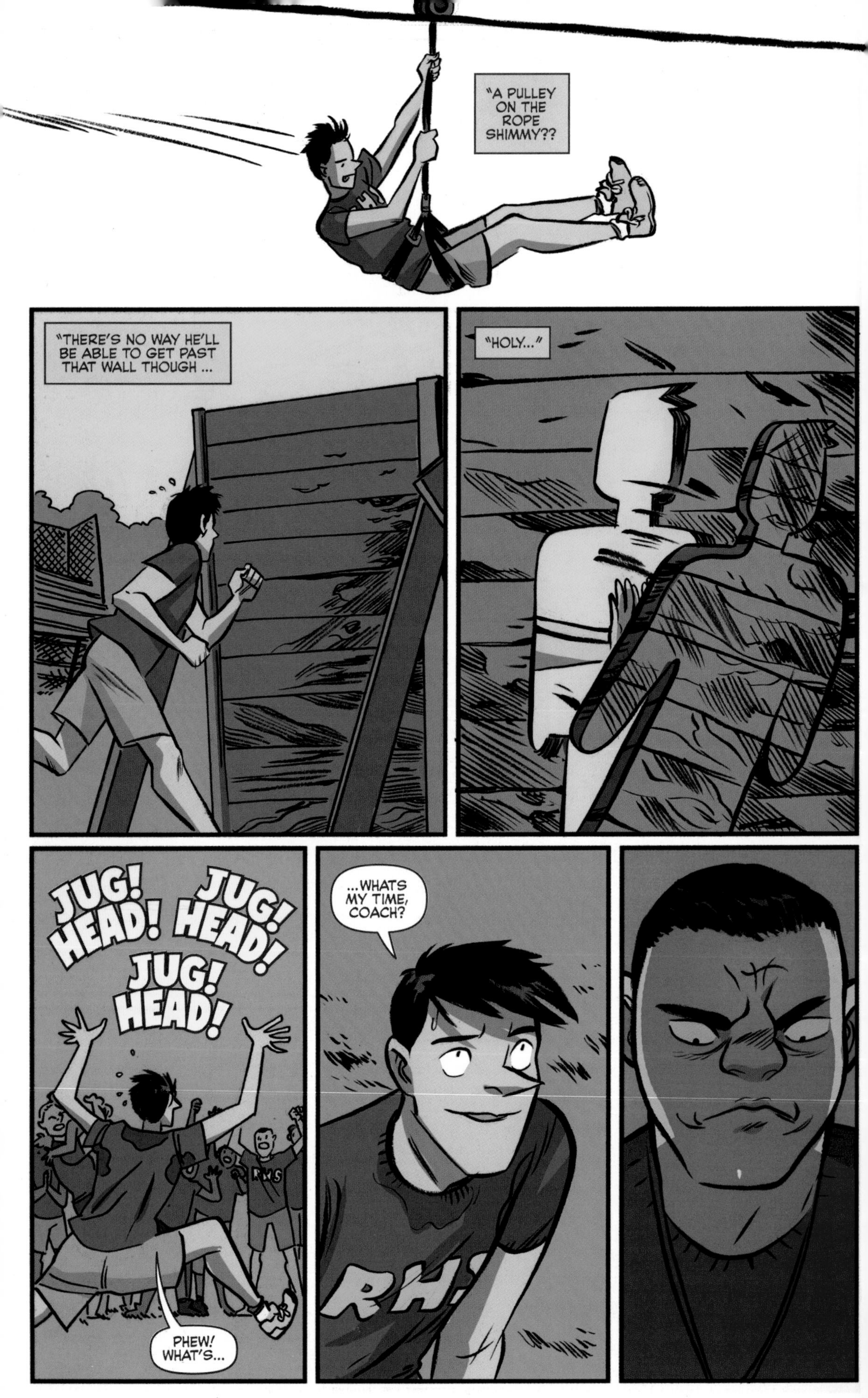
"A PULLEY ON THE ROPE SHIMMY??
"THERE'S NO WAY HE'LL BE ABLE TO GET PAST THAT WALL THOUGH ...
"HOLY..."
JUG! HEAD! JUG! HEAD! JUG! HEAD!
PHEW! WHAT'S...
...WHATS MY TIME, COACH?

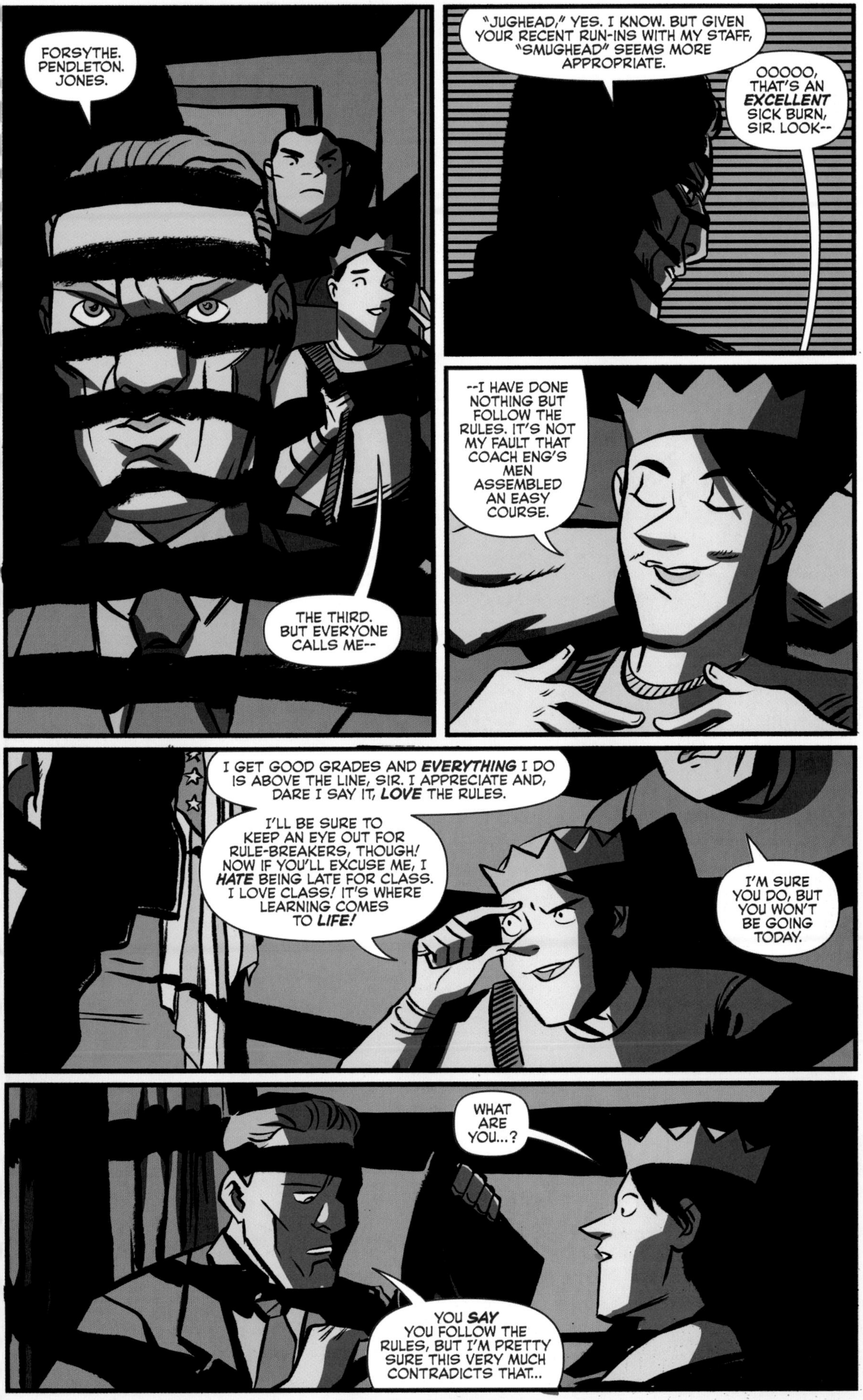

FORSYTHE. PENDLETON. JONES.
THE THIRD. BUT EVERYONE CALLS ME--
"JUGHEAD," YES. I KNOW. BUT GIVEN YOUR RECENT RUN-INS WITH MY STAFF, "SMUGHEAD" SEEMS MORE APPROPRIATE.
OOOOO, THAT'S AN **EXCELLENT** SICK BURN, SIR. LOOK--
--I HAVE DONE NOTHING BUT FOLLOW THE RULES. IT'S NOT MY FAULT THAT COACH ENG'S MEN ASSEMBLED AN EASY COURSE.
I GET GOOD GRADES AND **EVERYTHING** I DO IS ABOVE THE LINE, SIR. I APPRECIATE AND, DARE I SAY IT, **LOVE** THE RULES.
I'LL BE SURE TO KEEP AN EYE OUT FOR RULE-BREAKERS, THOUGH! NOW IF YOU'LL EXCUSE ME, I **HATE** BEING LATE FOR CLASS. I LOVE CLASS! IT'S WHERE LEARNING COMES TO **LIFE!**
I'M SURE YOU DO, BUT YOU WON'T BE GOING TODAY.
WHAT ARE YOU...?
YOU **SAY** YOU FOLLOW THE RULES, BUT I'M PRETTY SURE THIS VERY MUCH CONTRADICTS THAT...

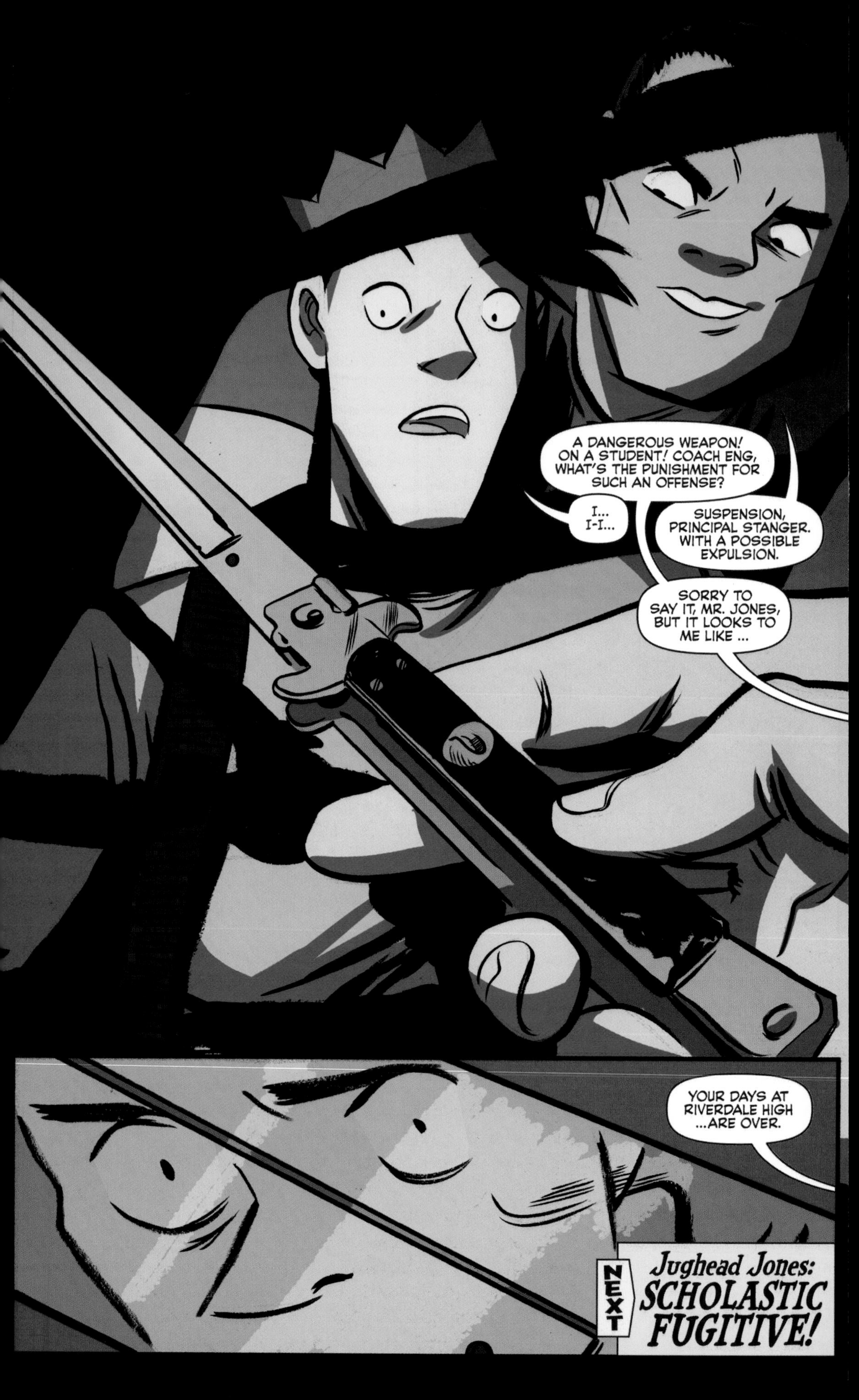
A DANGEROUS WEAPON! ON A STUDENT! COACH ENG, WHAT'S THE PUNISHMENT FOR SUCH AN OFFENSE?
I... I-I...
SUSPENSION, PRINCIPAL STANGER. WITH A POSSIBLE EXPULSION.
SORRY TO SAY IT, MR. JONES, BUT IT LOOKS TO ME LIKE ...
YOUR DAYS AT RIVERDALE HIGH ...ARE OVER.
NEXT Jughead Jones: SCHOLASTIC FUGITIVE!

TO BE
CONTINUED...

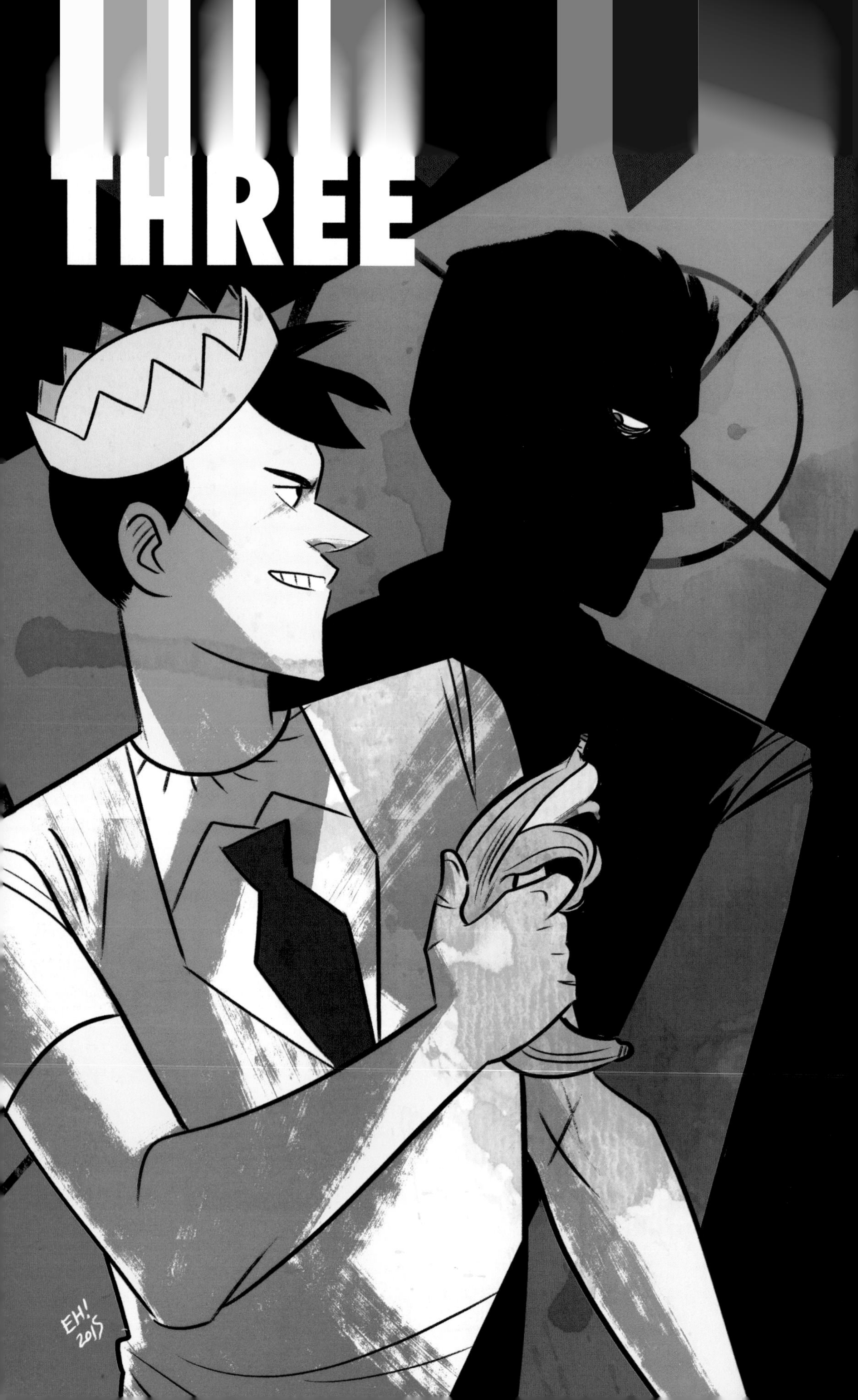
THREE
EH! 2015

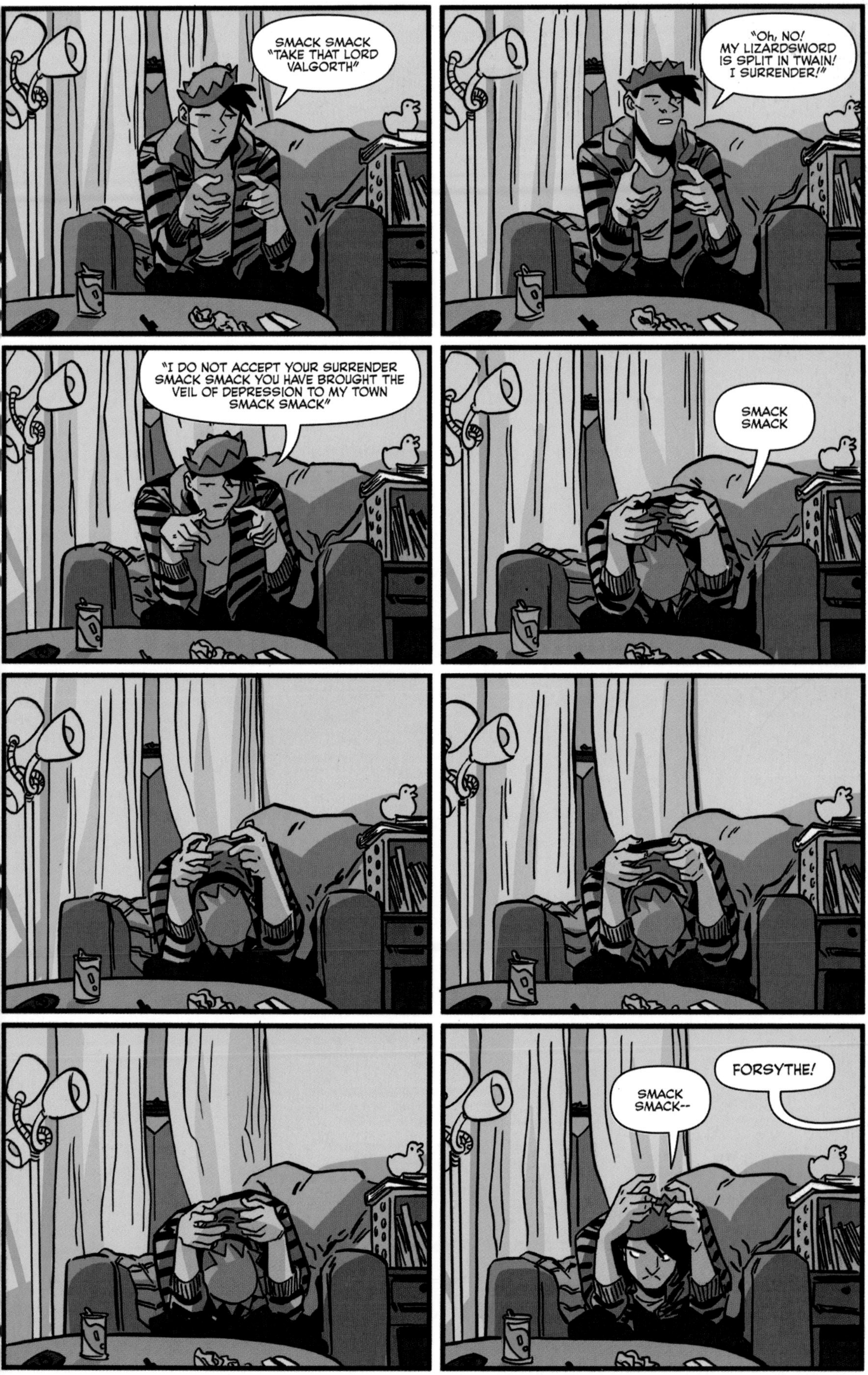
SMACK SMACK "TAKE THAT LORD VALGORTH"
"Oh, NO! MY LIZARDSWORD IS SPLIT IN TWAIN! I SURRENDER!"
"I DO NOT ACCEPT YOUR SURRENDER SMACK SMACK YOU HAVE BROUGHT THE VEIL OF DEPRESSION TO MY TOWN SMACK SMACK"
SMACK SMACK
SMACK SMACK--
FORSYTHE!

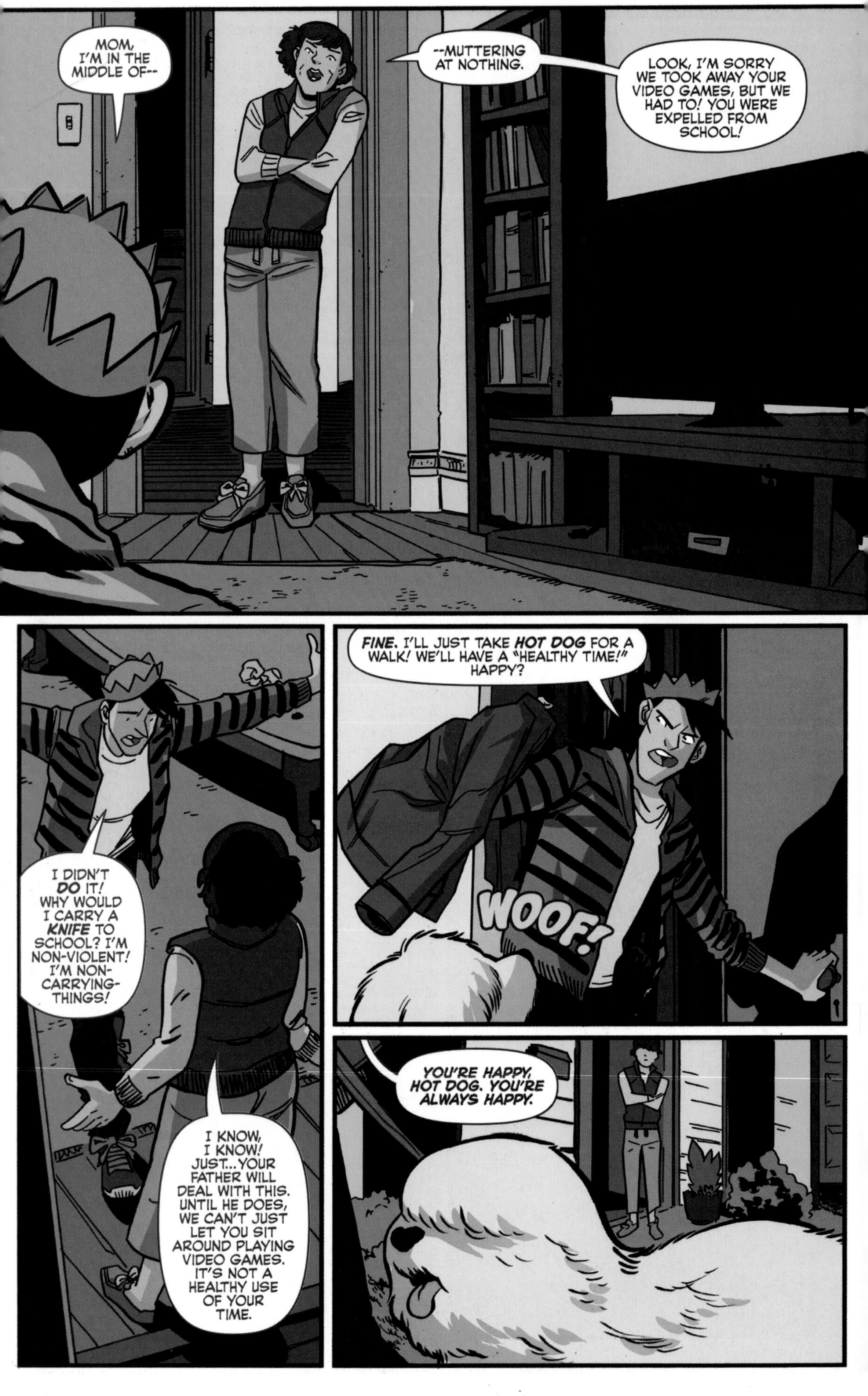
MOM, I'M IN THE MIDDLE OF--
--MUTTERING AT NOTHING.
LOOK, I'M SORRY WE TOOK AWAY YOUR VIDEO GAMES, BUT WE HAD TO! YOU WERE EXPELLED FROM SCHOOL!
I DIDN'T DO IT! WHY WOULD I CARRY A KNIFE TO SCHOOL? I'M NON-VIOLENT! I'M NON-CARRYING-THINGS!
I KNOW, I KNOW! JUST...YOUR FATHER WILL DEAL WITH THIS. UNTIL HE DOES, WE CAN'T JUST LET YOU SIT AROUND PLAYING VIDEO GAMES. IT'S NOT A HEALTHY USE OF YOUR TIME.
FINE. I'LL JUST TAKE HOT DOG FOR A WALK! WE'LL HAVE A "HEALTHY TIME!" HAPPY?
WOOF!
YOU'RE HAPPY, HOT DOG. YOU'RE ALWAYS HAPPY.

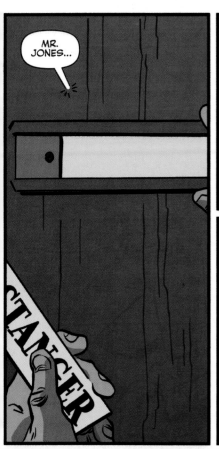

MR. JONES...

--PLEASE, PLEASE, CALL ME JONESY. IT'S TECH-NICALLY "FORSYTHE," LIKE MY SON, BUT, LIKE HIM, I ALSO DON'T GO BY IT. SO WHY WOULD WE NAME HIM THAT? WELL, IT'S A FUNNY STORY--

--MR. JONES. THIS IS A SERIOUS OFFENSE. RIVERDALE HIGH HAS A VERY STRICT POLICY AGAINST WEAPONS IN OUR HALLS.

OH, OF COURSE! TOTALLY REASONABLE! BUT IN *THIS* INSTANCE, I'M AFRAID--

--YOU HAVE THE WRONG GUY!

...I'M SORRY?

WELL, YOU SAID YOU FOUND IT IN MY SON'S BACKPACK, YES?

...YES.

AND THAT YOU NEVER SAW HIM TOUCH IT?

YES.

WELL, THAT'S BECAUSE HE DIDN'T KNOW IT WAS THERE! I SOMETIMES USE MY SON'S BACKPACK FOR MY FISHING TRIPS AND THOSE FISH AREN'T GOING TO GUT THEMSELVES, YOU KNOW?

ACTUALLY! YOU KNOW WHO ELSE WAS ON MY FISHING TRIP? SUPERINTENDENT HASSLE! HE'S *QUITE* THE FISHERMAN, LET ME TELL YOU...

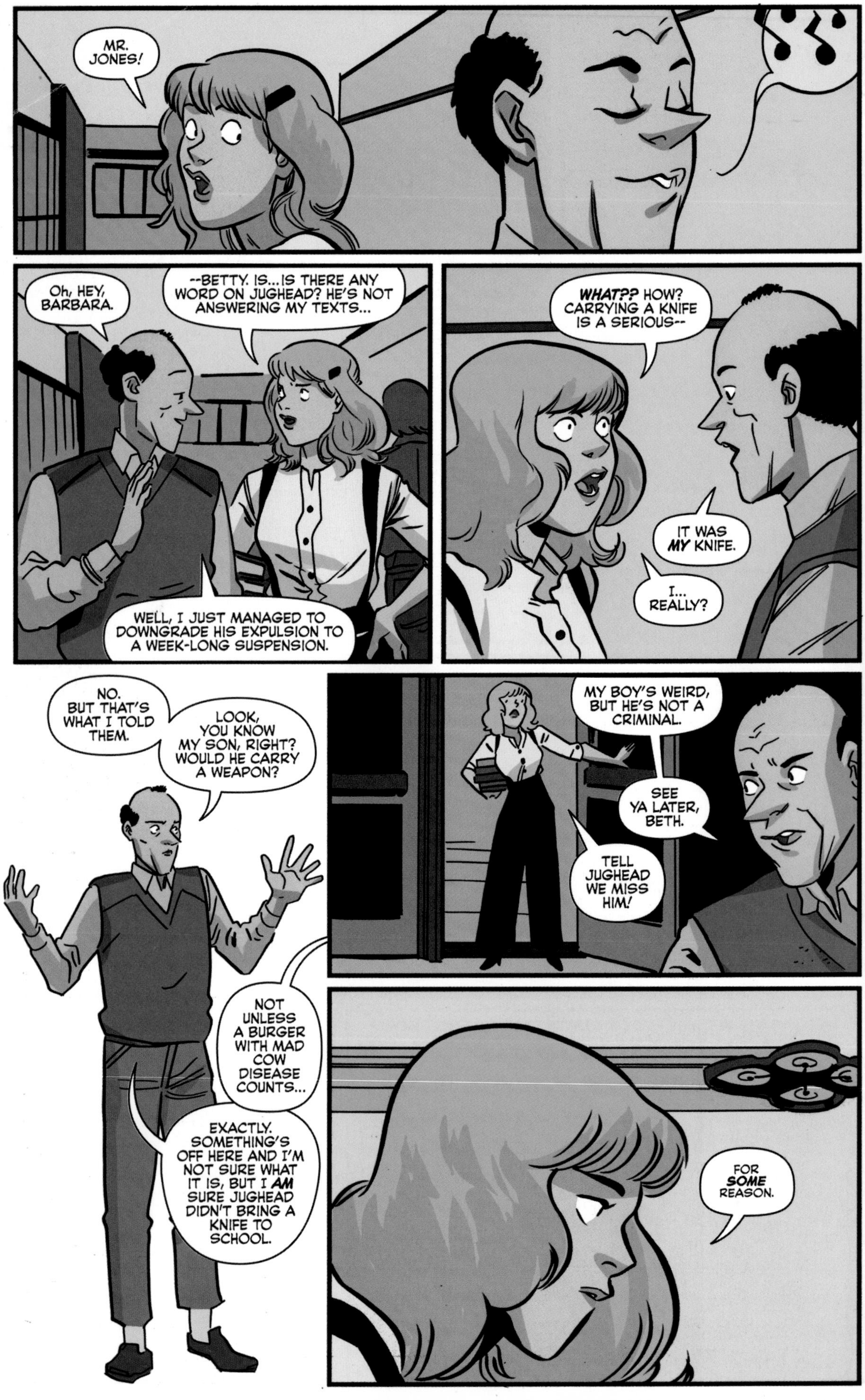
MR. JONES!
Oh, HEY, BARBARA.
--BETTY. IS...IS THERE ANY WORD ON JUGHEAD? HE'S NOT ANSWERING MY TEXTS...
WELL, I JUST MANAGED TO DOWNGRADE HIS EXPULSION TO A WEEK-LONG SUSPENSION.
WHAT?? HOW? CARRYING A KNIFE IS A SERIOUS--
IT WAS MY KNIFE.
I... REALLY?
NO. BUT THAT'S WHAT I TOLD THEM.
LOOK, YOU KNOW MY SON, RIGHT? WOULD HE CARRY A WEAPON?
NOT UNLESS A BURGER WITH MAD COW DISEASE COUNTS...
EXACTLY. SOMETHING'S OFF HERE AND I'M NOT SURE WHAT IT IS, BUT I AM SURE JUGHEAD DIDN'T BRING A KNIFE TO SCHOOL.
MY BOY'S WEIRD, BUT HE'S NOT A CRIMINAL.
SEE YA LATER, BETH.
TELL JUGHEAD WE MISS HIM!
FOR SOME REASON.

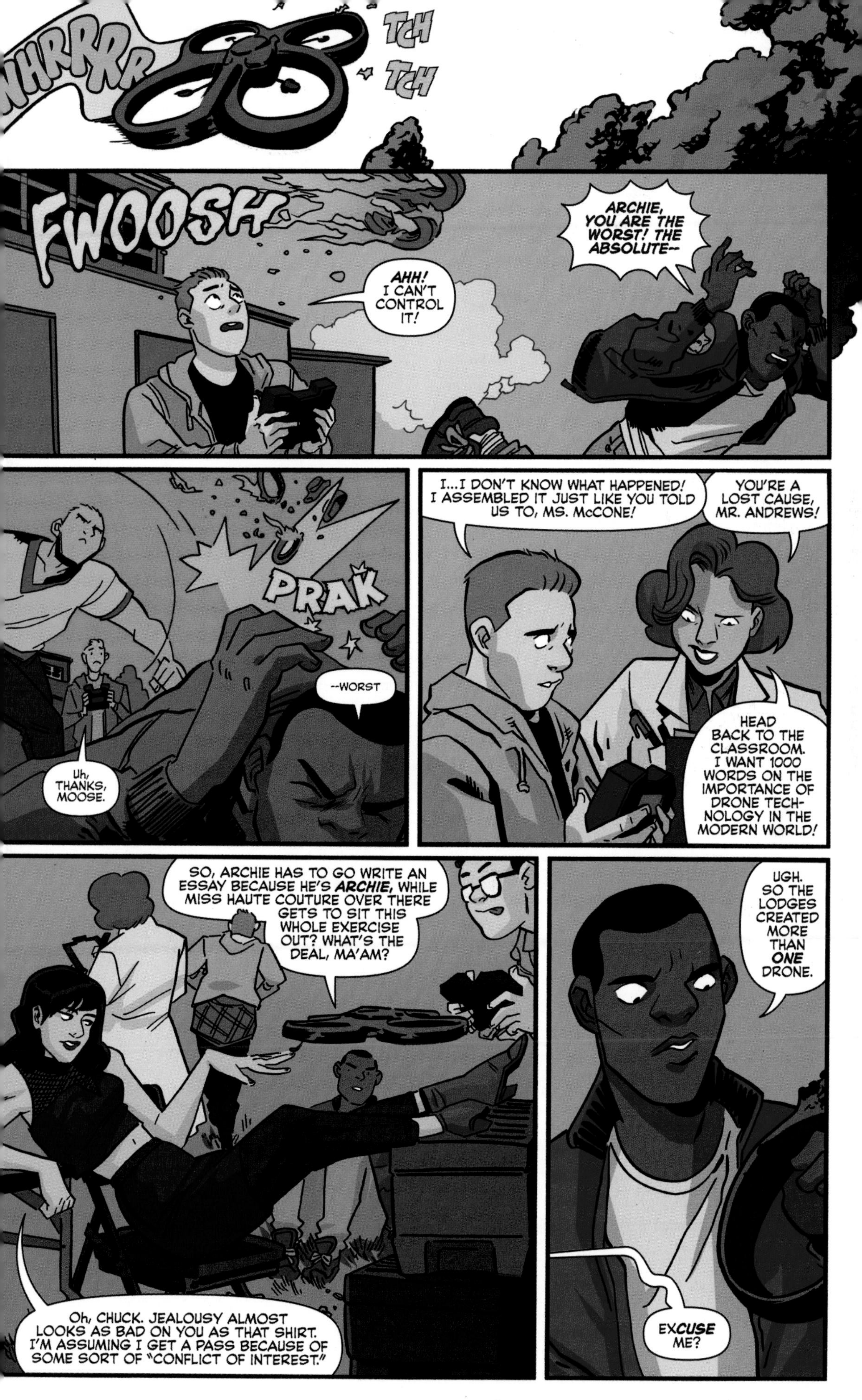
WHRRRRR
TCH
TCH
FWOOSH
AHH! I CAN'T CONTROL IT!
ARCHIE, YOU ARE THE WORST! THE ABSOLUTE--
PRAK
--WORST
Uh, THANKS, MOOSE.
I...I DON'T KNOW WHAT HAPPENED! I ASSEMBLED IT JUST LIKE YOU TOLD US TO, MS. McCONE!
YOU'RE A LOST CAUSE, MR. ANDREWS!
HEAD BACK TO THE CLASSROOM. I WANT 1000 WORDS ON THE IMPORTANCE OF DRONE TECH-NOLOGY IN THE MODERN WORLD!
SO, ARCHIE HAS TO GO WRITE AN ESSAY BECAUSE HE'S ARCHIE, WHILE MISS HAUTE COUTURE OVER THERE GETS TO SIT THIS WHOLE EXERCISE OUT? WHAT'S THE DEAL, MA'AM?
Oh, CHUCK. JEALOUSY ALMOST LOOKS AS BAD ON YOU AS THAT SHIRT. I'M ASSUMING I GET A PASS BECAUSE OF SOME SORT OF "CONFLICT OF INTEREST."
UGH. SO THE LODGES CREATED MORE THAN ONE DRONE.
EXCUSE ME?

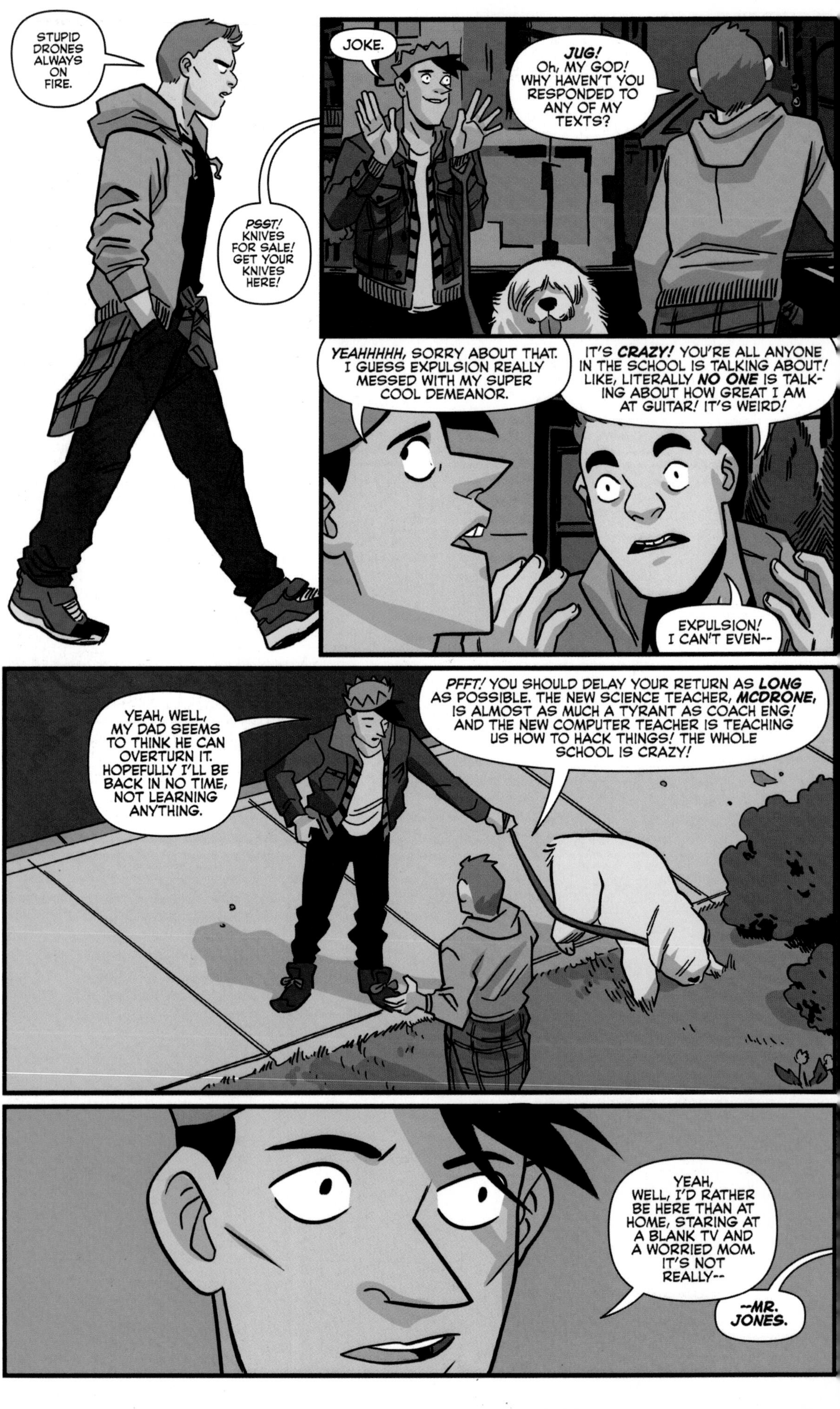
STUPID DRONES ALWAYS ON FIRE.
JOKE.
JUG! Oh, MY GOD! WHY HAVEN'T YOU RESPONDED TO ANY OF MY TEXTS?
PSST! KNIVES FOR SALE! GET YOUR KNIVES HERE!
YEAHHHHH, SORRY ABOUT THAT. I GUESS EXPULSION REALLY MESSED WITH MY SUPER COOL DEMEANOR.
IT'S CRAZY! YOU'RE ALL ANYONE IN THE SCHOOL IS TALKING ABOUT! LIKE, LITERALLY NO ONE IS TALK-ING ABOUT HOW GREAT I AM AT GUITAR! IT'S WEIRD!
EXPULSION! I CAN'T EVEN--
YEAH, WELL, MY DAD SEEMS TO THINK HE CAN OVERTURN IT. HOPEFULLY I'LL BE BACK IN NO TIME, NOT LEARNING ANYTHING.
PFFT! YOU SHOULD DELAY YOUR RETURN AS LONG AS POSSIBLE. THE NEW SCIENCE TEACHER, MCDRONE, IS ALMOST AS MUCH A TYRANT AS COACH ENG! AND THE NEW COMPUTER TEACHER IS TEACHING US HOW TO HACK THINGS! THE WHOLE SCHOOL IS CRAZY!
YEAH, WELL, I'D RATHER BE HERE THAN AT HOME, STARING AT A BLANK TV AND A WORRIED MOM. IT'S NOT REALLY--
--MR. JONES.

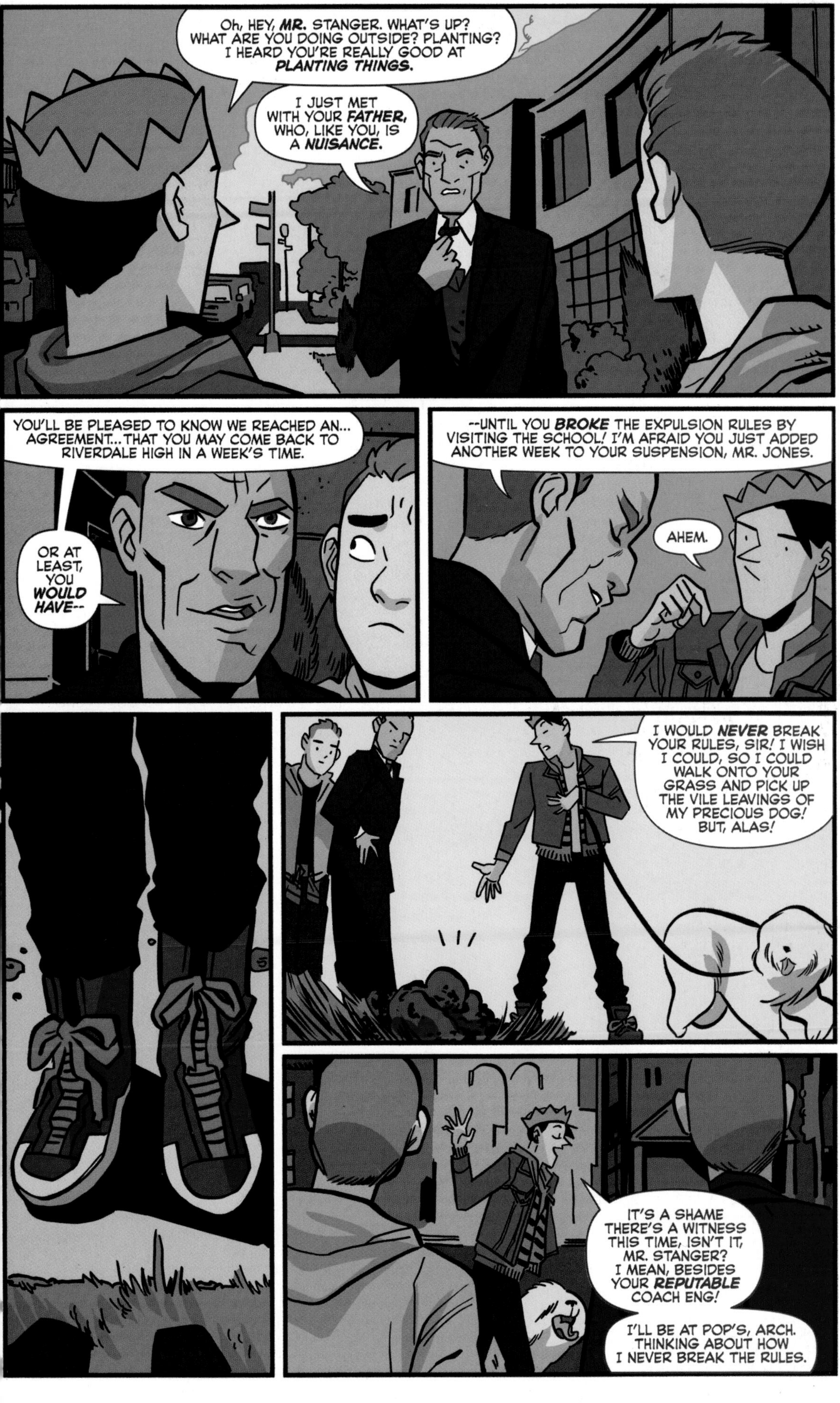
Oh, HEY, MR. STANGER. WHAT'S UP? WHAT ARE YOU DOING OUTSIDE? PLANTING? I HEARD YOU'RE REALLY GOOD AT PLANTING THINGS.
I JUST MET WITH YOUR FATHER, WHO, LIKE YOU, IS A NUISANCE.
YOU'LL BE PLEASED TO KNOW WE REACHED AN... AGREEMENT...THAT YOU MAY COME BACK TO RIVERDALE HIGH IN A WEEK'S TIME.
OR AT LEAST, YOU WOULD HAVE--
--UNTIL YOU BROKE THE EXPULSION RULES BY VISITING THE SCHOOL! I'M AFRAID YOU JUST ADDED ANOTHER WEEK TO YOUR SUSPENSION, MR. JONES.
AHEM.
I WOULD NEVER BREAK YOUR RULES, SIR! I WISH I COULD, SO I COULD WALK ONTO YOUR GRASS AND PICK UP THE VILE LEAVINGS OF MY PRECIOUS DOG! BUT, ALAS!
IT'S A SHAME THERE'S A WITNESS THIS TIME, ISN'T IT, MR. STANGER? I MEAN, BESIDES YOUR REPUTABLE COACH ENG!
I'LL BE AT POP'S, ARCH. THINKING ABOUT HOW I NEVER BREAK THE RULES.

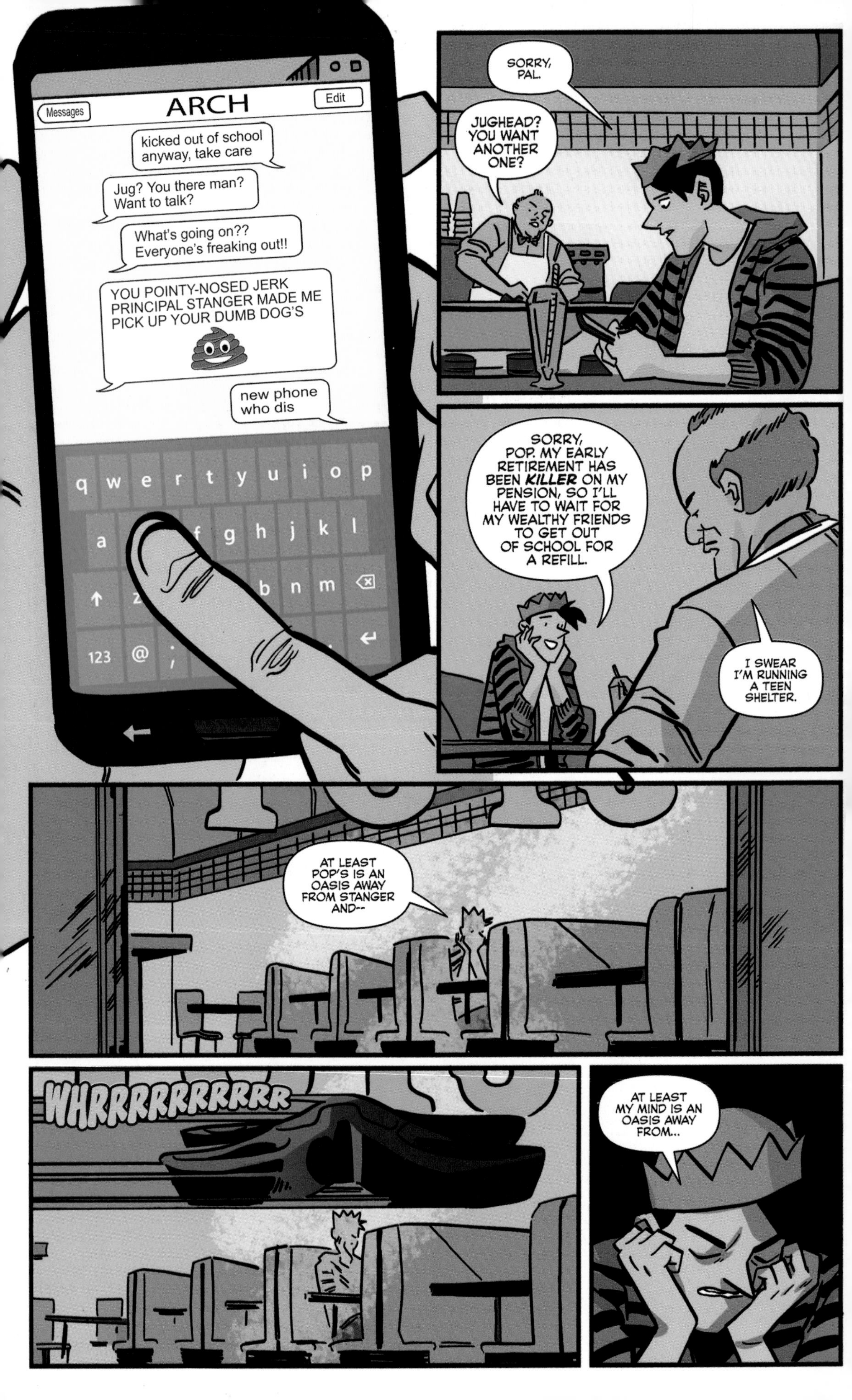

Messages
ARCH
Edit
kicked out of school anyway, take care
Jug? You there man? Want to talk?
What's going on?? Everyone's freaking out!!
YOU POINTY-NOSED JERK PRINCIPAL STANGER MADE ME PICK UP YOUR DUMB DOG'S
new phone who dis
SORRY, PAL.
JUGHEAD? YOU WANT ANOTHER ONE?
SORRY, POP. MY EARLY RETIREMENT HAS BEEN KILLER ON MY PENSION, SO I'LL HAVE TO WAIT FOR MY WEALTHY FRIENDS TO GET OUT OF SCHOOL FOR A REFILL.
I SWEAR I'M RUNNING A TEEN SHELTER.
AT LEAST POP'S IS AN OASIS AWAY FROM STANGER AND--
WHRRRRRRRRRR
AT LEAST MY MIND IS AN OASIS AWAY FROM...

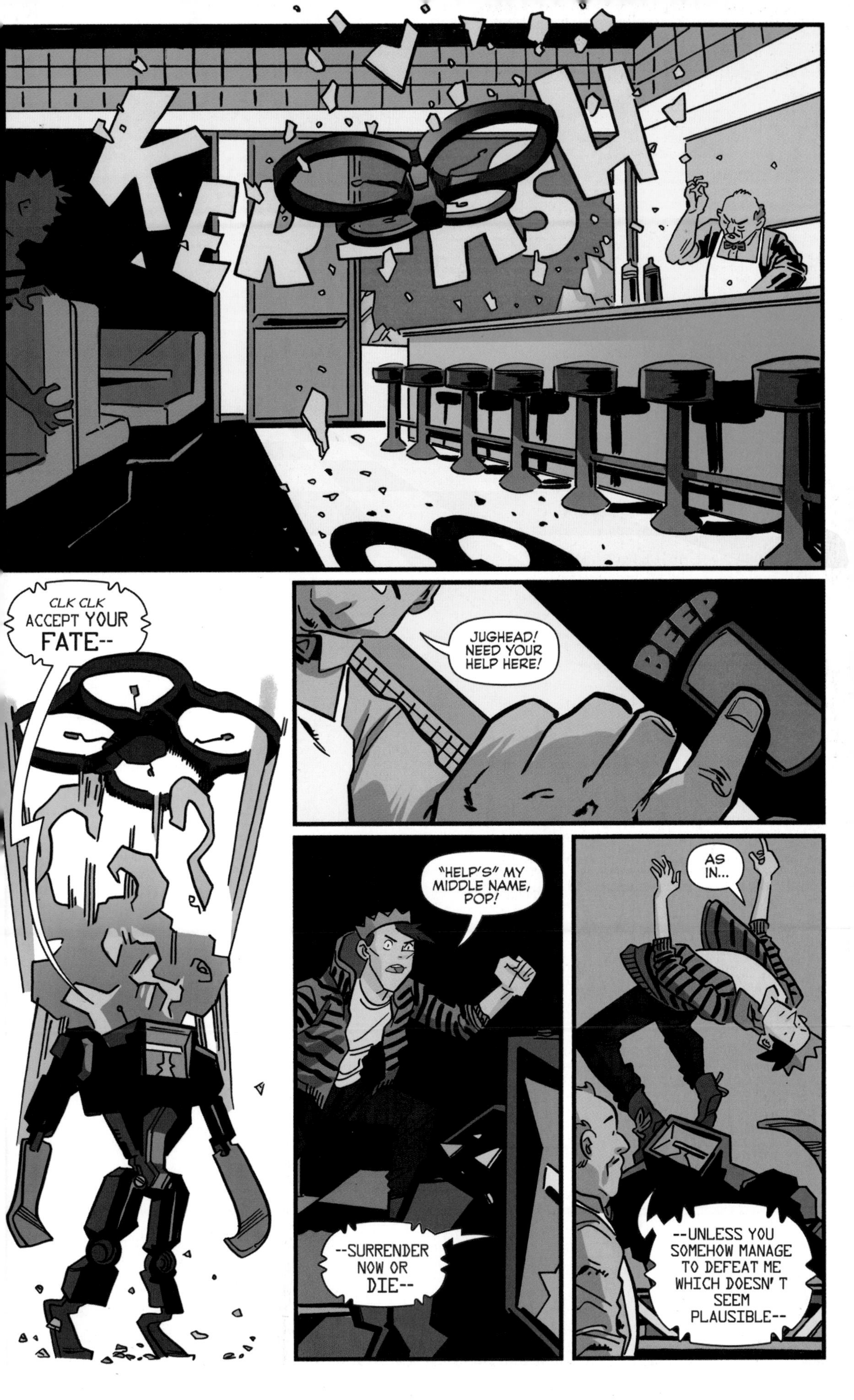
KERRASH
CLK CLK
ACCEPT YOUR FATE--
JUGHEAD! NEED YOUR HELP HERE!
BEEP
"HELP'S" MY MIDDLE NAME, POP!
--SURRENDER NOW OR DIE--
AS IN...
--UNLESS YOU SOMEHOW MANAGE TO DEFEAT ME WHICH DOESN'T SEEM PLAUSIBLE--

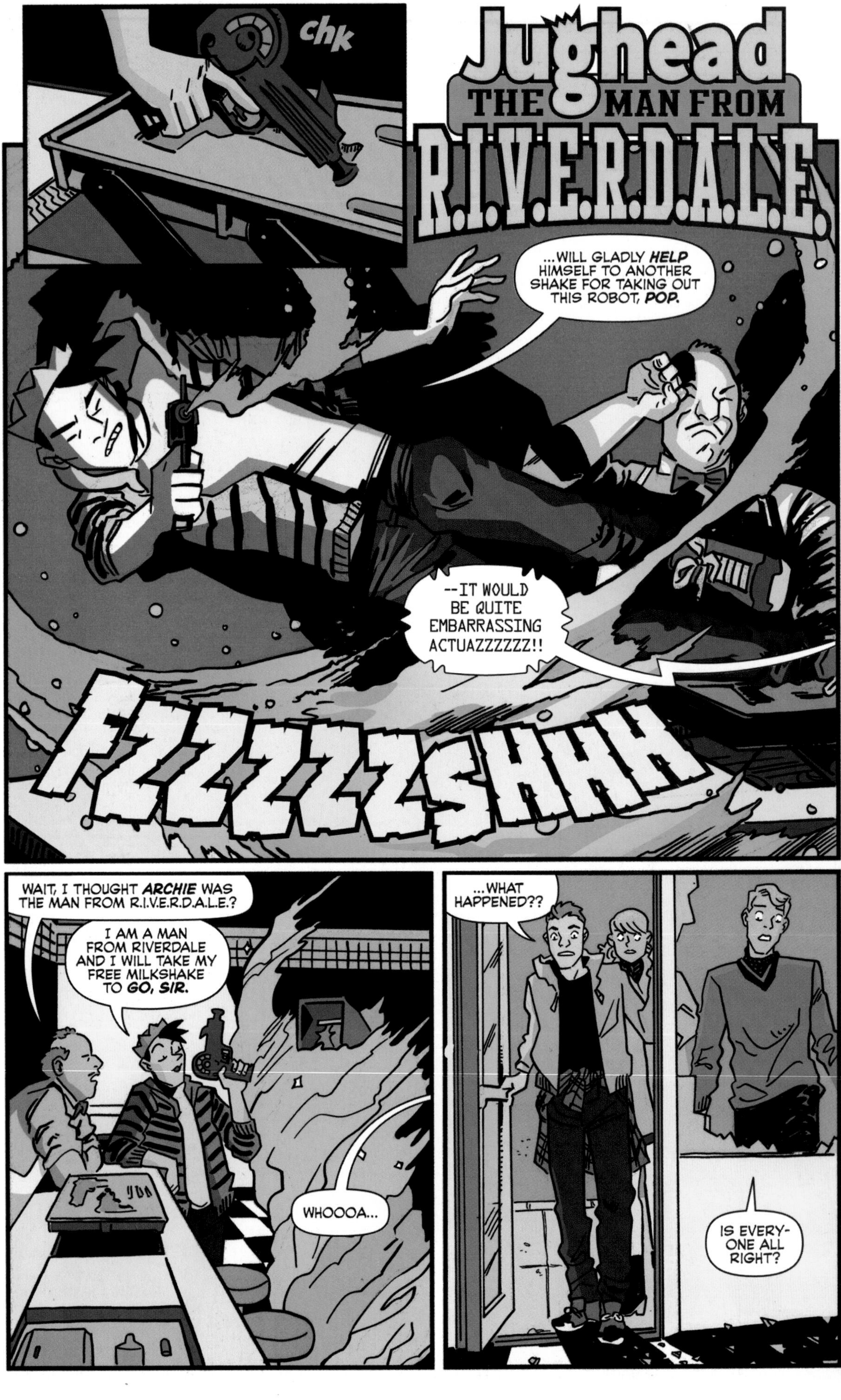
chk
Jughead THE MAN FROM R.I.V.E.R.D.A.L.E.
...WILL GLADLY HELP HIMSELF TO ANOTHER SHAKE FOR TAKING OUT THIS ROBOT, POP.
--IT WOULD BE QUITE EMBARRASSING ACTUAZZZZZZ!!
FZZZZZSHHH
WAIT, I THOUGHT ARCHIE WAS THE MAN FROM R.I.V.E.R.D.A.L.E.?
I AM A MAN FROM RIVERDALE AND I WILL TAKE MY FREE MILKSHAKE TO GO, SIR.
WHOOOA...
...WHAT HAPPENED??
IS EVERY-ONE ALL RIGHT?

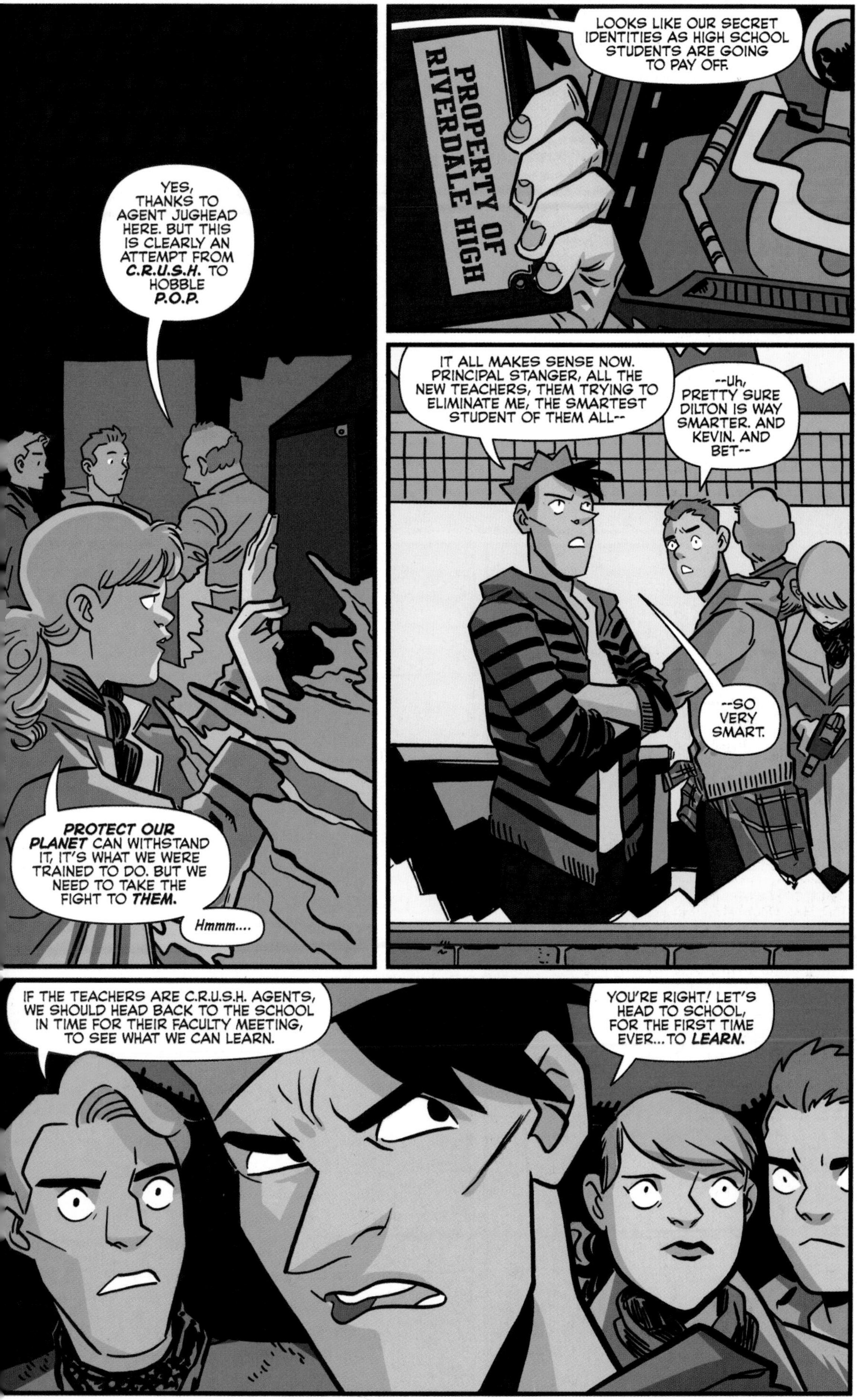
YES, THANKS TO AGENT JUGHEAD HERE. BUT THIS IS CLEARLY AN ATTEMPT FROM C.R.U.S.H. TO HOBBLE P.O.P.
PROTECT OUR PLANET CAN WITHSTAND IT, IT'S WHAT WE WERE TRAINED TO DO. BUT WE NEED TO TAKE THE FIGHT TO THEM.
Hmmm....
LOOKS LIKE OUR SECRET IDENTITIES AS HIGH SCHOOL STUDENTS ARE GOING TO PAY OFF.
PROPERTY OF RIVERDALE HIGH
IT ALL MAKES SENSE NOW. PRINCIPAL STANGER, ALL THE NEW TEACHERS, THEM TRYING TO ELIMINATE ME, THE SMARTEST STUDENT OF THEM ALL--
--Uh, PRETTY SURE DILTON IS WAY SMARTER. AND KEVIN. AND BET--
--SO VERY SMART.
IF THE TEACHERS ARE C.R.U.S.H. AGENTS, WE SHOULD HEAD BACK TO THE SCHOOL IN TIME FOR THEIR FACULTY MEETING, TO SEE WHAT WE CAN LEARN.
YOU'RE RIGHT! LET'S HEAD TO SCHOOL, FOR THE FIRST TIME EVER...TO LEARN.

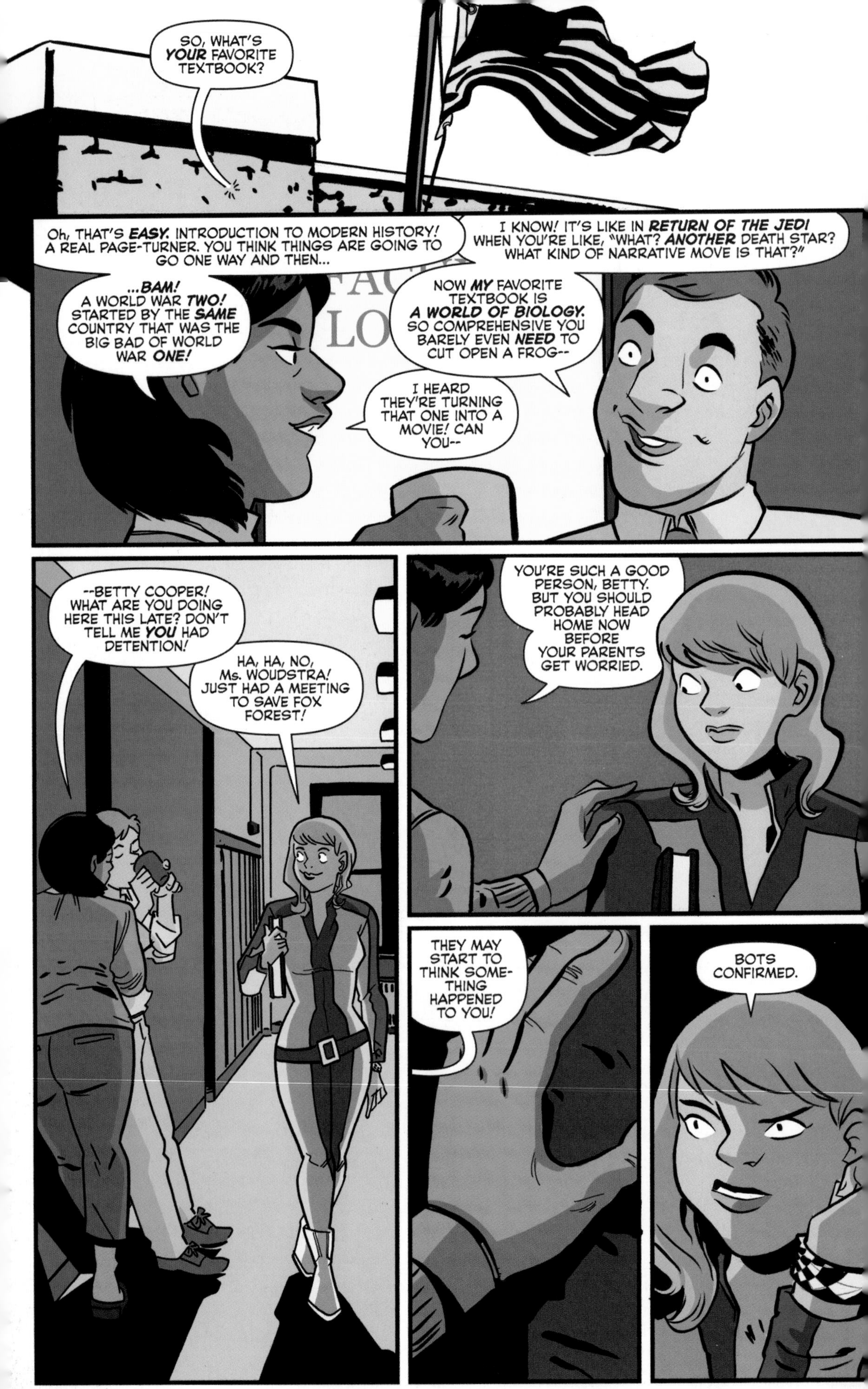
SO, WHAT'S **YOUR** FAVORITE TEXTBOOK?
Oh, THAT'S **EASY.** INTRODUCTION TO MODERN HISTORY! A REAL PAGE-TURNER. YOU THINK THINGS ARE GOING TO GO ONE WAY AND THEN...
...**BAM!** A WORLD WAR **TWO!** STARTED BY THE **SAME** COUNTRY THAT WAS THE BIG BAD OF WORLD WAR **ONE!**
I KNOW! IT'S LIKE IN **RETURN OF THE JEDI** WHEN YOU'RE LIKE, "WHAT? **ANOTHER** DEATH STAR? WHAT KIND OF NARRATIVE MOVE IS THAT?"
NOW **MY** FAVORITE TEXTBOOK IS **A WORLD OF BIOLOGY.** SO COMPREHENSIVE YOU BARELY EVEN **NEED** TO CUT OPEN A FROG--
I HEARD THEY'RE TURNING THAT ONE INTO A MOVIE! CAN YOU--
--BETTY COOPER! WHAT ARE YOU DOING HERE THIS LATE? DON'T TELL ME **YOU** HAD DETENTION!
HA, HA, NO, Ms. WOUDSTRA! JUST HAD A MEETING TO SAVE FOX FOREST!
YOU'RE SUCH A GOOD PERSON, BETTY. BUT YOU SHOULD PROBABLY HEAD HOME NOW BEFORE YOUR PARENTS GET WORRIED.
THEY MAY START TO THINK SOME-THING HAPPENED TO YOU!
BOTS CONFIRMED.

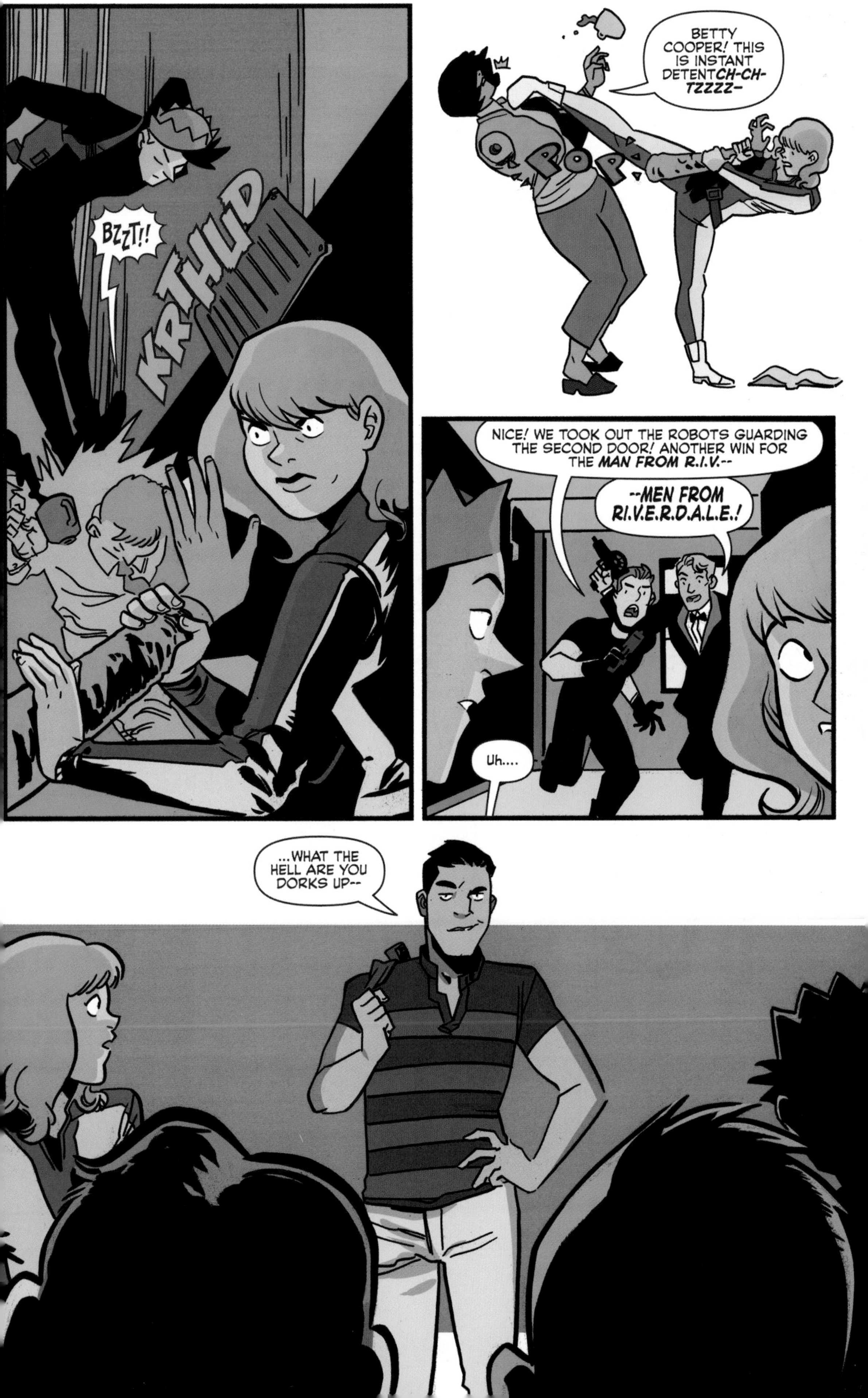
BZZT!!
KRTHUD
BETTY COOPER! THIS IS INSTANT DETENTCH-CH-TZZZZ--
POP
NICE! WE TOOK OUT THE ROBOTS GUARDING THE SECOND DOOR! ANOTHER WIN FOR THE MAN FROM R.I.V.--
--MEN FROM R.I.V.E.R.D.A.L.E.!
Uh....
...WHAT THE HELL ARE YOU DORKS UP--

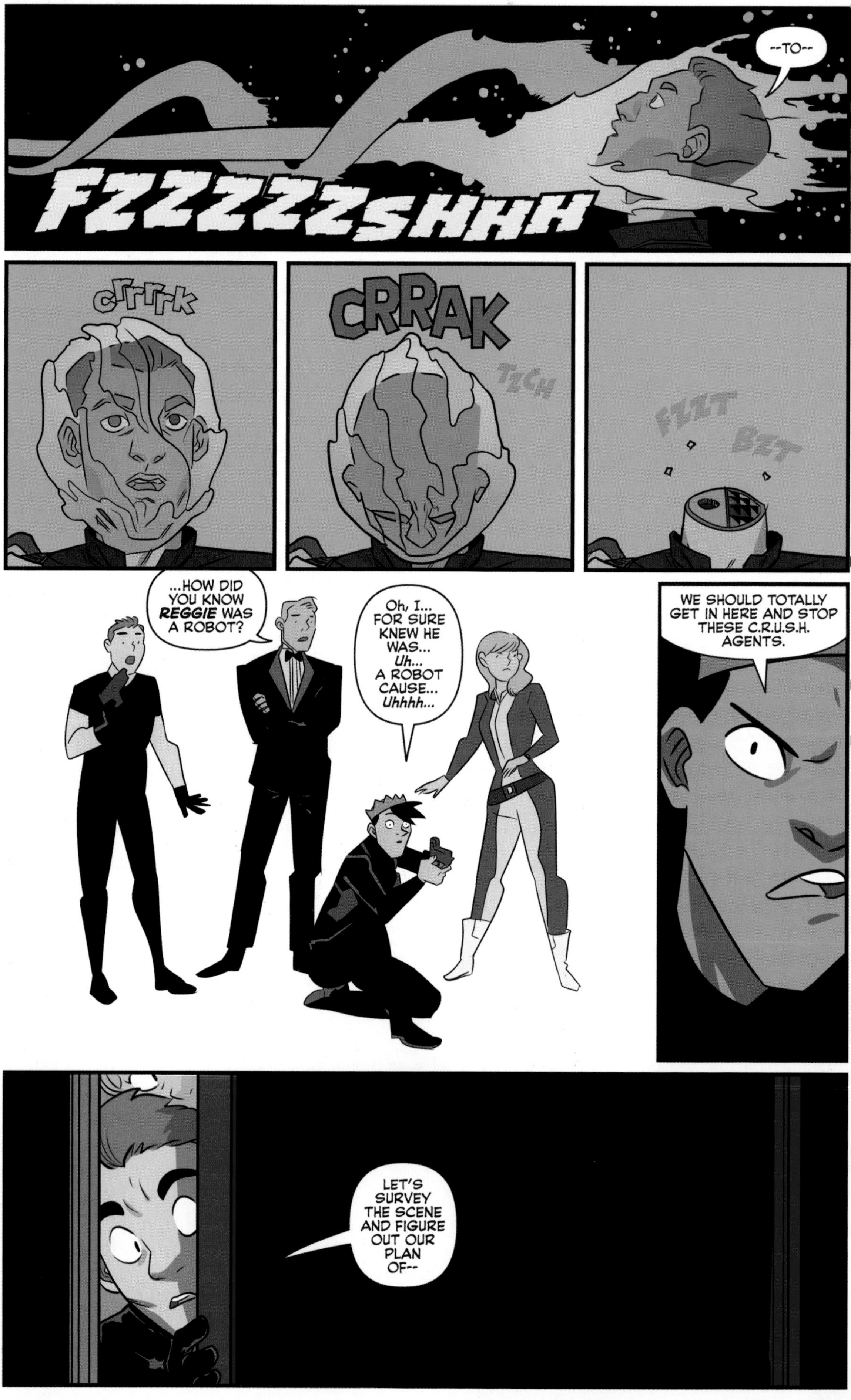
--TO--
FZZZZZSHHH
crrrrk
CRRAK
TZCH
FZZT
BZT
...HOW DID YOU KNOW *REGGIE* WAS A ROBOT?
Oh, I... FOR SURE KNEW HE WAS... *Uh...* A ROBOT CAUSE... *Uhhhh...*
WE SHOULD TOTALLY GET IN HERE AND STOP THESE C.R.U.S.H. AGENTS.
LET'S SURVEY THE SCENE AND FIGURE OUT OUR PLAN OF--

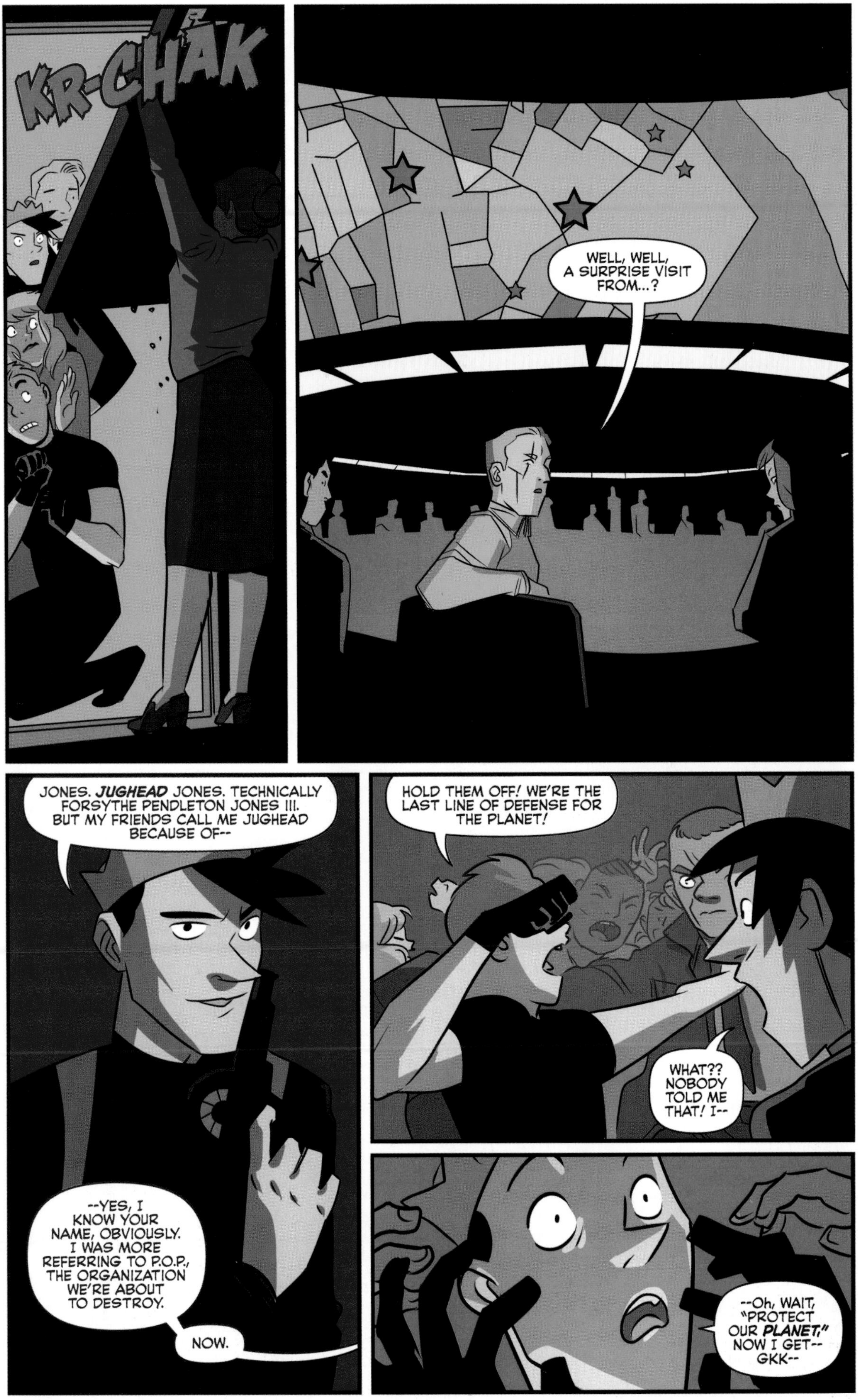
KR-CHAK
WELL, WELL, A SURPRISE VISIT FROM...?
JONES. JUGHEAD JONES. TECHNICALLY FORSYTHE PENDLETON JONES III. BUT MY FRIENDS CALL ME JUGHEAD BECAUSE OF--
--YES, I KNOW YOUR NAME, OBVIOUSLY. I WAS MORE REFERRING TO P.O.P., THE ORGANIZATION WE'RE ABOUT TO DESTROY.
NOW.
HOLD THEM OFF! WE'RE THE LAST LINE OF DEFENSE FOR THE PLANET!
WHAT?? NOBODY TOLD ME THAT! I--
--Oh, WAIT, "PROTECT OUR PLANET," NOW I GET-- GKK--

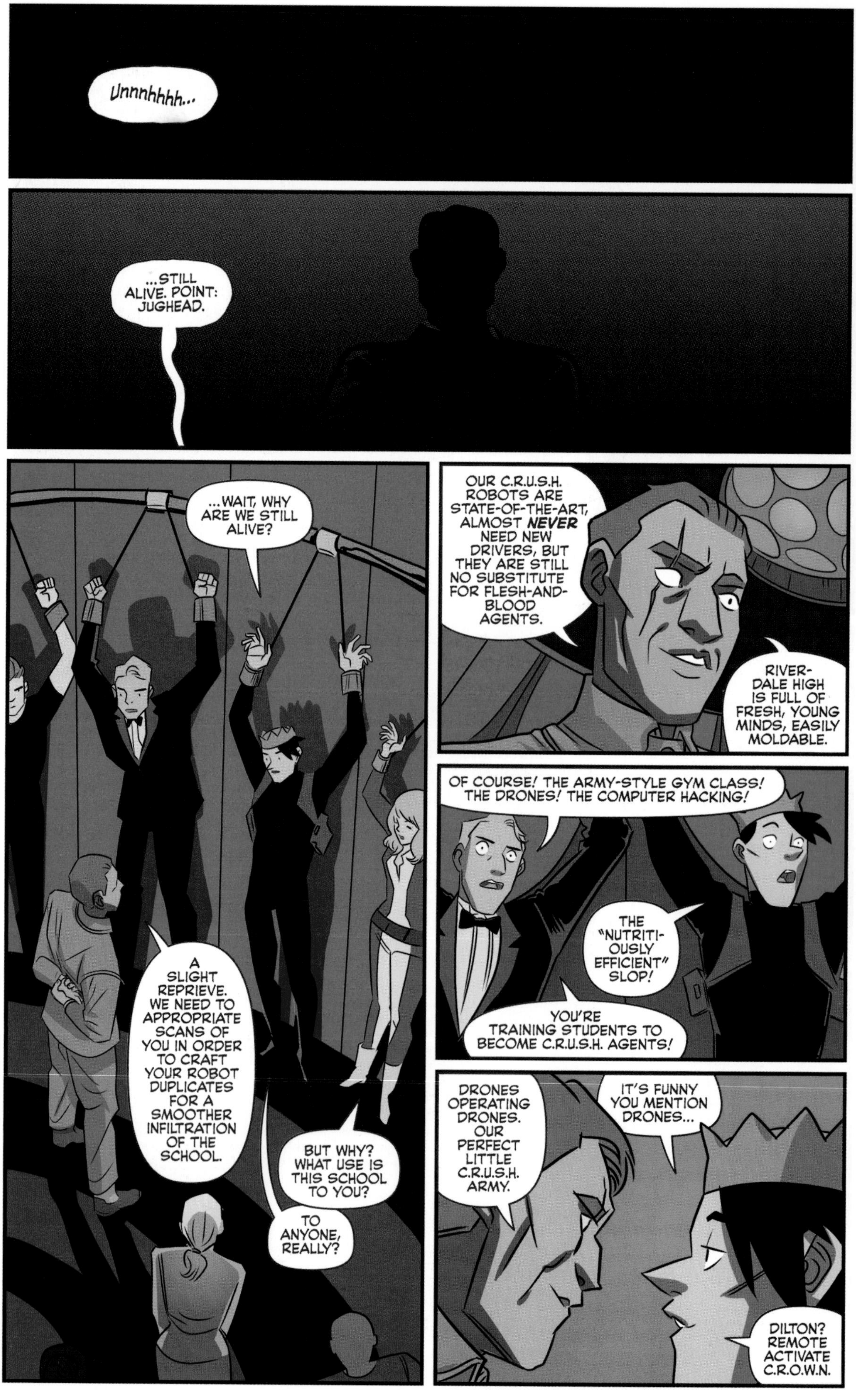
Unnnhhhh...
...STILL ALIVE. POINT: JUGHEAD.
...WAIT, WHY ARE WE STILL ALIVE?
A SLIGHT REPRIEVE. WE NEED TO APPROPRIATE SCANS OF YOU IN ORDER TO CRAFT YOUR ROBOT DUPLICATES FOR A SMOOTHER INFILTRATION OF THE SCHOOL.
BUT WHY? WHAT USE IS THIS SCHOOL TO YOU?
TO ANYONE, REALLY?
OUR C.R.U.S.H. ROBOTS ARE STATE-OF-THE-ART, ALMOST NEVER NEED NEW DRIVERS, BUT THEY ARE STILL NO SUBSTITUTE FOR FLESH-AND-BLOOD AGENTS.
RIVER-DALE HIGH IS FULL OF FRESH, YOUNG MINDS, EASILY MOLDABLE.
OF COURSE! THE ARMY-STYLE GYM CLASS! THE DRONES! THE COMPUTER HACKING!
THE "NUTRITI-OUSLY EFFICIENT" SLOP!
YOU'RE TRAINING STUDENTS TO BECOME C.R.U.S.H. AGENTS!
DRONES OPERATING DRONES. OUR PERFECT LITTLE C.R.U.S.H. ARMY.
IT'S FUNNY YOU MENTION DRONES...
DILTON? REMOTE ACTIVATE C.R.O.W.N.

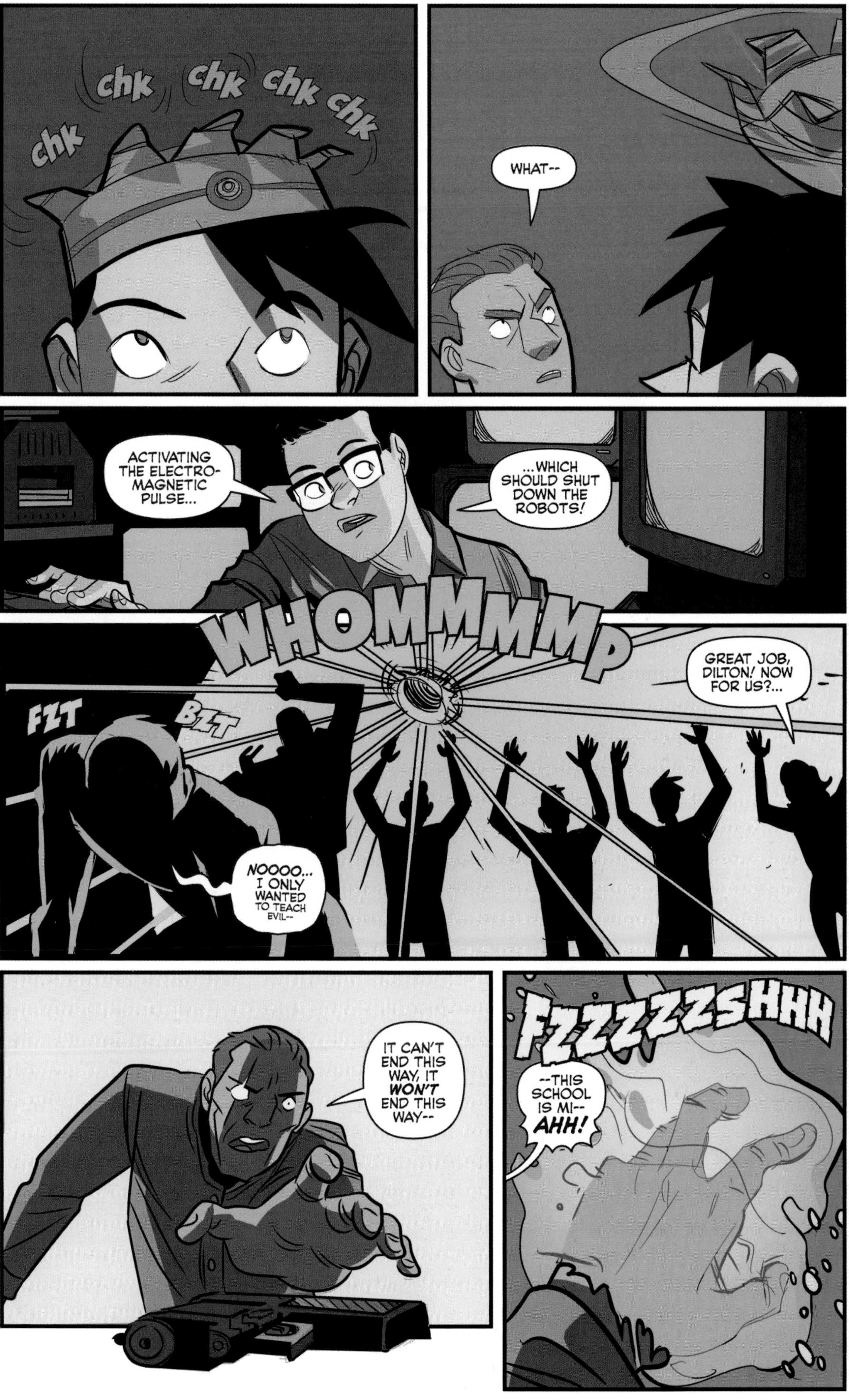
chk chk chk chk chk
WHAT--
ACTIVATING THE ELECTRO-MAGNETIC PULSE...
...WHICH SHOULD SHUT DOWN THE ROBOTS!
WHOMMMMP
FZT
BZT
GREAT JOB, DILTON! NOW FOR US?...
NOOOO... I ONLY WANTED TO TEACH EVIL--
IT CAN'T END THIS WAY, IT WON'T END THIS WAY--
FZZZZZSHHH
--THIS SCHOOL IS MI-- AHH!

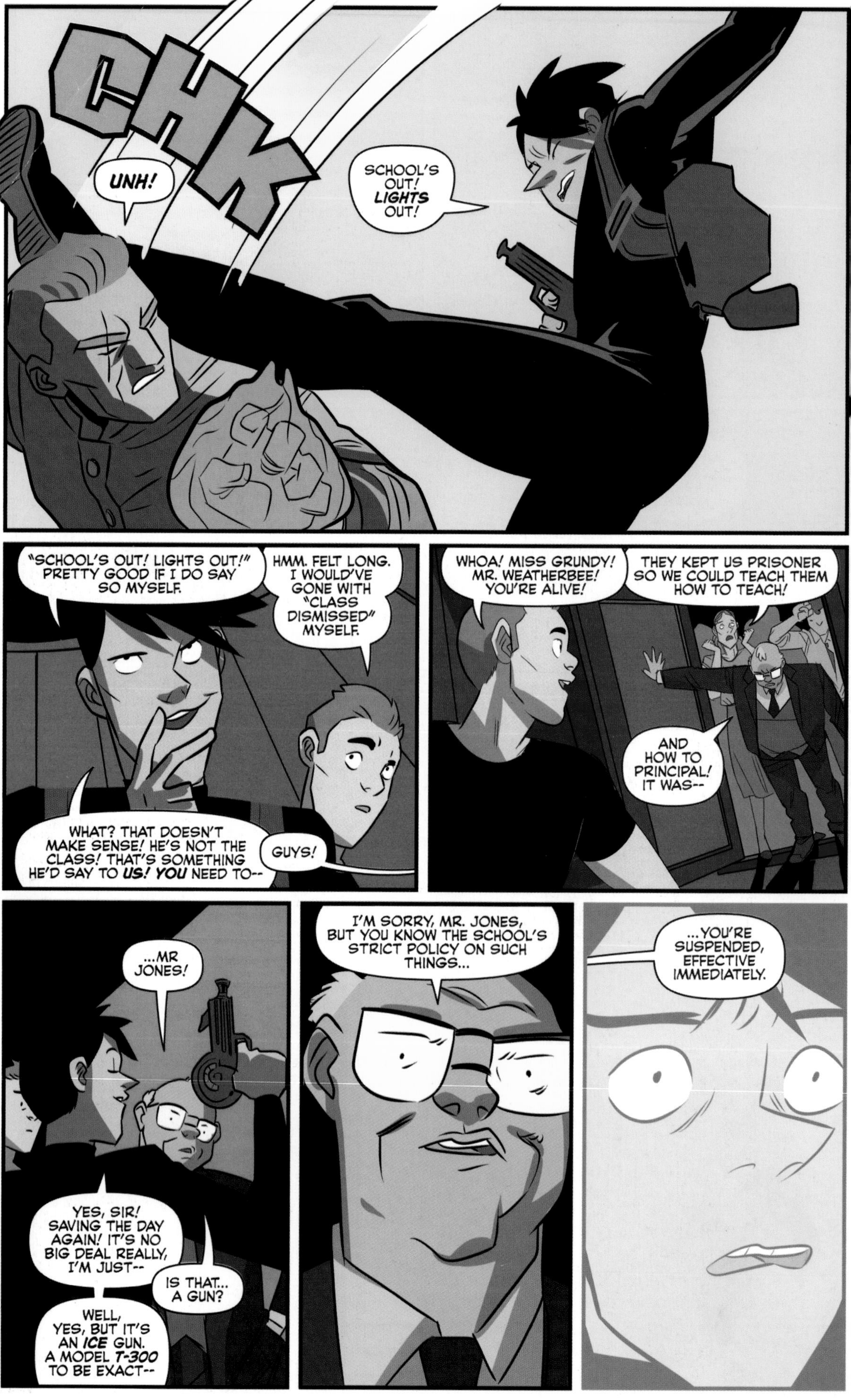
CHK
UNH!
SCHOOL'S OUT! LIGHTS OUT!
"SCHOOL'S OUT! LIGHTS OUT!" PRETTY GOOD IF I DO SAY SO MYSELF.
HMM. FELT LONG. I WOULD'VE GONE WITH "CLASS DISMISSED" MYSELF.
WHAT? THAT DOESN'T MAKE SENSE! HE'S NOT THE CLASS! THAT'S SOMETHING HE'D SAY TO US! YOU NEED TO--
GUYS!
WHOA! MISS GRUNDY! MR. WEATHERBEE! YOU'RE ALIVE!
THEY KEPT US PRISONER SO WE COULD TEACH THEM HOW TO TEACH!
AND HOW TO PRINCIPAL! IT WAS--
...MR JONES!
YES, SIR! SAVING THE DAY AGAIN! IT'S NO BIG DEAL REALLY, I'M JUST--
IS THAT... A GUN?
WELL, YES, BUT IT'S AN ICE GUN. A MODEL T-300 TO BE EXACT--
I'M SORRY, MR. JONES, BUT YOU KNOW THE SCHOOL'S STRICT POLICY ON SUCH THINGS...
...YOU'RE SUSPENDED, EFFECTIVE IMMEDIATELY.

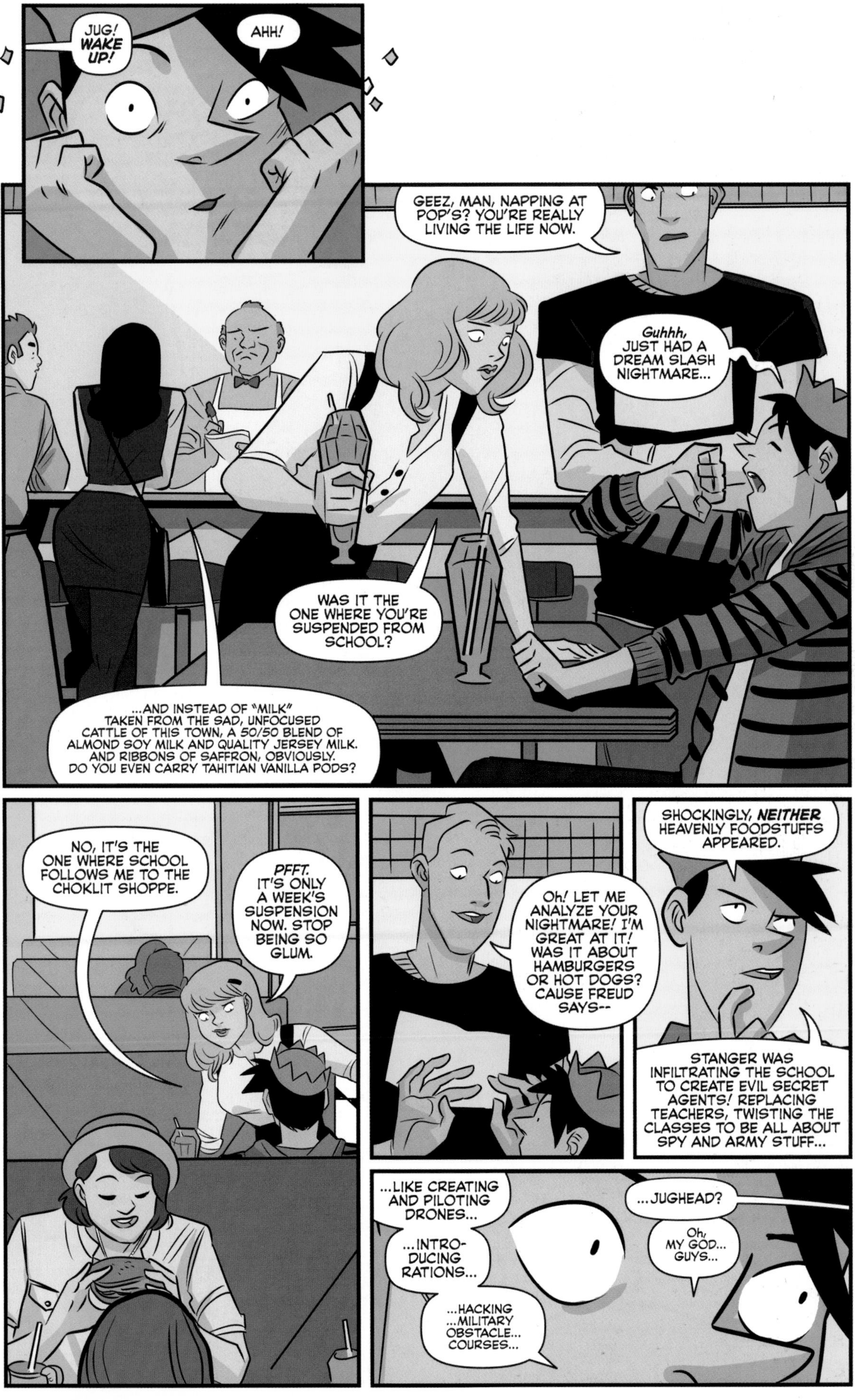
JUG! WAKE UP!
AHH!
GEEZ, MAN, NAPPING AT POP'S? YOU'RE REALLY LIVING THE LIFE NOW.
Guhhh, JUST HAD A DREAM SLASH NIGHTMARE...
WAS IT THE ONE WHERE YOU'RE SUSPENDED FROM SCHOOL?
...AND INSTEAD OF "MILK" TAKEN FROM THE SAD, UNFOCUSED CATTLE OF THIS TOWN, A 50/50 BLEND OF ALMOND SOY MILK AND QUALITY JERSEY MILK. AND RIBBONS OF SAFFRON, OBVIOUSLY. DO YOU EVEN CARRY TAHITIAN VANILLA PODS?
NO, IT'S THE ONE WHERE SCHOOL FOLLOWS ME TO THE CHOKLIT SHOPPE.
PFFT. IT'S ONLY A WEEK'S SUSPENSION NOW. STOP BEING SO GLUM.
Oh! LET ME ANALYZE YOUR NIGHTMARE! I'M GREAT AT IT! WAS IT ABOUT HAMBURGERS OR HOT DOGS? CAUSE FREUD SAYS--
SHOCKINGLY, NEITHER HEAVENLY FOODSTUFFS APPEARED.
STANGER WAS INFILTRATING THE SCHOOL TO CREATE EVIL SECRET AGENTS! REPLACING TEACHERS, TWISTING THE CLASSES TO BE ALL ABOUT SPY AND ARMY STUFF...
...LIKE CREATING AND PILOTING DRONES...
...INTRO-DUCING RATIONS...
...HACKING ...MILITARY OBSTACLE... COURSES...
...JUGHEAD?
Oh, MY GOD... GUYS...

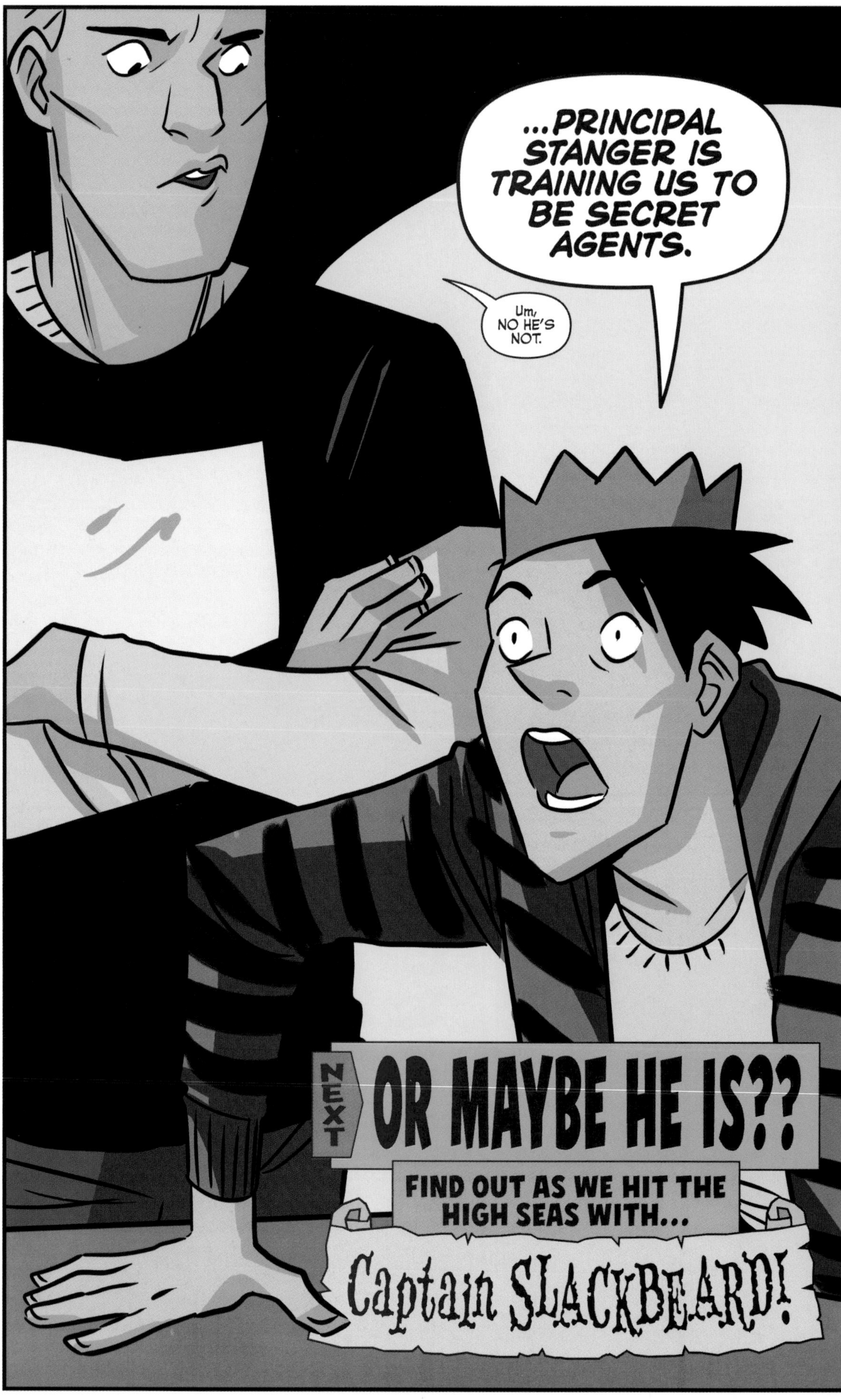
...PRINCIPAL STANGER IS TRAINING US TO BE SECRET AGENTS.
Um, NO HE'S NOT.
NEXT
OR MAYBE HE IS??
FIND OUT AS WE HIT THE HIGH SEAS WITH...
Captain SLACKBEARD!

TO BE
CONTINUED...

ISSUE FOUR

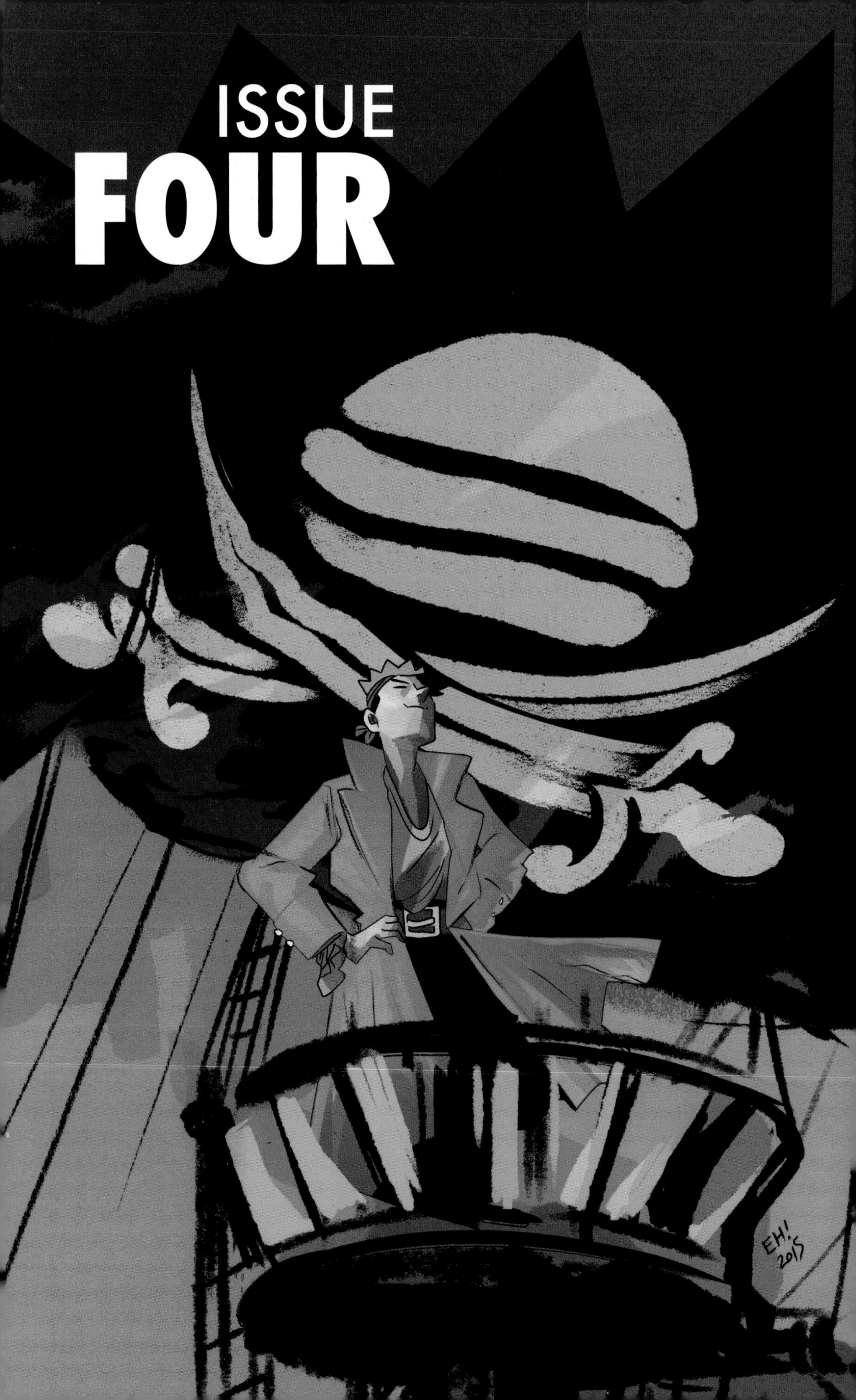
EH!
2015

LOOK, HEAR ME OUT. IT ALL MAKES SENSE.

WHY WOULD THEY REPLACE PRINCIPAL WEATHERBEE WITH STANGER? RIVERDALE HIGH'S TEST SCORES ARE TOTALLY ABOVE AVERAGE! YOU DON'T FIRE A PRINCIPAL FOR DOING WELL!

AND ALL THE TEACHERS STANGER REPLACED! WITH...WITH CRAZY INTENSE INSTRUCTORS! TEACHING THINGS LIKE *DRONE OPERATION* AND *ARMY OBSTACLE COURSES!*

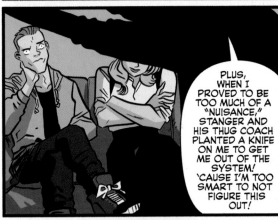

PLUS, WHEN I PROVED TO BE TOO MUCH OF A "NUISANCE," STANGER AND HIS THUG COACH PLANTED A KNIFE ON ME TO GET ME OUT OF THE SYSTEM! 'CAUSE I'M TOO SMART TO NOT FIGURE THIS OUT!

AND, WORST OF ALL, THEY REPLACED DECENT, NORMAL FOOD WITH HIGH-NUTRITION RATIONS!

SO, CALL ME PARANOID, CALL ME CRAZY, BUT I THINK THE EVIDENCE SPEAKS FOR ITSELF...

...RIVERDALE HIGH IS BEING TRANSFORMED INTO A TRAINING GROUND FOR SECRET AGENTS.

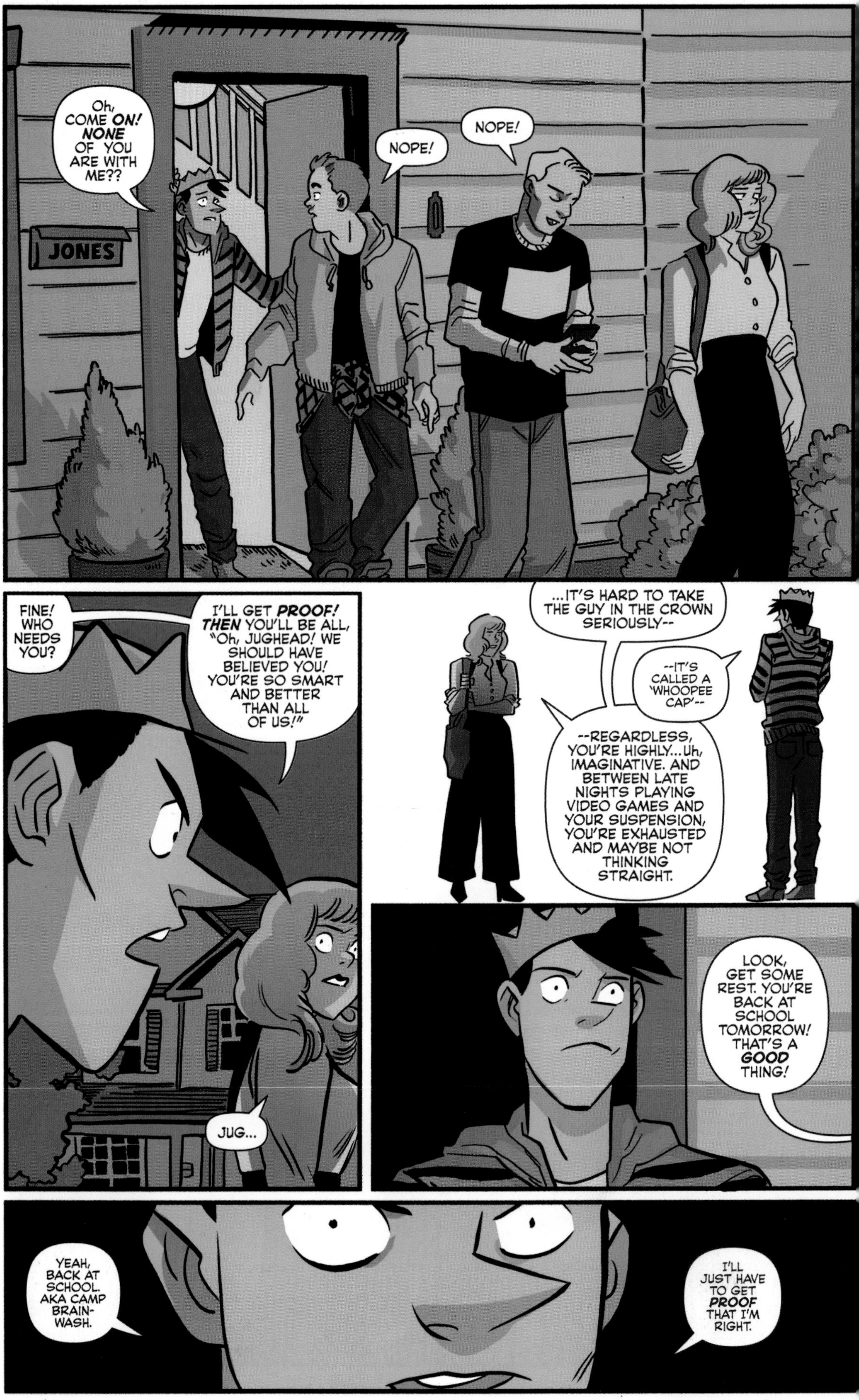
Oh, COME ON! NONE OF YOU ARE WITH ME??
NOPE!
NOPE!
JONES
FINE! WHO NEEDS YOU?
I'LL GET PROOF! THEN YOU'LL BE ALL, "Oh, JUGHEAD! WE SHOULD HAVE BELIEVED YOU! YOU'RE SO SMART AND BETTER THAN ALL OF US!"
JUG...
...IT'S HARD TO TAKE THE GUY IN THE CROWN SERIOUSLY--
--IT'S CALLED A 'WHOOPEE CAP'--
--REGARDLESS, YOU'RE HIGHLY...Uh, IMAGINATIVE. AND BETWEEN LATE NIGHTS PLAYING VIDEO GAMES AND YOUR SUSPENSION, YOU'RE EXHAUSTED AND MAYBE NOT THINKING STRAIGHT.
LOOK, GET SOME REST. YOU'RE BACK AT SCHOOL TOMORROW! THAT'S A GOOD THING!
YEAH, BACK AT SCHOOL. AKA CAMP BRAIN-WASH.
I'LL JUST HAVE TO GET PROOF THAT I'M RIGHT.

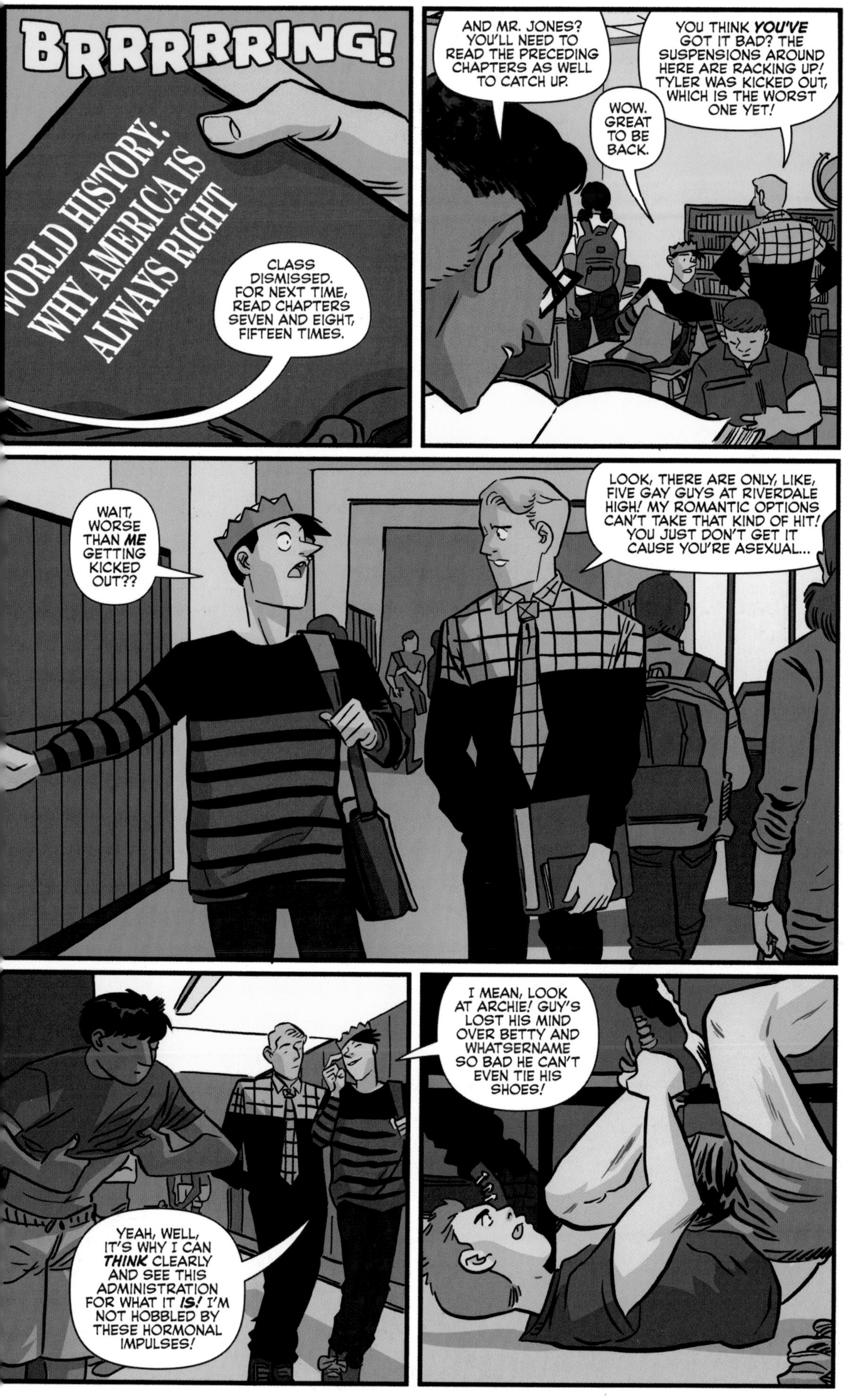
BRRRRRING!
WORLD HISTORY: WHY AMERICA IS ALWAYS RIGHT
CLASS DISMISSED. FOR NEXT TIME, READ CHAPTERS SEVEN AND EIGHT, FIFTEEN TIMES.
AND MR. JONES? YOU'LL NEED TO READ THE PRECEDING CHAPTERS AS WELL TO CATCH UP.
WOW. GREAT TO BE BACK.
YOU THINK YOU'VE GOT IT BAD? THE SUSPENSIONS AROUND HERE ARE RACKING UP! TYLER WAS KICKED OUT, WHICH IS THE WORST ONE YET!
WAIT, WORSE THAN ME GETTING KICKED OUT??
LOOK, THERE ARE ONLY, LIKE, FIVE GAY GUYS AT RIVERDALE HIGH! MY ROMANTIC OPTIONS CAN'T TAKE THAT KIND OF HIT! YOU JUST DON'T GET IT CAUSE YOU'RE ASEXUAL...
YEAH, WELL, IT'S WHY I CAN THINK CLEARLY AND SEE THIS ADMINISTRATION FOR WHAT IT IS! I'M NOT HOBBLED BY THESE HORMONAL IMPULSES!
I MEAN, LOOK AT ARCHIE! GUY'S LOST HIS MIND OVER BETTY AND WHATSERNAME SO BAD HE CAN'T EVEN TIE HIS SHOES!

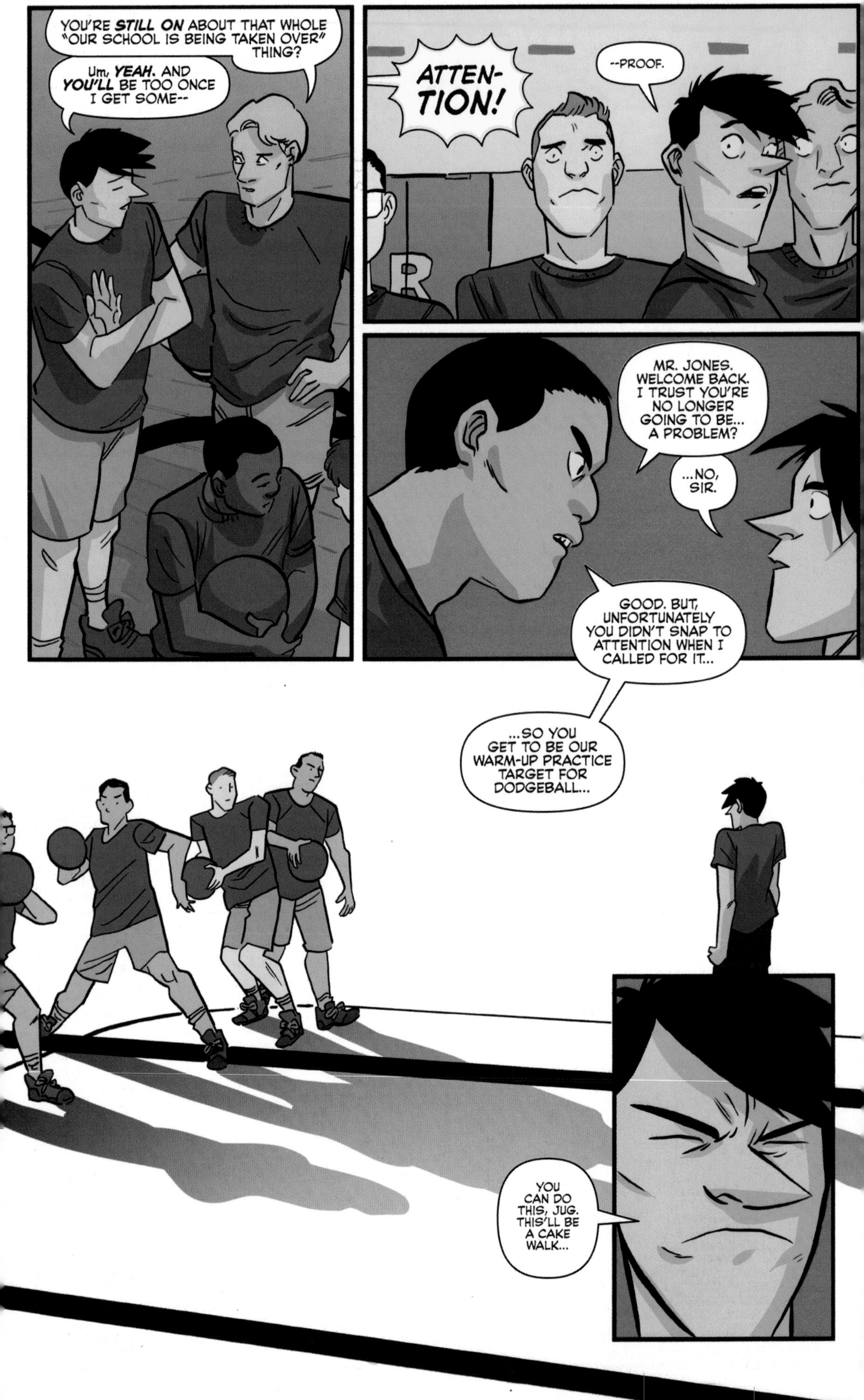
YOU'RE STILL ON ABOUT THAT WHOLE "OUR SCHOOL IS BEING TAKEN OVER" THING?
Um, YEAH. AND YOU'LL BE TOO ONCE I GET SOME--
ATTEN-TION!
--PROOF.
MR. JONES. WELCOME BACK. I TRUST YOU'RE NO LONGER GOING TO BE... A PROBLEM?
...NO, SIR.
GOOD. BUT, UNFORTUNATELY YOU DIDN'T SNAP TO ATTENTION WHEN I CALLED FOR IT...
...SO YOU GET TO BE OUR WARM-UP PRACTICE TARGET FOR DODGEBALL...
YOU CAN DO THIS, JUG. THIS'LL BE A CAKE WALK...

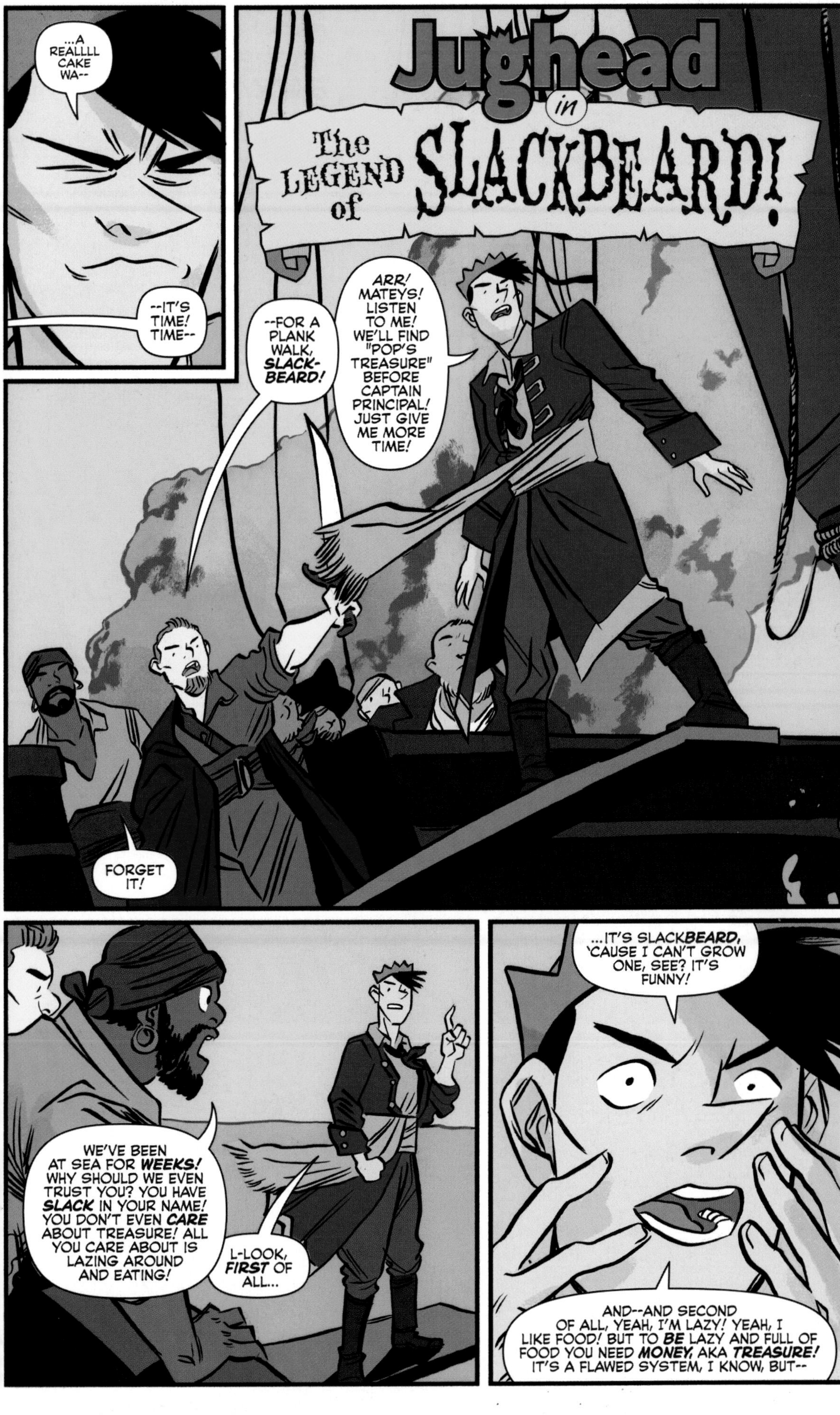
...A REALLLL CAKE WA--
--IT'S TIME! TIME--
Jughead in
The LEGEND of SLACKBEARD!
--FOR A PLANK WALK, SLACK-BEARD!
ARR! MATEYS! LISTEN TO ME! WE'LL FIND "POP'S TREASURE" BEFORE CAPTAIN PRINCIPAL! JUST GIVE ME MORE TIME!
FORGET IT!
WE'VE BEEN AT SEA FOR WEEKS! WHY SHOULD WE EVEN TRUST YOU? YOU HAVE SLACK IN YOUR NAME! YOU DON'T EVEN CARE ABOUT TREASURE! ALL YOU CARE ABOUT IS LAZING AROUND AND EATING!
L-LOOK, FIRST OF ALL...
...IT'S SLACKBEARD, 'CAUSE I CAN'T GROW ONE, SEE? IT'S FUNNY!
AND--AND SECOND OF ALL, YEAH, I'M LAZY! YEAH, I LIKE FOOD! BUT TO BE LAZY AND FULL OF FOOD YOU NEED MONEY, AKA TREASURE! IT'S A FLAWED SYSTEM, I KNOW, BUT--

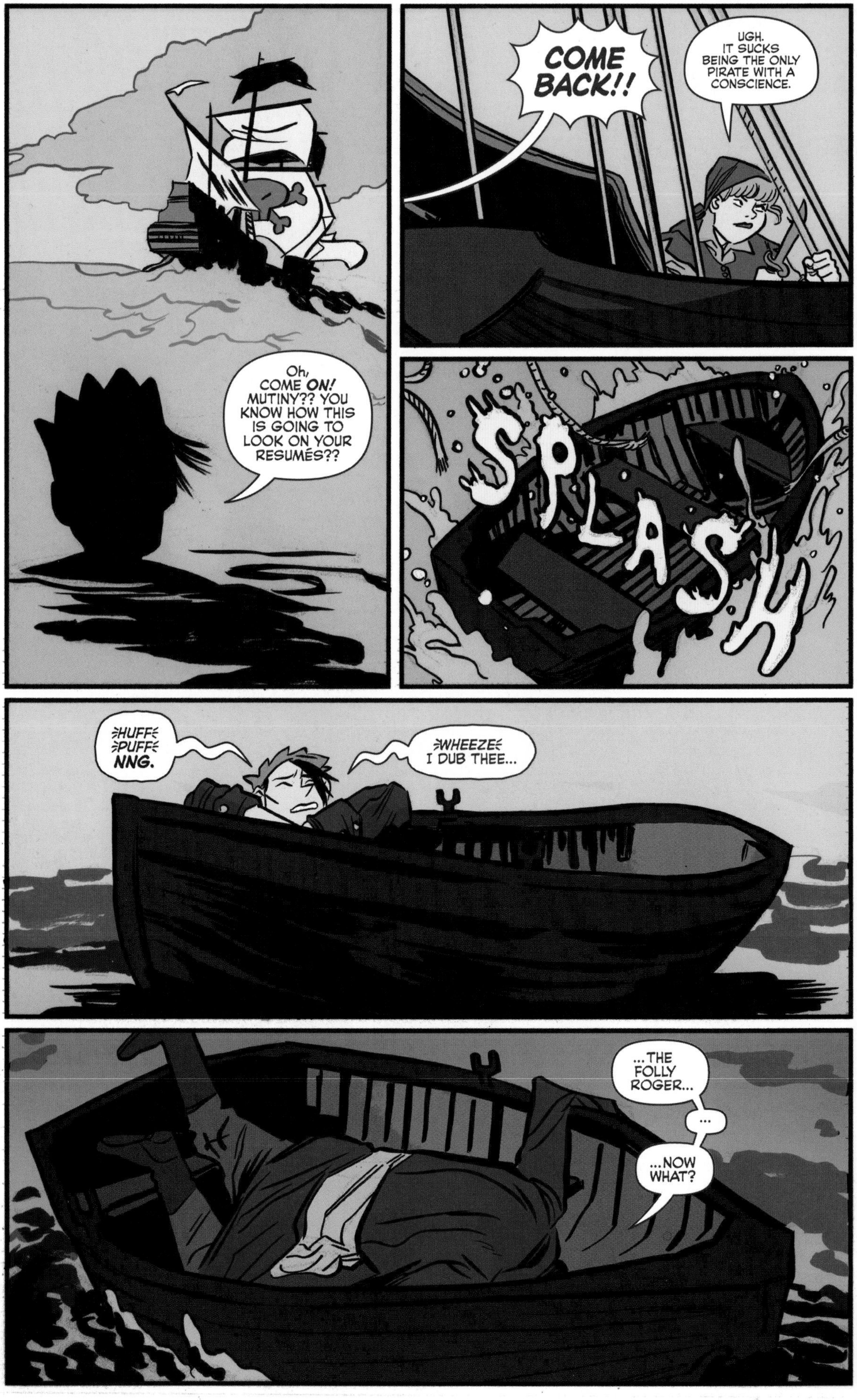
COME BACK!!
UGH. IT SUCKS BEING THE ONLY PIRATE WITH A CONSCIENCE.
Oh, COME ON! MUTINY?? YOU KNOW HOW THIS IS GOING TO LOOK ON YOUR RESUMÉS??
SPLASH
HUFF PUFF NNG.
WHEEZE I DUB THEE...
...THE FOLLY ROGER...
...
...NOW WHAT?

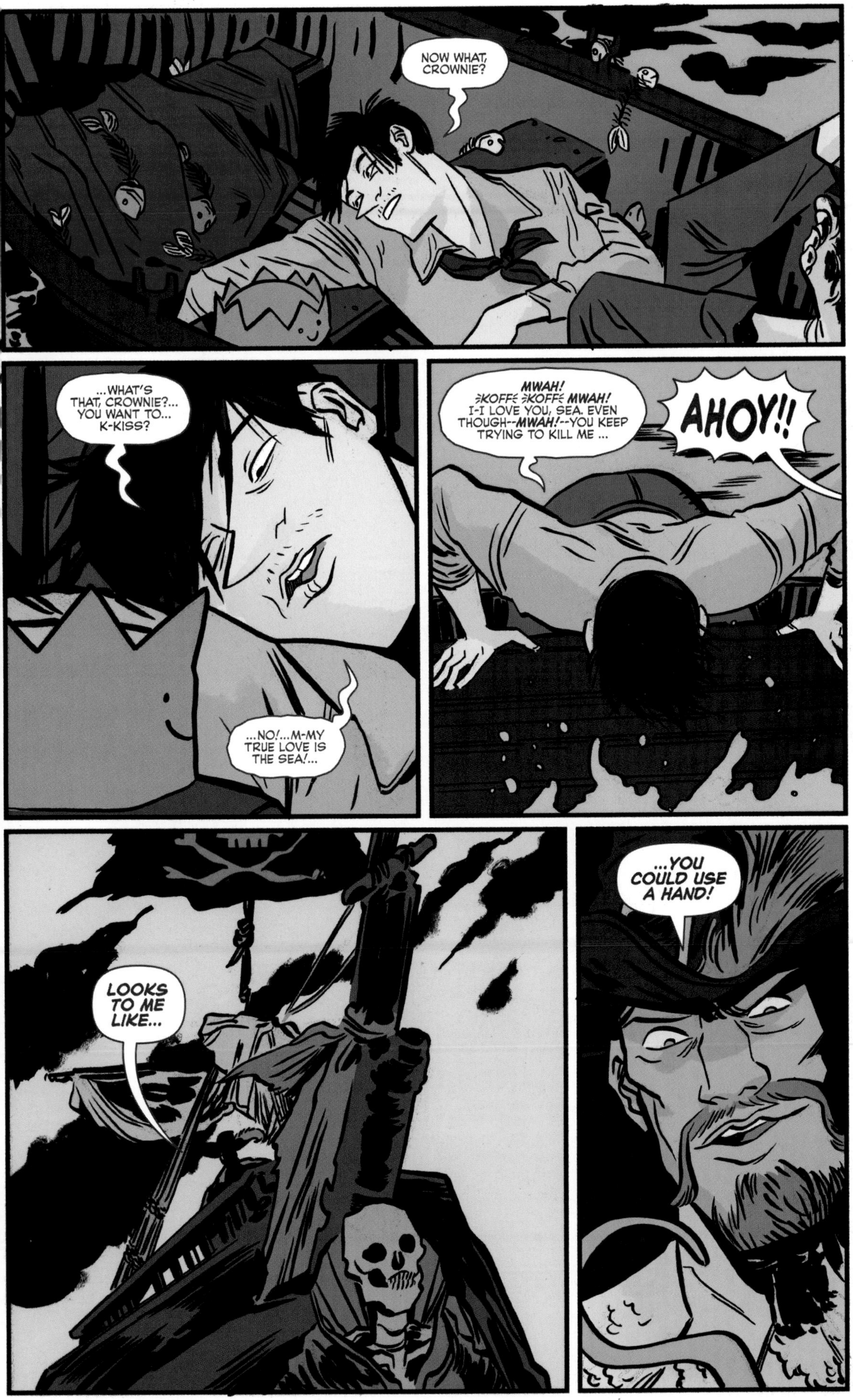
NOW WHAT, CROWNIE?
...WHAT'S THAT, CROWNIE?... YOU WANT TO... K-KISS?
...NO!...M-MY TRUE LOVE IS THE SEA!...
MWAH! KOFF KOFF MWAH! I-I LOVE YOU, SEA. EVEN THOUGH--MWAH!--YOU KEEP TRYING TO KILL ME ...
AHOY!!
LOOKS TO ME LIKE...
...YOU COULD USE A HAND!

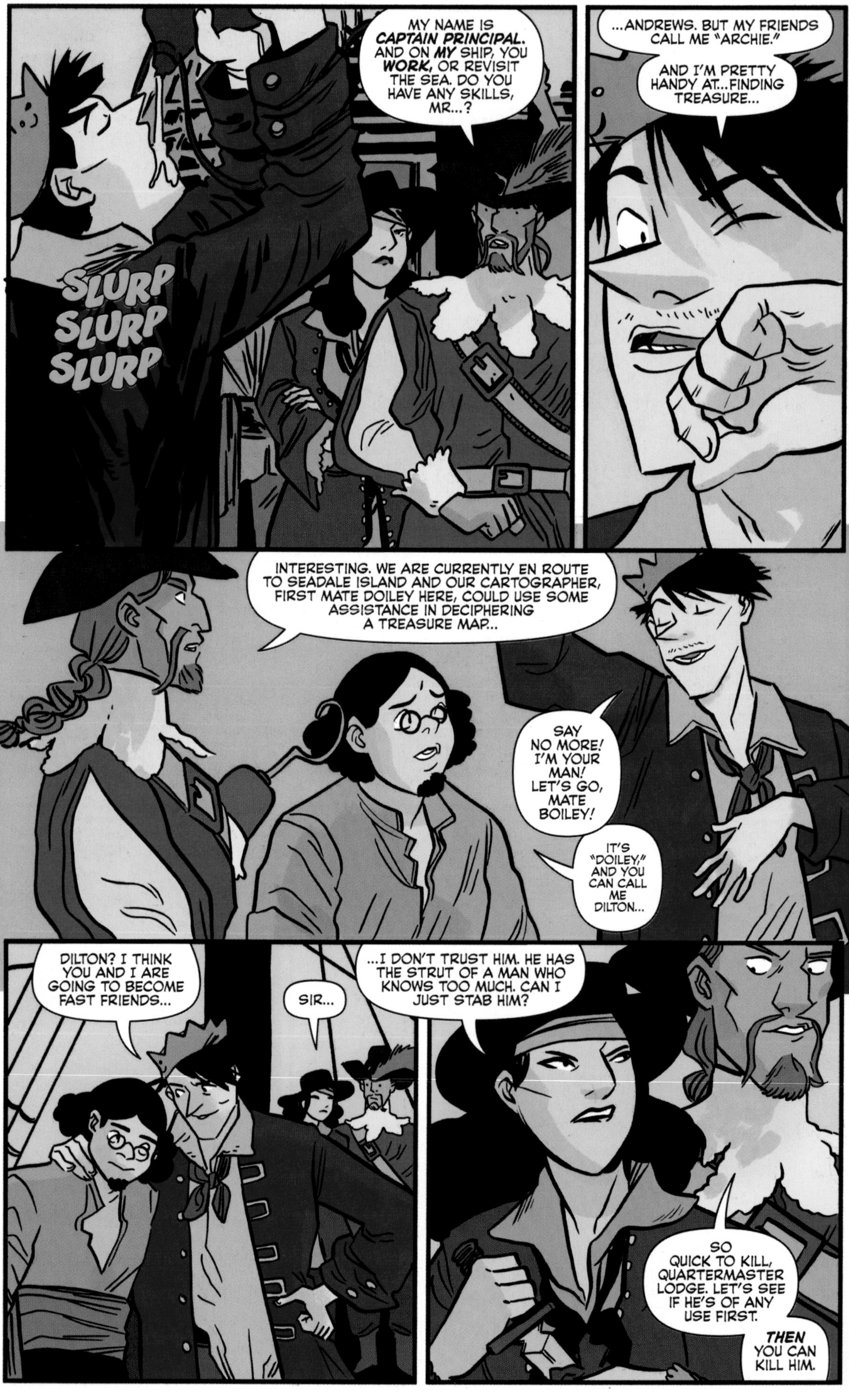
SLURP SLURP SLURP
MY NAME IS CAPTAIN PRINCIPAL. AND ON MY SHIP, YOU WORK, OR REVISIT THE SEA. DO YOU HAVE ANY SKILLS, MR...?
...ANDREWS. BUT MY FRIENDS CALL ME "ARCHIE."
AND I'M PRETTY HANDY AT...FINDING TREASURE...
INTERESTING. WE ARE CURRENTLY EN ROUTE TO SEADALE ISLAND AND OUR CARTOGRAPHER, FIRST MATE DOILEY HERE, COULD USE SOME ASSISTANCE IN DECIPHERING A TREASURE MAP...
SAY NO MORE! I'M YOUR MAN! LET'S GO, MATE BOILEY!
IT'S "DOILEY," AND YOU CAN CALL ME DILTON...
DILTON? I THINK YOU AND I ARE GOING TO BECOME FAST FRIENDS...
SIR...
...I DON'T TRUST HIM. HE HAS THE STRUT OF A MAN WHO KNOWS TOO MUCH. CAN I JUST STAB HIM?
SO QUICK TO KILL, QUARTERMASTER LODGE. LET'S SEE IF HE'S OF ANY USE FIRST.
THEN YOU CAN KILL HIM.

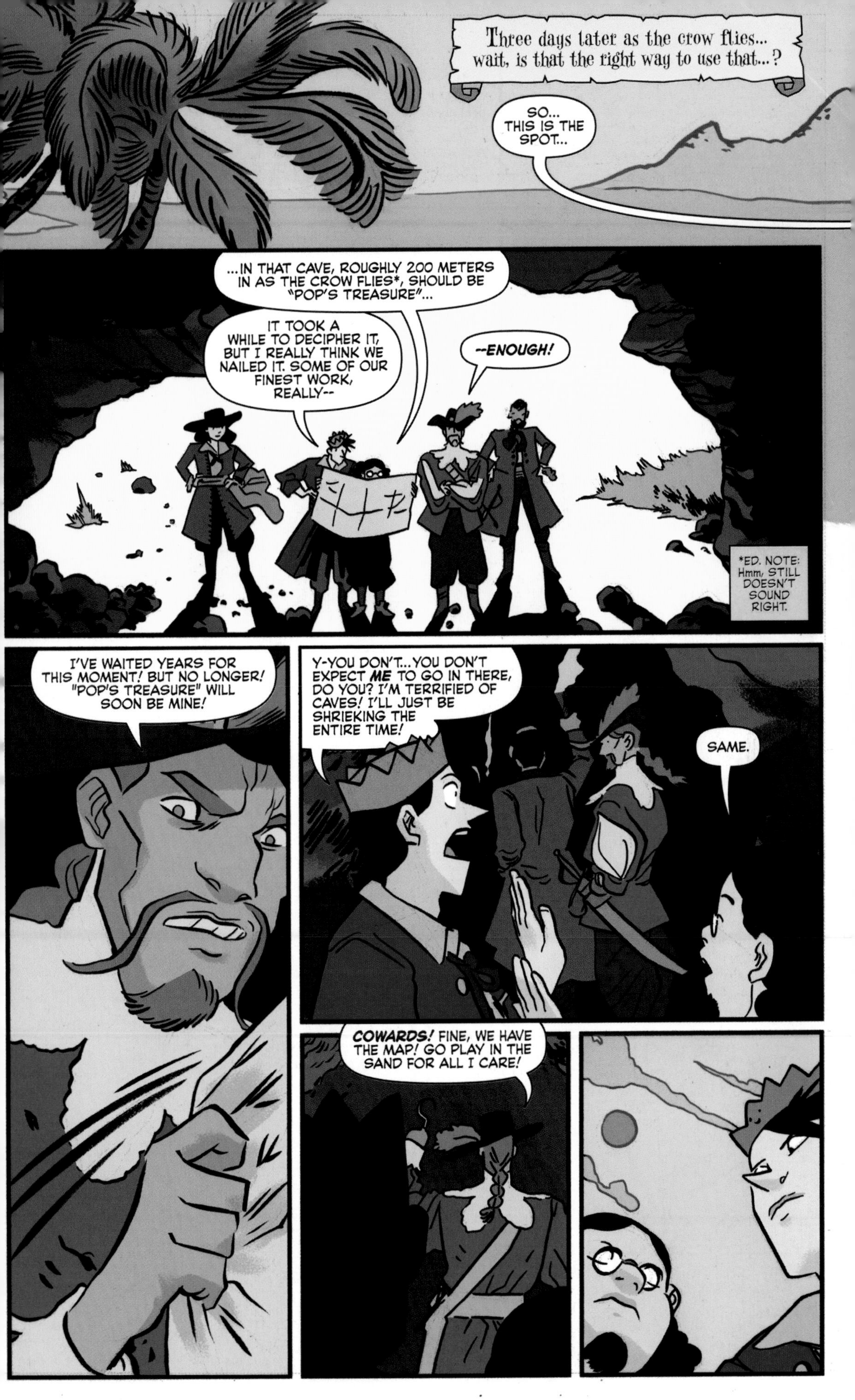

Three days later as the crow flies... wait, is that the right way to use that...?
SO... THIS IS THE SPOT...
...IN THAT CAVE, ROUGHLY 200 METERS IN AS THE CROW FLIES*, SHOULD BE "POP'S TREASURE"...
IT TOOK A WHILE TO DECIPHER IT, BUT I REALLY THINK WE NAILED IT. SOME OF OUR FINEST WORK, REALLY--
--ENOUGH!
*ED. NOTE: Hmm, STILL DOESN'T SOUND RIGHT.
I'VE WAITED YEARS FOR THIS MOMENT! BUT NO LONGER! "POP'S TREASURE" WILL SOON BE MINE!
Y-YOU DON'T...YOU DON'T EXPECT ME TO GO IN THERE, DO YOU? I'M TERRIFIED OF CAVES! I'LL JUST BE SHRIEKING THE ENTIRE TIME!
SAME.
COWARDS! FINE, WE HAVE THE MAP! GO PLAY IN THE SAND FOR ALL I CARE!

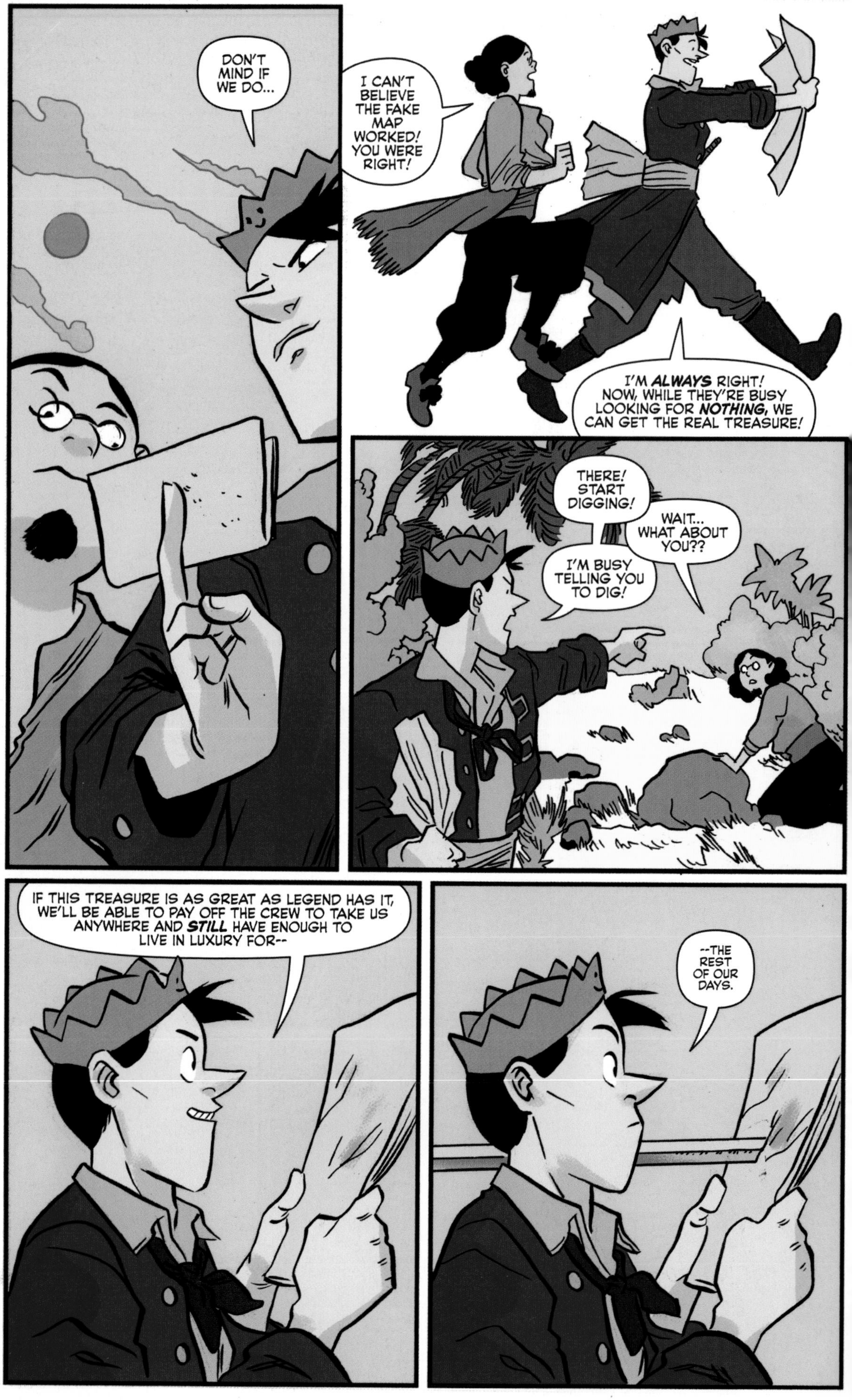
DON'T MIND IF WE DO...
I CAN'T BELIEVE THE FAKE MAP WORKED! YOU WERE RIGHT!
I'M ALWAYS RIGHT! NOW, WHILE THEY'RE BUSY LOOKING FOR NOTHING, WE CAN GET THE REAL TREASURE!
THERE! START DIGGING!
WAIT... WHAT ABOUT YOU??
I'M BUSY TELLING YOU TO DIG!
IF THIS TREASURE IS AS GREAT AS LEGEND HAS IT, WE'LL BE ABLE TO PAY OFF THE CREW TO TAKE US ANYWHERE AND STILL HAVE ENOUGH TO LIVE IN LUXURY FOR--
--THE REST OF OUR DAYS.

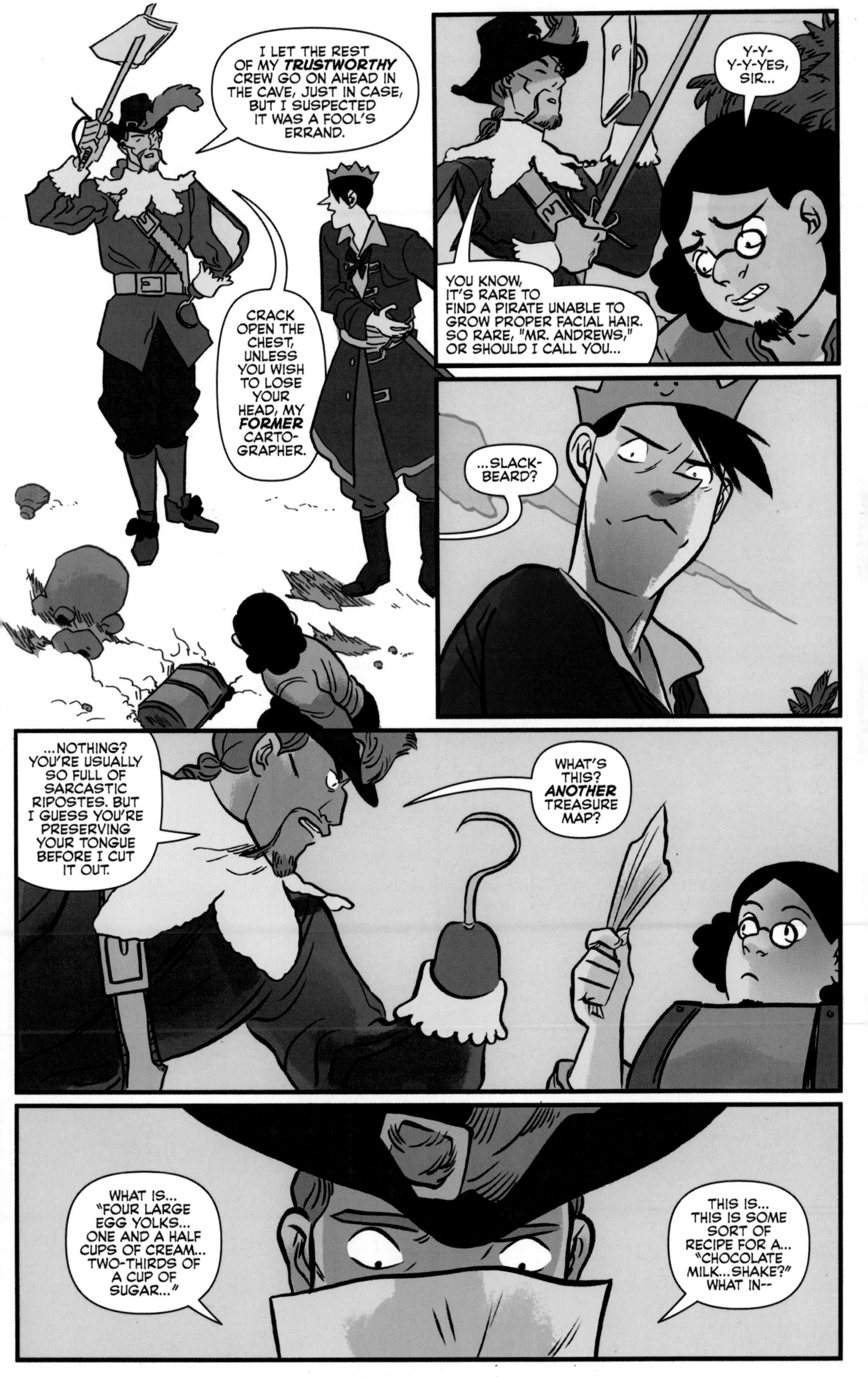

I LET THE REST OF MY TRUSTWORTHY CREW GO ON AHEAD IN THE CAVE, JUST IN CASE, BUT I SUSPECTED IT WAS A FOOL'S ERRAND.
CRACK OPEN THE CHEST, UNLESS YOU WISH TO LOSE YOUR HEAD, MY FORMER CARTOGRAPHER.
Y-Y-Y-Y-YES, SIR...
YOU KNOW, IT'S RARE TO FIND A PIRATE UNABLE TO GROW PROPER FACIAL HAIR. SO RARE, "MR. ANDREWS," OR SHOULD I CALL YOU...
...SLACK-BEARD?
...NOTHING? YOU'RE USUALLY SO FULL OF SARCASTIC RIPOSTES. BUT I GUESS YOU'RE PRESERVING YOUR TONGUE BEFORE I CUT IT OUT.
WHAT'S THIS? ANOTHER TREASURE MAP?
WHAT IS... "FOUR LARGE EGG YOLKS... ONE AND A HALF CUPS OF CREAM... TWO-THIRDS OF A CUP OF SUGAR..."
THIS IS... THIS IS SOME SORT OF RECIPE FOR A... "CHOCOLATE MILK...SHAKE?" WHAT IN--

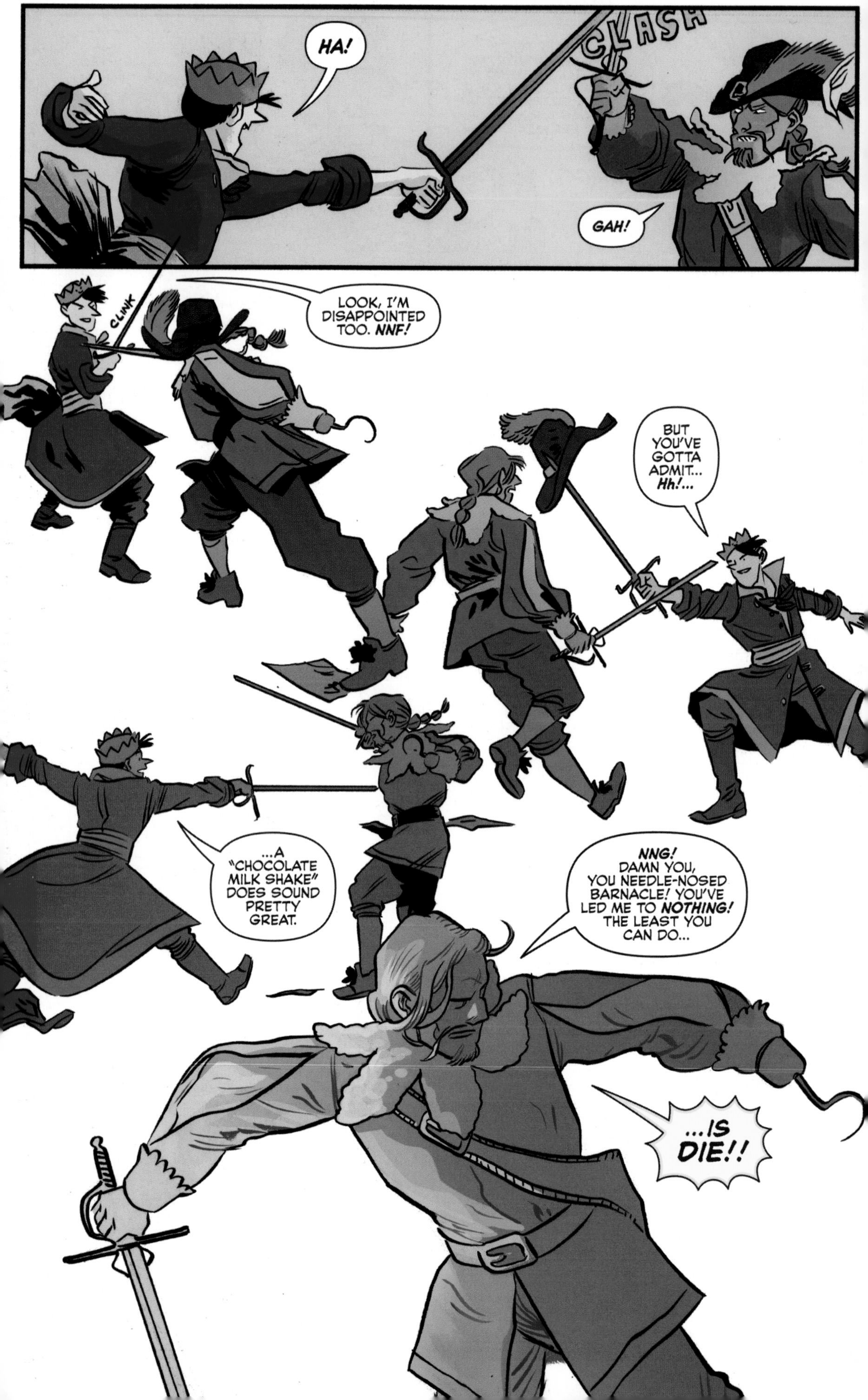
HA!
CLASH
GAH!
CLINK
LOOK, I'M DISAPPOINTED TOO. NNF!
BUT YOU'VE GOTTA ADMIT... Hh!...
...A "CHOCOLATE MILK SHAKE" DOES SOUND PRETTY GREAT.
NNG! DAMN YOU, YOU NEEDLE-NOSED BARNACLE! YOU'VE LED ME TO NOTHING! THE LEAST YOU CAN DO...
...IS DIE!!

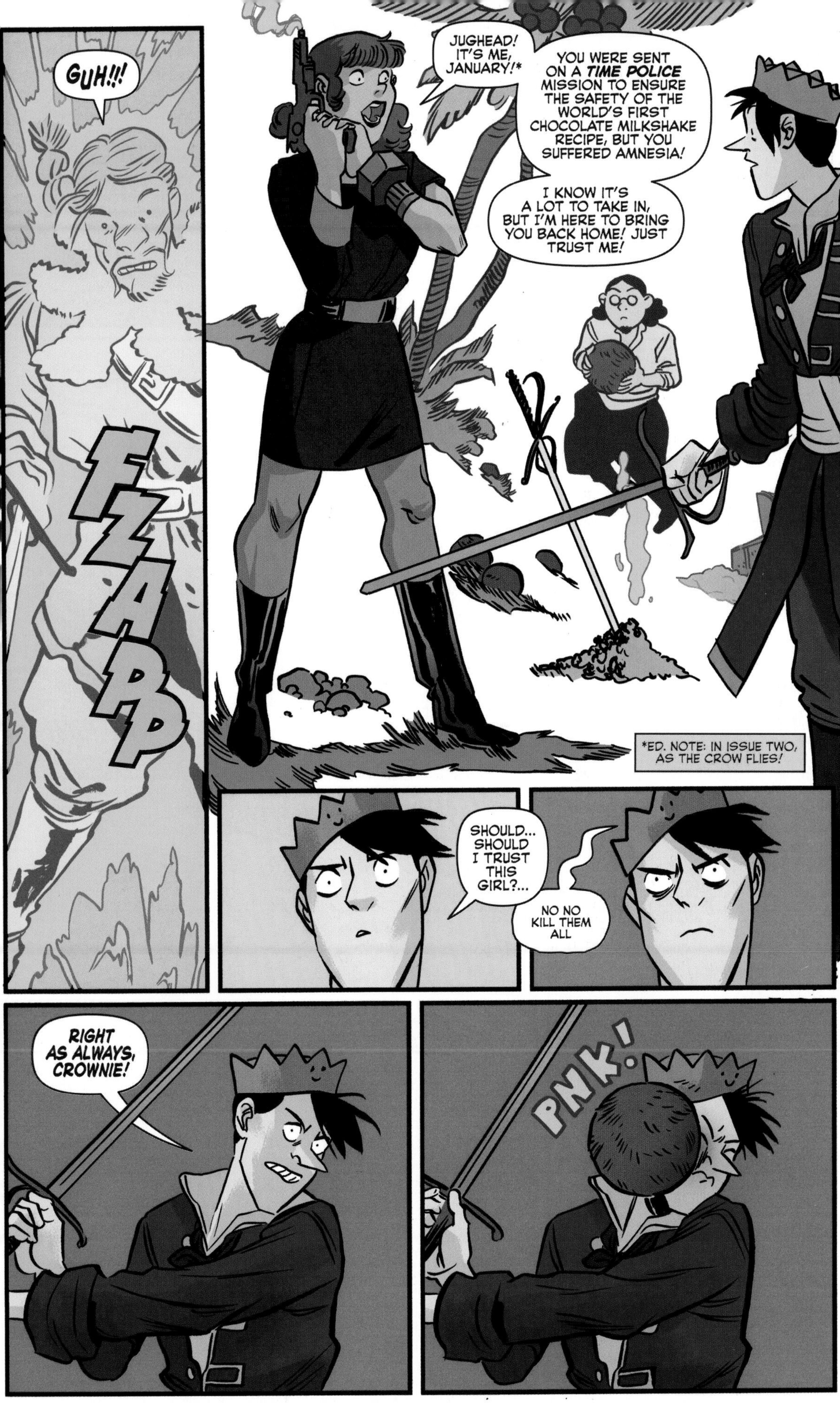
GUH!!!
FZAPP
JUGHEAD! IT'S ME, JANUARY!*
YOU WERE SENT ON A *TIME POLICE* MISSION TO ENSURE THE SAFETY OF THE WORLD'S FIRST CHOCOLATE MILKSHAKE RECIPE, BUT YOU SUFFERED AMNESIA!
I KNOW IT'S A LOT TO TAKE IN, BUT I'M HERE TO BRING YOU BACK HOME! JUST TRUST ME!
*ED. NOTE: IN ISSUE TWO, AS THE CROW FLIES!
SHOULD... SHOULD I TRUST THIS GIRL?...
NO NO KILL THEM ALL
RIGHT AS ALWAYS, CROWNIE!
PNK!

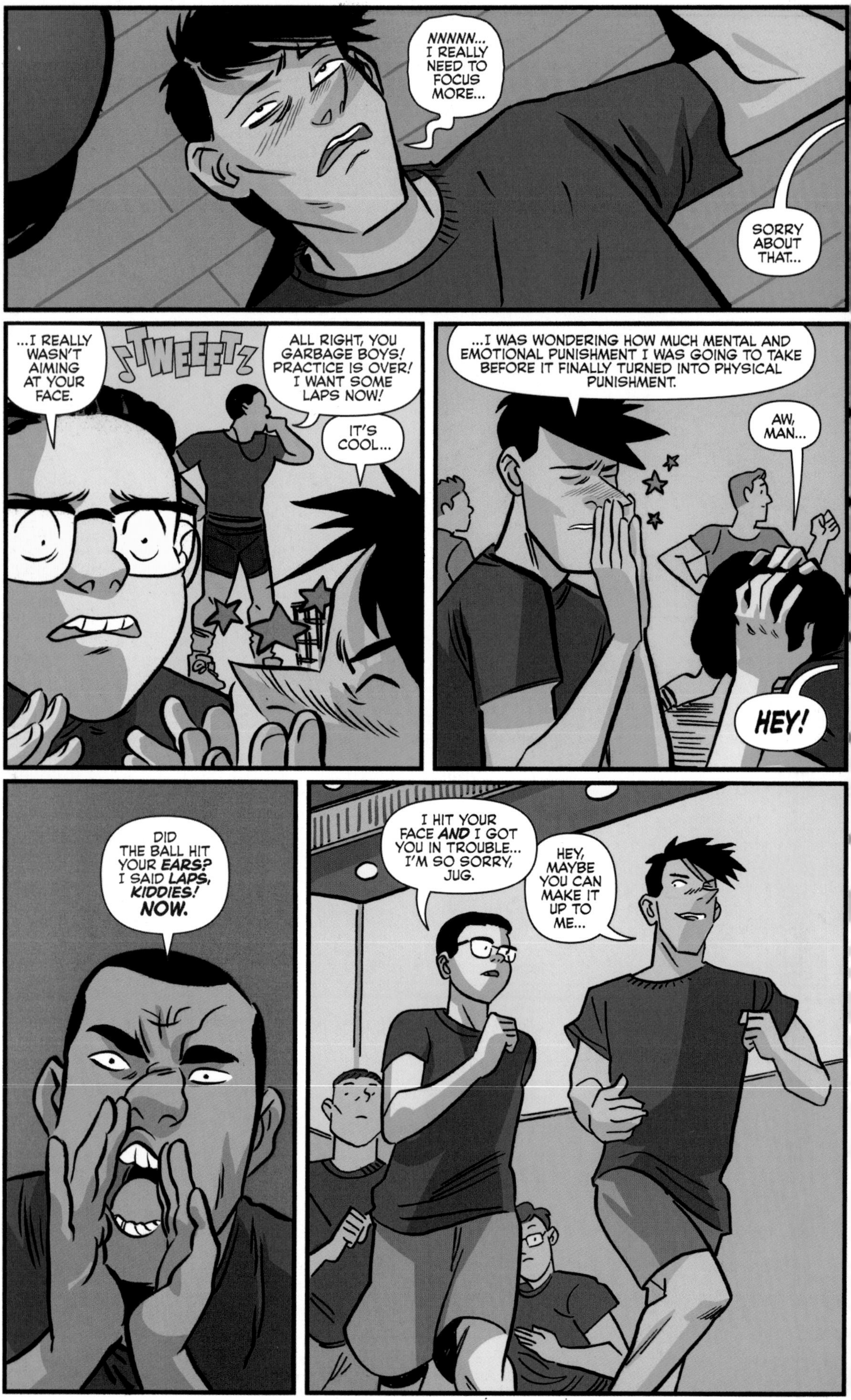

NNNNN... I REALLY NEED TO FOCUS MORE...
SORRY ABOUT THAT...
...I REALLY WASN'T AIMING AT YOUR FACE.
TWEEET
ALL RIGHT, YOU GARBAGE BOYS! PRACTICE IS OVER! I WANT SOME LAPS NOW!
IT'S COOL...
...I WAS WONDERING HOW MUCH MENTAL AND EMOTIONAL PUNISHMENT I WAS GOING TO TAKE BEFORE IT FINALLY TURNED INTO PHYSICAL PUNISHMENT.
AW, MAN...
HEY!
DID THE BALL HIT YOUR EARS? I SAID LAPS, KIDDIES! NOW.
I HIT YOUR FACE AND I GOT YOU IN TROUBLE... I'M SO SORRY, JUG.
HEY, MAYBE YOU CAN MAKE IT UP TO ME...

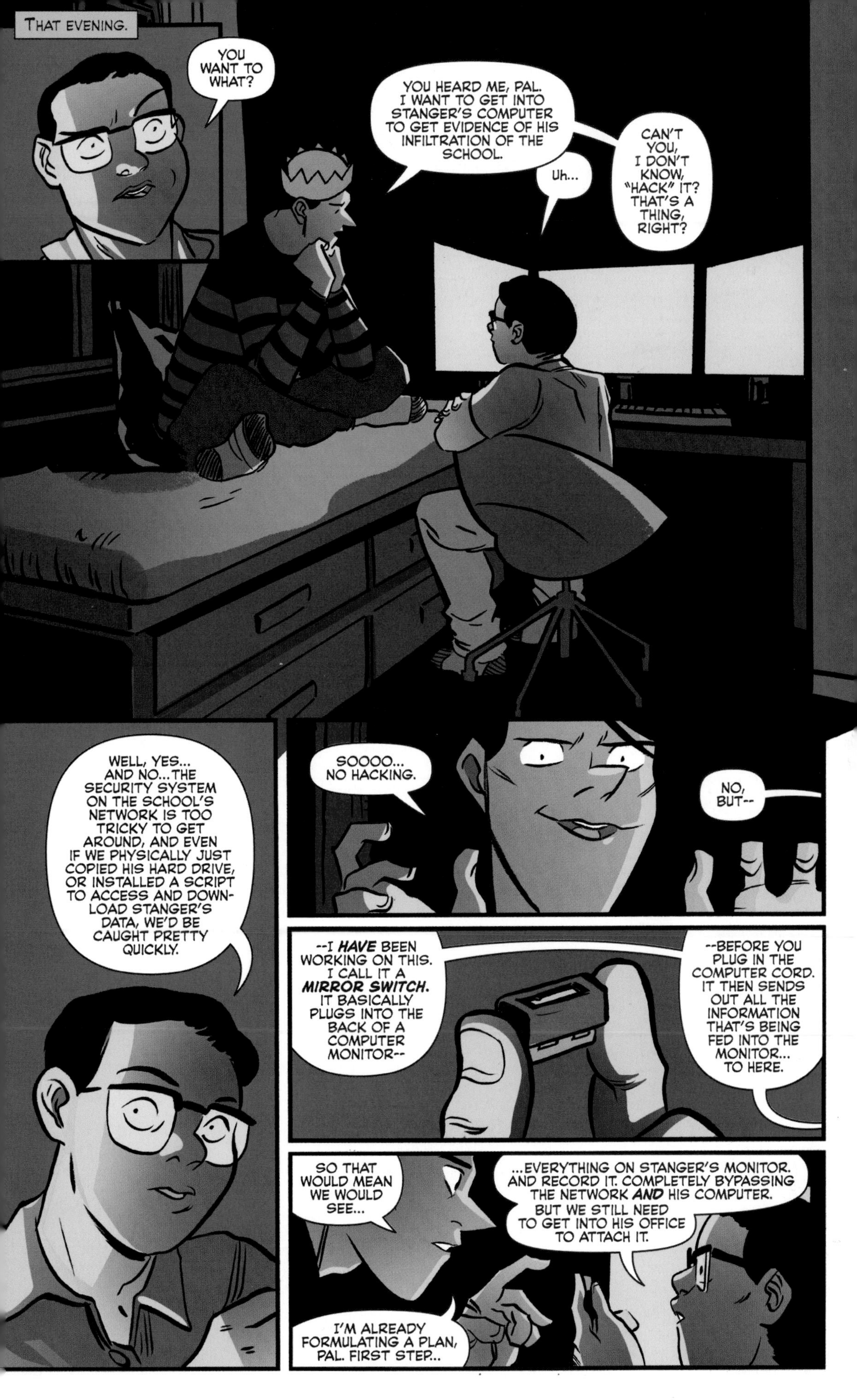

THAT EVENING.
YOU WANT TO WHAT?
YOU HEARD ME, PAL. I WANT TO GET INTO STANGER'S COMPUTER TO GET EVIDENCE OF HIS INFILTRATION OF THE SCHOOL.
Uh...
CAN'T YOU, I DON'T KNOW, "HACK" IT? THAT'S A THING, RIGHT?
WELL, YES... AND NO... THE SECURITY SYSTEM ON THE SCHOOL'S NETWORK IS TOO TRICKY TO GET AROUND, AND EVEN IF WE PHYSICALLY JUST COPIED HIS HARD DRIVE, OR INSTALLED A SCRIPT TO ACCESS AND DOWN-LOAD STANGER'S DATA, WE'D BE CAUGHT PRETTY QUICKLY.
SOOOO... NO HACKING.
NO, BUT--
--I HAVE BEEN WORKING ON THIS. I CALL IT A MIRROR SWITCH. IT BASICALLY PLUGS INTO THE BACK OF A COMPUTER MONITOR--
--BEFORE YOU PLUG IN THE COMPUTER CORD. IT THEN SENDS OUT ALL THE INFORMATION THAT'S BEING FED INTO THE MONITOR... TO HERE.
SO THAT WOULD MEAN WE WOULD SEE...
...EVERYTHING ON STANGER'S MONITOR. AND RECORD IT. COMPLETELY BYPASSING THE NETWORK AND HIS COMPUTER. BUT WE STILL NEED TO GET INTO HIS OFFICE TO ATTACH IT.
I'M ALREADY FORMULATING A PLAN, PAL. FIRST STEP...

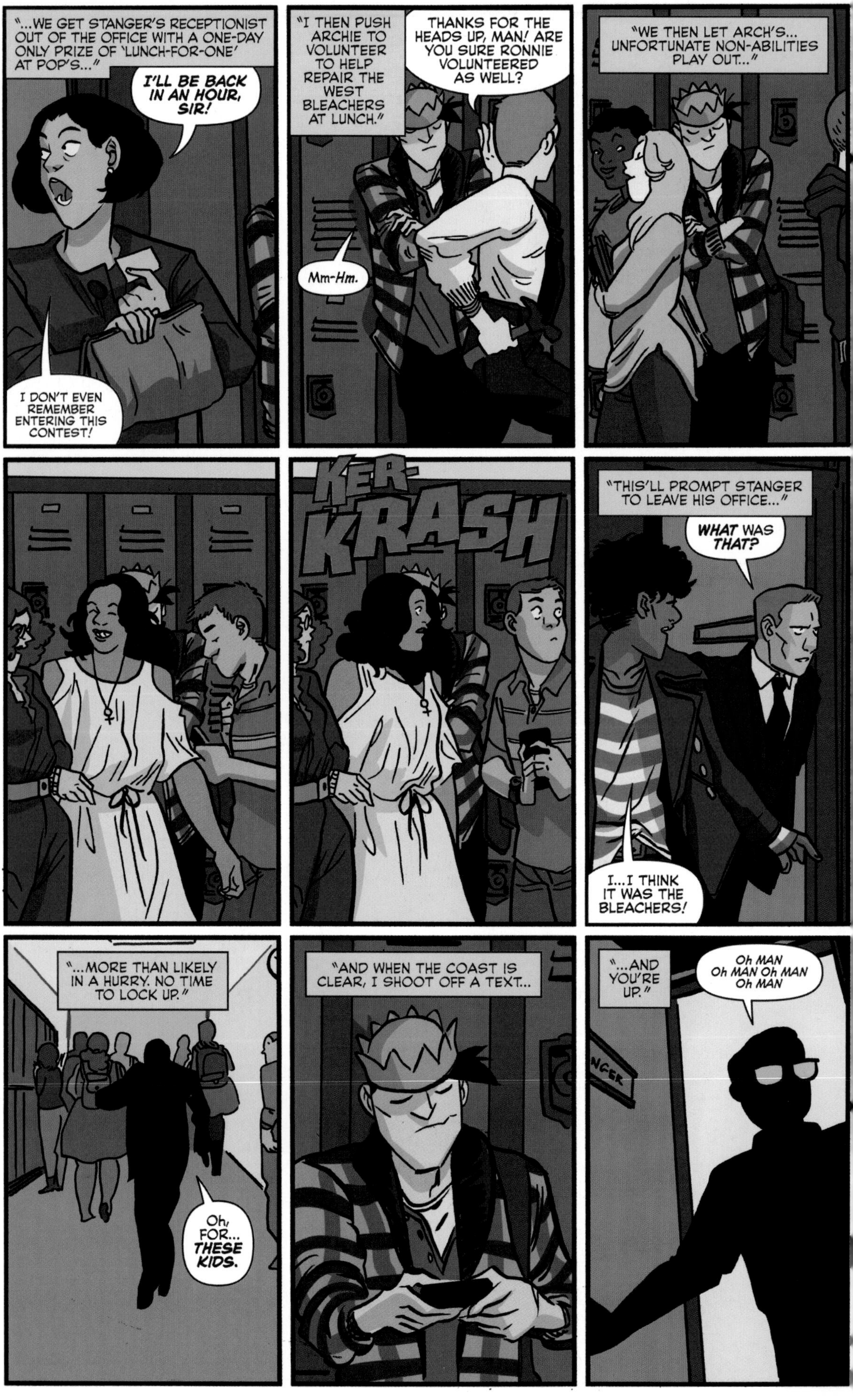
"...WE GET STANGER'S RECEPTIONIST OUT OF THE OFFICE WITH A ONE-DAY ONLY PRIZE OF 'LUNCH-FOR-ONE' AT POP'S..."
I'LL BE BACK IN AN HOUR, SIR!
I DON'T EVEN REMEMBER ENTERING THIS CONTEST!
"I THEN PUSH ARCHIE TO VOLUNTEER TO HELP REPAIR THE WEST BLEACHERS AT LUNCH."
THANKS FOR THE HEADS UP, MAN! ARE YOU SURE RONNIE VOLUNTEERED AS WELL?
Mm-Hm.
"WE THEN LET ARCH'S... UNFORTUNATE NON-ABILITIES PLAY OUT..."
KER-KRASH
"THIS'LL PROMPT STANGER TO LEAVE HIS OFFICE..."
WHAT WAS THAT?
I...I THINK IT WAS THE BLEACHERS!
"...MORE THAN LIKELY IN A HURRY. NO TIME TO LOCK UP."
Oh, FOR... THESE KIDS.
"AND WHEN THE COAST IS CLEAR, I SHOOT OFF A TEXT...
"...AND YOU'RE UP."
Oh MAN
Oh MAN Oh MAN
Oh MAN

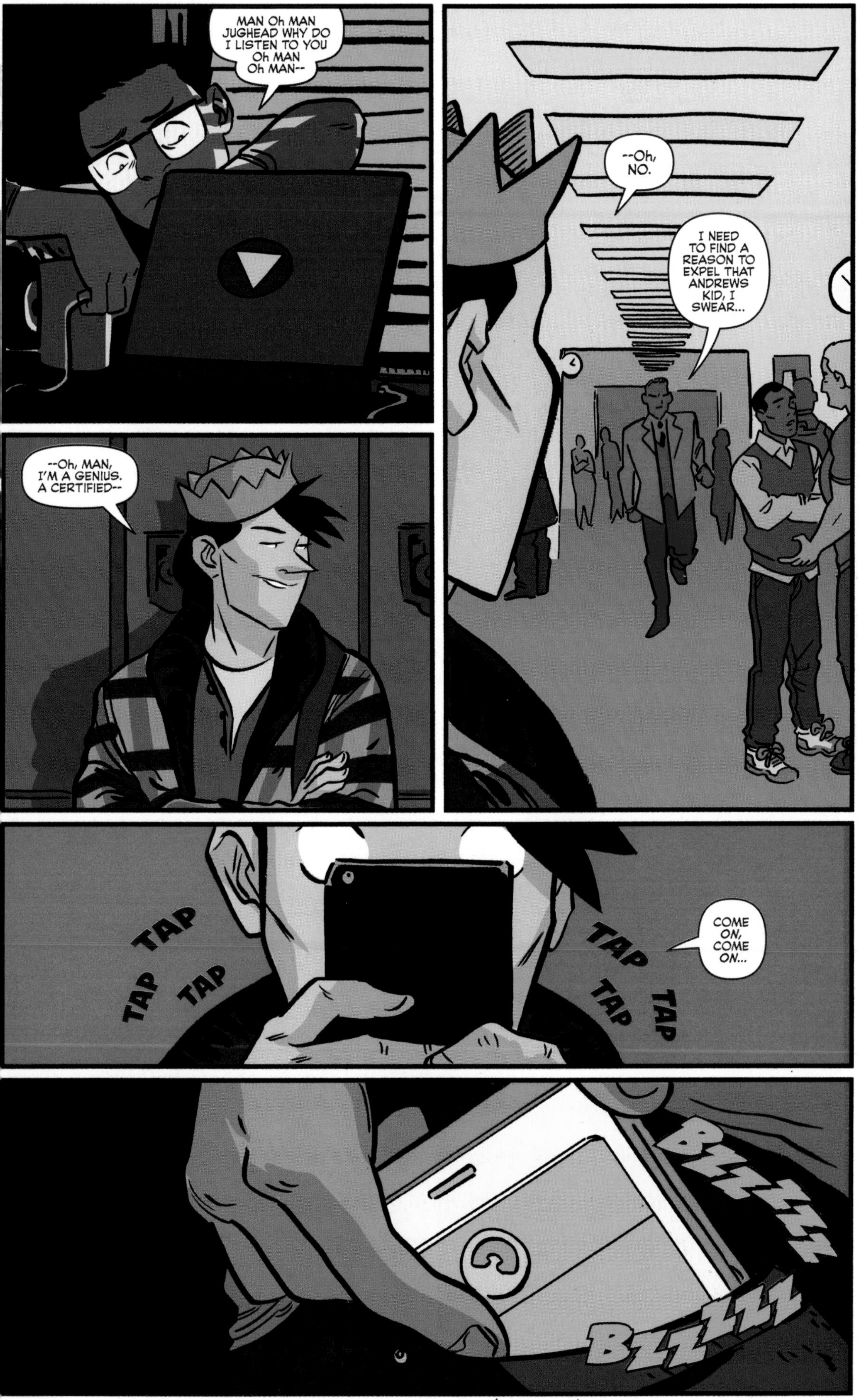
MAN Oh MAN JUGHEAD WHY DO I LISTEN TO YOU Oh MAN Oh MAN--
--Oh, MAN, I'M A GENIUS. A CERTIFIED--
--Oh, NO.
I NEED TO FIND A REASON TO EXPEL THAT ANDREWS KID, I SWEAR...
TAP TAP TAP TAP
TAP TAP TAP TAP
COME ON, COME ON...
BZZZZZZ
BZZZZZZ

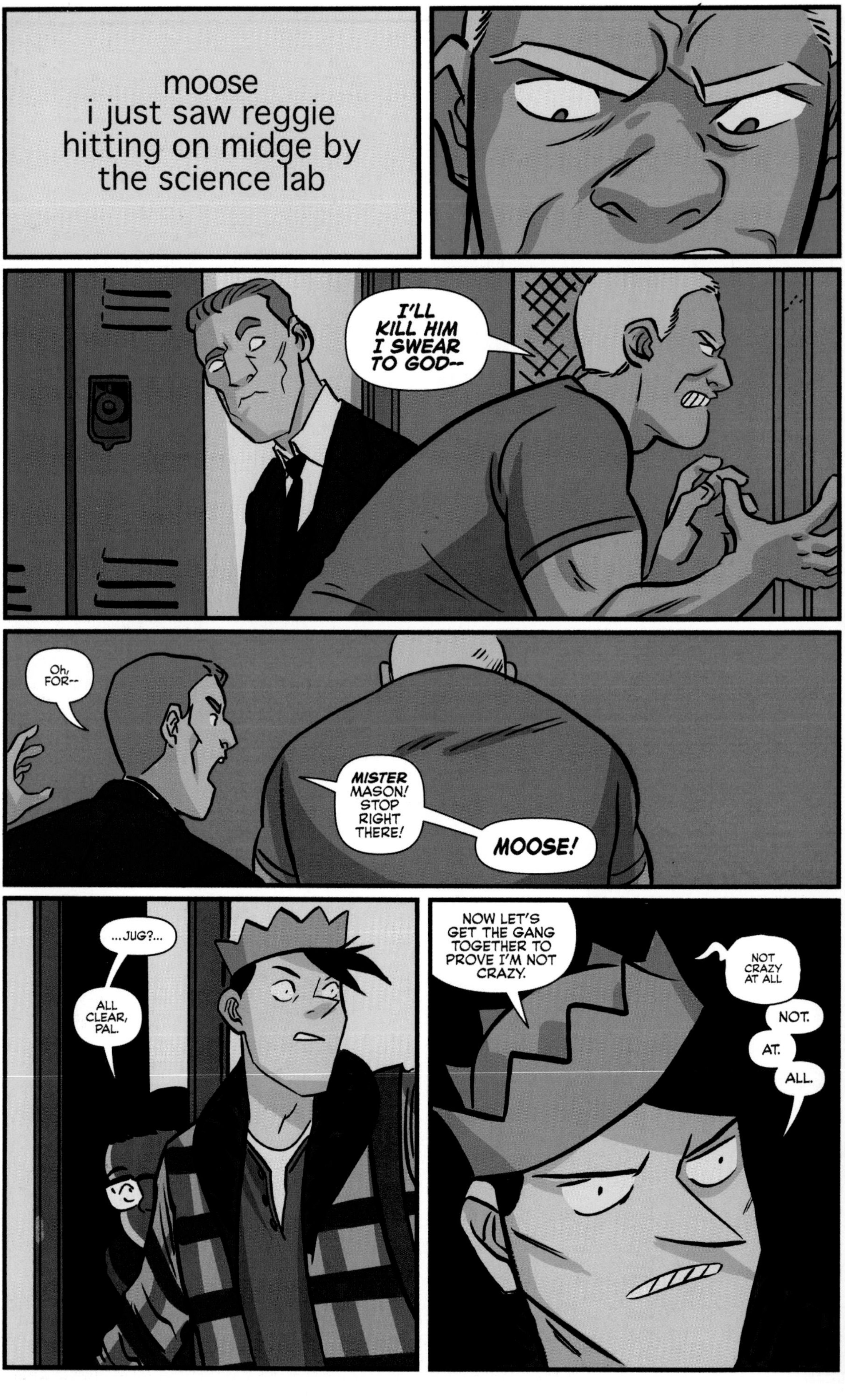
moose
i just saw reggie
hitting on midge by
the science lab
I'LL KILL HIM I SWEAR TO GOD--
Oh, FOR--
MISTER MASON! STOP RIGHT THERE!
MOOSE!
...JUG?...
ALL CLEAR, PAL.
NOW LET'S GET THE GANG TOGETHER TO PROVE I'M NOT CRAZY.
NOT CRAZY AT ALL
NOT.
AT.
ALL.

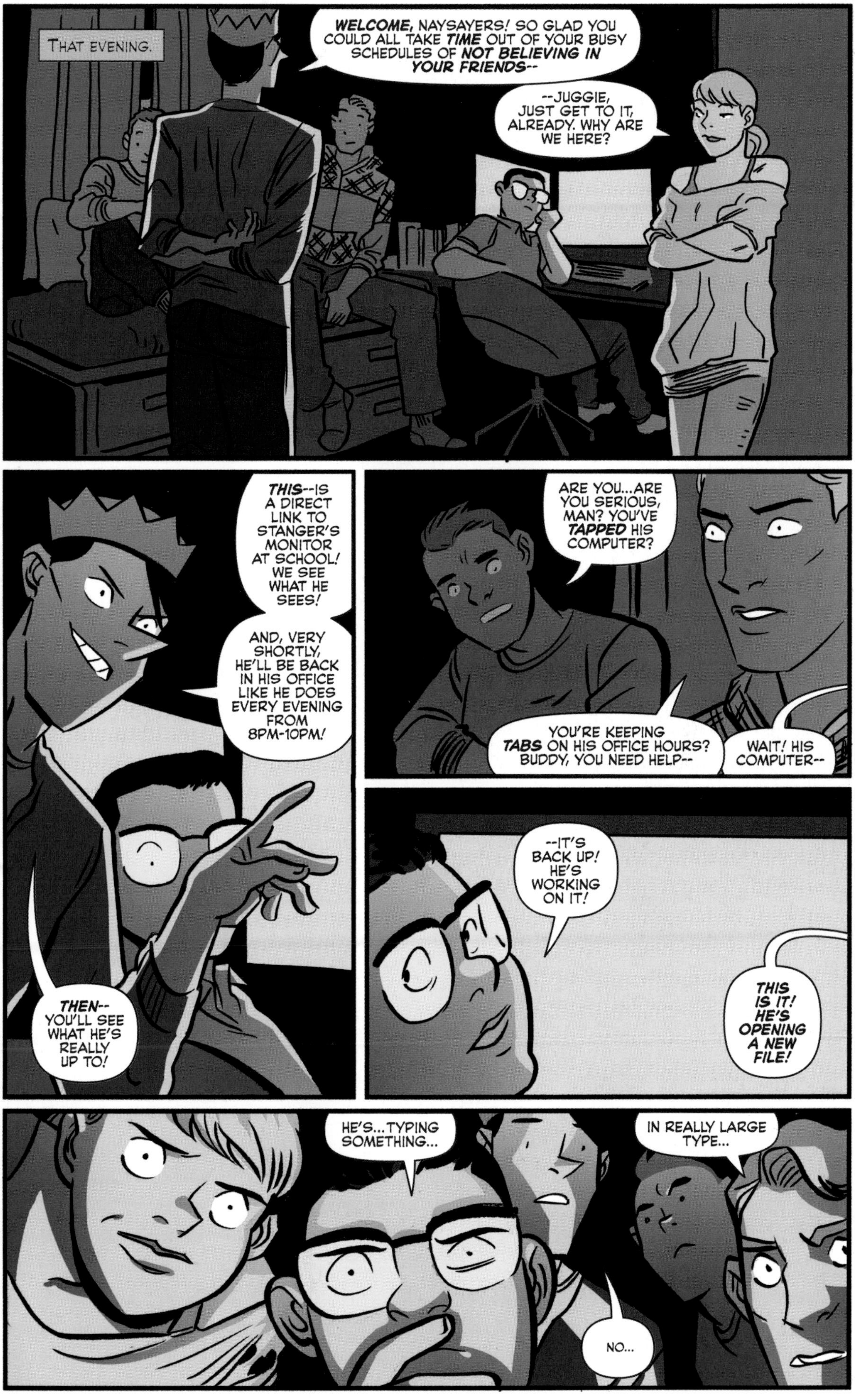
THAT EVENING.
WELCOME, NAYSAYERS! SO GLAD YOU COULD ALL TAKE TIME OUT OF YOUR BUSY SCHEDULES OF NOT BELIEVING IN YOUR FRIENDS--
--JUGGIE, JUST GET TO IT, ALREADY. WHY ARE WE HERE?
THIS--IS A DIRECT LINK TO STANGER'S MONITOR AT SCHOOL! WE SEE WHAT HE SEES!
AND, VERY SHORTLY, HE'LL BE BACK IN HIS OFFICE LIKE HE DOES EVERY EVENING FROM 8PM-10PM!
THEN--YOU'LL SEE WHAT HE'S REALLY UP TO!
ARE YOU...ARE YOU SERIOUS, MAN? YOU'VE TAPPED HIS COMPUTER?
YOU'RE KEEPING TABS ON HIS OFFICE HOURS? BUDDY, YOU NEED HELP--
WAIT! HIS COMPUTER--
--IT'S BACK UP! HE'S WORKING ON IT!
THIS IS IT! HE'S OPENING A NEW FILE!
HE'S...TYPING SOMETHING...
IN REALLY LARGE TYPE...
NO...

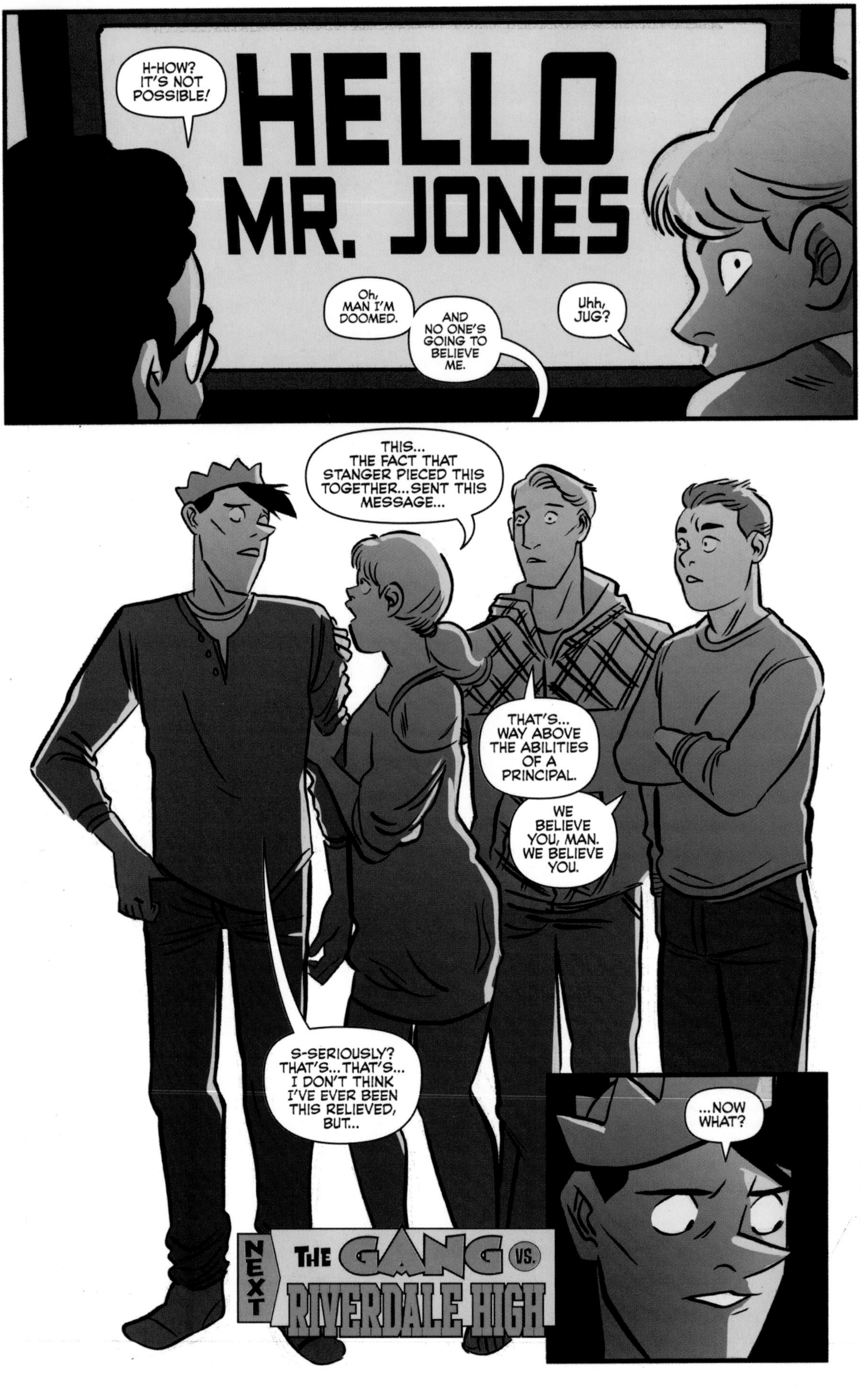

H-HOW? IT'S NOT POSSIBLE!
HELLO MR. JONES
Oh, MAN I'M DOOMED.
AND NO ONE'S GOING TO BELIEVE ME.
Uhh, JUG?
THIS... THE FACT THAT STANGER PIECED THIS TOGETHER...SENT THIS MESSAGE...
THAT'S... WAY ABOVE THE ABILITIES OF A PRINCIPAL.
WE BELIEVE YOU, MAN. WE BELIEVE YOU.
S-SERIOUSLY? THAT'S...THAT'S... I DON'T THINK I'VE EVER BEEN THIS RELIEVED, BUT...
...NOW WHAT?
NEXT
THE GANG VS. RIVERDALE HIGH

TO BE
CONTINUED...

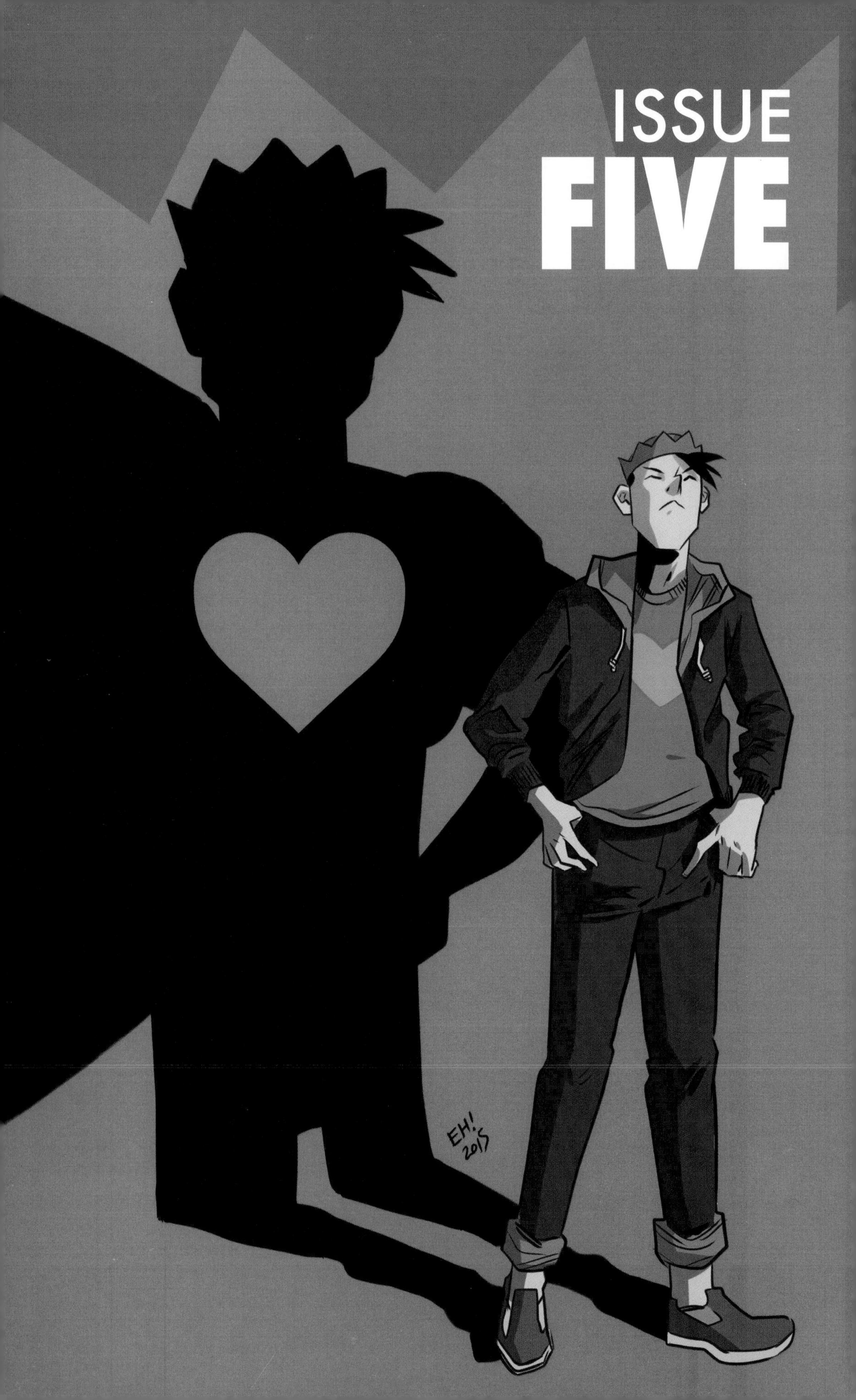
ISSUE
FIVE
EH!
2015

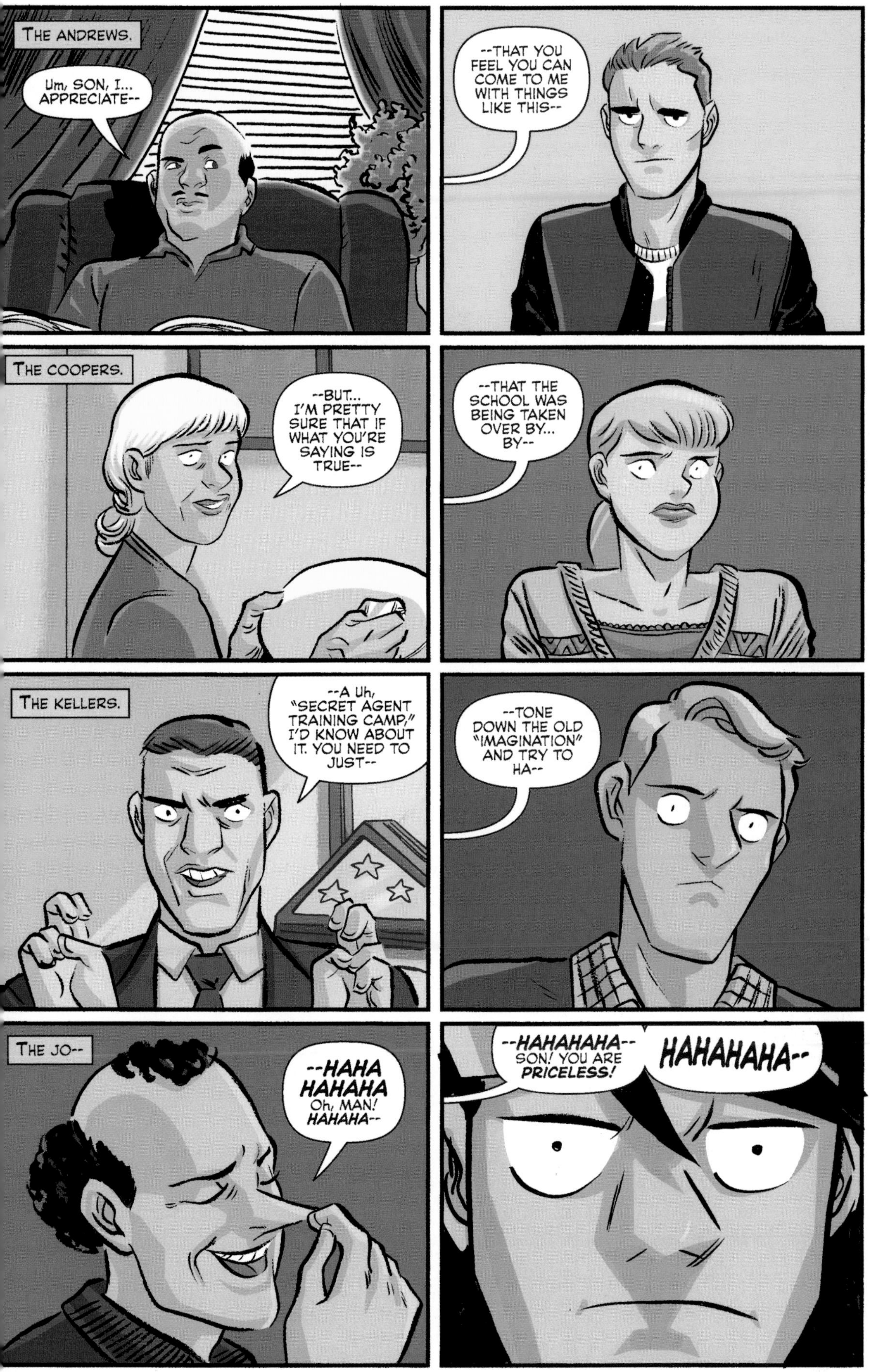
THE ANDREWS.
Um, SON, I... APPRECIATE--
--THAT YOU FEEL YOU CAN COME TO ME WITH THINGS LIKE THIS--
THE COOPERS.
--BUT... I'M PRETTY SURE THAT IF WHAT YOU'RE SAYING IS TRUE--
--THAT THE SCHOOL WAS BEING TAKEN OVER BY... BY--
THE KELLERS.
--A Uh, "SECRET AGENT TRAINING CAMP," I'D KNOW ABOUT IT. YOU NEED TO JUST--
--TONE DOWN THE OLD "IMAGINATION" AND TRY TO HA--
THE JO--
--HAHA HAHAHA Oh, MAN! HAHAHA--
--HAHAHAHA-- SON! YOU ARE PRICELESS!
HAHAHAHA--

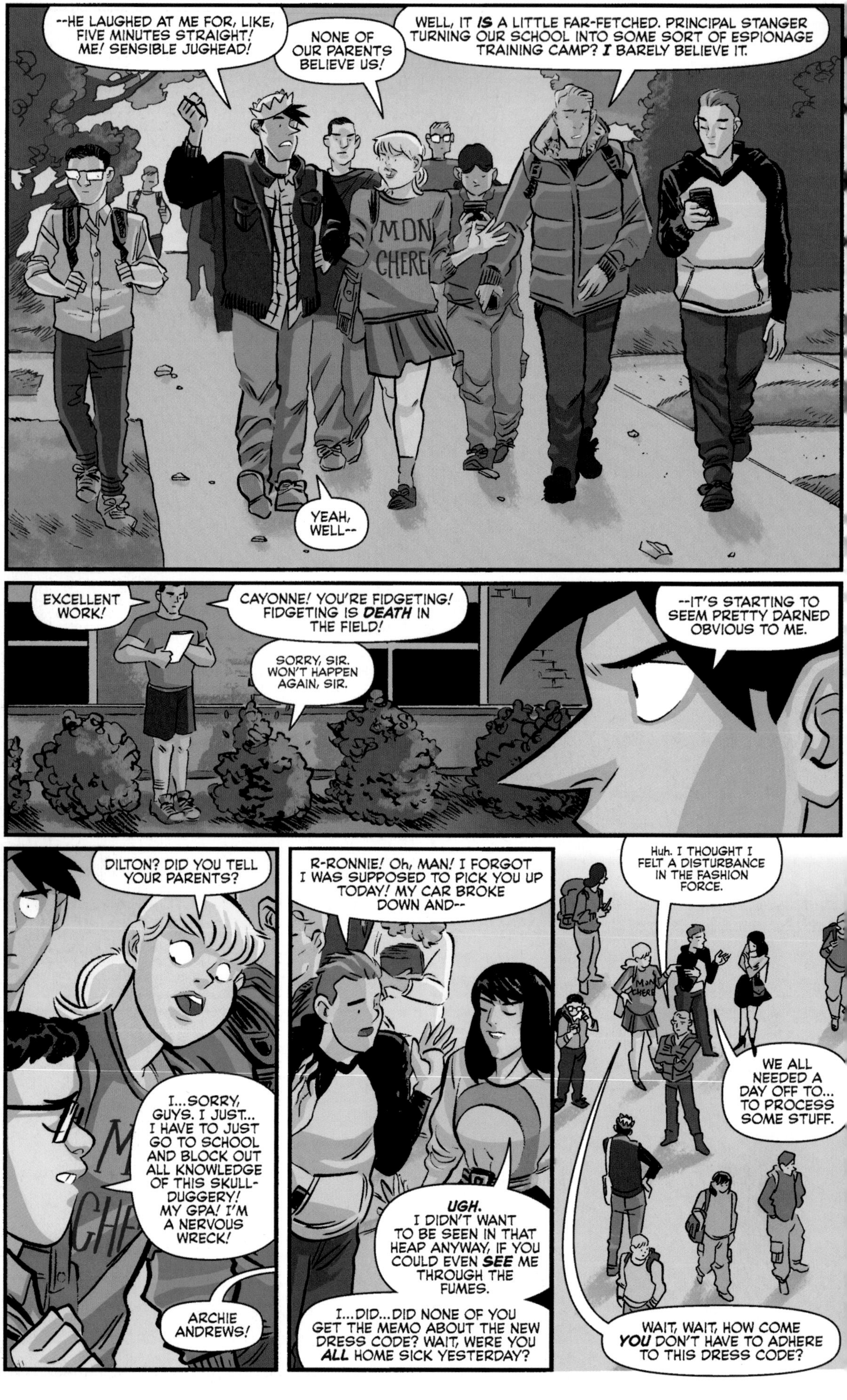
--HE LAUGHED AT ME FOR, LIKE, FIVE MINUTES STRAIGHT! ME! SENSIBLE JUGHEAD!
NONE OF OUR PARENTS BELIEVE US!
WELL, IT *IS* A LITTLE FAR-FETCHED. PRINCIPAL STANGER TURNING OUR SCHOOL INTO SOME SORT OF ESPIONAGE TRAINING CAMP? *I* BARELY BELIEVE IT.
MON CHERE
YEAH, WELL--
EXCELLENT WORK!
CAYONNE! YOU'RE FIDGETING! FIDGETING IS *DEATH* IN THE FIELD!
SORRY, SIR. WON'T HAPPEN AGAIN, SIR.
--IT'S STARTING TO SEEM PRETTY DARNED OBVIOUS TO ME.
DILTON? DID YOU TELL YOUR PARENTS?
I...SORRY, GUYS. I JUST... I HAVE TO JUST GO TO SCHOOL AND BLOCK OUT ALL KNOWLEDGE OF THIS SKULL-DUGGERY! MY GPA! I'M A NERVOUS WRECK!
ARCHIE ANDREWS!
R-RONNIE! Oh, MAN! I FORGOT I WAS SUPPOSED TO PICK YOU UP TODAY! MY CAR BROKE DOWN AND--
UGH. I DIDN'T WANT TO BE SEEN IN THAT HEAP ANYWAY, IF YOU COULD EVEN *SEE* ME THROUGH THE FUMES.
I...DID...DID NONE OF YOU GET THE MEMO ABOUT THE NEW DRESS CODE? WAIT, WERE YOU *ALL* HOME SICK YESTERDAY?
Huh. I THOUGHT I FELT A DISTURBANCE IN THE FASHION FORCE.
WE ALL NEEDED A DAY OFF TO... TO PROCESS SOME STUFF.
WAIT, WAIT, HOW COME *YOU* DON'T HAVE TO ADHERE TO THIS DRESS CODE?

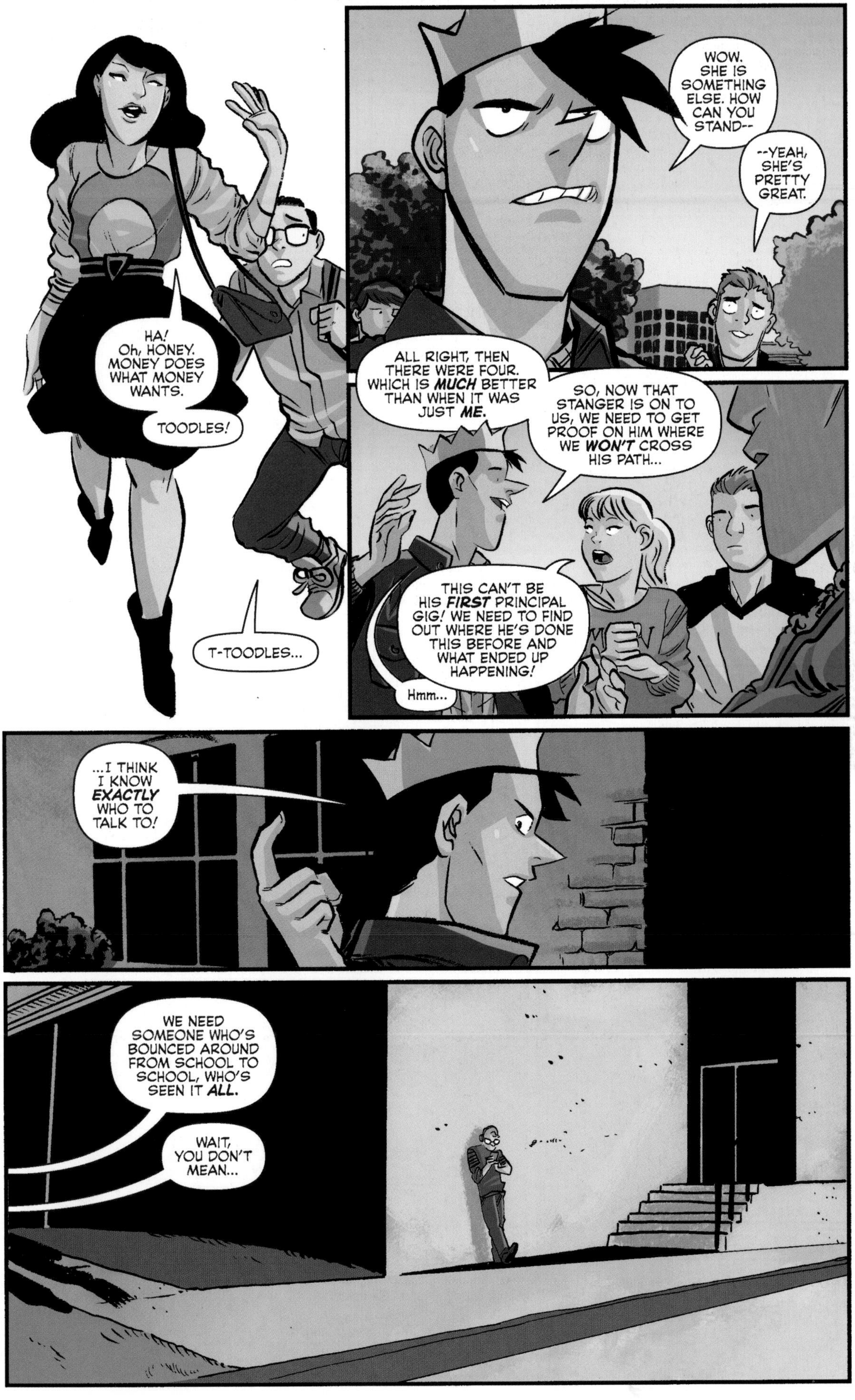
HA! Oh, HONEY. MONEY DOES WHAT MONEY WANTS.
TOODLES!
T-TOODLES...
WOW. SHE IS SOMETHING ELSE. HOW CAN YOU STAND--
--YEAH, SHE'S PRETTY GREAT.
ALL RIGHT, THEN THERE WERE FOUR. WHICH IS MUCH BETTER THAN WHEN IT WAS JUST ME.
SO, NOW THAT STANGER IS ON TO US, WE NEED TO GET PROOF ON HIM WHERE WE WON'T CROSS HIS PATH...
THIS CAN'T BE HIS FIRST PRINCIPAL GIG! WE NEED TO FIND OUT WHERE HE'S DONE THIS BEFORE AND WHAT ENDED UP HAPPENING!
Hmm...
...I THINK I KNOW EXACTLY WHO TO TALK TO!
WE NEED SOMEONE WHO'S BOUNCED AROUND FROM SCHOOL TO SCHOOL, WHO'S SEEN IT ALL.
WAIT, YOU DON'T MEAN...

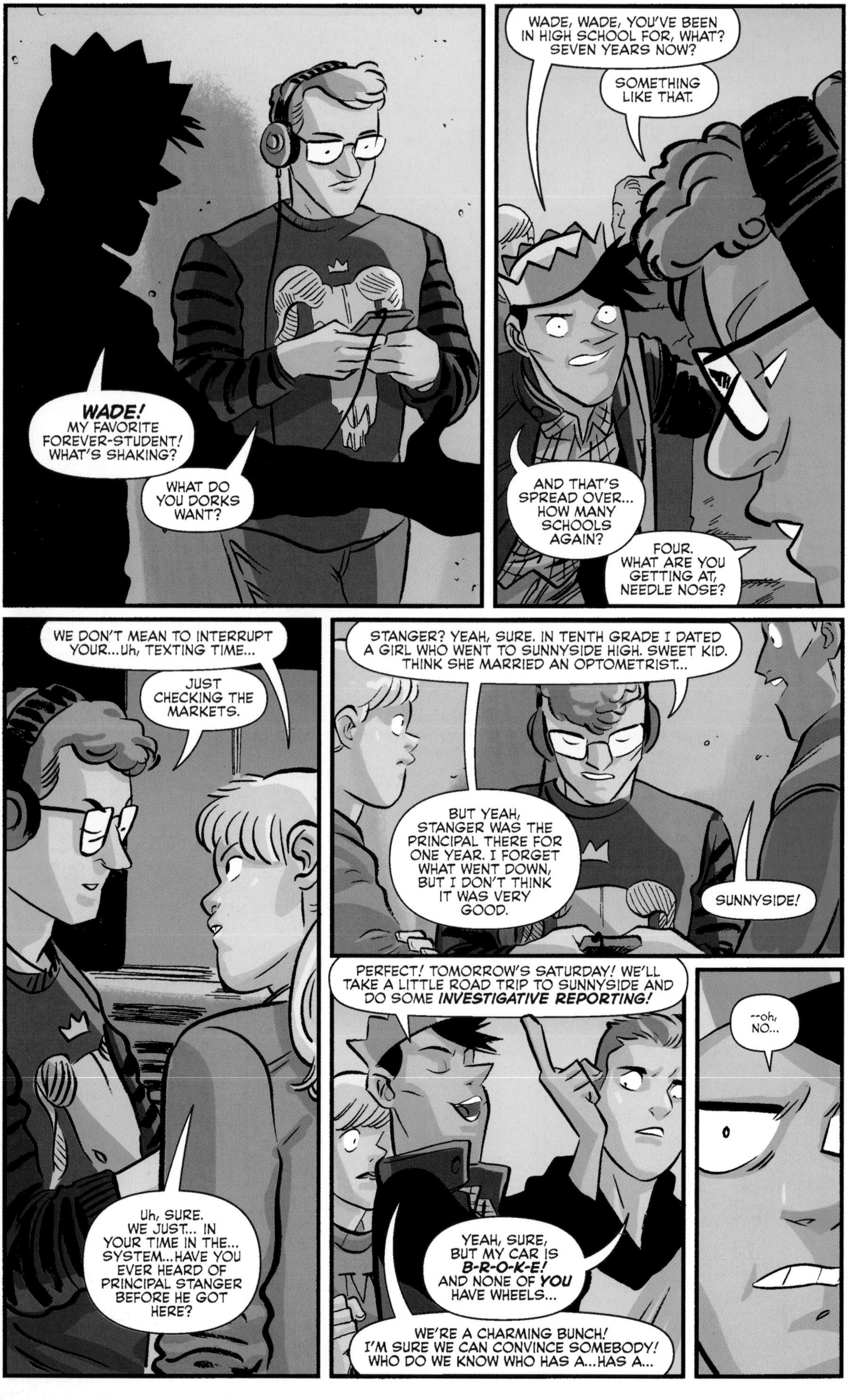
WADE! MY FAVORITE FOREVER-STUDENT! WHAT'S SHAKING?
WHAT DO YOU DORKS WANT?
WADE, WADE, YOU'VE BEEN IN HIGH SCHOOL FOR, WHAT? SEVEN YEARS NOW?
SOMETHING LIKE THAT.
AND THAT'S SPREAD OVER... HOW MANY SCHOOLS AGAIN?
FOUR. WHAT ARE YOU GETTING AT, NEEDLE NOSE?
WE DON'T MEAN TO INTERRUPT YOUR...Uh, TEXTING TIME...
JUST CHECKING THE MARKETS.
Uh, SURE. WE JUST... IN YOUR TIME IN THE... SYSTEM...HAVE YOU EVER HEARD OF PRINCIPAL STANGER BEFORE HE GOT HERE?
STANGER? YEAH, SURE. IN TENTH GRADE I DATED A GIRL WHO WENT TO SUNNYSIDE HIGH. SWEET KID. THINK SHE MARRIED AN OPTOMETRIST...
BUT YEAH, STANGER WAS THE PRINCIPAL THERE FOR ONE YEAR. I FORGET WHAT WENT DOWN, BUT I DON'T THINK IT WAS VERY GOOD.
SUNNYSIDE!
PERFECT! TOMORROW'S SATURDAY! WE'LL TAKE A LITTLE ROAD TRIP TO SUNNYSIDE AND DO SOME INVESTIGATIVE REPORTING!
YEAH, SURE, BUT MY CAR IS B-R-O-K-E! AND NONE OF YOU HAVE WHEELS...
WE'RE A CHARMING BUNCH! I'M SURE WE CAN CONVINCE SOMEBODY! WHO DO WE KNOW WHO HAS A...HAS A...
--oh, NO...

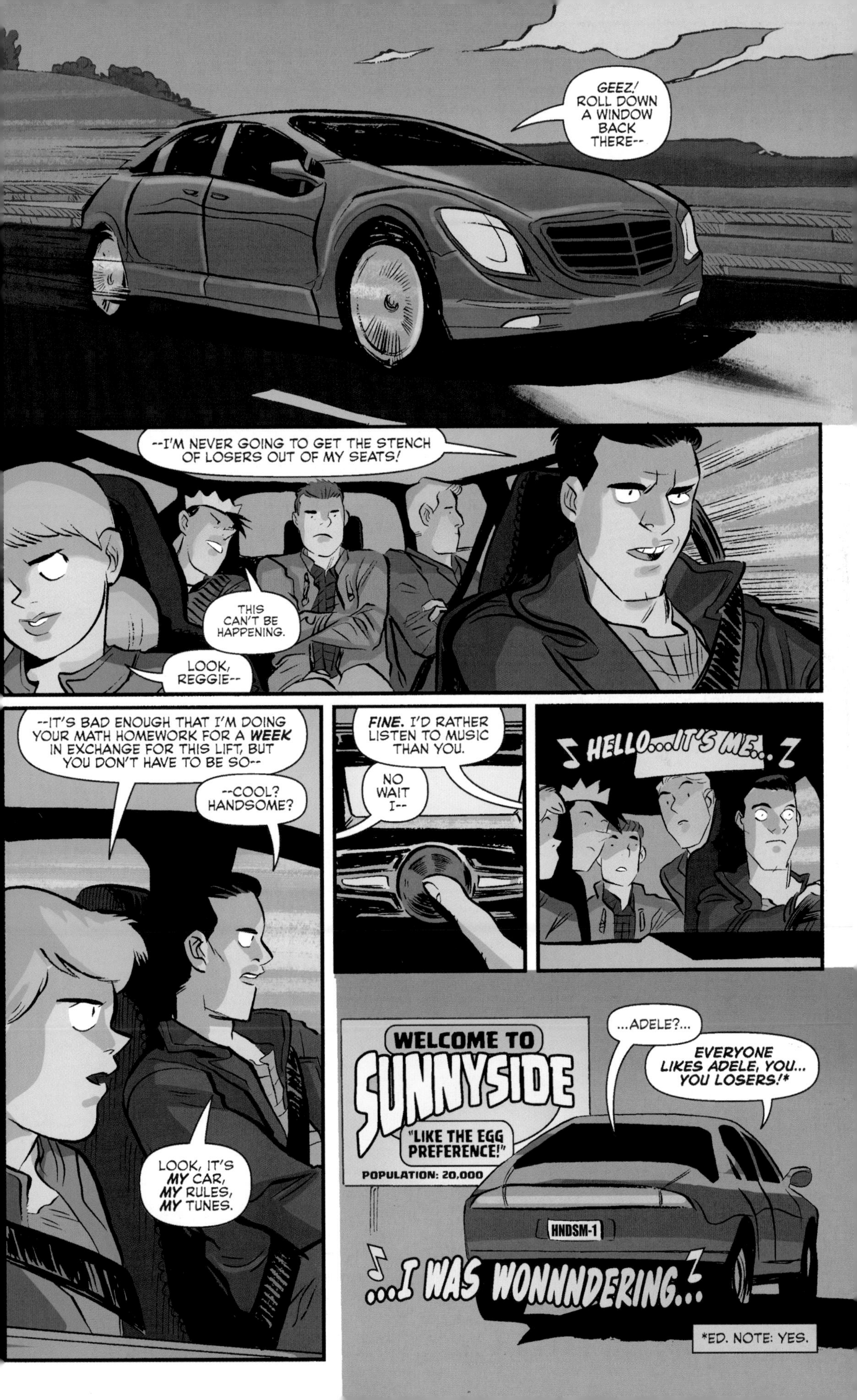
GEEZ! ROLL DOWN A WINDOW BACK THERE--
--I'M NEVER GOING TO GET THE STENCH OF LOSERS OUT OF MY SEATS!
THIS CAN'T BE HAPPENING.
LOOK, REGGIE--
--IT'S BAD ENOUGH THAT I'M DOING YOUR MATH HOMEWORK FOR A WEEK IN EXCHANGE FOR THIS LIFT, BUT YOU DON'T HAVE TO BE SO--
--COOL? HANDSOME?
LOOK, IT'S MY CAR, MY RULES, MY TUNES.
FINE. I'D RATHER LISTEN TO MUSIC THAN YOU.
NO WAIT I--
HELLO...IT'S ME...
WELCOME TO
SUNNYSIDE
"LIKE THE EGG PREFERENCE!"
POPULATION: 20,000
...ADELE?...
EVERYONE LIKES ADELE, YOU... YOU LOSERS!*
HNDSM-1
...I WAS WONNNDERING...
*ED. NOTE: YES.

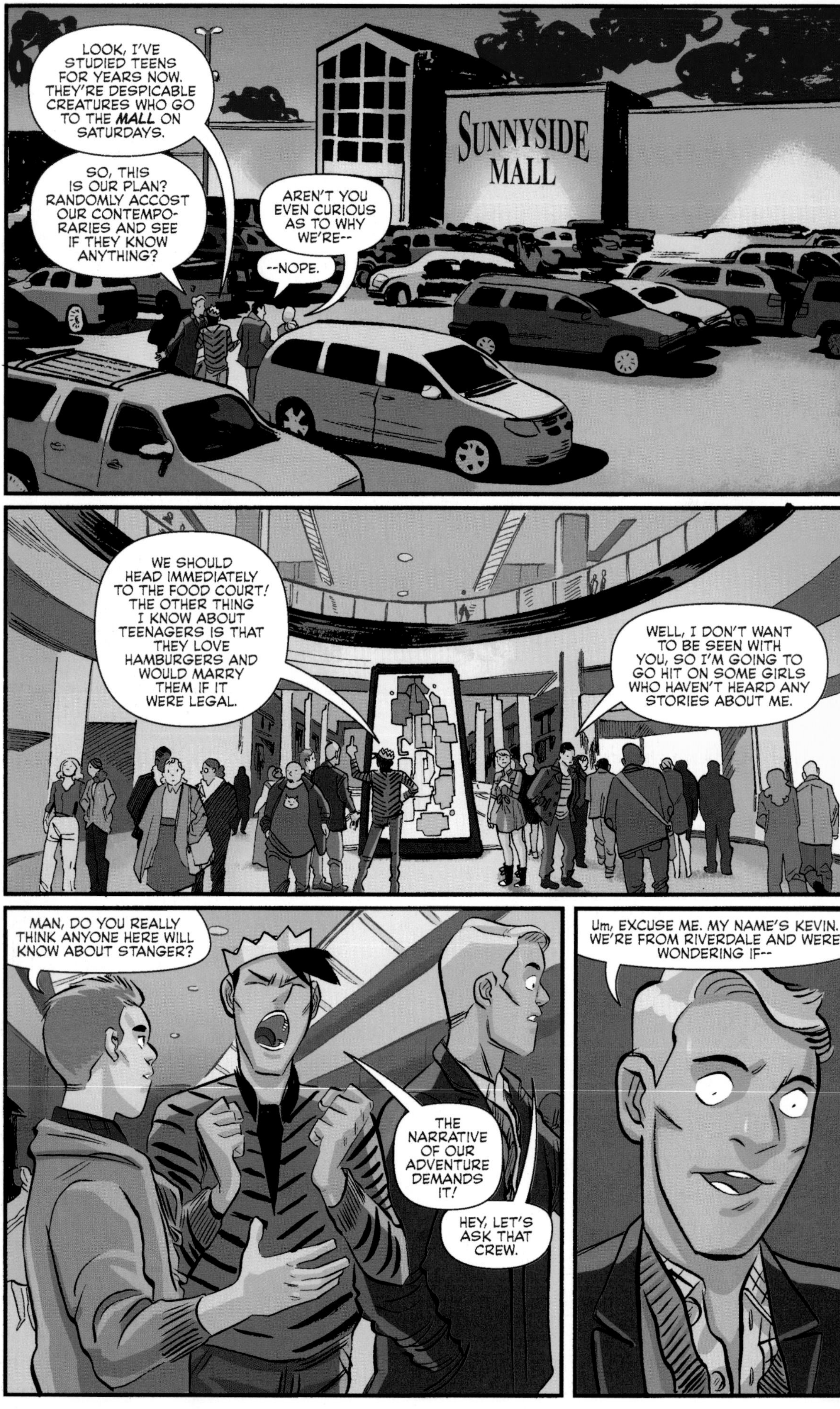
LOOK, I'VE STUDIED TEENS FOR YEARS NOW. THEY'RE DESPICABLE CREATURES WHO GO TO THE *MALL* ON SATURDAYS.
SUNNYSIDE MALL
SO, THIS IS OUR PLAN? RANDOMLY ACCOST OUR CONTEMPO-RARIES AND SEE IF THEY KNOW ANYTHING?
AREN'T YOU EVEN CURIOUS AS TO WHY WE'RE--
--NOPE.
WE SHOULD HEAD IMMEDIATELY TO THE FOOD COURT! THE OTHER THING I KNOW ABOUT TEENAGERS IS THAT THEY LOVE HAMBURGERS AND WOULD MARRY THEM IF IT WERE LEGAL.
WELL, I DON'T WANT TO BE SEEN WITH YOU, SO I'M GOING TO GO HIT ON SOME GIRLS WHO HAVEN'T HEARD ANY STORIES ABOUT ME.
MAN, DO YOU REALLY THINK ANYONE HERE WILL KNOW ABOUT STANGER?
THE NARRATIVE OF OUR ADVENTURE DEMANDS IT!
HEY, LET'S ASK THAT CREW.
Um, EXCUSE ME. MY NAME'S KEVIN. WE'RE FROM RIVERDALE AND WERE WONDERING IF--

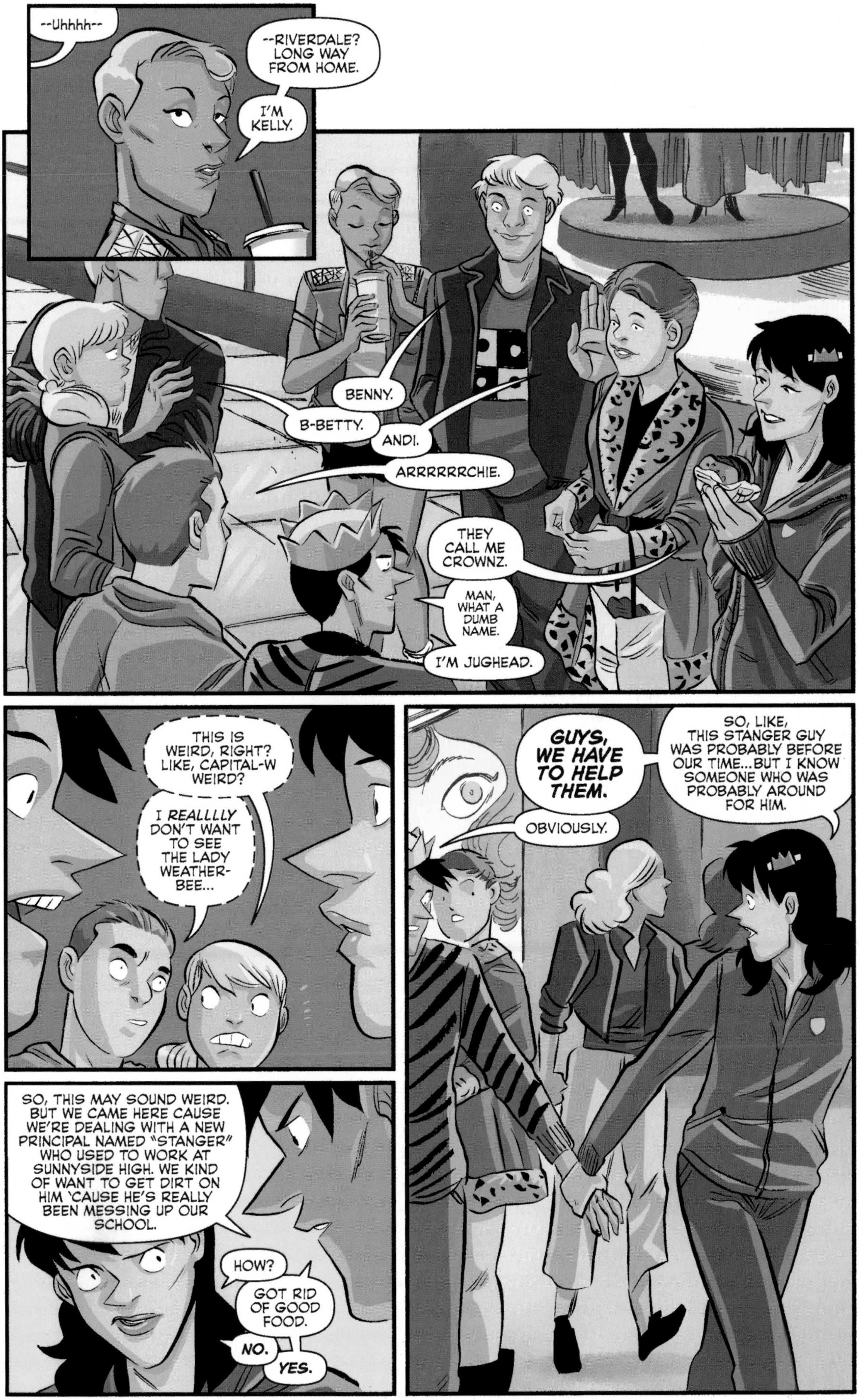
--Uhhhh--
--RIVERDALE? LONG WAY FROM HOME.
I'M KELLY.
BENNY.
B-BETTY.
ANDI.
ARRRRRRCHIE.
THEY CALL ME CROWNZ.
MAN, WHAT A DUMB NAME.
I'M JUGHEAD.
THIS IS WEIRD, RIGHT? LIKE, CAPITAL-W WEIRD?
I REALLLLY DON'T WANT TO SEE THE LADY WEATHER-BEE...
SO, THIS MAY SOUND WEIRD. BUT WE CAME HERE CAUSE WE'RE DEALING WITH A NEW PRINCIPAL NAMED "STANGER" WHO USED TO WORK AT SUNNYSIDE HIGH. WE KIND OF WANT TO GET DIRT ON HIM 'CAUSE HE'S REALLY BEEN MESSING UP OUR SCHOOL.
HOW?
GOT RID OF GOOD FOOD.
NO.
YES.
GUYS, WE HAVE TO HELP THEM.
OBVIOUSLY.
SO, LIKE, THIS STANGER GUY WAS PROBABLY BEFORE OUR TIME...BUT I KNOW SOMEONE WHO WAS PROBABLY AROUND FOR HIM.

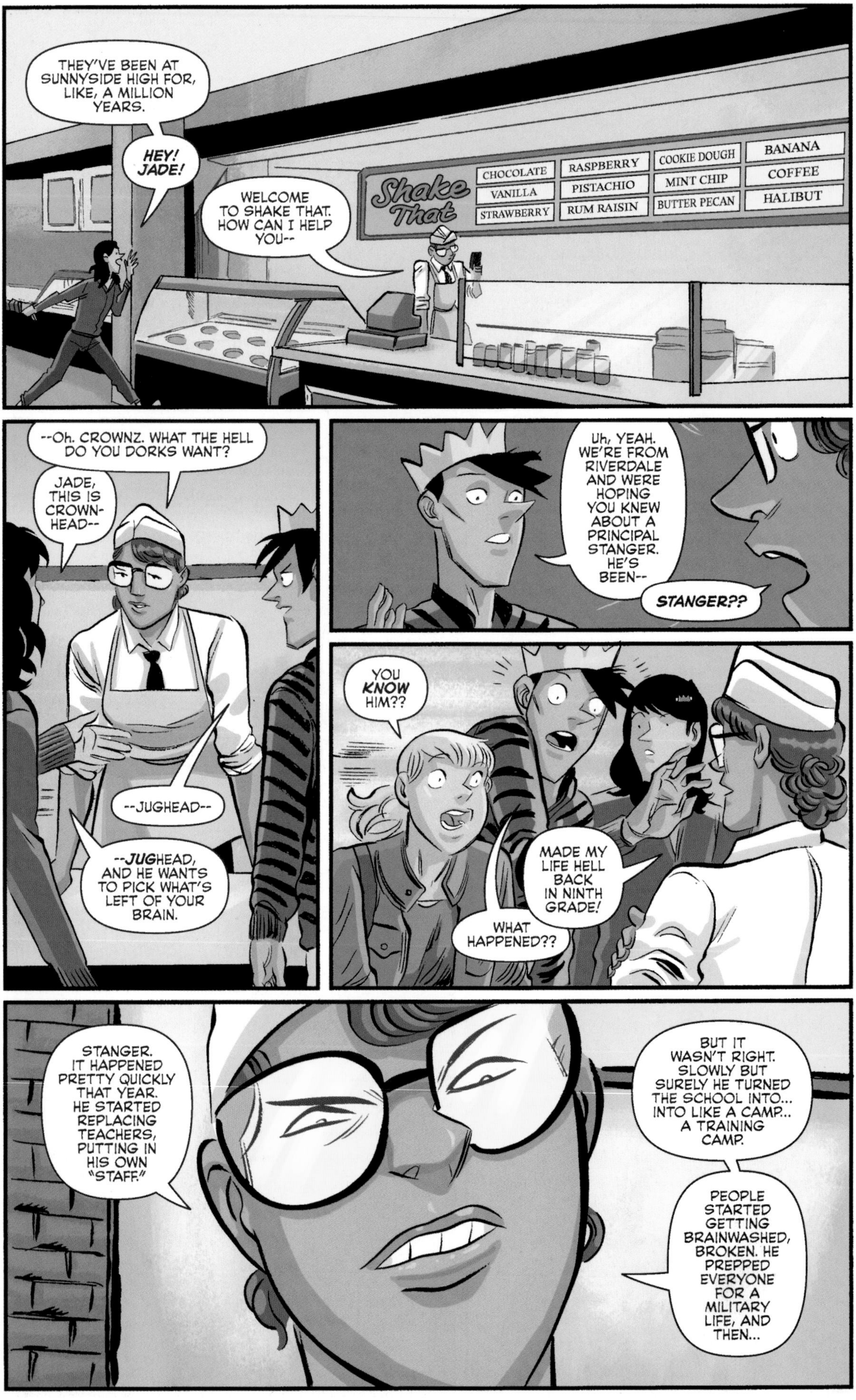
THEY'VE BEEN AT SUNNYSIDE HIGH FOR, LIKE, A MILLION YEARS.
HEY! JADE!
WELCOME TO SHAKE THAT. HOW CAN I HELP YOU--
Shake That
CHOCOLATE
VANILLA
STRAWBERRY
RASPBERRY
PISTACHIO
RUM RAISIN
COOKIE DOUGH
MINT CHIP
BUTTER PECAN
BANANA
COFFEE
HALIBUT
--Oh. CROWNZ. WHAT THE HELL DO YOU DORKS WANT?
JADE, THIS IS CROWN-HEAD--
--JUGHEAD--
--JUGHEAD, AND HE WANTS TO PICK WHAT'S LEFT OF YOUR BRAIN.
Uh, YEAH. WE'RE FROM RIVERDALE AND WERE HOPING YOU KNEW ABOUT A PRINCIPAL STANGER. HE'S BEEN--
STANGER??
YOU KNOW HIM??
MADE MY LIFE HELL BACK IN NINTH GRADE!
WHAT HAPPENED??
STANGER. IT HAPPENED PRETTY QUICKLY THAT YEAR. HE STARTED REPLACING TEACHERS, PUTTING IN HIS OWN "STAFF."
BUT IT WASN'T RIGHT. SLOWLY BUT SURELY HE TURNED THE SCHOOL INTO... INTO LIKE A CAMP... A TRAINING CAMP.
PEOPLE STARTED GETTING BRAINWASHED, BROKEN. HE PREPPED EVERYONE FOR A MILITARY LIFE, AND THEN...

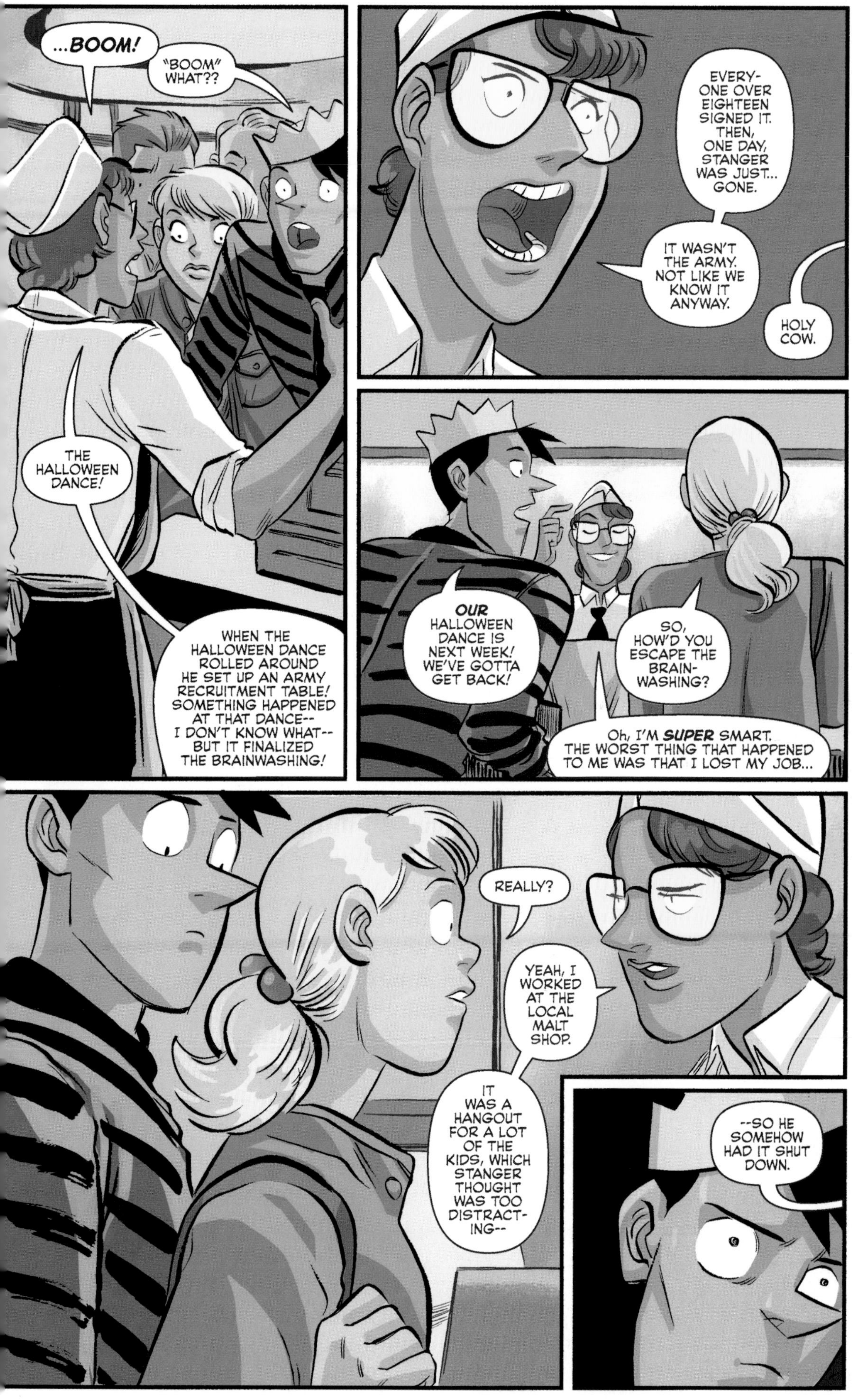
...BOOM!
"BOOM" WHAT??
THE HALLOWEEN DANCE!
WHEN THE HALLOWEEN DANCE ROLLED AROUND HE SET UP AN ARMY RECRUITMENT TABLE! SOMETHING HAPPENED AT THAT DANCE-- I DON'T KNOW WHAT-- BUT IT FINALIZED THE BRAINWASHING!
EVERY-ONE OVER EIGHTEEN SIGNED IT. THEN, ONE DAY, STANGER WAS JUST... GONE.
IT WASN'T THE ARMY. NOT LIKE WE KNOW IT ANYWAY.
HOLY COW.
OUR HALLOWEEN DANCE IS NEXT WEEK! WE'VE GOTTA GET BACK!
SO, HOW'D YOU ESCAPE THE BRAIN-WASHING?
Oh, I'M SUPER SMART. THE WORST THING THAT HAPPENED TO ME WAS THAT I LOST MY JOB...
REALLY?
YEAH, I WORKED AT THE LOCAL MALT SHOP.
IT WAS A HANGOUT FOR A LOT OF THE KIDS, WHICH STANGER THOUGHT WAS TOO DISTRACT-ING--
--SO HE SOMEHOW HAD IT SHUT DOWN.

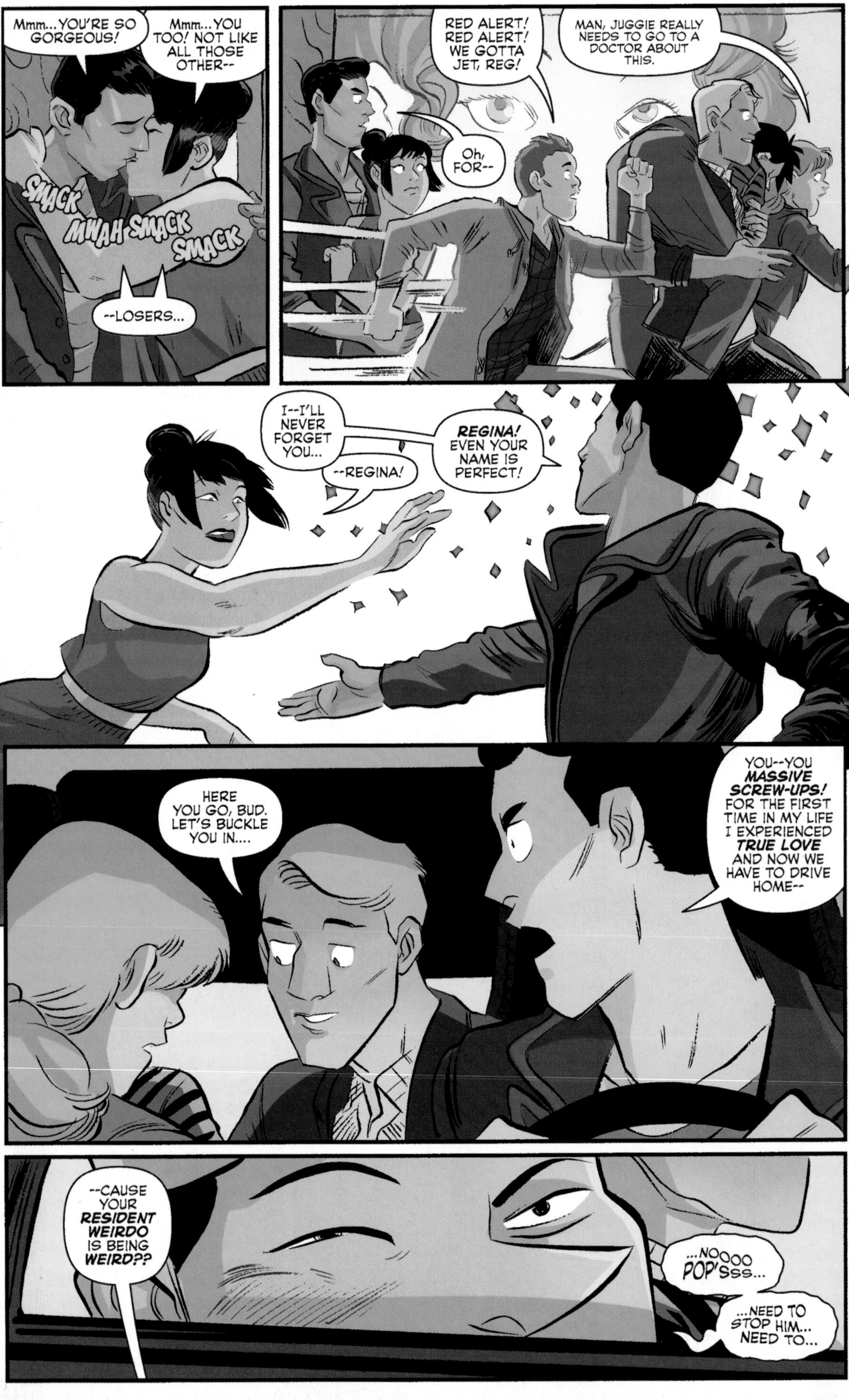
Mmm...YOU'RE SO GORGEOUS!
Mmm...YOU TOO! NOT LIKE ALL THOSE OTHER--
SMACK MWAH SMACK SMACK
--LOSERS...
RED ALERT! RED ALERT! WE GOTTA JET, REG!
MAN, JUGGIE REALLY NEEDS TO GO TO A DOCTOR ABOUT THIS.
Oh, FOR--
I--I'LL NEVER FORGET YOU...
--REGINA!
REGINA! EVEN YOUR NAME IS PERFECT!
HERE YOU GO, BUD. LET'S BUCKLE YOU IN....
YOU--YOU MASSIVE SCREW-UPS! FOR THE FIRST TIME IN MY LIFE I EXPERIENCED TRUE LOVE AND NOW WE HAVE TO DRIVE HOME--
--CAUSE YOUR RESIDENT WEIRDO IS BEING WEIRD??
...NOOOO POP'Sss...
...NEED TO STOP HIM... NEED TO...

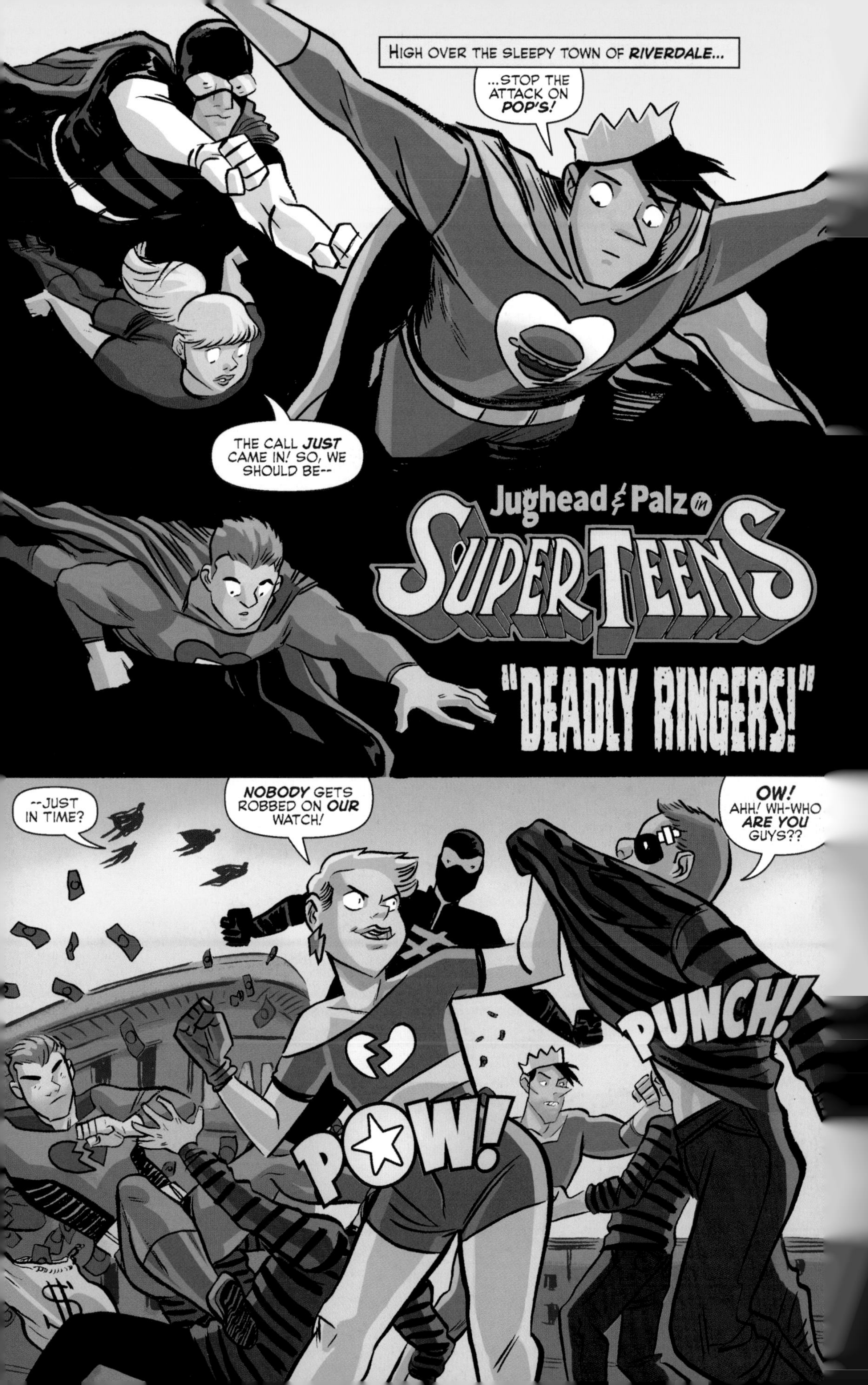

HIGH OVER THE SLEEPY TOWN OF RIVERDALE...
...STOP THE ATTACK ON POP'S!
THE CALL JUST CAME IN! SO, WE SHOULD BE--
Jughead & Palz in
SUPER TEENS
"DEADLY RINGERS!"
--JUST IN TIME?
NOBODY GETS ROBBED ON OUR WATCH!
OW! AHH! WH-WHO ARE YOU GUYS??
PUNCH!
POW!

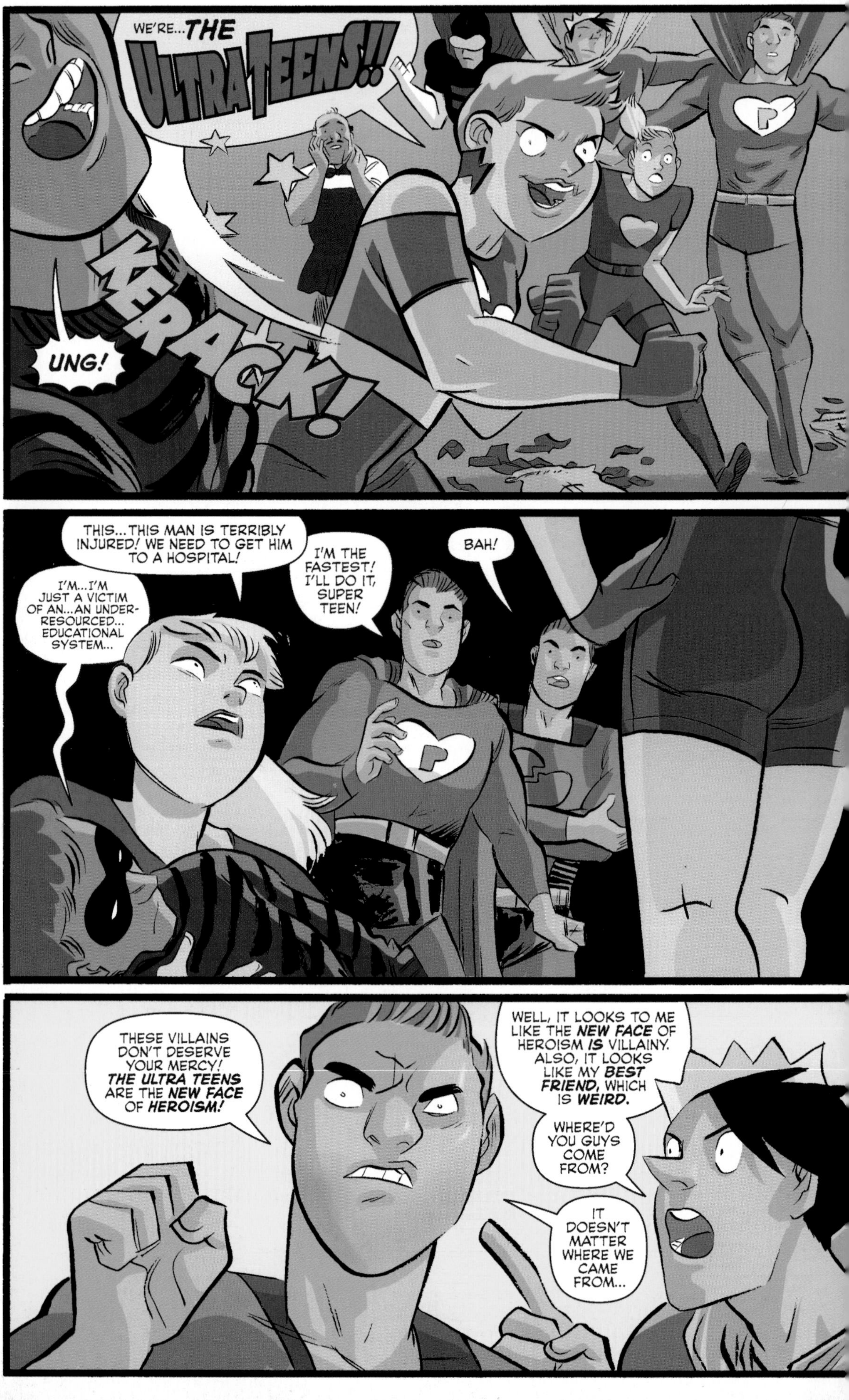

WE'RE...THE ULTRA TEENS!!
KERACK!
UNG!
THIS...THIS MAN IS TERRIBLY INJURED! WE NEED TO GET HIM TO A HOSPITAL!
I'M...I'M JUST A VICTIM OF AN...AN UNDER-RESOURCED... EDUCATIONAL SYSTEM...
I'M THE FASTEST! I'LL DO IT, SUPER TEEN!
BAH!
THESE VILLAINS DON'T DESERVE YOUR MERCY! THE ULTRA TEENS ARE THE NEW FACE OF HEROISM!
WELL, IT LOOKS TO ME LIKE THE NEW FACE OF HEROISM IS VILLAINY. ALSO, IT LOOKS LIKE MY BEST FRIEND, WHICH IS WEIRD.
WHERE'D YOU GUYS COME FROM?
IT DOESN'T MATTER WHERE WE CAME FROM...

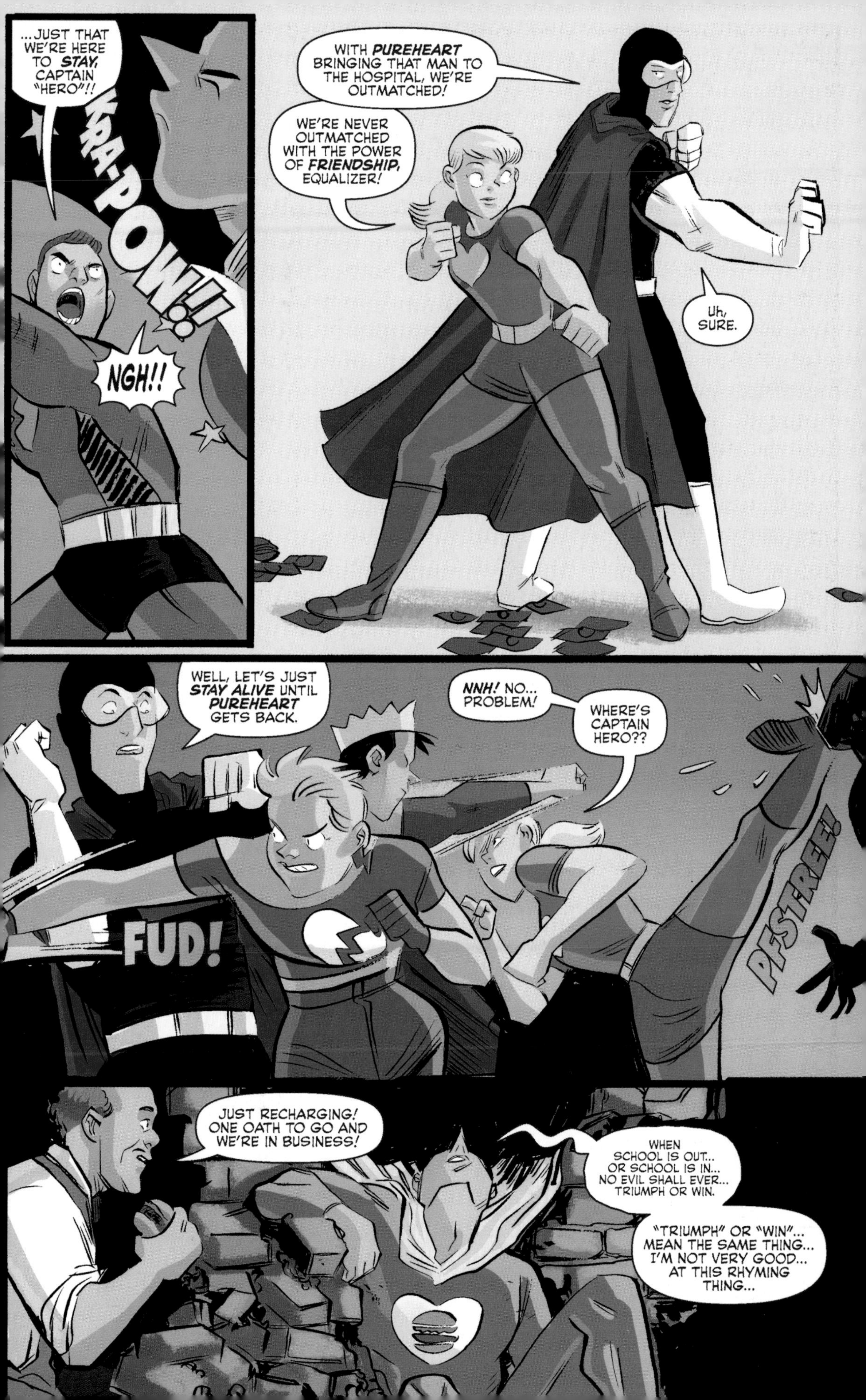

...JUST THAT WE'RE HERE TO STAY, CAPTAIN "HERO"!!
KRA-POW!!
NGH!!
WITH PUREHEART BRINGING THAT MAN TO THE HOSPITAL, WE'RE OUTMATCHED!
WE'RE NEVER OUTMATCHED WITH THE POWER OF FRIENDSHIP, EQUALIZER!
Uh, SURE.
WELL, LET'S JUST STAY ALIVE UNTIL PUREHEART GETS BACK.
NNH! NO... PROBLEM!
WHERE'S CAPTAIN HERO??
FUD!
PFSTREEE!
JUST RECHARGING! ONE OATH TO GO AND WE'RE IN BUSINESS!
WHEN SCHOOL IS OUT... OR SCHOOL IS IN... NO EVIL SHALL EVER... TRIUMPH OR WIN.
"TRIUMPH" OR "WIN"... MEAN THE SAME THING... I'M NOT VERY GOOD... AT THIS RHYMING THING...

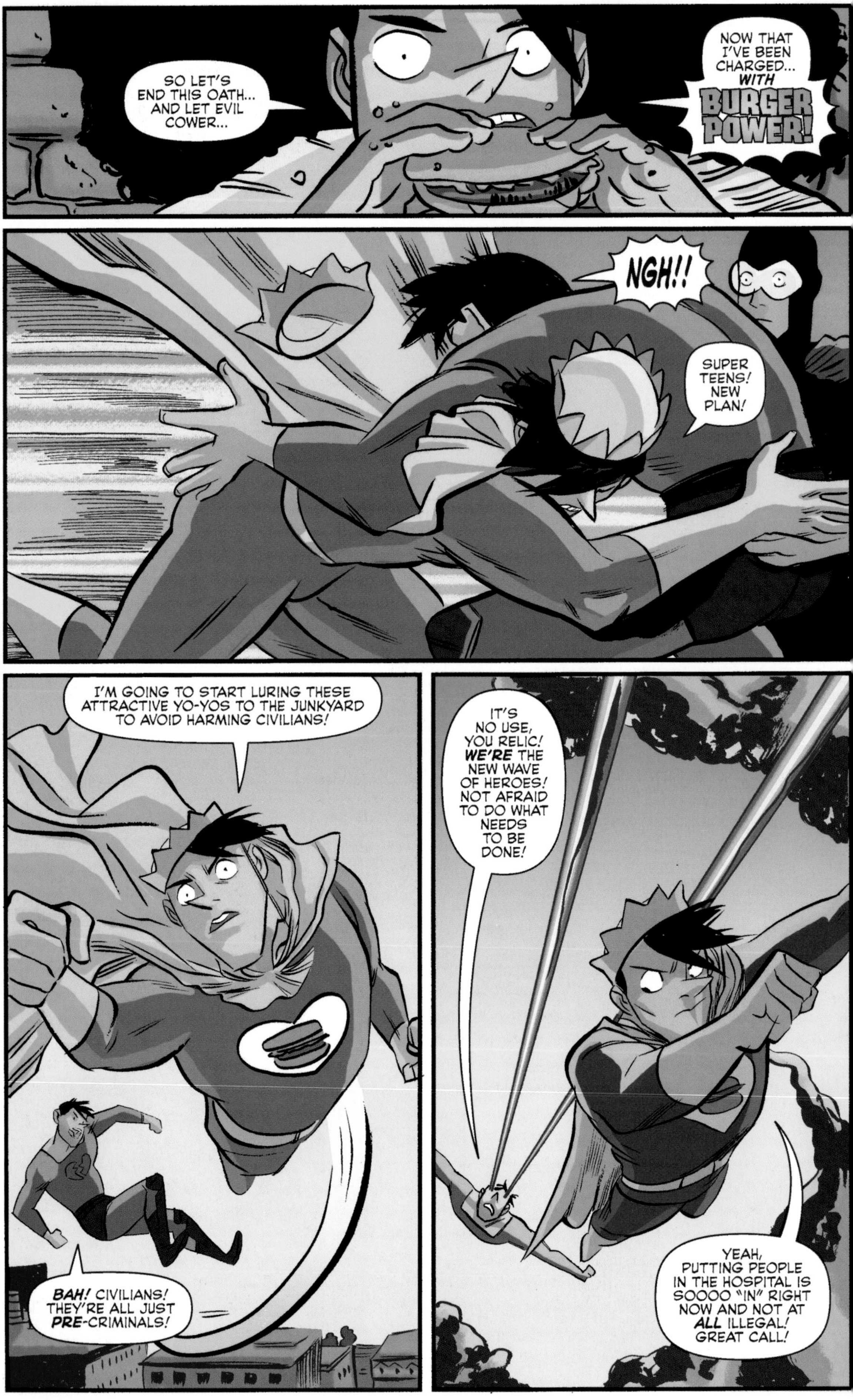
SO LET'S END THIS OATH... AND LET EVIL COWER...
NOW THAT I'VE BEEN CHARGED... WITH
BURGER POWER!
NGH!!
SUPER TEENS! NEW PLAN!
I'M GOING TO START LURING THESE ATTRACTIVE YO-YOS TO THE JUNKYARD TO AVOID HARMING CIVILIANS!
BAH! CIVILIANS! THEY'RE ALL JUST PRE-CRIMINALS!
IT'S NO USE, YOU RELIC! WE'RE THE NEW WAVE OF HEROES! NOT AFRAID TO DO WHAT NEEDS TO BE DONE!
YEAH, PUTTING PEOPLE IN THE HOSPITAL IS SOOOO "IN" RIGHT NOW AND NOT AT ALL ILLEGAL! GREAT CALL!

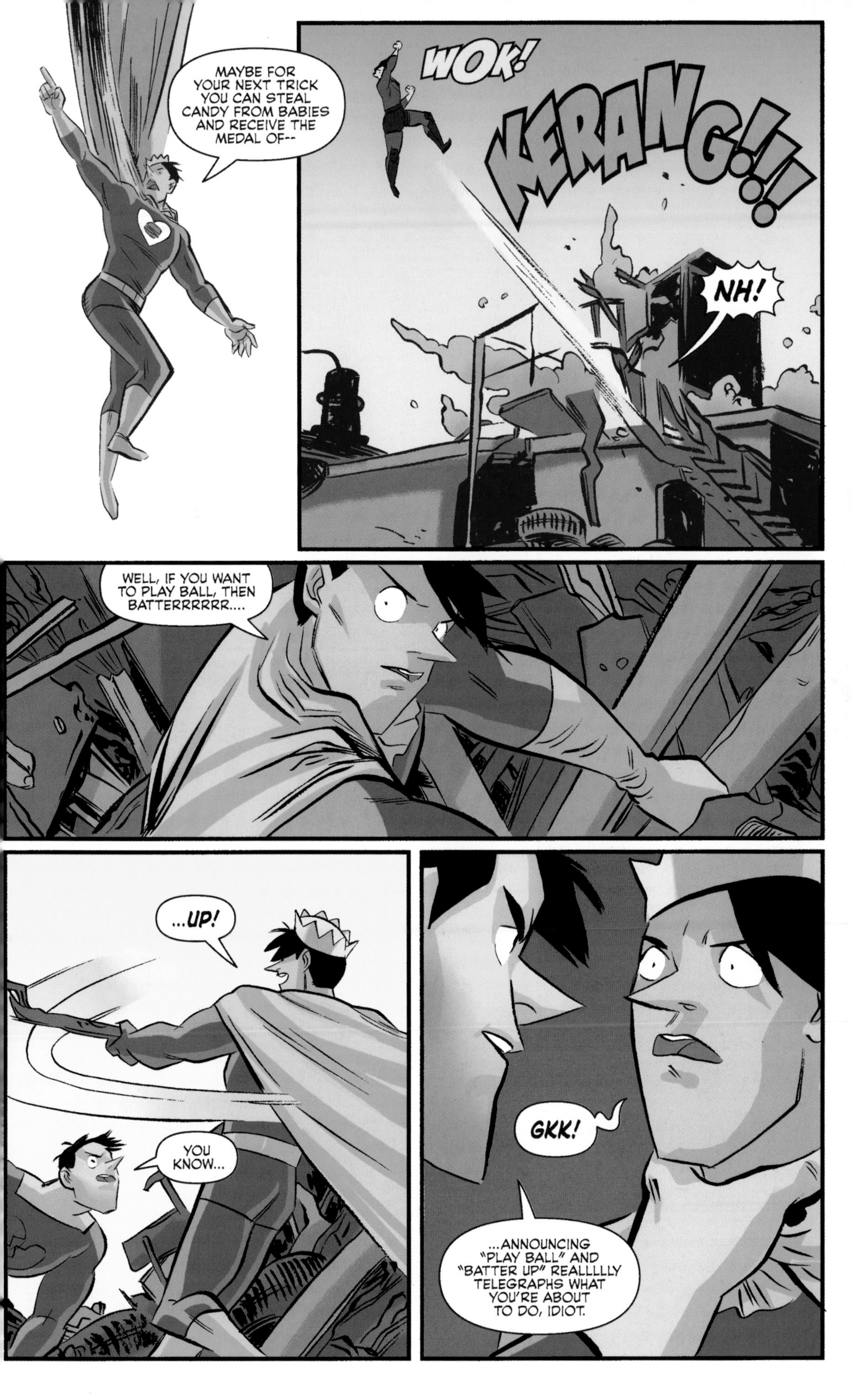
MAYBE FOR YOUR NEXT TRICK YOU CAN STEAL CANDY FROM BABIES AND RECEIVE THE MEDAL OF--
WOK!
KERANG!!!
NH!
WELL, IF YOU WANT TO PLAY BALL, THEN BATTERRRRRR....
...UP!
YOU KNOW...
GKK!
...ANNOUNCING "PLAY BALL" AND "BATTER UP" REALLLLLY TELEGRAPHS WHAT YOU'RE ABOUT TO DO, IDIOT.

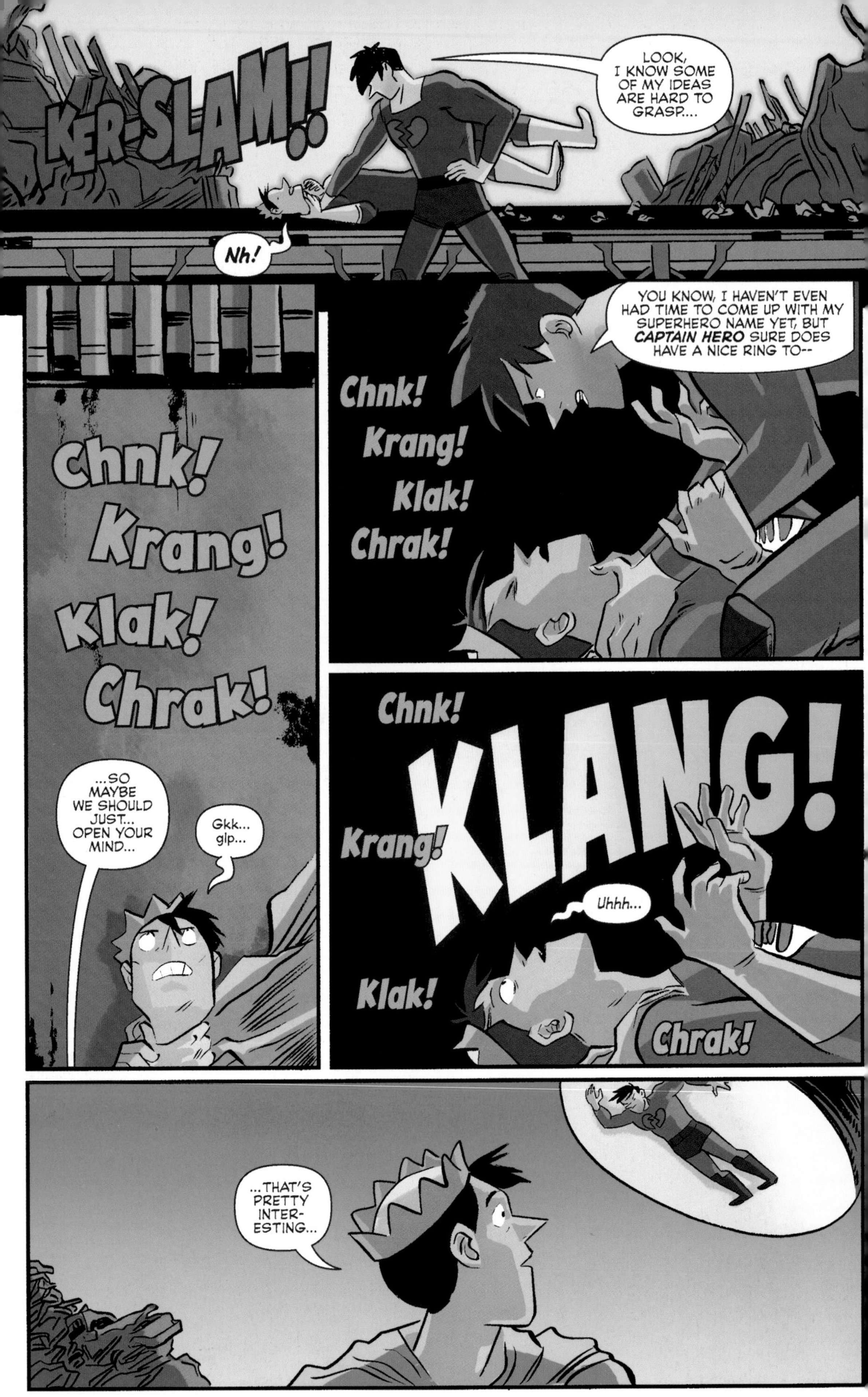
KER-SLAM!!
LOOK, I KNOW SOME OF MY IDEAS ARE HARD TO GRASP....
Nh!
YOU KNOW, I HAVEN'T EVEN HAD TIME TO COME UP WITH MY SUPERHERO NAME YET, BUT CAPTAIN HERO SURE DOES HAVE A NICE RING TO--
Chnk!
Krang!
Klak!
Chrak!
Chnk!
Krang!
Klak!
Chrak!
...SO MAYBE WE SHOULD JUST... OPEN YOUR MIND...
Gkk... glp...
Chnk!
KLANG!
Krang!
Uhhh...
Klak!
Chrak!
...THAT'S PRETTY INTER-ESTING...

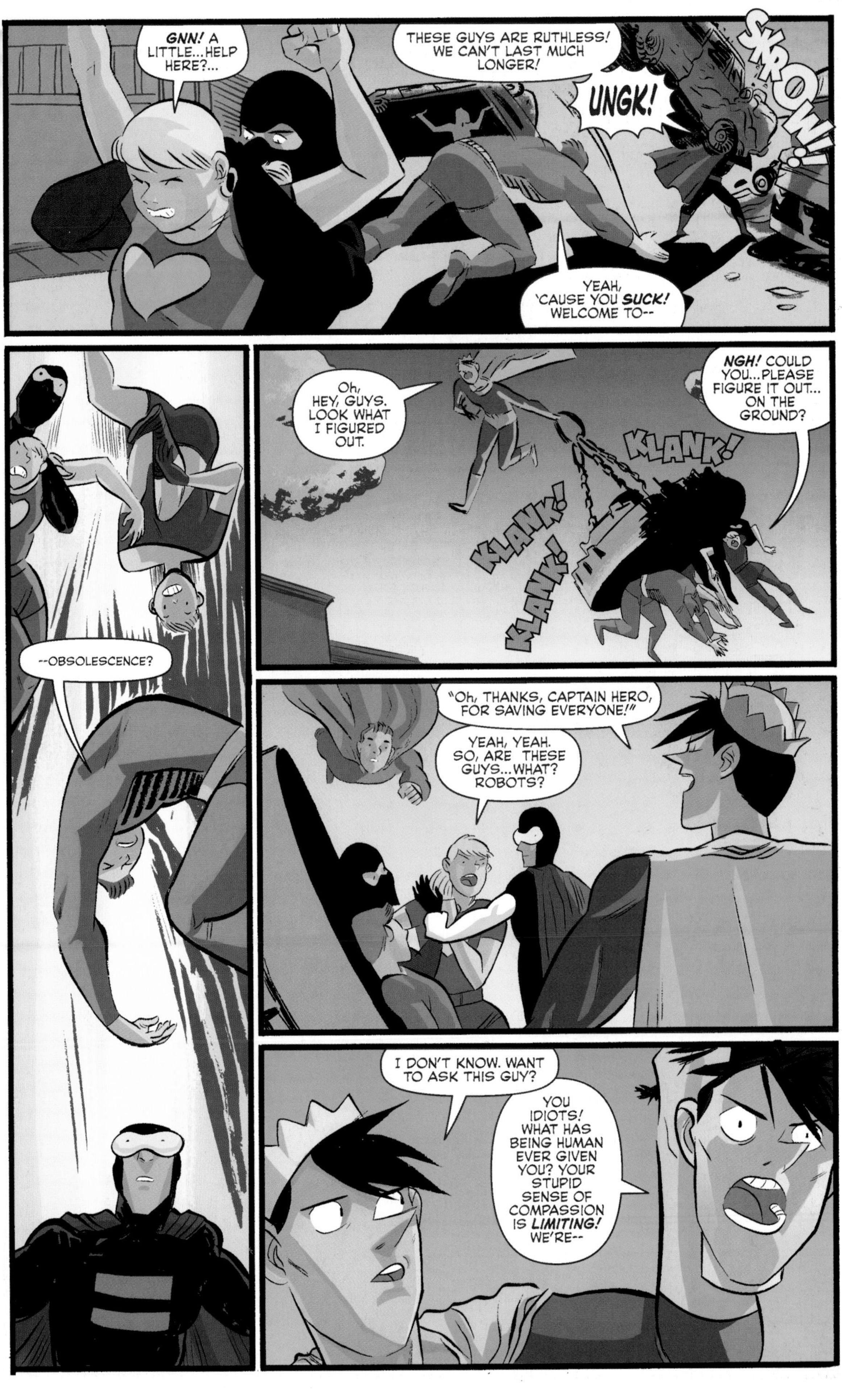
GNN! A LITTLE...HELP HERE?...
THESE GUYS ARE RUTHLESS! WE CAN'T LAST MUCH LONGER!
UNGK!
SKROW!
YEAH, 'CAUSE YOU SUCK! WELCOME TO--
--OBSOLESCENCE?
Oh, HEY, GUYS. LOOK WHAT I FIGURED OUT.
NGH! COULD YOU...PLEASE FIGURE IT OUT... ON THE GROUND?
KLANK!
KLANK!
KLANK!
"Oh, THANKS, CAPTAIN HERO, FOR SAVING EVERYONE!"
YEAH, YEAH. SO, ARE THESE GUYS...WHAT? ROBOTS?
I DON'T KNOW. WANT TO ASK THIS GUY?
YOU IDIOTS! WHAT HAS BEING HUMAN EVER GIVEN YOU? YOUR STUPID SENSE OF COMPASSION IS LIMITING! WE'RE--

OR BETTER YET, WE CAN ASK *THIS* GUY...

--HEY! DON'T TILT ME OVER WHEN I'M YELLING AT YOU! THAT'S INCREDIBLY RUDE!

WAIT...MANTLE INDUSTRIES??

THAT'S RIGHT...

MANTLE INDUSTRIES

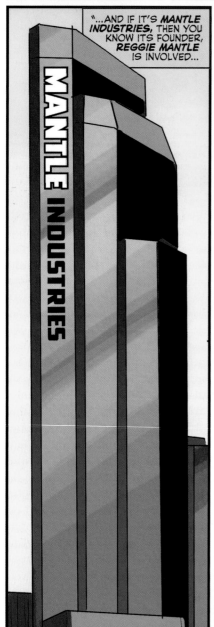

"...AND IF IT'S *MANTLE INDUSTRIES*, THEN YOU KNOW ITS FOUNDER, *REGGIE MANTLE* IS INVOLVED...

MANTLE INDUSTRIES

"...AND IF *REGGIE MANTLE* IS INVOLVED, THEN WE HAVE TO DEAL WITH...

"...*IRON MANTLE*"

"TO BE CONTINUED, LOSER!! HEY! LOSER! I'M TALKING TO YOU~"

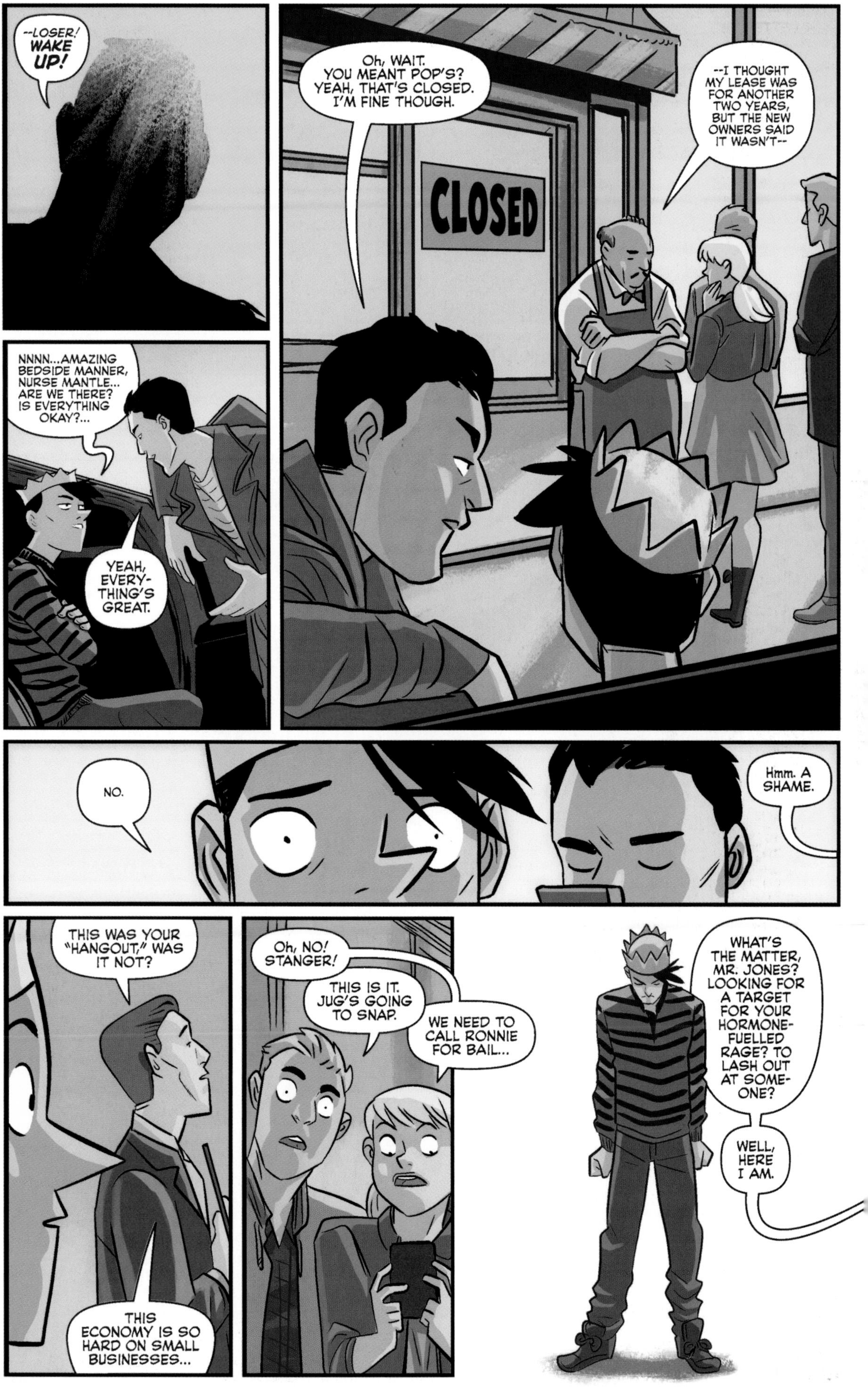
--LOSER! WAKE UP!
Oh, WAIT. YOU MEANT POP'S? YEAH, THAT'S CLOSED. I'M FINE THOUGH.
--I THOUGHT MY LEASE WAS FOR ANOTHER TWO YEARS, BUT THE NEW OWNERS SAID IT WASN'T--
CLOSED
NNNN...AMAZING BEDSIDE MANNER, NURSE MANTLE... ARE WE THERE? IS EVERYTHING OKAY?...
YEAH, EVERYTHING'S GREAT.
NO.
Hmm. A SHAME.
THIS WAS YOUR "HANGOUT," WAS IT NOT?
THIS ECONOMY IS SO HARD ON SMALL BUSINESSES...
Oh, NO! STANGER!
THIS IS IT. JUG'S GOING TO SNAP.
WE NEED TO CALL RONNIE FOR BAIL...
WHAT'S THE MATTER, MR. JONES? LOOKING FOR A TARGET FOR YOUR HORMONE-FUELLED RAGE? TO LASH OUT AT SOMEONE?
WELL, HERE I AM.

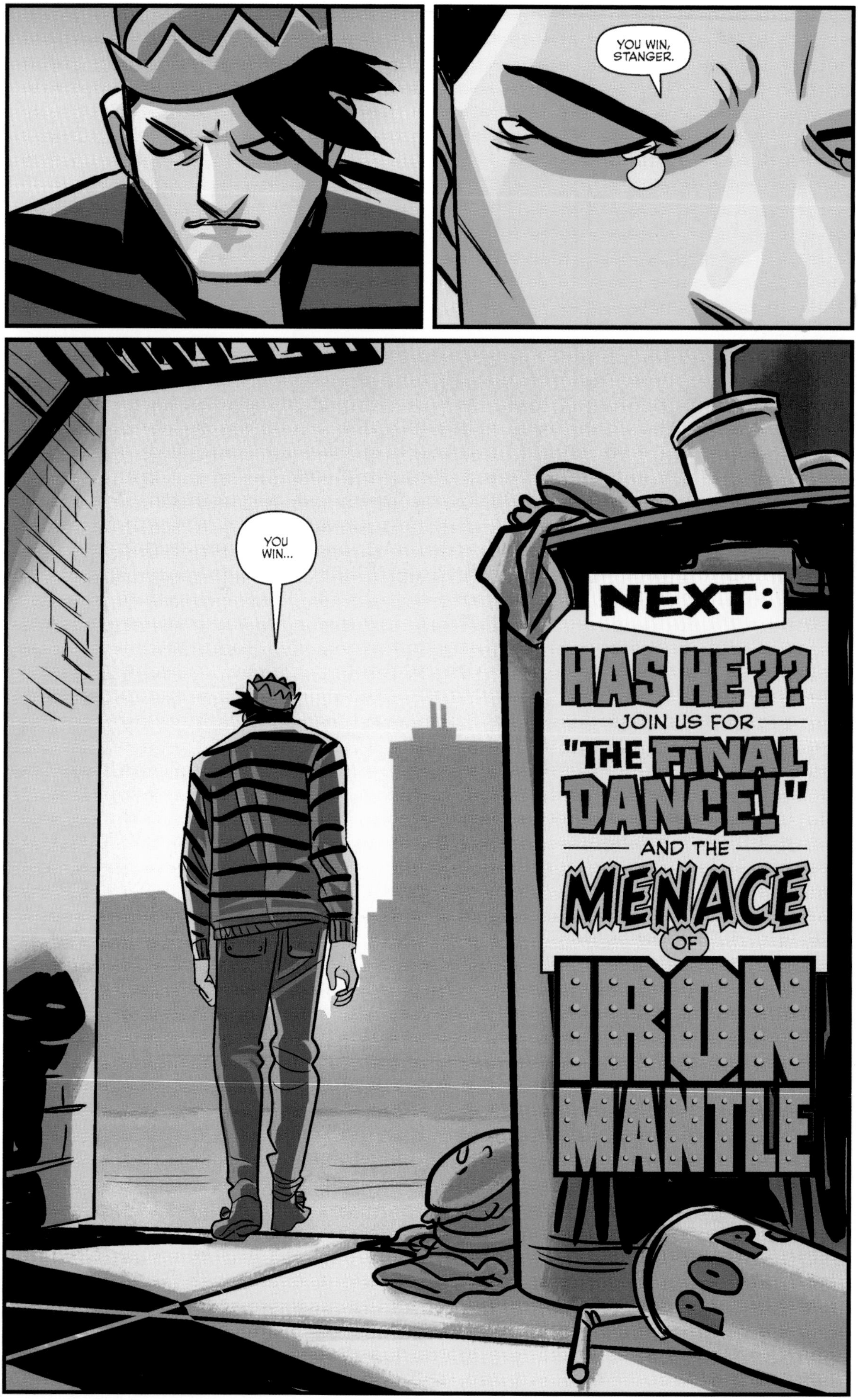
YOU WIN, STANGER.
YOU WIN...
NEXT:
HAS HE??
JOIN US FOR
"THE FINAL DANCE!"
AND THE
MENACE
OF
IRON MANTLE
POP

TO BE
CONTINUED...

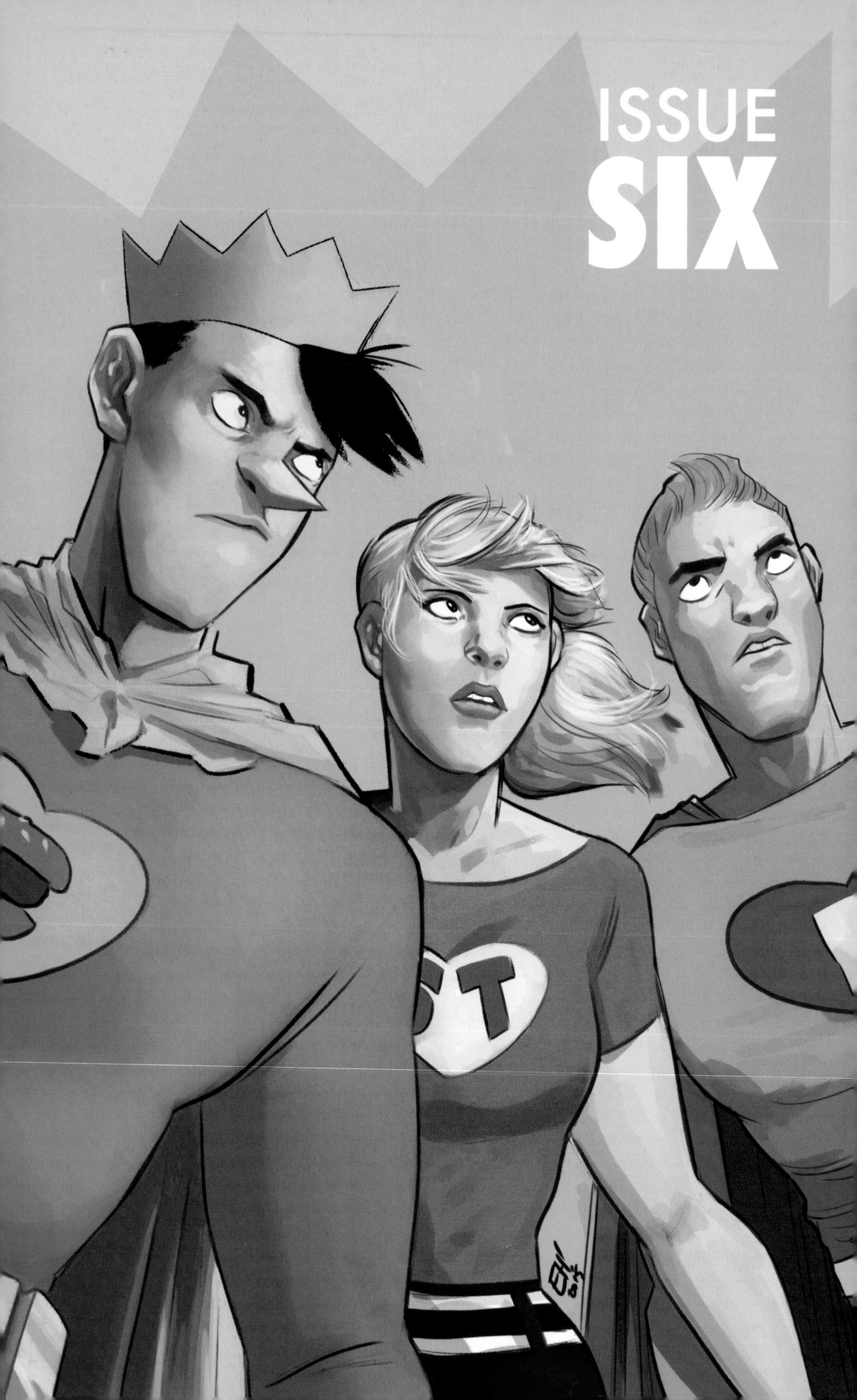
ISSUE
SIX

Jughead in SUPERTEENAGE DAYDREAM!

I KNOW *IRON MANTLE* CREATED THOSE... THOSE *ANTI*-HEROES, THE *ULTRA TEENS*,* BUT SHOULD WE REALLY TAKE HIM ON WITHOUT A PLAN?

THERE'S NO TIME! HE'S GIVING A *MANTLE INDUSTRIES* SPEECH AT CITY HALL, SO WE NEED TO SEIZE THIS CHANCE TO TAKE HIM DOWN!

*IN THE *WILDLY* POPULAR LAST ISSUE! I'D BE SURPRISED IF YOU COULD EVEN FIND ONE AT THIS POINT! QUICK! TO EBAY!

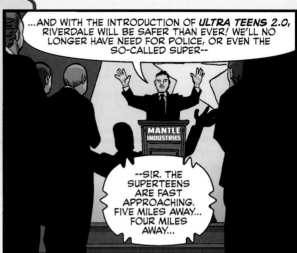

...AND WITH THE INTRODUCTION OF *ULTRA TEENS 2.0*, RIVERDALE WILL BE SAFER THAN EVER! WE'LL NO LONGER HAVE NEED FOR POLICE, OR EVEN THE SO-CALLED SUPER--

--SIR. THE SUPERTEENS ARE FAST APPROACHING. FIVE MILES AWAY... FOUR MILES AWAY...

MANTLE INDUSTRIES

...THREE MILES... TWO MILES...

APOLOGIES, EVERYONE...

CHOK

CHOK

...ONE MILE...

KLK KLAK KLK

KLIK KLAK KLK

...BUT IT APPEARS WE HAVE SOME UN-SCHEDULED...

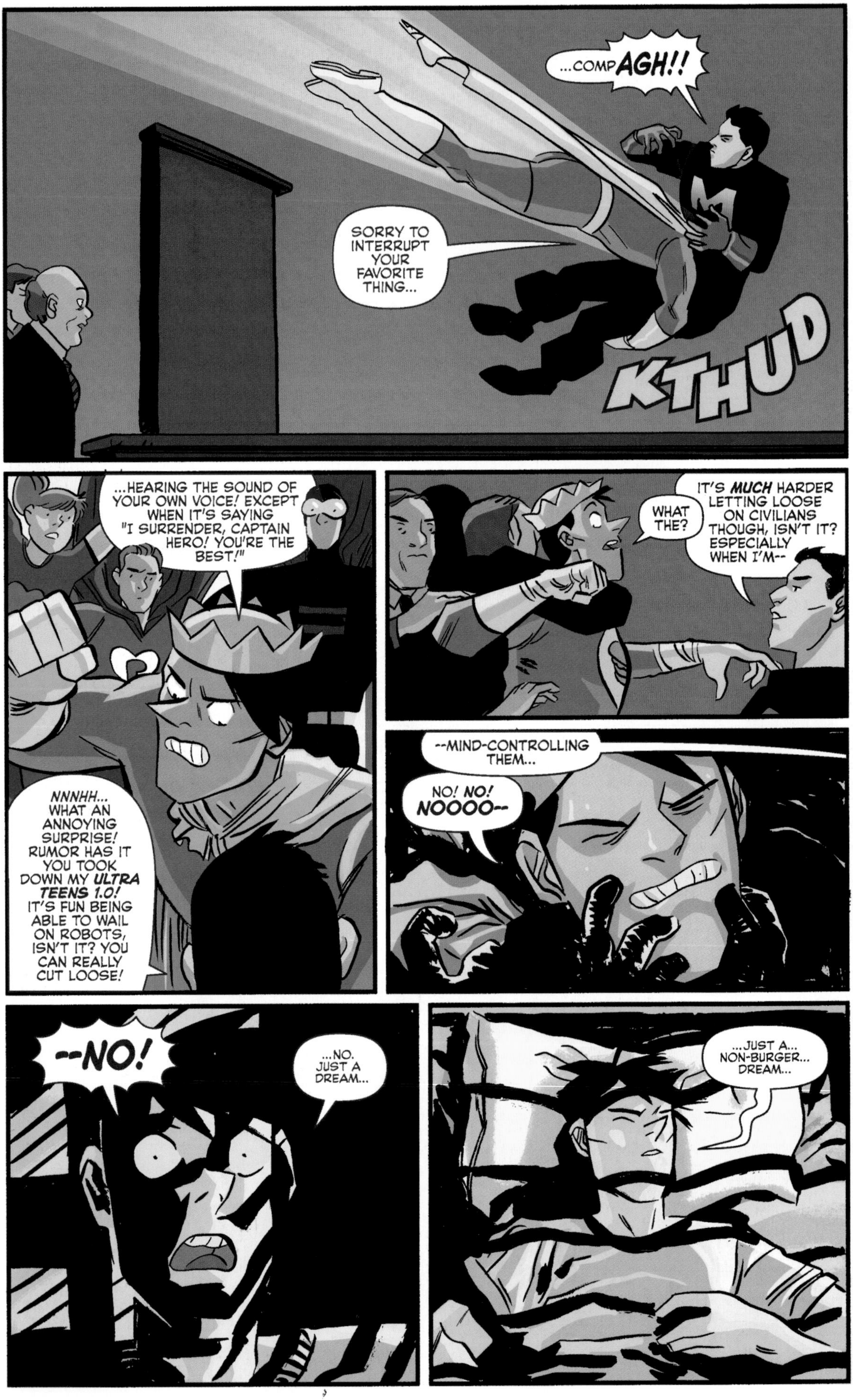
...COMPAGH!!
SORRY TO INTERRUPT YOUR FAVORITE THING...
KTHUD
...HEARING THE SOUND OF YOUR OWN VOICE! EXCEPT WHEN IT'S SAYING "I SURRENDER, CAPTAIN HERO! YOU'RE THE BEST!"
NNNHH... WHAT AN ANNOYING SURPRISE! RUMOR HAS IT YOU TOOK DOWN MY ULTRA TEENS 1.0! IT'S FUN BEING ABLE TO WAIL ON ROBOTS, ISN'T IT? YOU CAN REALLY CUT LOOSE!
WHAT THE?
IT'S MUCH HARDER LETTING LOOSE ON CIVILIANS THOUGH, ISN'T IT? ESPECIALLY WHEN I'M--
--MIND-CONTROLLING THEM...
NO! NO! NOOOO--
--NO!
...NO. JUST A DREAM...
...JUST A... NON-BURGER... DREAM...

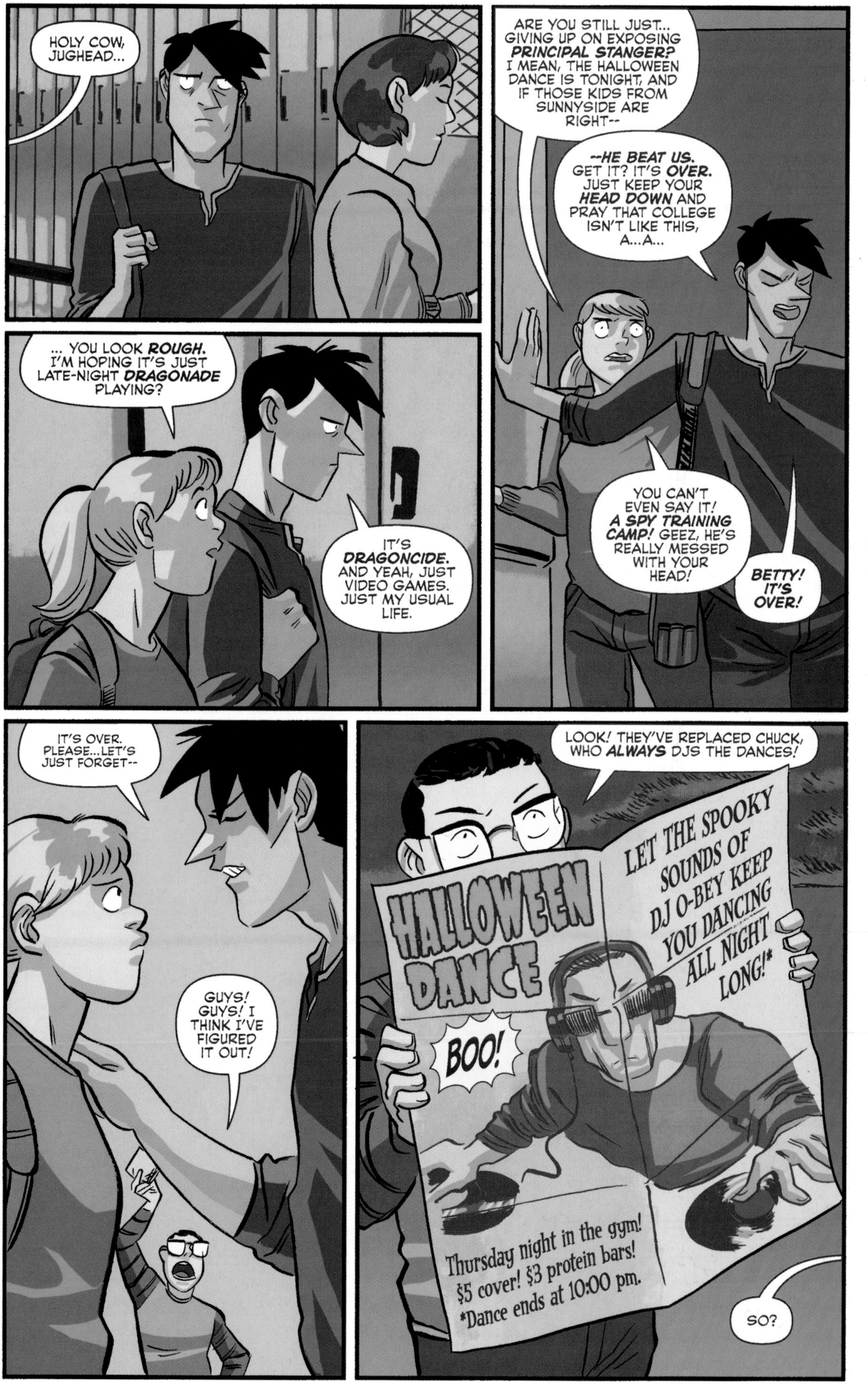
HOLY COW, JUGHEAD...
... YOU LOOK ROUGH. I'M HOPING IT'S JUST LATE-NIGHT DRAGONADE PLAYING?
IT'S DRAGONCIDE. AND YEAH, JUST VIDEO GAMES. JUST MY USUAL LIFE.
ARE YOU STILL JUST... GIVING UP ON EXPOSING PRINCIPAL STANGER? I MEAN, THE HALLOWEEN DANCE IS TONIGHT, AND IF THOSE KIDS FROM SUNNYSIDE ARE RIGHT--
--HE BEAT US. GET IT? IT'S OVER. JUST KEEP YOUR HEAD DOWN AND PRAY THAT COLLEGE ISN'T LIKE THIS, A...A...
YOU CAN'T EVEN SAY IT! A SPY TRAINING CAMP! GEEZ, HE'S REALLY MESSED WITH YOUR HEAD!
BETTY! IT'S OVER!
IT'S OVER. PLEASE...LET'S JUST FORGET--
GUYS! GUYS! I THINK I'VE FIGURED IT OUT!
LOOK! THEY'VE REPLACED CHUCK, WHO ALWAYS DJS THE DANCES!
HALLOWEEN DANCE
LET THE SPOOKY SOUNDS OF DJ O-BEY KEEP YOU DANCING ALL NIGHT LONG!*
BOO!
Thursday night in the gym! $5 cover! $3 protein bars! *Dance ends at 10:00 pm.
SO?

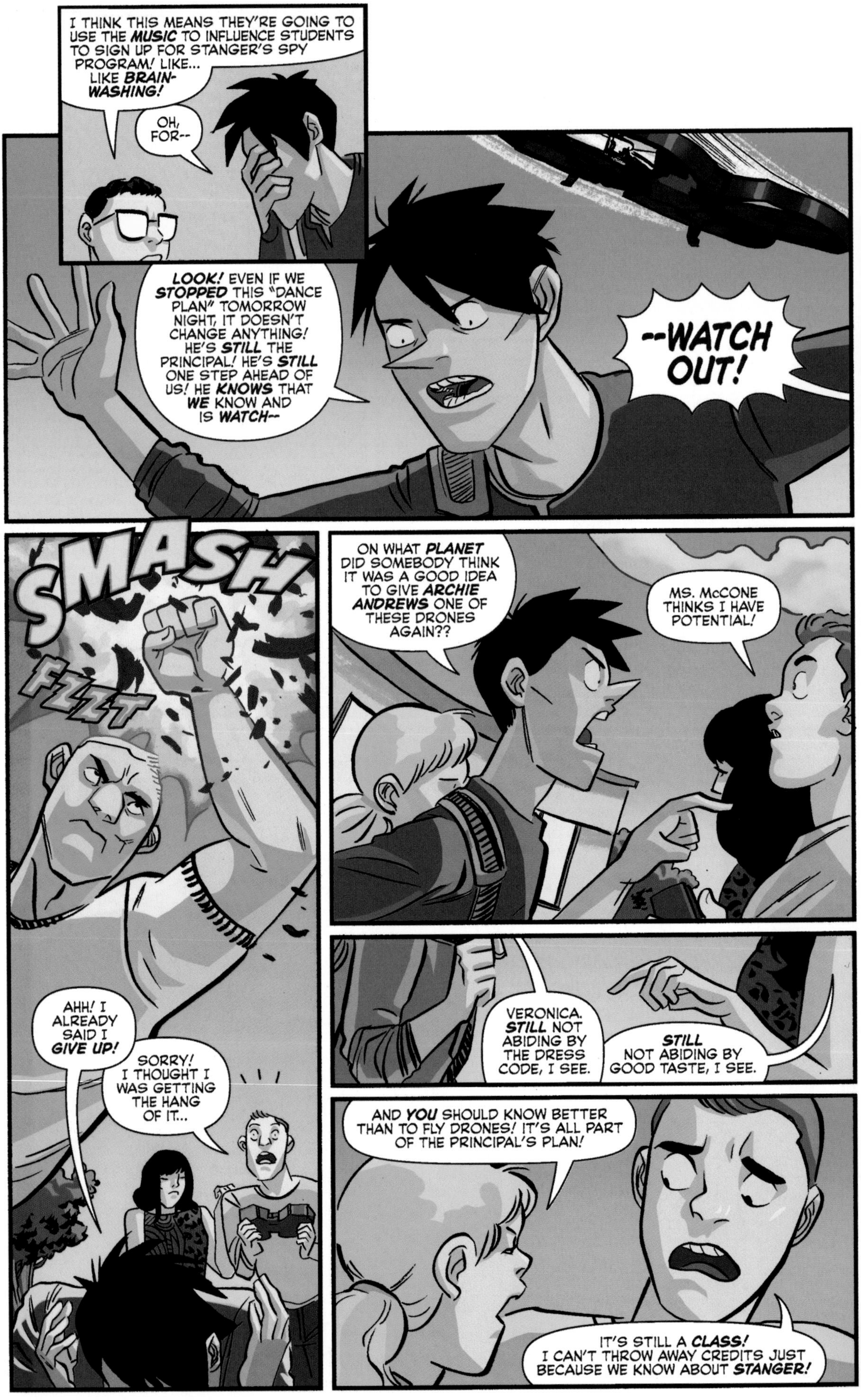
I THINK THIS MEANS THEY'RE GOING TO USE THE MUSIC TO INFLUENCE STUDENTS TO SIGN UP FOR STANGER'S SPY PROGRAM! LIKE... LIKE BRAIN-WASHING!
OH, FOR--
LOOK! EVEN IF WE STOPPED THIS "DANCE PLAN" TOMORROW NIGHT, IT DOESN'T CHANGE ANYTHING! HE'S STILL THE PRINCIPAL! HE'S STILL ONE STEP AHEAD OF US! HE KNOWS THAT WE KNOW AND IS WATCH--
--WATCH OUT!
SMASH
FZZT
AHH! I ALREADY SAID I GIVE UP!
SORRY! I THOUGHT I WAS GETTING THE HANG OF IT...
ON WHAT PLANET DID SOMEBODY THINK IT WAS A GOOD IDEA TO GIVE ARCHIE ANDREWS ONE OF THESE DRONES AGAIN??
MS. McCONE THINKS I HAVE POTENTIAL!
VERONICA. STILL NOT ABIDING BY THE DRESS CODE, I SEE.
STILL NOT ABIDING BY GOOD TASTE, I SEE.
AND YOU SHOULD KNOW BETTER THAN TO FLY DRONES! IT'S ALL PART OF THE PRINCIPAL'S PLAN!
IT'S STILL A CLASS! I CAN'T THROW AWAY CREDITS JUST BECAUSE WE KNOW ABOUT STANGER!

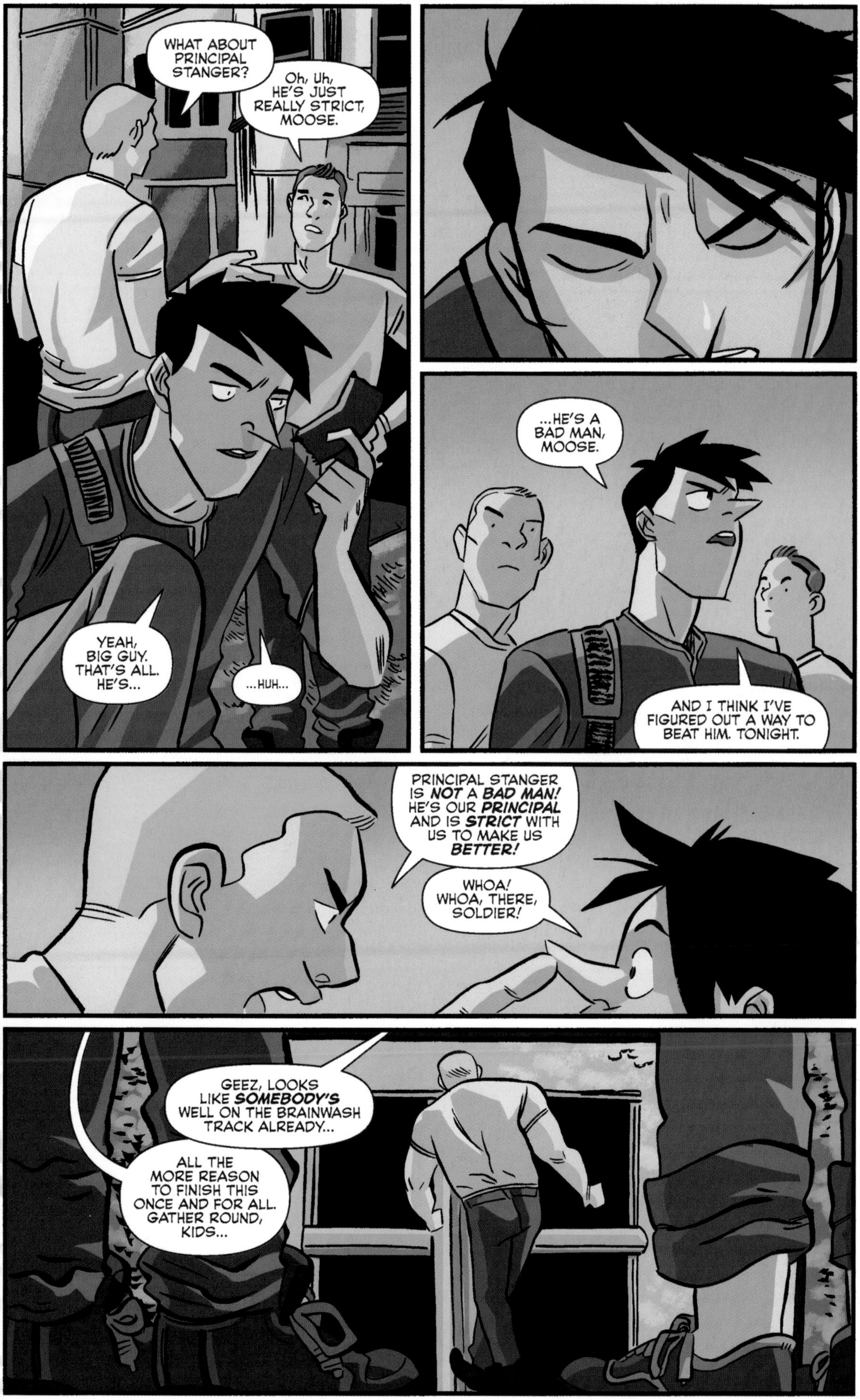
WHAT ABOUT PRINCIPAL STANGER?
Oh, Uh, HE'S JUST REALLY STRICT, MOOSE.
YEAH, BIG GUY. THAT'S ALL. HE'S...
...HUH...
...HE'S A BAD MAN, MOOSE.
AND I THINK I'VE FIGURED OUT A WAY TO BEAT HIM. TONIGHT.
PRINCIPAL STANGER IS NOT A BAD MAN! HE'S OUR PRINCIPAL AND IS STRICT WITH US TO MAKE US BETTER!
WHOA! WHOA, THERE, SOLDIER!
GEEZ, LOOKS LIKE SOMEBODY'S WELL ON THE BRAINWASH TRACK ALREADY...
ALL THE MORE REASON TO FINISH THIS ONCE AND FOR ALL. GATHER ROUND, KIDS...

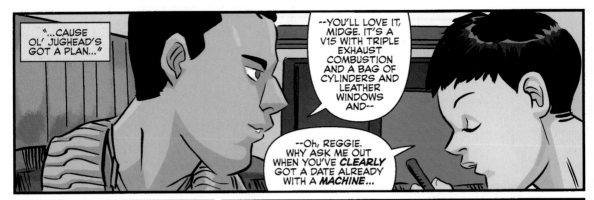

"...CAUSE OL' JUGHEAD'S GOT A PLAN..."

--YOU'LL LOVE IT, MIDGE. IT'S A V15 WITH TRIPLE EXHAUST COMBUSTION AND A BAG OF CYLINDERS AND LEATHER WINDOWS AND--

--OH, REGGIE. WHY ASK ME OUT WHEN YOU'VE *CLEARLY* GOT A DATE ALREADY WITH A *MACHINE*...

HEY, A MAN CAN HAVE MANY LOVES, I-YI-YI-*YI!* *M-MOOSE!* I W-W-W-WASN'T--

...WASN'T... OH, MY GOD... I MUST HAVE DIED AND I'M A GHOST...

PLEASE STOP HAUNTING ME.

PRINCIPAL STANGER

AH, MR. MASON. CAN I HELP YOU?

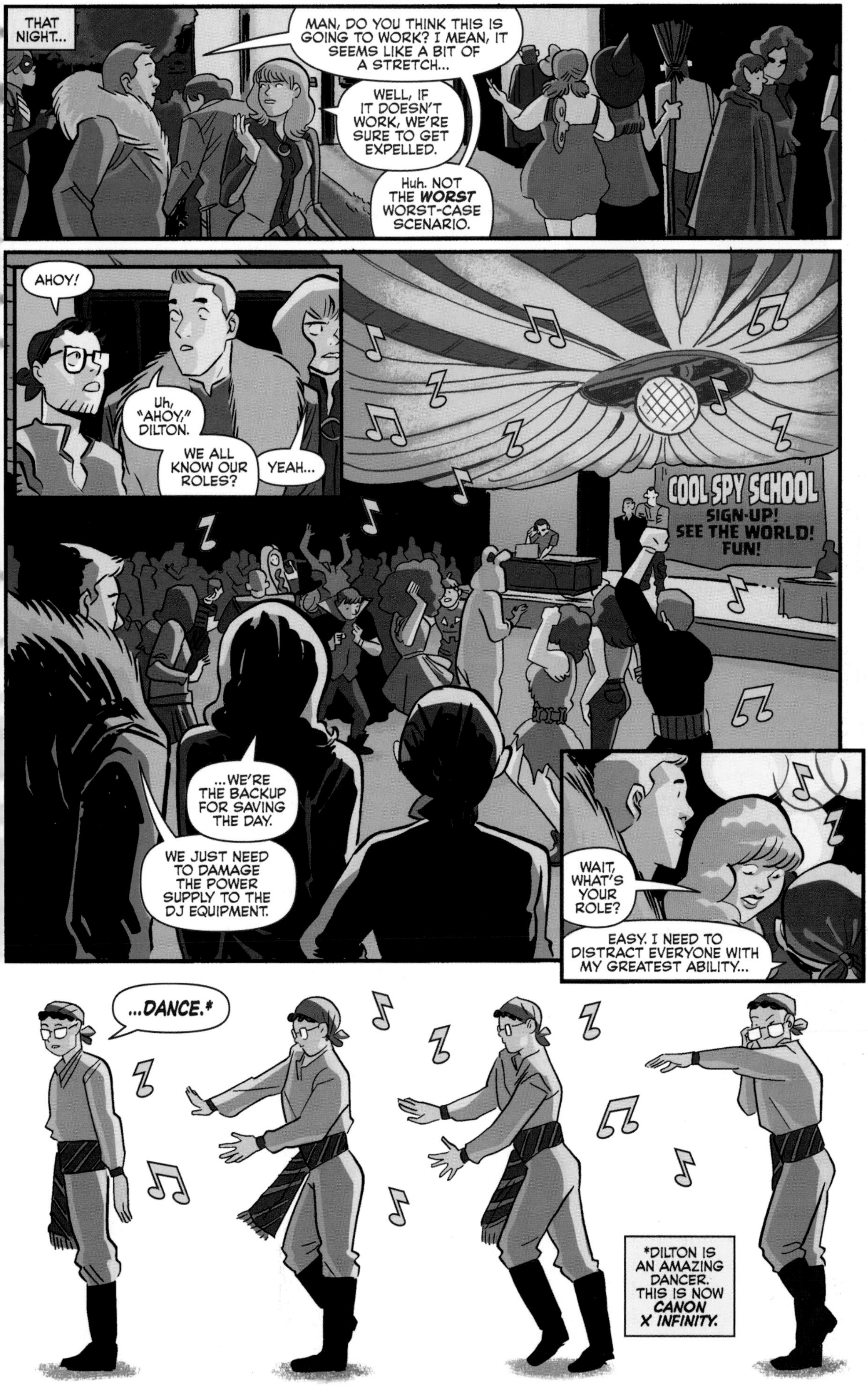
THAT NIGHT...
MAN, DO YOU THINK THIS IS GOING TO WORK? I MEAN, IT SEEMS LIKE A BIT OF A STRETCH...
WELL, IF IT DOESN'T WORK, WE'RE SURE TO GET EXPELLED.
Huh. NOT THE WORST WORST-CASE SCENARIO.
AHOY!
Uh, "AHOY," DILTON.
WE ALL KNOW OUR ROLES?
YEAH...
COOL SPY SCHOOL
SIGN-UP! SEE THE WORLD! FUN!
...WE'RE THE BACKUP FOR SAVING THE DAY.
WE JUST NEED TO DAMAGE THE POWER SUPPLY TO THE DJ EQUIPMENT.
WAIT, WHAT'S YOUR ROLE?
EASY. I NEED TO DISTRACT EVERYONE WITH MY GREATEST ABILITY...
...DANCE.*
*DILTON IS AN AMAZING DANCER. THIS IS NOW CANON X INFINITY.

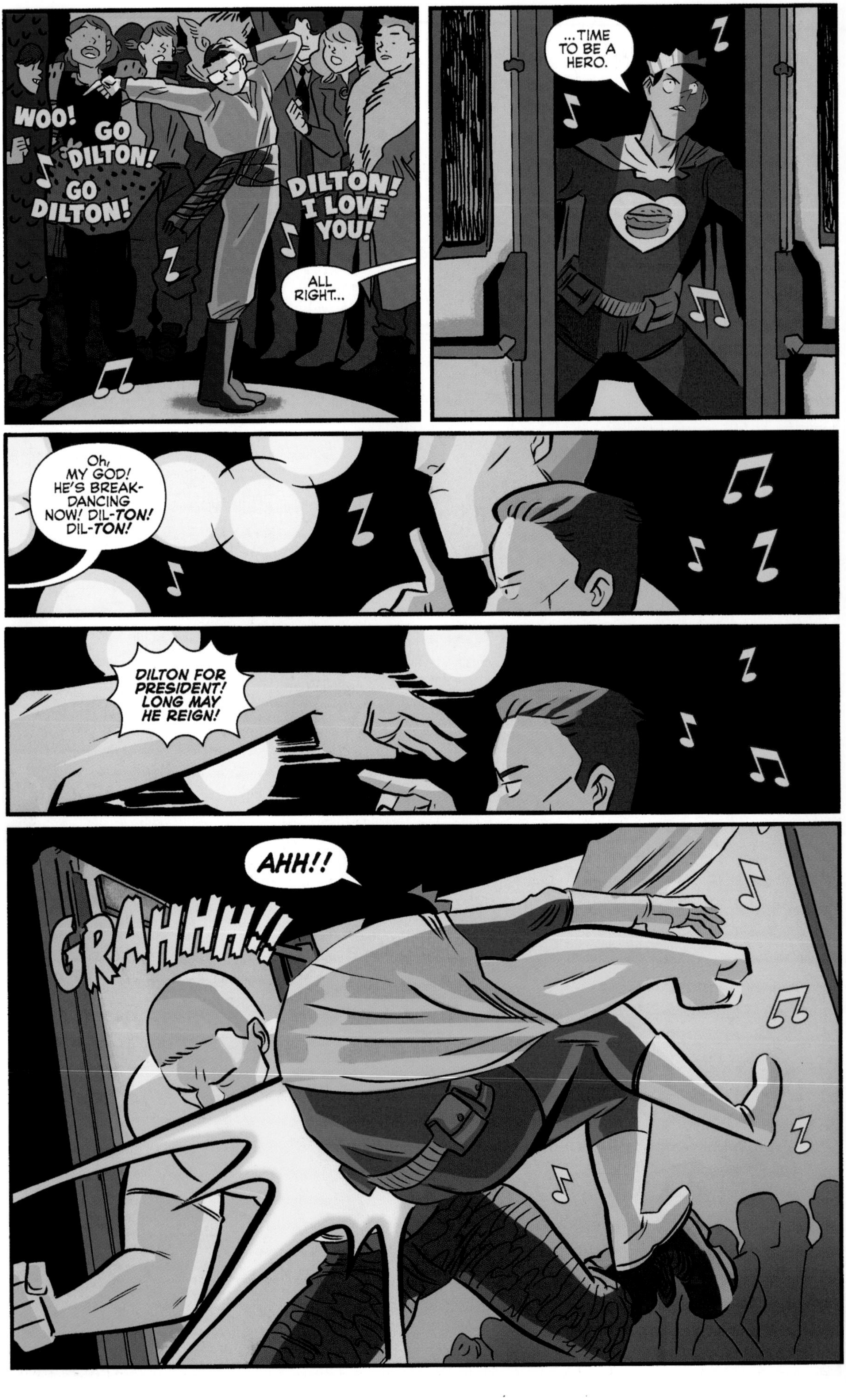
WOO!
GO DILTON!
GO DILTON!
DILTON! I LOVE YOU!
ALL RIGHT...
...TIME TO BE A HERO.
Oh, MY GOD! HE'S BREAK-DANCING NOW! DIL-TON! DIL-TON!
DILTON FOR PRESIDENT! LONG MAY HE REIGN!
AHH!!
GRAHHH!!

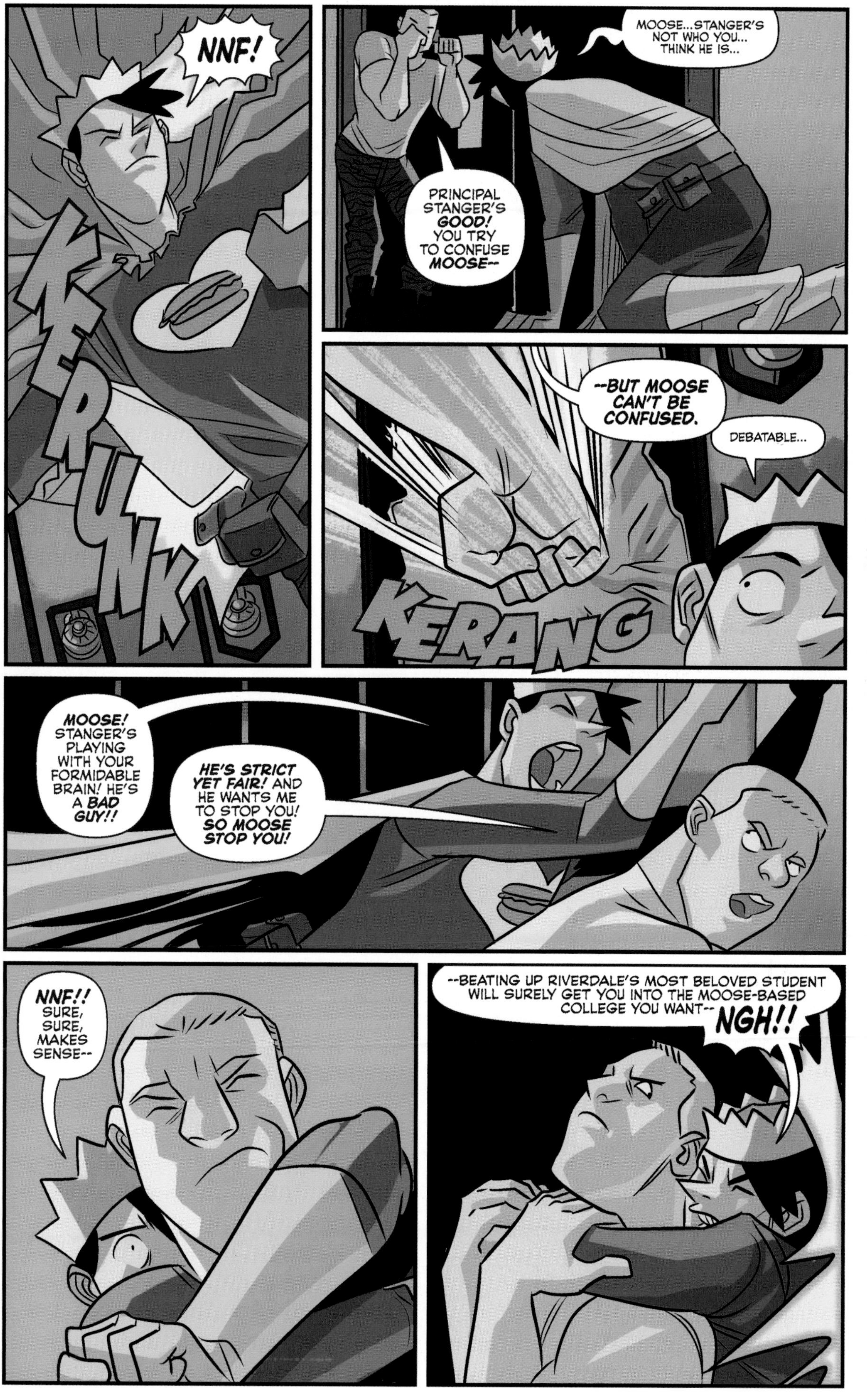
NNF!
KERRUNK
MOOSE...STANGER'S NOT WHO YOU... THINK HE IS...
PRINCIPAL STANGER'S GOOD! YOU TRY TO CONFUSE MOOSE--
--BUT MOOSE CAN'T BE CONFUSED.
DEBATABLE...
KERANG
MOOSE! STANGER'S PLAYING WITH YOUR FORMIDABLE BRAIN! HE'S A BAD GUY!!
HE'S STRICT YET FAIR! AND HE WANTS ME TO STOP YOU! SO MOOSE STOP YOU!
NNF!! SURE, SURE, MAKES SENSE--
--BEATING UP RIVERDALE'S MOST BELOVED STUDENT WILL SURELY GET YOU INTO THE MOOSE-BASED COLLEGE YOU WANT--
NGH!!

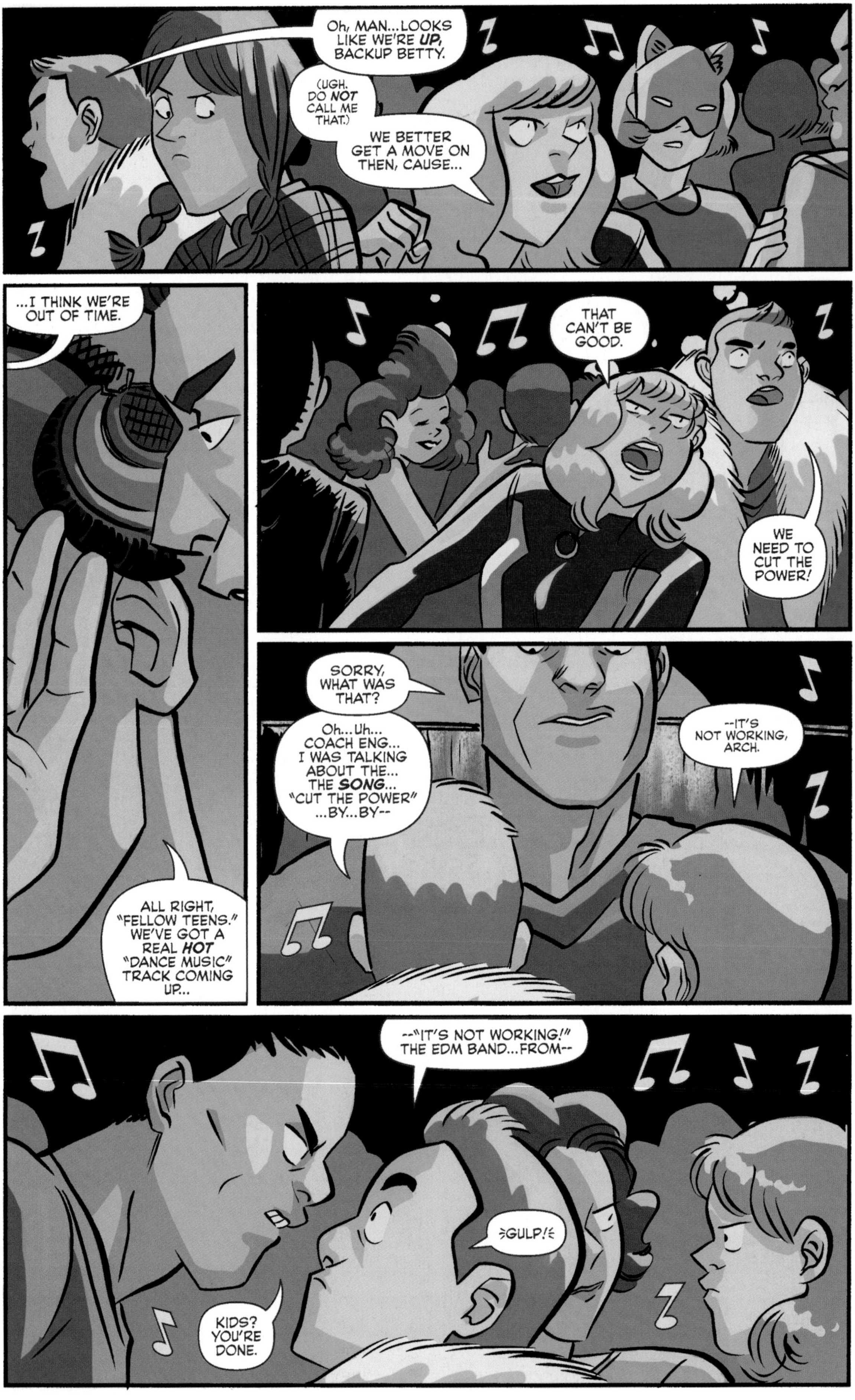
Oh, MAN...LOOKS LIKE WE'RE UP, BACKUP BETTY.
(UGH. DO NOT CALL ME THAT.)
WE BETTER GET A MOVE ON THEN, CAUSE...
...I THINK WE'RE OUT OF TIME.
THAT CAN'T BE GOOD.
WE NEED TO CUT THE POWER!
SORRY, WHAT WAS THAT?
Oh...Uh... COACH ENG... I WAS TALKING ABOUT THE... THE SONG... "CUT THE POWER" ...BY...BY--
--IT'S NOT WORKING, ARCH.
ALL RIGHT, "FELLOW TEENS." WE'VE GOT A REAL HOT "DANCE MUSIC" TRACK COMING UP...
--"IT'S NOT WORKING!" THE EDM BAND...FROM--
GULP!
KIDS? YOU'RE DONE.

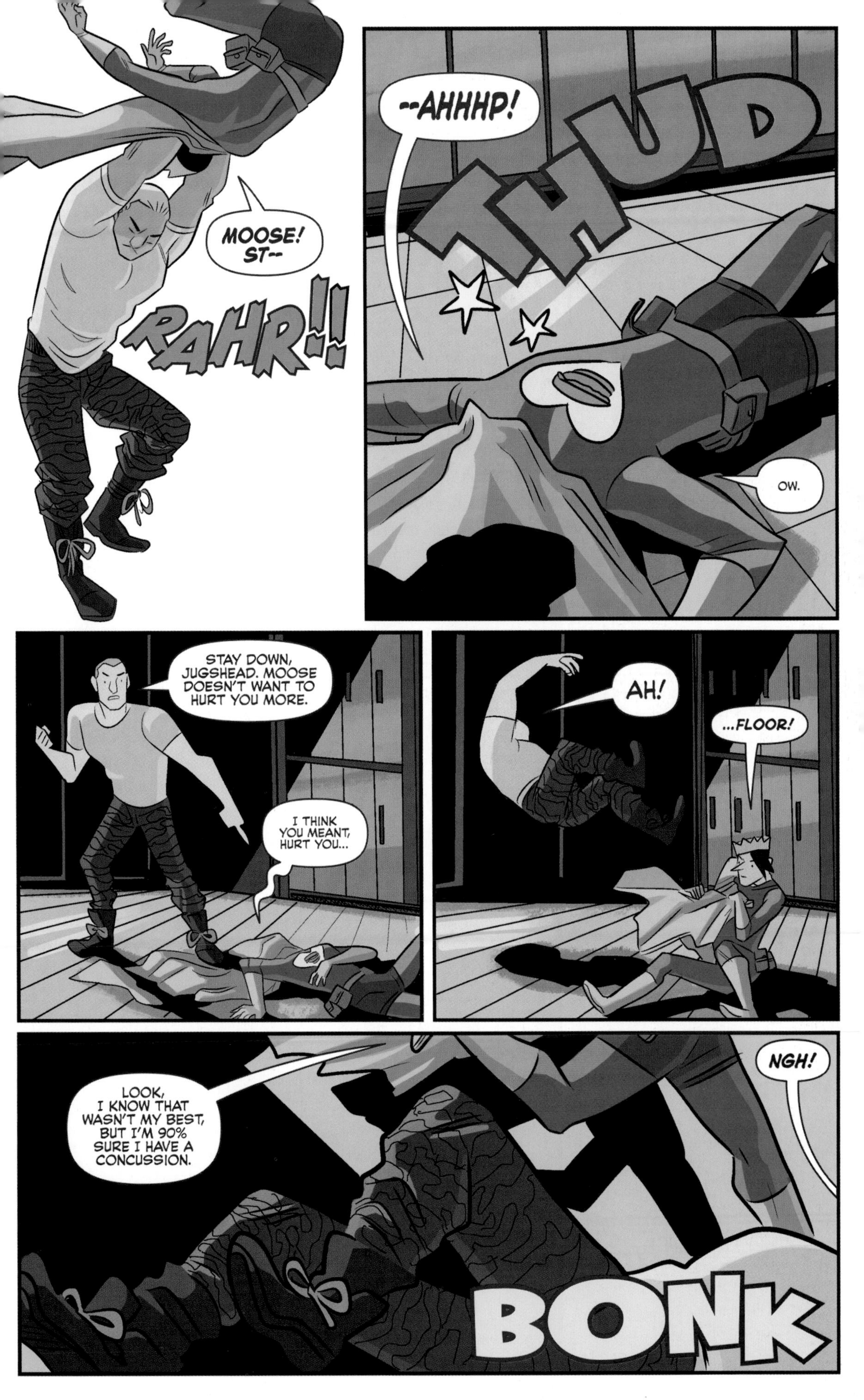
MOOSE!
ST--
RAHR!!
--AHHHP!
THUD
OW.
STAY DOWN, JUGSHEAD. MOOSE DOESN'T WANT TO HURT YOU MORE.
I THINK YOU MEANT, HURT YOU...
AH!
...FLOOR!
LOOK, I KNOW THAT WASN'T MY BEST, BUT I'M 90% SURE I HAVE A CONCUSSION.
NGH!
BONK

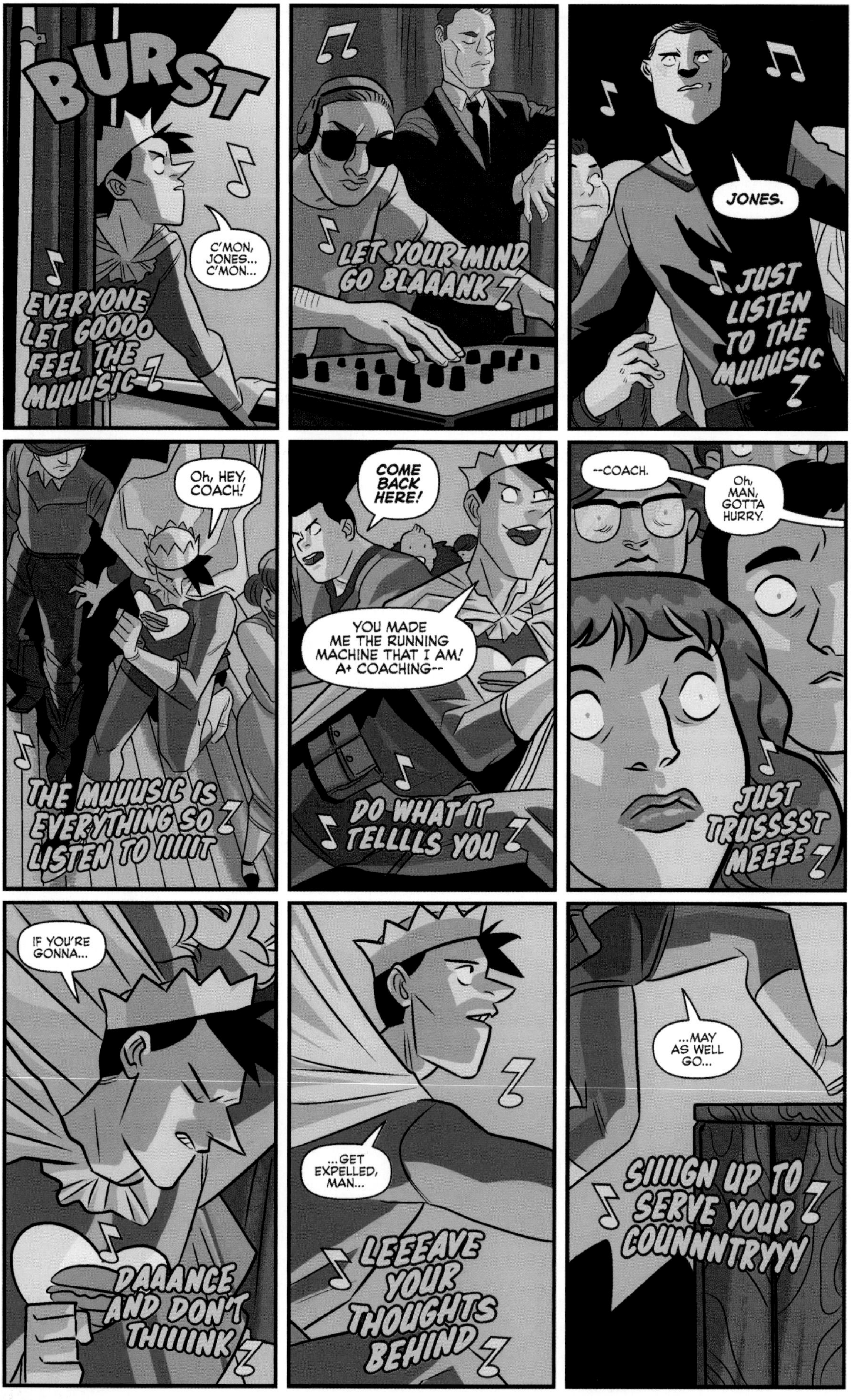
BURST
C'MON, JONES... C'MON...
EVERYONE LET GOOOO FEEL THE MUUUSIC
LET YOUR MIND GO BLAAANK
JONES.
JUST LISTEN TO THE MUUUSIC
Oh, HEY, COACH!
THE MUUUSIC IS EVERYTHING SO LISTEN TO IIIIIT
COME BACK HERE!
YOU MADE ME THE RUNNING MACHINE THAT I AM! A+ COACHING--
DO WHAT IT TELLLLS YOU
--COACH.
Oh, MAN, GOTTA HURRY.
JUST TRUSSSST MEEEE
IF YOU'RE GONNA...
DAAANCE AND DON'T THIIIINK
...GET EXPELLED, MAN...
LEEEAVE YOUR THOUGHTS BEHIND
...MAY AS WELL GO...
SIIIIGN UP TO SERVE YOUR COUNNNTRYYY

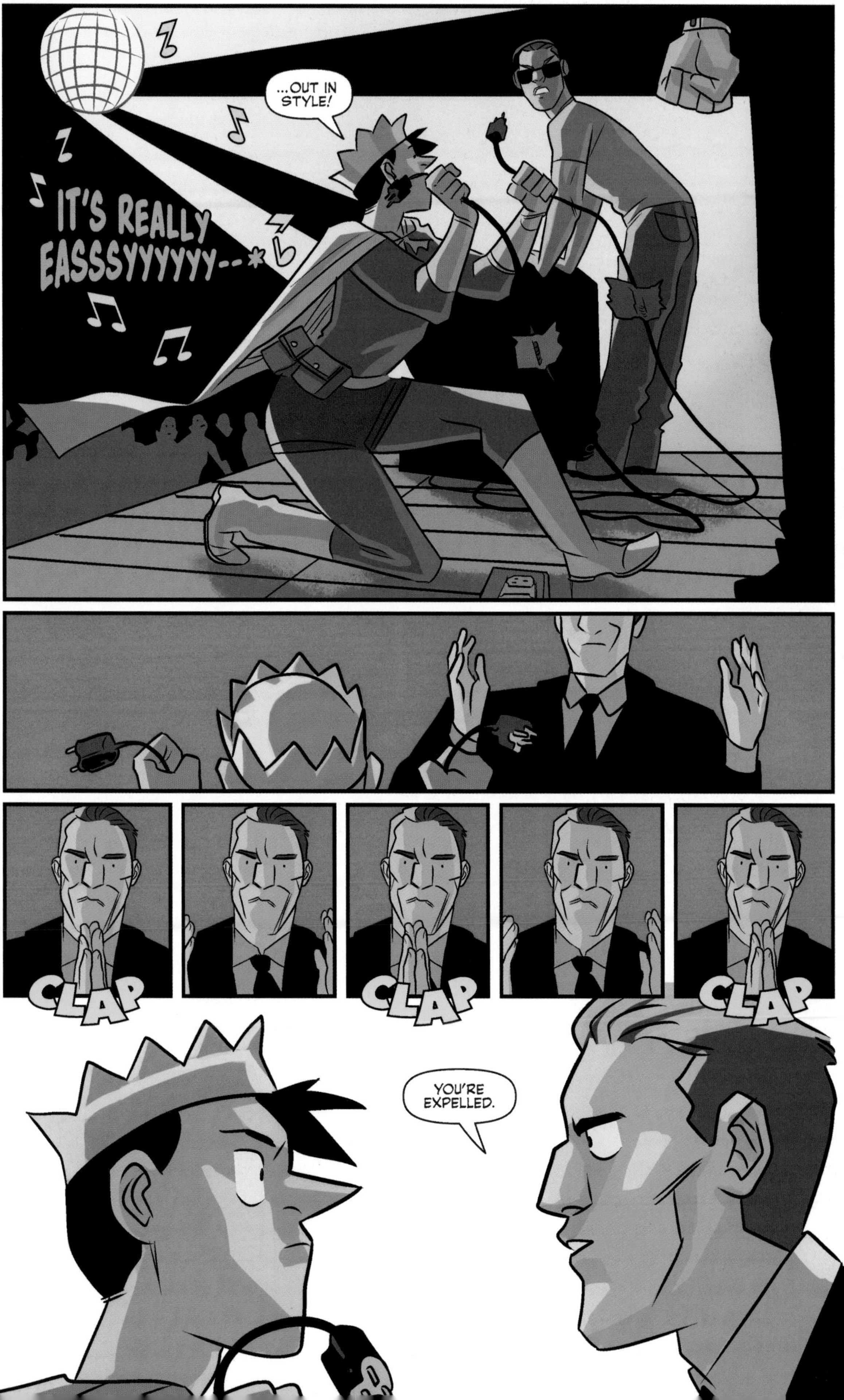
...OUT IN STYLE!
IT'S REALLY EASSSYYYYYY--*
CLAP
CLAP
CLAP
YOU'RE EXPELLED.

YEAH, I KIND OF FIGURED.

AND FOR WHAT?

YOU RUIN ONE DANCE? THERE'LL BE ANOTHER. WHILE YOU'RE SERVING BURGERS DOWN THE STREET.

THAT *DOES* SOUND AMAZING...

I WIN.

YOU WIN AT LOSING, YOU LOSING-WINNER...

...NOBODY MAY BELIEVE ME WHEN I SAY YOU'RE TURNING OUR SCHOOL INTO A SPY CAMP...

JUGHEAD'S FINALLY LOST HIS MIND!

HA HA! HIS CROWN'S ON TOO TIGHT!

THAT SOUNDS PRETTY COOL, ACTUALLY!

SURE, MY FRIENDS HAVE MY BACK, 'CAUSE THEY'RE MY FRIENDS...

...BUT WHO'S GOING TO BELIEVE A BUNCH OF *VERY* COOL TEEN-AGERS?

SO, WE TOLD OUR PARENTS, BUT *THEY* DIDN'T BELIEVE US EITHER...

SO THAT'S WHEN I REALIZED SOMETHING...

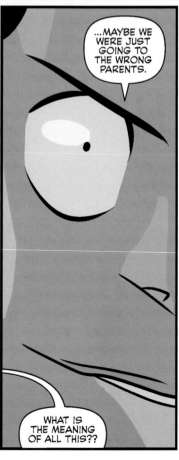

...MAYBE WE WERE JUST GOING TO THE WRONG PARENTS.

WHAT IS THE MEANING OF ALL THIS??

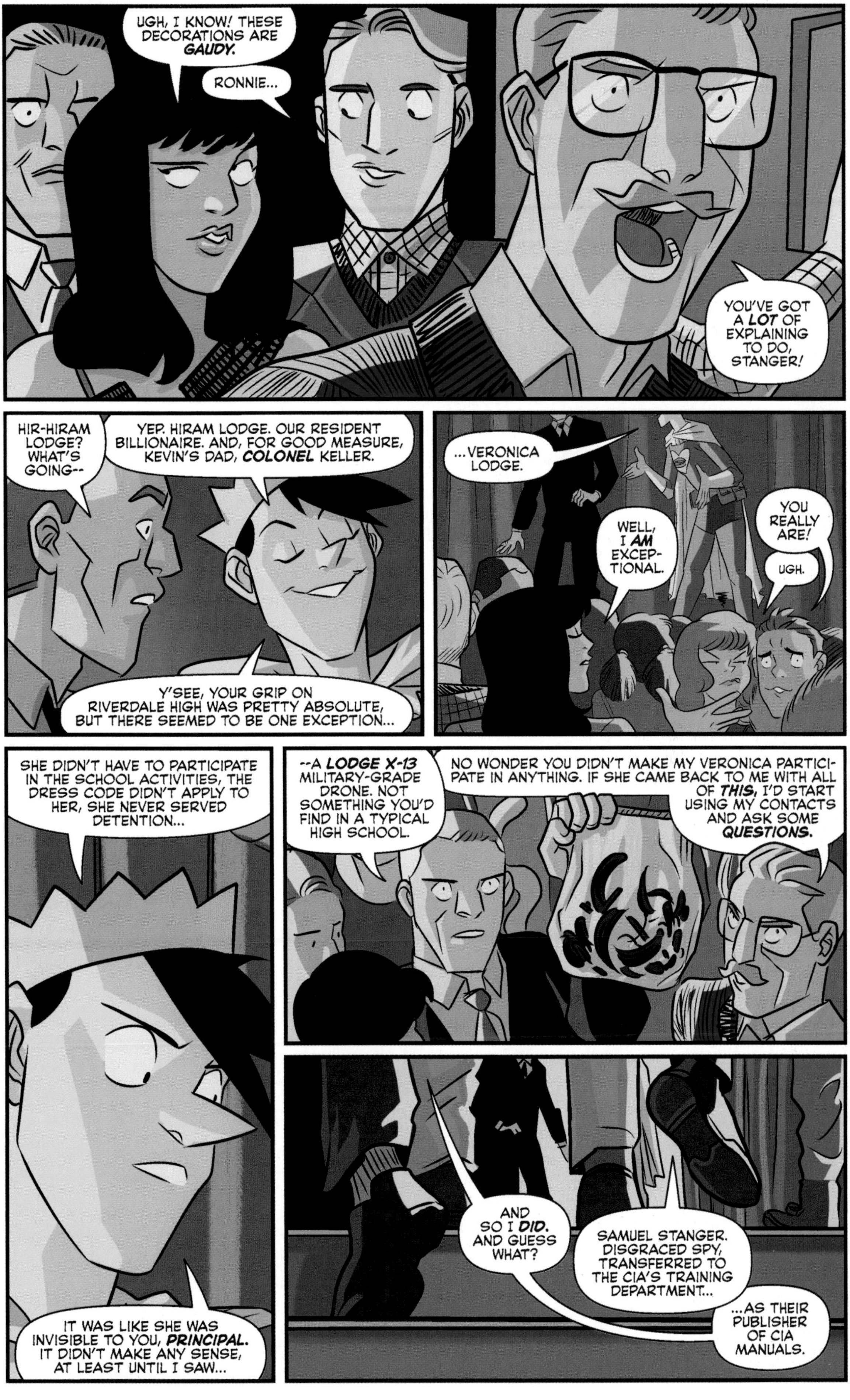
UGH, I KNOW! THESE DECORATIONS ARE GAUDY.
RONNIE...
YOU'VE GOT A LOT OF EXPLAINING TO DO, STANGER!
HIR-HIRAM LODGE? WHAT'S GOING--
YEP. HIRAM LODGE. OUR RESIDENT BILLIONAIRE. AND, FOR GOOD MEASURE, KEVIN'S DAD, COLONEL KELLER.
Y'SEE, YOUR GRIP ON RIVERDALE HIGH WAS PRETTY ABSOLUTE, BUT THERE SEEMED TO BE ONE EXCEPTION...
...VERONICA LODGE.
WELL, I AM EXCEPTIONAL.
YOU REALLY ARE!
UGH.
SHE DIDN'T HAVE TO PARTICIPATE IN THE SCHOOL ACTIVITIES, THE DRESS CODE DIDN'T APPLY TO HER, SHE NEVER SERVED DETENTION...
IT WAS LIKE SHE WAS INVISIBLE TO YOU, PRINCIPAL. IT DIDN'T MAKE ANY SENSE, AT LEAST UNTIL I SAW...
--A LODGE X-13 MILITARY-GRADE DRONE. NOT SOMETHING YOU'D FIND IN A TYPICAL HIGH SCHOOL.
NO WONDER YOU DIDN'T MAKE MY VERONICA PARTICIPATE IN ANYTHING. IF SHE CAME BACK TO ME WITH ALL OF THIS, I'D START USING MY CONTACTS AND ASK SOME QUESTIONS.
AND SO I DID. AND GUESS WHAT?
SAMUEL STANGER. DISGRACED SPY, TRANSFERRED TO THE CIA'S TRAINING DEPARTMENT...
...AS THEIR PUBLISHER OF CIA MANUALS.

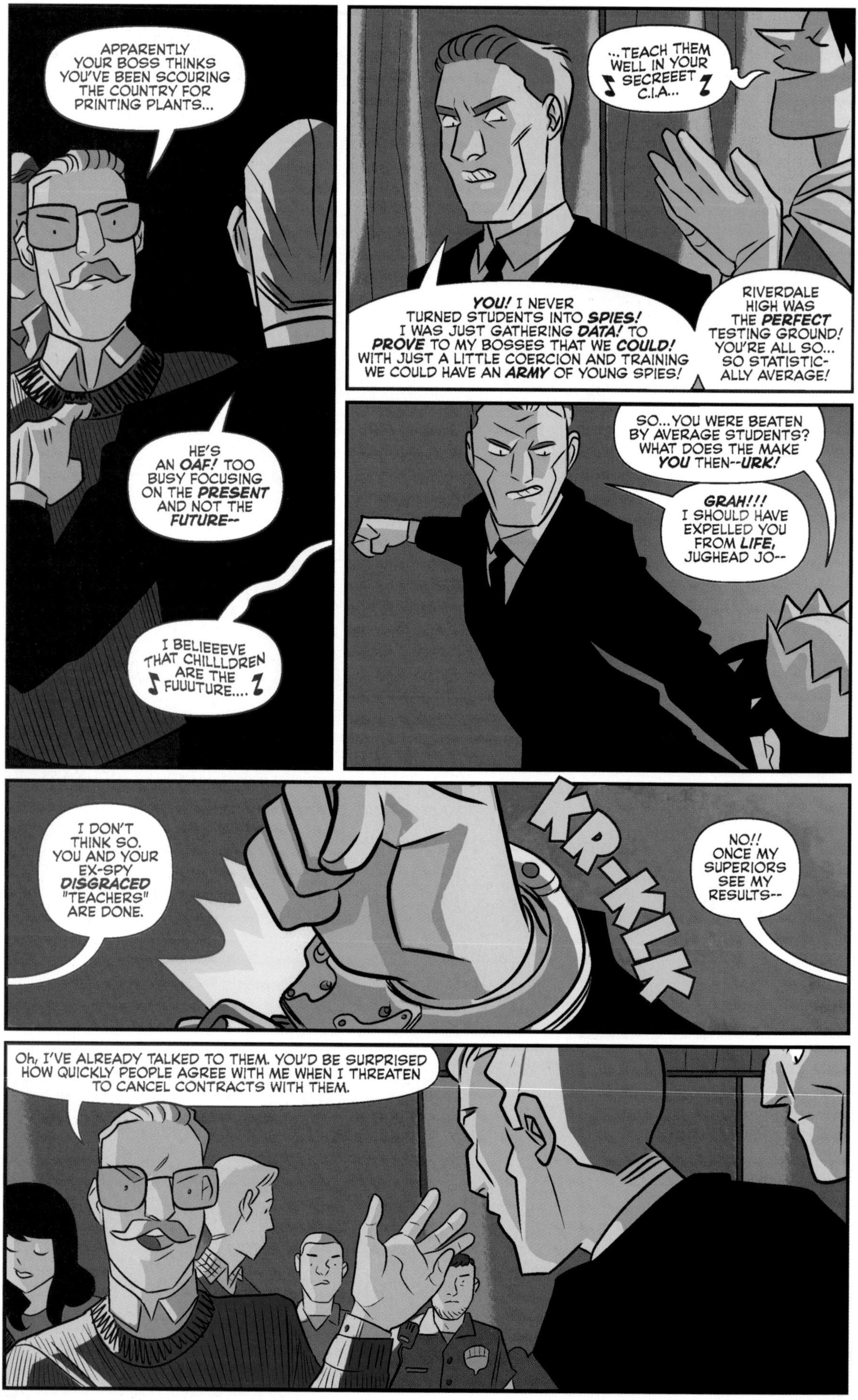
APPARENTLY YOUR BOSS THINKS YOU'VE BEEN SCOURING THE COUNTRY FOR PRINTING PLANTS...
HE'S AN OAF! TOO BUSY FOCUSING ON THE PRESENT AND NOT THE FUTURE--
I BELIEEEVE THAT CHILLLDREN ARE THE FUUUTURE....
...TEACH THEM WELL IN YOUR SECREEET C.I.A...
YOU! I NEVER TURNED STUDENTS INTO SPIES! I WAS JUST GATHERING DATA! TO PROVE TO MY BOSSES THAT WE COULD! WITH JUST A LITTLE COERCION AND TRAINING WE COULD HAVE AN ARMY OF YOUNG SPIES!
RIVERDALE HIGH WAS THE PERFECT TESTING GROUND! YOU'RE ALL SO... SO STATISTIC-ALLY AVERAGE!
SO...YOU WERE BEATEN BY AVERAGE STUDENTS? WHAT DOES THE MAKE YOU THEN--URK!
GRAH!!! I SHOULD HAVE EXPELLED YOU FROM LIFE, JUGHEAD JO--
I DON'T THINK SO. YOU AND YOUR EX-SPY DISGRACED "TEACHERS" ARE DONE.
KR-KLIK
NO!! ONCE MY SUPERIORS SEE MY RESULTS--
Oh, I'VE ALREADY TALKED TO THEM. YOU'D BE SURPRISED HOW QUICKLY PEOPLE AGREE WITH ME WHEN I THREATEN TO CANCEL CONTRACTS WITH THEM.

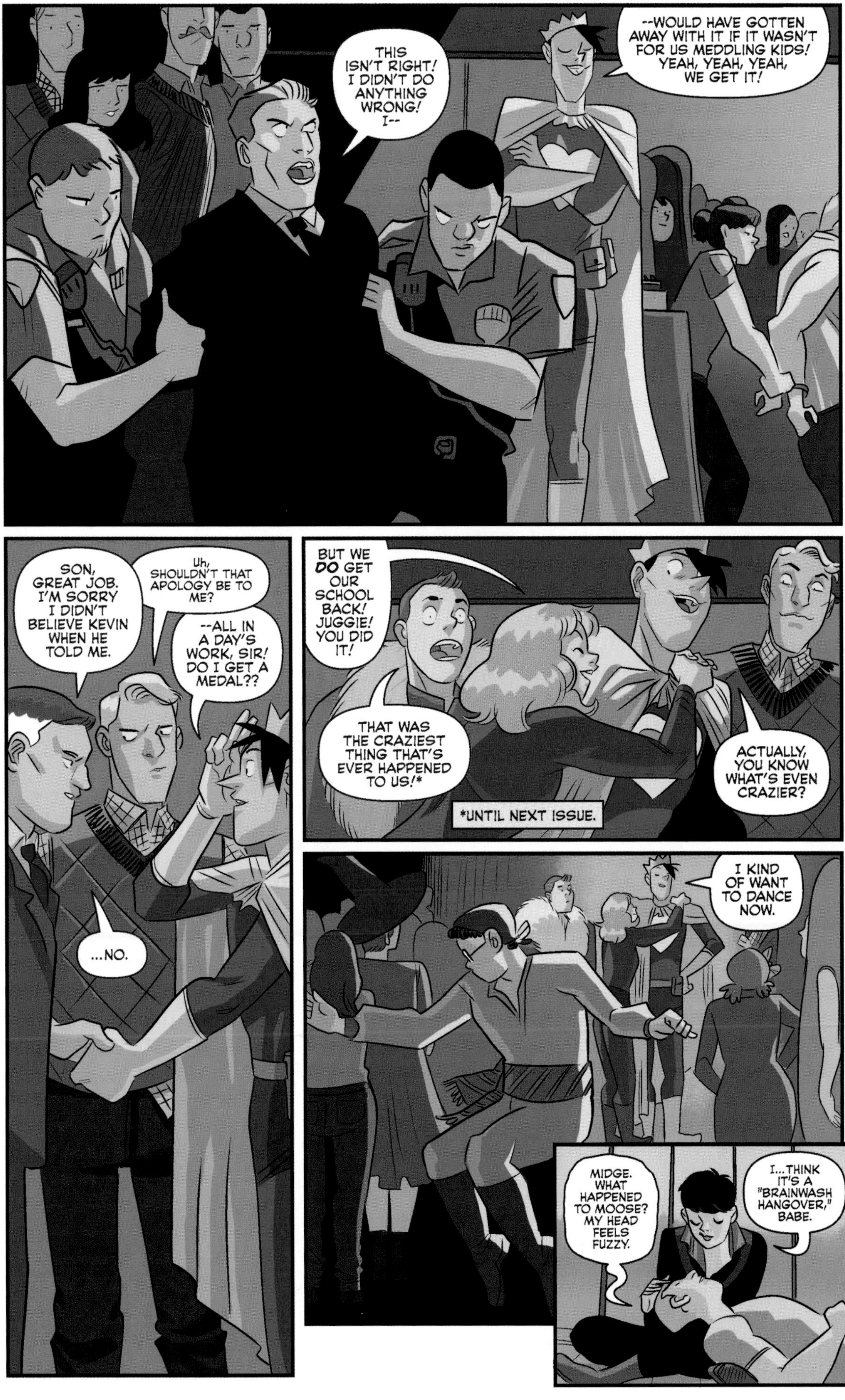
THIS ISN'T RIGHT! I DIDN'T DO ANYTHING WRONG! I--
--WOULD HAVE GOTTEN AWAY WITH IT IF IT WASN'T FOR US MEDDLING KIDS! YEAH, YEAH, YEAH, WE GET IT!
SON, GREAT JOB. I'M SORRY I DIDN'T BELIEVE KEVIN WHEN HE TOLD ME.
Uh, SHOULDN'T THAT APOLOGY BE TO ME?
--ALL IN A DAY'S WORK, SIR! DO I GET A MEDAL??
...NO.
BUT WE DO GET OUR SCHOOL BACK! JUGGIE! YOU DID IT!
THAT WAS THE CRAZIEST THING THAT'S EVER HAPPENED TO US!*
ACTUALLY, YOU KNOW WHAT'S EVEN CRAZIER?
*UNTIL NEXT ISSUE.
I KIND OF WANT TO DANCE NOW.
MIDGE. WHAT HAPPENED TO MOOSE? MY HEAD FEELS FUZZY.
I...THINK IT'S A "BRAINWASH HANGOVER," BABE.

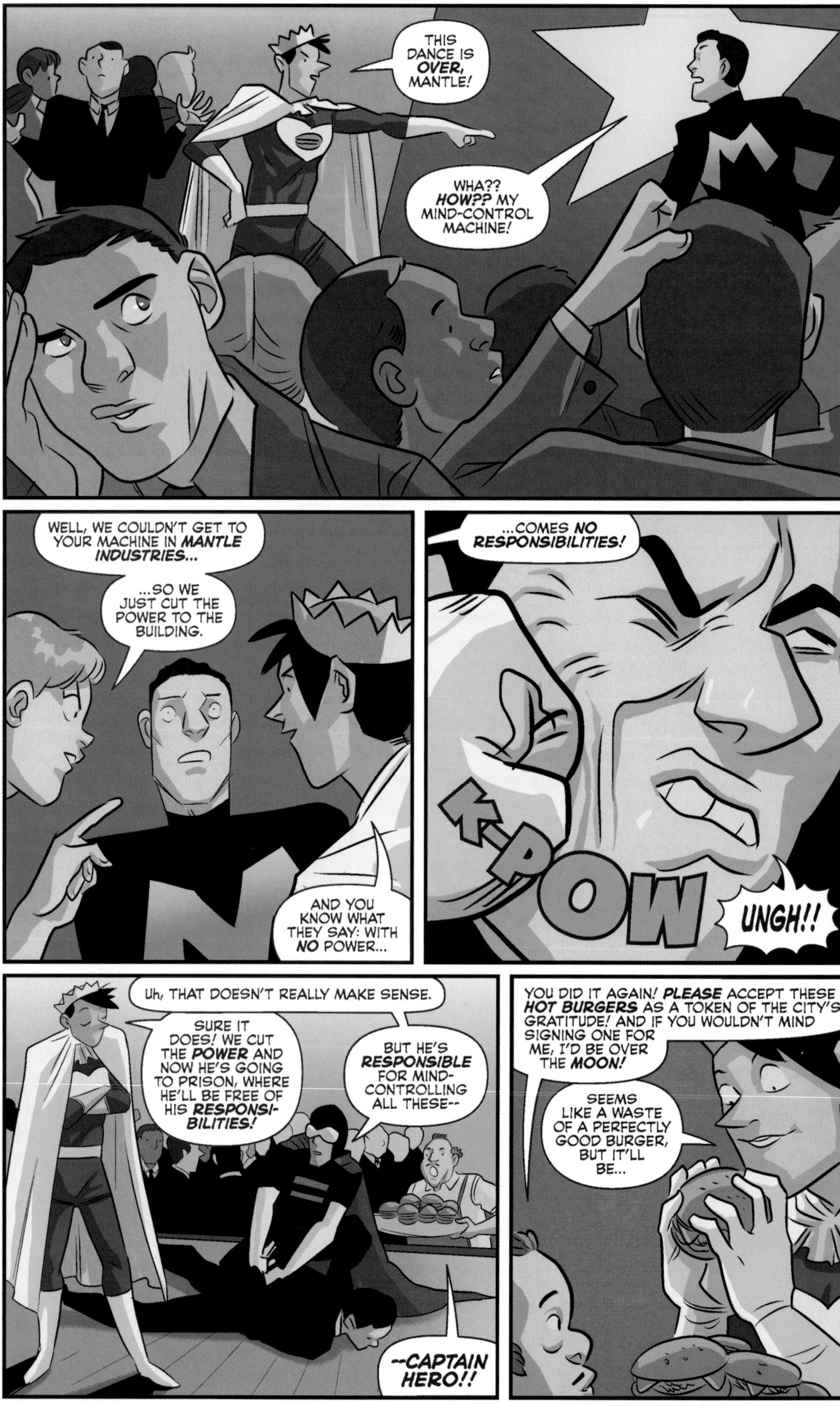
THIS DANCE IS OVER, MANTLE!
WHA?? HOW?? MY MIND-CONTROL MACHINE!
WELL, WE COULDN'T GET TO YOUR MACHINE IN MANTLE INDUSTRIES...
...SO WE JUST CUT THE POWER TO THE BUILDING.
AND YOU KNOW WHAT THEY SAY: WITH NO POWER...
...COMES NO RESPONSIBILITIES!
K-POW
UNGH!!
Uh, THAT DOESN'T REALLY MAKE SENSE.
SURE IT DOES! WE CUT THE POWER AND NOW HE'S GOING TO PRISON, WHERE HE'LL BE FREE OF HIS RESPONSI-BILITIES!
BUT HE'S RESPONSIBLE FOR MIND-CONTROLLING ALL THESE--
--CAPTAIN HERO!!
YOU DID IT AGAIN! PLEASE ACCEPT THESE HOT BURGERS AS A TOKEN OF THE CITY'S GRATITUDE! AND IF YOU WOULDN'T MIND SIGNING ONE FOR ME, I'D BE OVER THE MOON!
SEEMS LIKE A WASTE OF A PERFECTLY GOOD BURGER, BUT IT'LL BE...

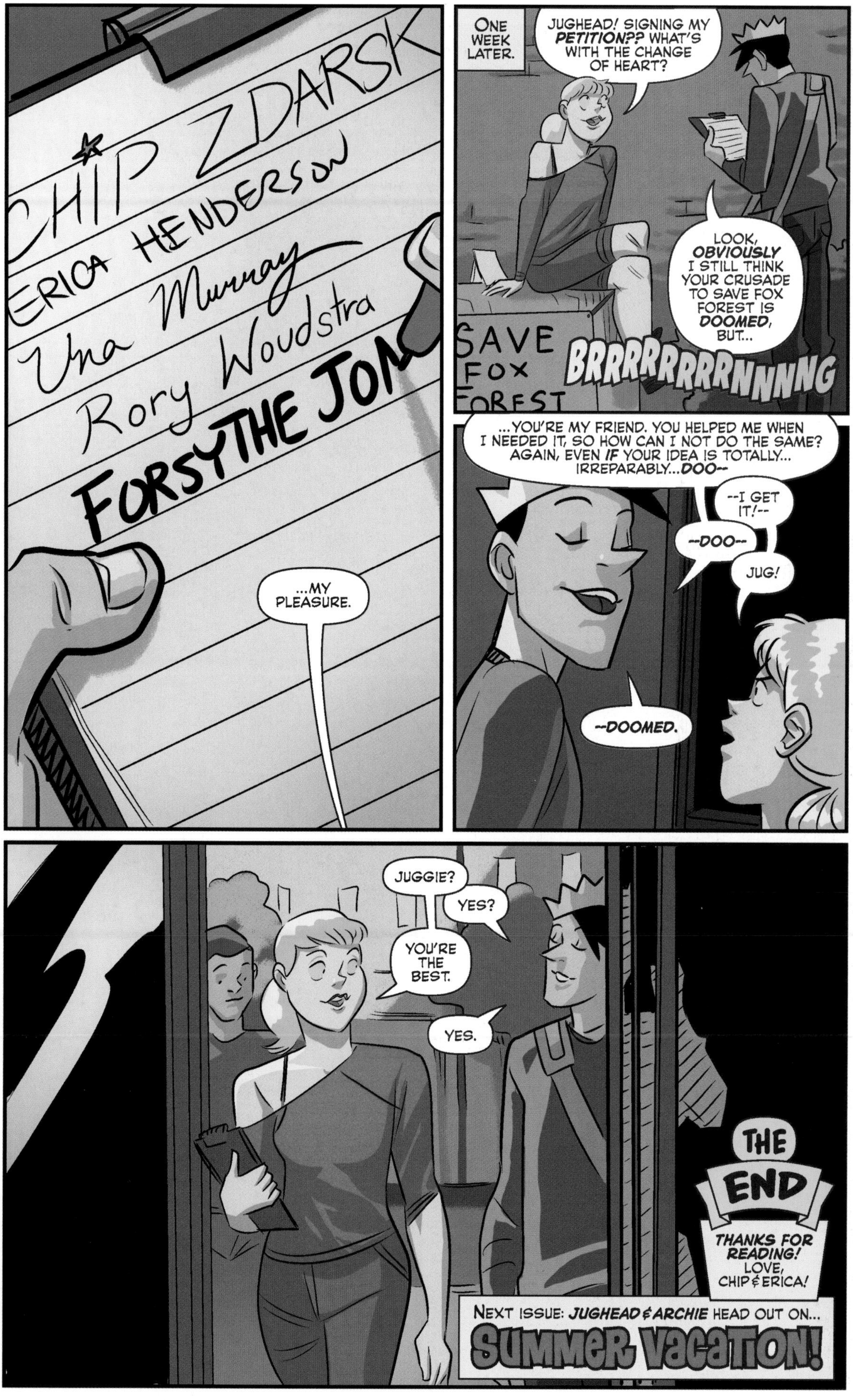
CHIP ZDARSK
ERICA HENDERSON
Una Murray
Rory Woudstra
FORSYTHE JO
...MY PLEASURE.
ONE WEEK LATER.
JUGHEAD! SIGNING MY PETITION?? WHAT'S WITH THE CHANGE OF HEART?
LOOK, OBVIOUSLY I STILL THINK YOUR CRUSADE TO SAVE FOX FOREST IS DOOMED, BUT...
SAVE FOX FOREST
BRRRRRRRRNNNNG
...YOU'RE MY FRIEND. YOU HELPED ME WHEN I NEEDED IT, SO HOW CAN I NOT DO THE SAME? AGAIN, EVEN IF YOUR IDEA IS TOTALLY... IRREPARABLY...DOO--
--I GET IT!--
--DOO--
JUG!
--DOOMED.
JUGGIE?
YES?
YOU'RE THE BEST.
YES.
THE END
THANKS FOR READING! LOVE, CHIP & ERICA!
NEXT ISSUE: JUGHEAD & ARCHIE HEAD OUT ON...
SUMMER VACATION!

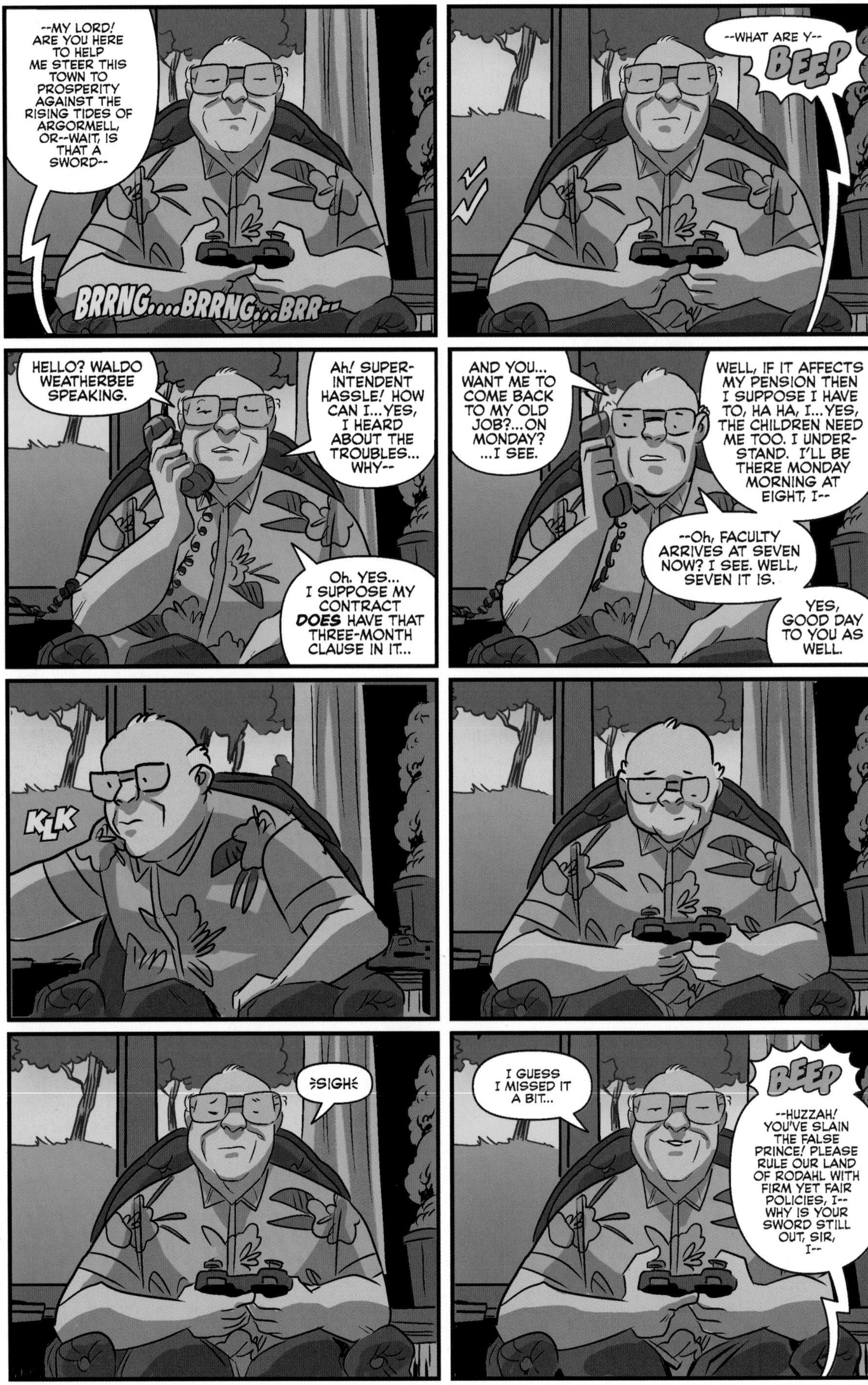
--MY LORD! ARE YOU HERE TO HELP ME STEER THIS TOWN TO PROSPERITY AGAINST THE RISING TIDES OF ARGORMELL, OR--WAIT, IS THAT A SWORD--
BRRNG....BRRNG...BRR--
--WHAT ARE Y--
BEEP
HELLO? WALDO WEATHERBEE SPEAKING.
Ah! SUPER-INTENDENT HASSLE! HOW CAN I...YES, I HEARD ABOUT THE TROUBLES... WHY--
Oh. YES... I SUPPOSE MY CONTRACT DOES HAVE THAT THREE-MONTH CLAUSE IN IT...
AND YOU... WANT ME TO COME BACK TO MY OLD JOB?...ON MONDAY? ...I SEE.
WELL, IF IT AFFECTS MY PENSION THEN I SUPPOSE I HAVE TO, HA HA, I...YES, THE CHILDREN NEED ME TOO. I UNDER-STAND. I'LL BE THERE MONDAY MORNING AT EIGHT, I--
--Oh, FACULTY ARRIVES AT SEVEN NOW? I SEE. WELL, SEVEN IT IS.
YES, GOOD DAY TO YOU AS WELL.
KLK
SIGH
I GUESS I MISSED IT A BIT...
BEEP
--HUZZAH! YOU'VE SLAIN THE FALSE PRINCE! PLEASE RULE OUR LAND OF RODAHL WITH FIRM YET FAIR POLICIES, I-- WHY IS YOUR SWORD STILL OUT, SIR, I--

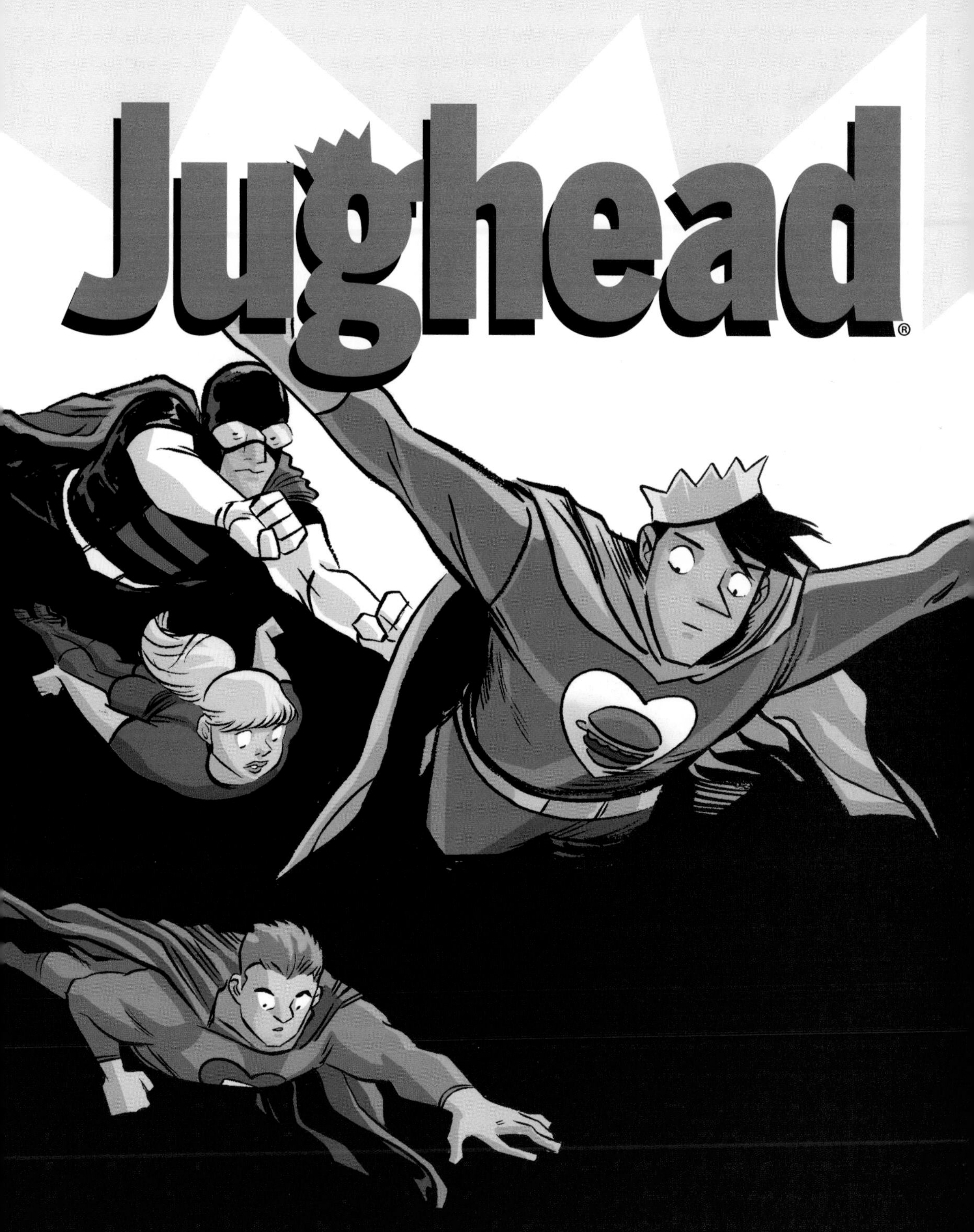
Jughead®

SPECIAL FEATURES

CHARACTER
SKETCHES

Where it all began! When Erica's fantastic variant cover for *Archie* #2 landed her the coveted spot as the *Jughead* series artist, she whipped up these awesome original character sketches of Archie, Veronica, Betty and—your hero—Jughead!

ARCHIE ANDREWS **VERONICA** LODGE **BETTY** COOPER **JUGHEAD** JONES

Jughead

COVER GALLERY

ISSUE ONE

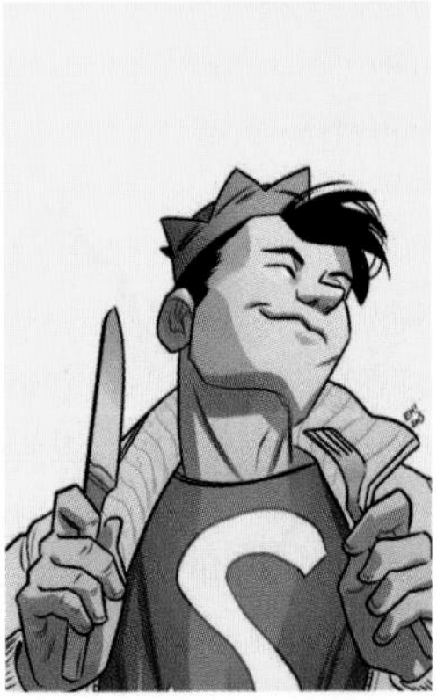

ERICA HENDERSON

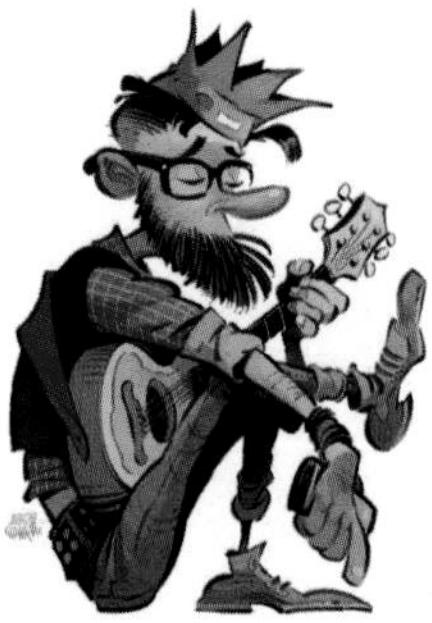

ANTON EMDIN

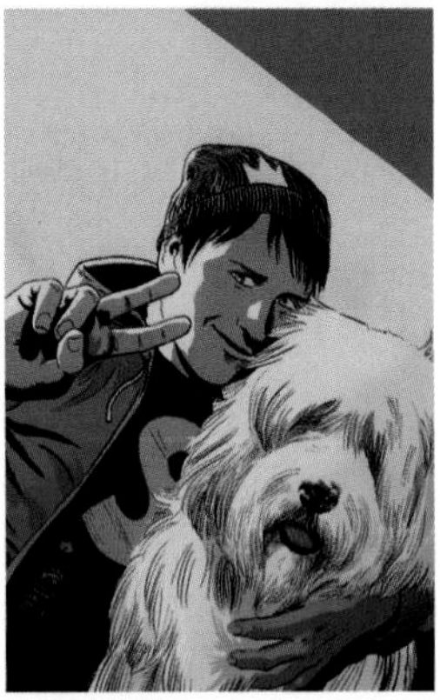

FRANCESCO FRANCAVILLA

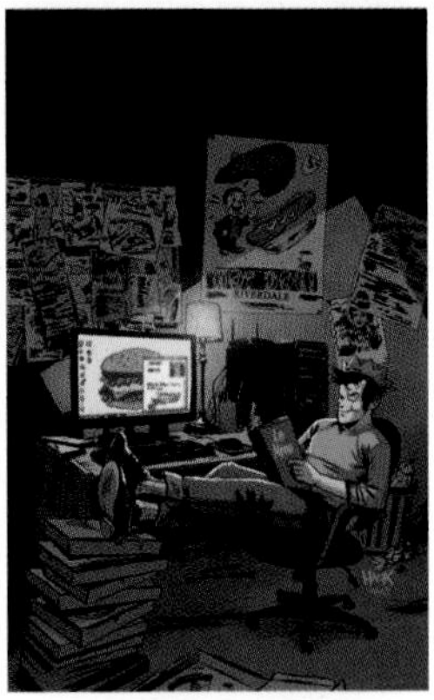

ROBERT HACK

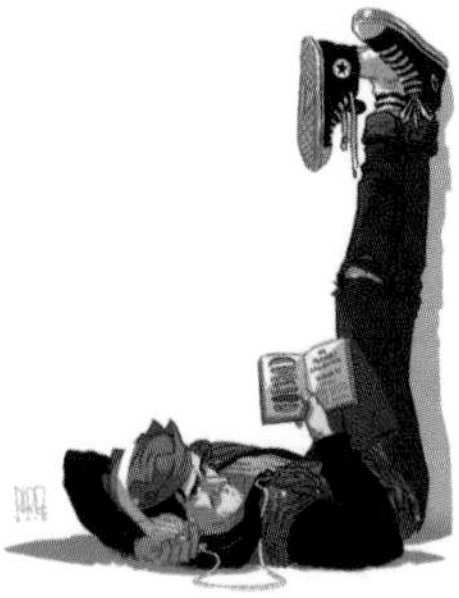

RAMON PEREZ

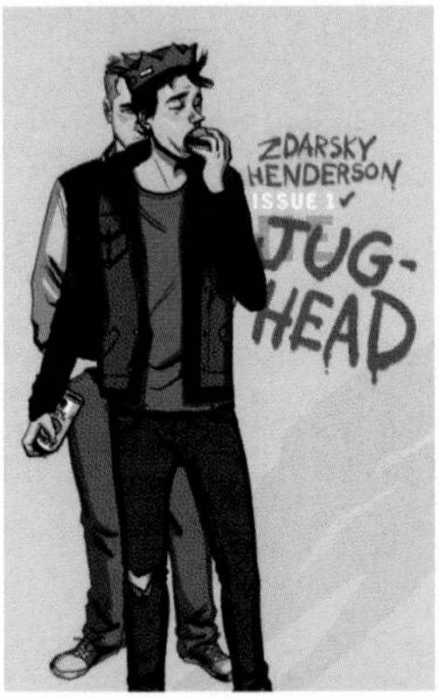
ZDARSKY
HENDERSON
ISSUE 1
JUG-HEAD

CHIP ZDARSKY

ISSUE TWO

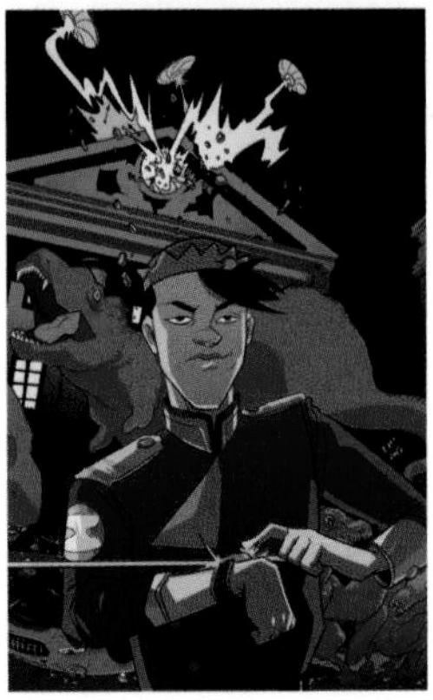

ERICA HENDERSON

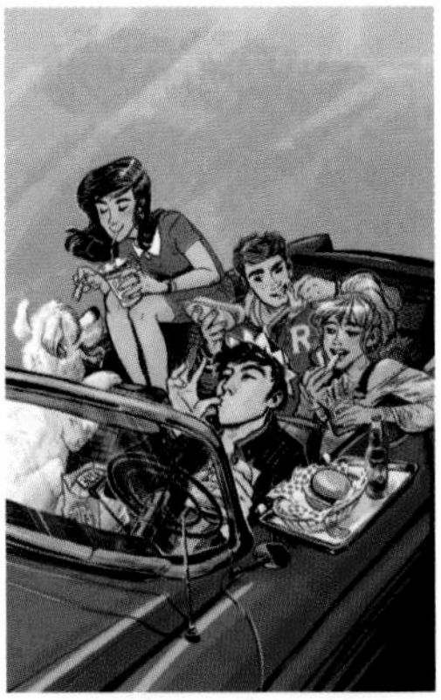

VERONICA FISH

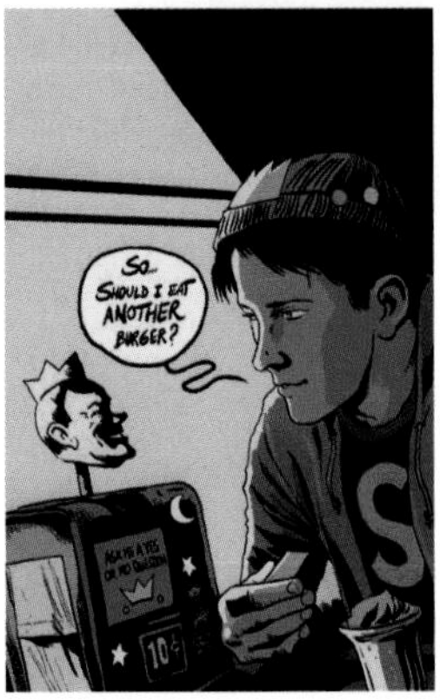
So... SHOULD I EAT ANOTHER BURGER?

FRANCESCO FRANCAVILLA

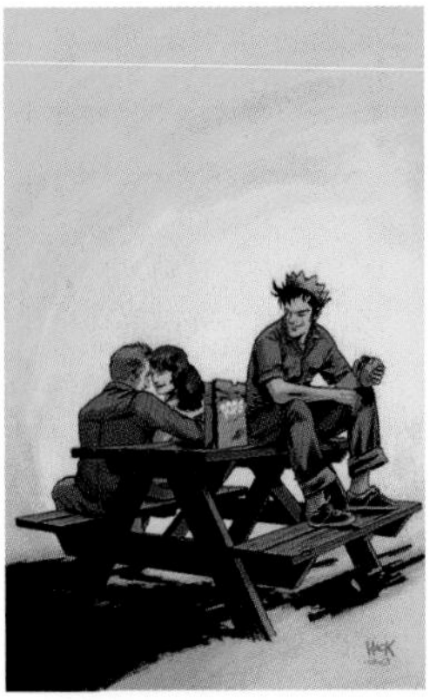

ROBERT HACK

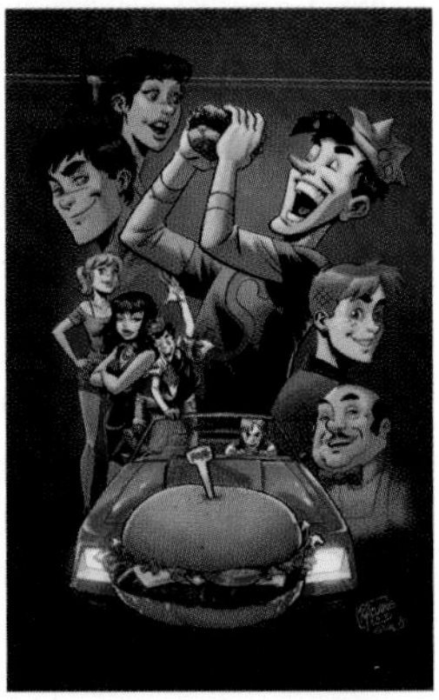

LES MCCLAINE

ISSUE THREE

ERICA HENDERSON

KHARY RANDOLPH

TY TEMPLETON

ISSUE FOUR

ERICA HENDERSON

J. BONE

DAVID MACK

ISSUE FIVE

ERICA HENDERSON

ELLIOT FERNANDEZ

THOMAS PITILLI

ISSUE SIX

ERICA HENDERSON

CLIFF CHIANG

RAMON PEREZ

ORIGINAL SCRIPTS

Receiving a new script each month is always exciting, but Chip's scripts always managed to bring a little extra fun to the table. Check out these excerpts from some of our favorite moments, followed by a look at how the script was transformed in the final art pages.

JUGHEAD #1 - PAGE ONE

JUGHEAD #1
BY CHIP ZDARSKY. HA HA HA HA
May 26, 2015

PAGE ONE

Erica! This page is broken up into eight static-ish panels! Which hopefully isn't too boring for you. There's a dragon later, so, yeah. Give me a shout if anything is confusing due to me being bad writer! Or, just give me a shout for no reason. I'm pretty lonely.

1.1 JUG just slouched into a couch, playing a video game. As the panels go on, we see an increase in take-out boxes, pop cans, chip bags, etc. In 1.1 it's light out, then it moves into dusk, then darkness, then hints of light, then it's fully daytime again. We can see JUG's phone in each panel. And obviously there's a window here.

TV (quiet): —my lord, the town of Tragroth is in need of your blade! Please collect 400 spookleberries and then walk exactly along this clearly marked path to find the magician Gareth who will—

1.2 (progression)

TV (quiet): —thank you, good knight. The dragon has been slain. Here are seven dragondollars for your trouble from my pouch full of dragondollars, I—wait, what are you doing with your sword, I—no! No, please—

--MY LORD, THE TOWN OF TRAGROTH IS IN NEED OF YOUR BLADE! PLEASE COLLECT 400 SPOOKLEBERRIES AND THEN WALK EXACTLY ALONG THIS CLEARLY MARKED PATH TO FIND THE MAGICIAN GARETH WHO WILL--
--THANK YOU, GOOD KNIGHT. THE DRAGON HAS BEEN SLAIN. HERE ARE SEVEN DRAGONDOLLARS FOR YOUR TROUBLE FROM MY POUCH FULL OF DRAGONDOLLARS, I--WAIT, WHAT ARE YOU DOING WITH YOUR SWORD, I--NO! NO, PLEASE--
FAMILY

10.1 A small, possibly inset, shot of JUGHEAD's hand grabbing a gun from the counter.

SFX: chk

10.2 A nice big shot of JUGHEAD, blasting the ROBOT with a freeze ray from the gun (even though there are a bunch of weapons in the counter, none of them fire actual bullets. THINK OF THE CHILDREN, ERICA.)

TITLE/JUGHEAD (large, as a part of JUGHEAD's caption): …THE MAN FROM R.I.V.E.R.D.A.L.E…

JUGHEAD: …will gladly HELP himself to another shake for taking out this robot, POP.

ROBOT: —IT WOULD BE QUITE EMBARASSING ACTUAZzzzzzZ!!!

SFX: FZZZZZSHHH!!!

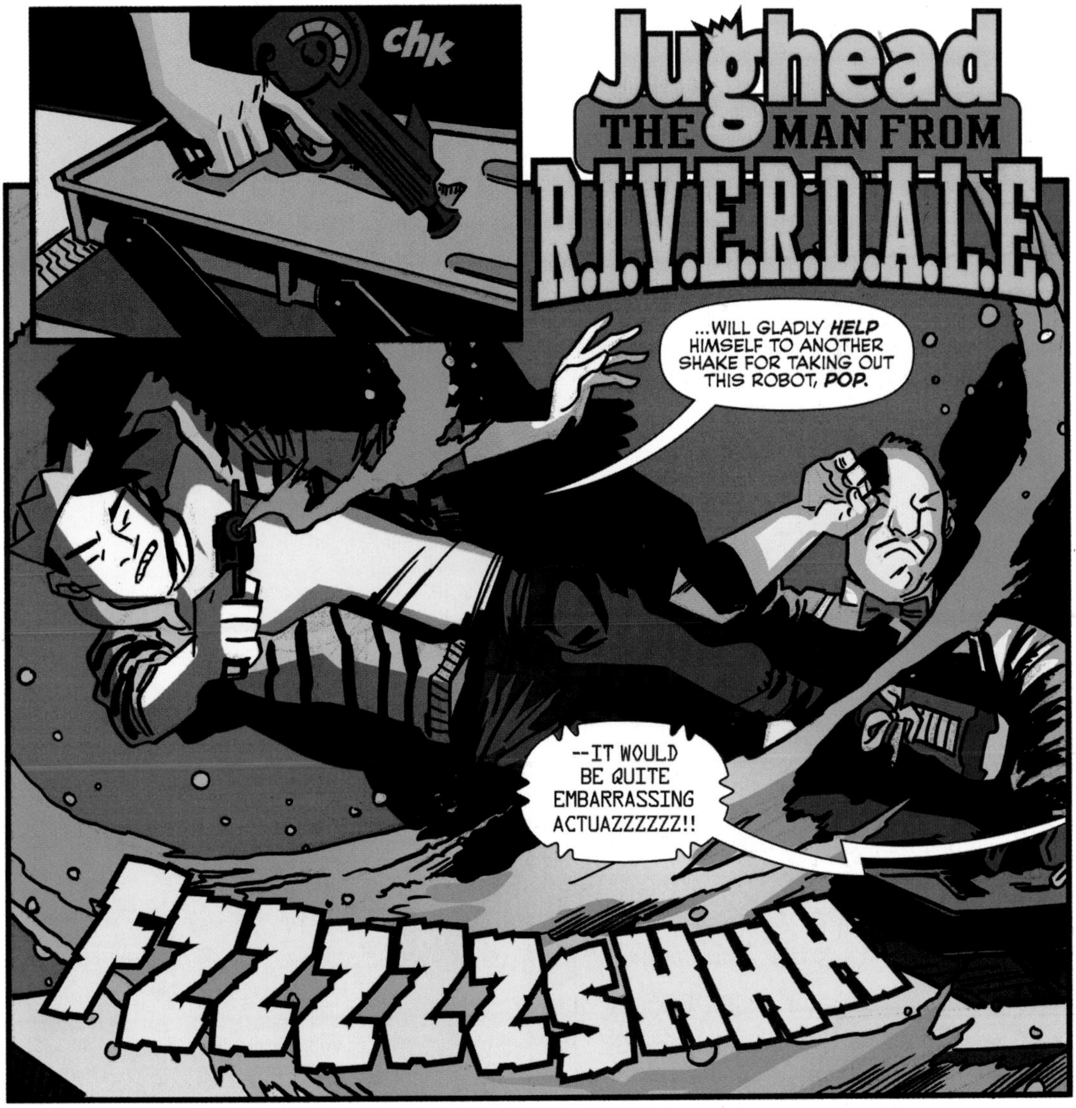
chk
Jughead THE MAN FROM R.I.V.E.R.D.A.L.E.
...WILL GLADLY HELP HIMSELF TO ANOTHER SHAKE FOR TAKING OUT THIS ROBOT, POP.
--IT WOULD BE QUITE EMBARRASSING ACTUAZZZZZZ!!
FZZZZZSHHH

JUGHEAD #4 - PAGE ONE

JUGGIE JONEZ 4
CHIP ZDARSKYYYY
November 24, 2015

PAGE ONE

We're emulating the opening of issue one again here. Eight static panels that take place in JUGHEAD's living room. On the couch we see ARCHIE, BETTY and KEVIN. ARCHIE looks bored, BETTY has her arms crossed and KEVIN is entertaining JUGHEAD's rant to be polite. The angle of the shot may have to change slightly to better incorporate JUGHEAD's silhouette in some panels, which comes in and out of frame. Its not super necessary to have his head in the shot, really. Does that make sense? Of course it does! I'm a good explainer man!

1.1 JUGHEAD: Look, hear me out. It all makes sense.

1.2 JUGHEAD: Why would they replace Principal Weatherbee with Stanger? Riverdale High's test score are totally above average! You don't fire a principal for doing well!

1.3 JUGHEAD: And all the teachers Stanger replaced! With … with crazy intense instructors! Teaching things like DRONE OPERATION and ARMY OBSTACLE COURSES!

1.4 JUGHEAD: Plus, when I proved to be too much of a "nuisance," Stanger and his thug coach planted a knife on me to get me out of the system! Cause I'm too smart to not figure this out!

LOOK, HEAR ME OUT. IT ALL MAKES SENSE.
WHY WOULD THEY REPLACE PRINCIPAL WEATHERBEE WITH STANGER? RIVERDALE HIGH'S TEST SCORES ARE TOTALLY ABOVE AVERAGE! YOU DON'T FIRE A PRINCIPAL FOR DOING WELL!
AND ALL THE TEACHERS STANGER REPLACED! WITH...WITH CRAZY INTENSE INSTRUCTORS! TEACHING THINGS LIKE DRONE OPERATION AND ARMY OBSTACLE COURSES!
PLUS, WHEN I PROVED TO BE TOO MUCH OF A "NUISANCE," STANGER AND HIS THUG COACH PLANTED A KNIFE ON ME TO GET ME OUT OF THE SYSTEM! 'CAUSE I'M TOO SMART TO NOT FIGURE THIS OUT!

JUGHEAD #5 - PAGE FOUR

PAGE FOUR

4.1 We now see who they're referring to. WADE. He's a 20-year-old version of Mark Waid, the oldest "kid" at RIVERDALE HIGH. I just want to mess with Mark. He's wearing a heavy metal band t-shirt and he's world-weary. Playing on his phone before the bell.

JUGHEAD: WADE! My favourite forever-student! What's shaking?

WADE: What do you dorks want?

4.2 JUGHEAD buttering him up, kind of.

JUGHEAD: Wade, Wade, you've been in high school for, what? Seven years now?

WADE: Something like that.

JUGHEAD: And that's spread over … how many schools again?

WADE: Four. What are you getting at, needle nose?

WADE! MY FAVORITE FOREVER-STUDENT! WHAT'S SHAKING?
WHAT DO YOU DORKS WANT?
WADE, WADE, YOU'VE BEEN IN HIGH SCHOOL FOR, WHAT? SEVEN YEARS NOW?
SOMETHING LIKE THAT.
AND THAT'S SPREAD OVER... HOW MANY SCHOOLS AGAIN?
FOUR. WHAT ARE YOU GETTING AT, NEEDLE NOSE?

PAGE NINETEEN

19.1 Close on a signature form. We see a hand writing out "FORSYTHE JONES" underneath "RORY WOUDSTRA" (a ten-year old Archie fan!) and "UNA MURRAY" (my MOMMY) and whoever you'd like, Erica. This is our chance for eternal glory, if space allows.

JUGHEAD (OP): …my pleasure.

19.2 We pull out to see JUGHEAD has just signed the SAVE FOX FOREST petition. We're just outside the school. BETTY is in front of the setup with JUGHEAD, elated he's signed on. BEHIND them we see BRIGITTE packing up cause school's about to start.

CAPTION: ONE WEEK LATER.

BETTY: Jughead! Signing my PETITION?? What's with the change of heart?

JUGHEAD: Look, OBVIOUSLY I still think your crusade to save Fox Forest is DOOMED, but …

SFX (school bell): BRrRrRrRrNnNnG

CHIP ZDARSK
ERICA HENDERSON
Una Murray
Rory Woudstra
FORSYTHE JON
...MY PLEASURE.
ONE WEEK LATER.
JUGHEAD! SIGNING MY PETITION?? WHAT'S WITH THE CHANGE OF HEART?
LOOK, OBVIOUSLY I STILL THINK YOUR CRUSADE TO SAVE FOX FOREST IS DOOMED, BUT...
SAVE FOX FOREST
BRRRRRRRRRNNNNG

SPECIAL **BONUS ISSUE**

ARCHIE®

ARCHIE VOL. 1 features issues #1 - #6 of the hit series, and can be found at finer book stores everywhere right now! If you've already enjoyed the first volume, then you'll love this special BONUS ISSUE featuring the first chapter of ARCHIE VOL. 2!

We'll, what are you waiting for? Let's get ready to roll...

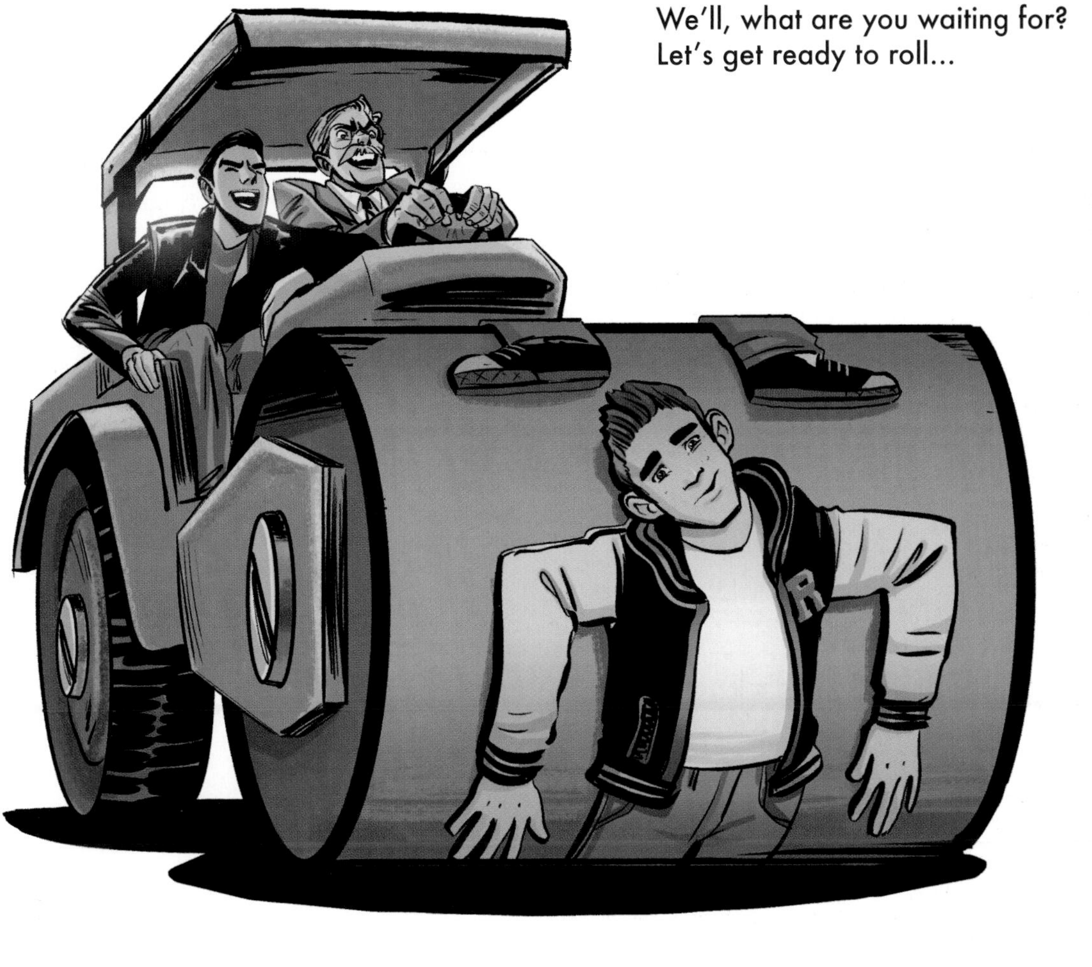

R

STORY BY
MARK WAID

ART BY
VERONICA FISH

COLORING BY
ANDRE SZYMANOWICZ
WITH **JEN VAUGHN**

LETTERING BY
JACK MORELLI

ISSUE SEVEN

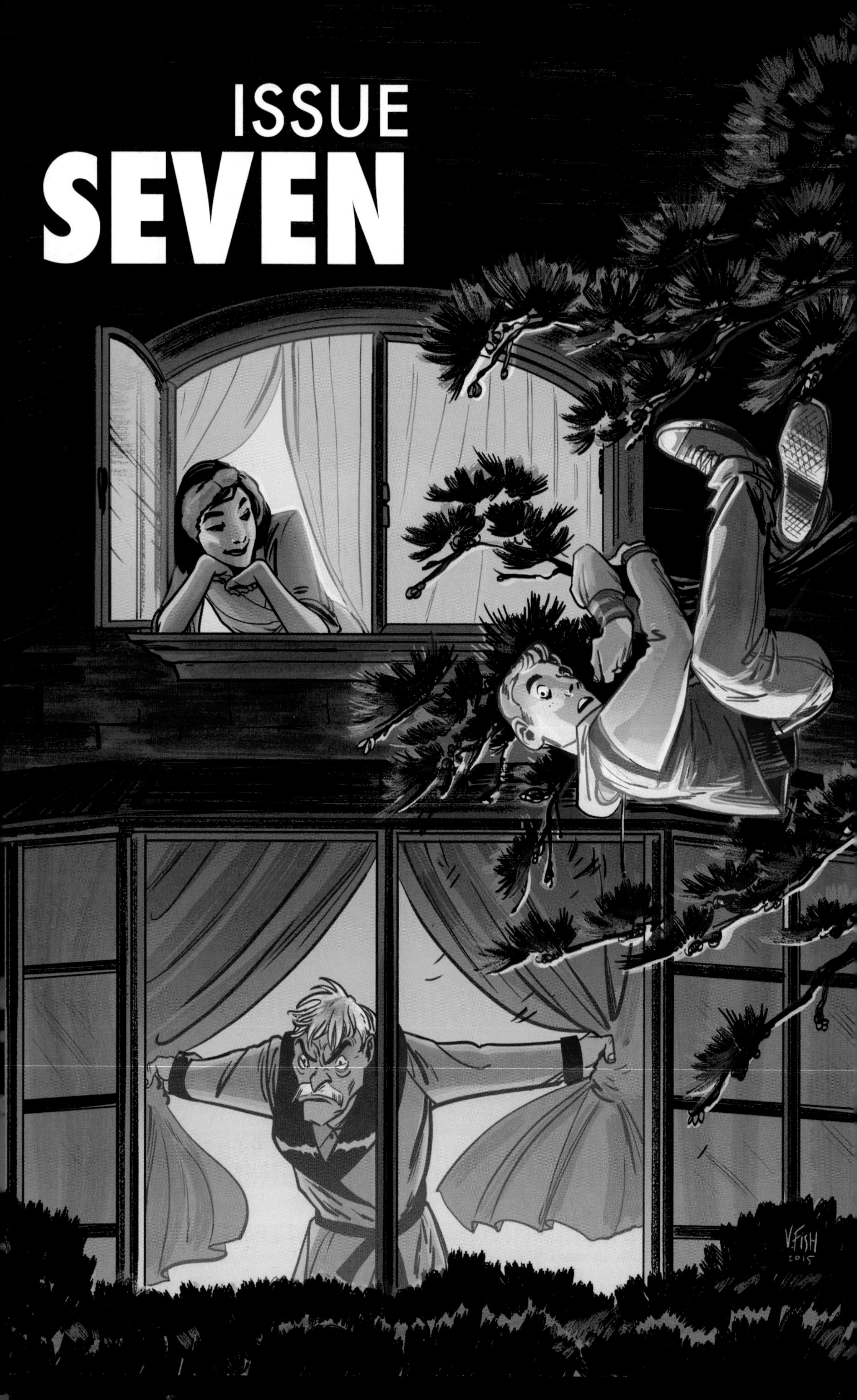
V.FISH
2015

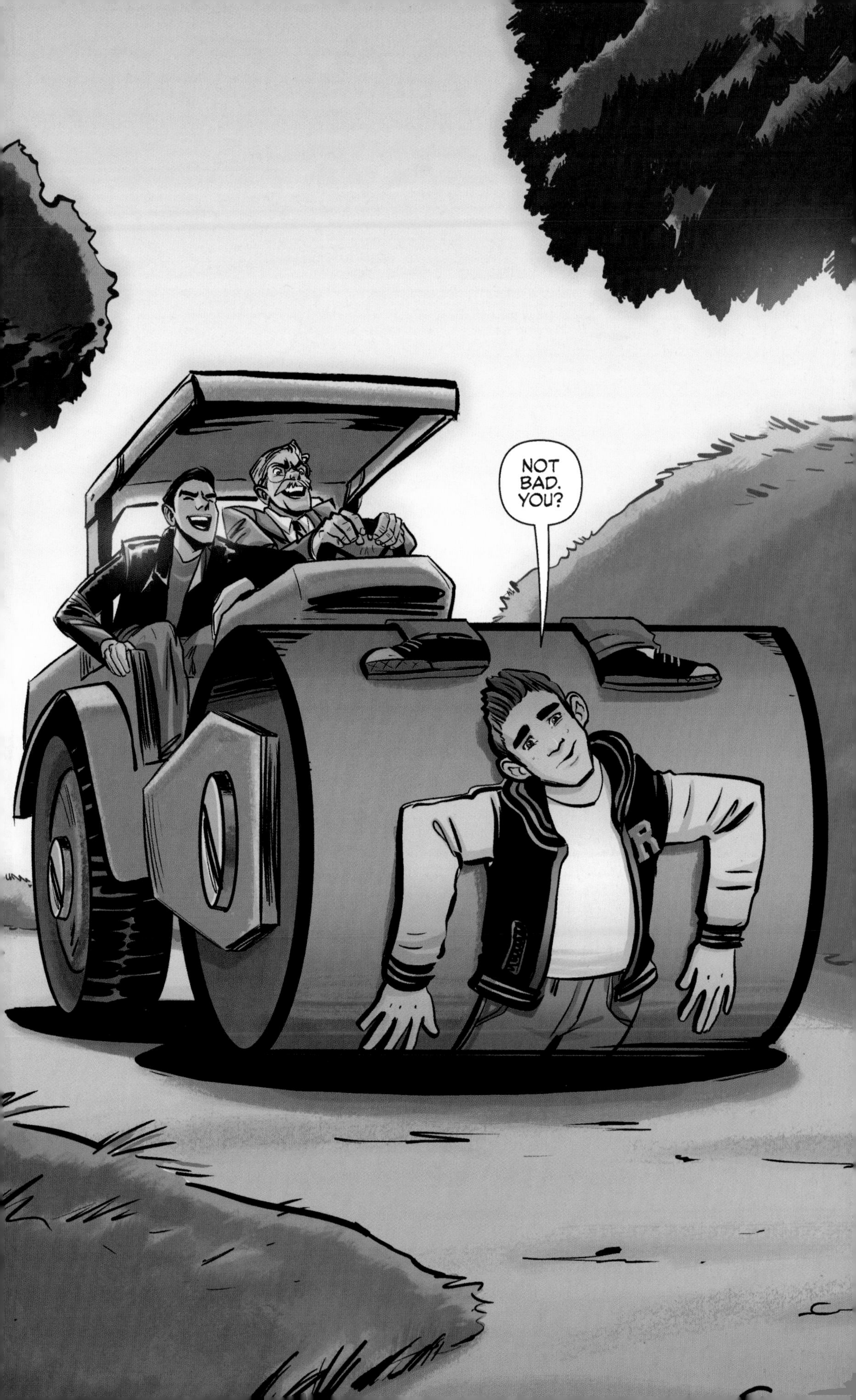
NOT BAD. YOU?

CHAPTER ONE: FAMILY TIME!

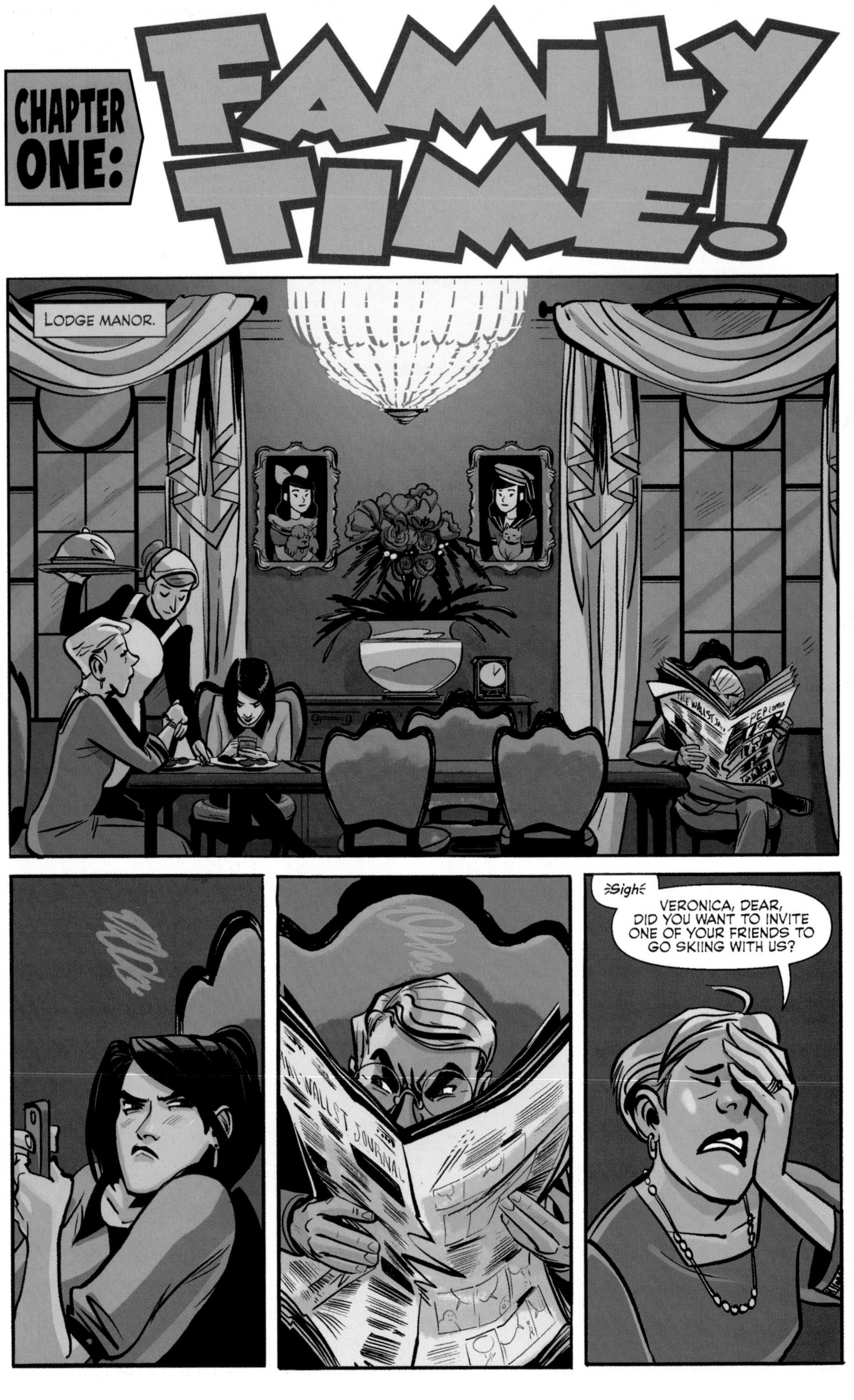
LODGE MANOR.
Sigh
VERONICA, DEAR, DID YOU WANT TO INVITE ONE OF YOUR FRIENDS TO GO SKIING WITH US?

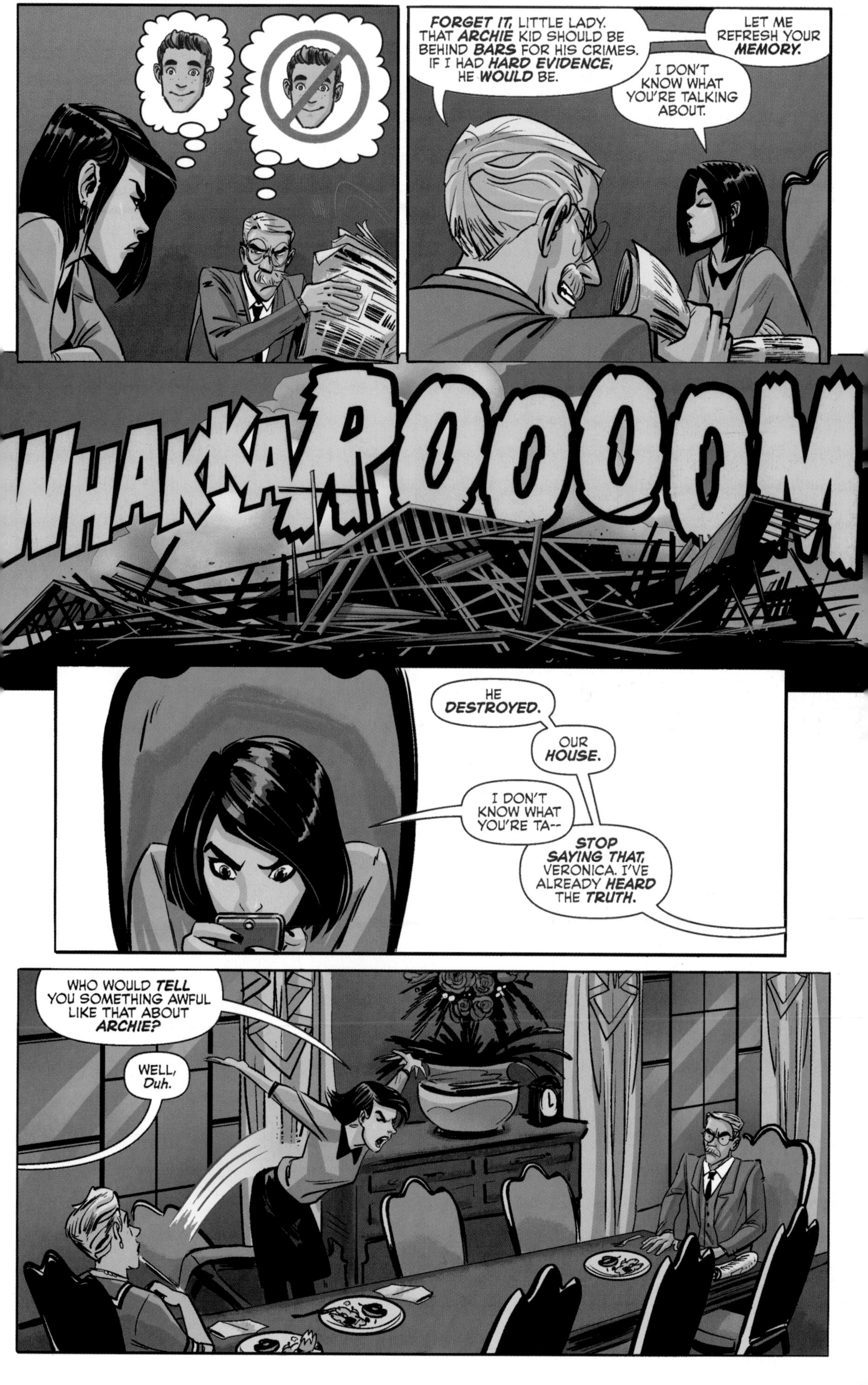
FORGET IT, LITTLE LADY. THAT ARCHIE KID SHOULD BE BEHIND BARS FOR HIS CRIMES. IF I HAD HARD EVIDENCE, HE WOULD BE.
LET ME REFRESH YOUR MEMORY.
I DON'T KNOW WHAT YOU'RE TALKING ABOUT.
WHAKKAROOOOM
HE DESTROYED.
OUR HOUSE.
I DON'T KNOW WHAT YOU'RE TA--
STOP SAYING THAT, VERONICA. I'VE ALREADY HEARD THE TRUTH.
WHO WOULD TELL YOU SOMETHING AWFUL LIKE THAT ABOUT ARCHIE?
WELL, Duh.

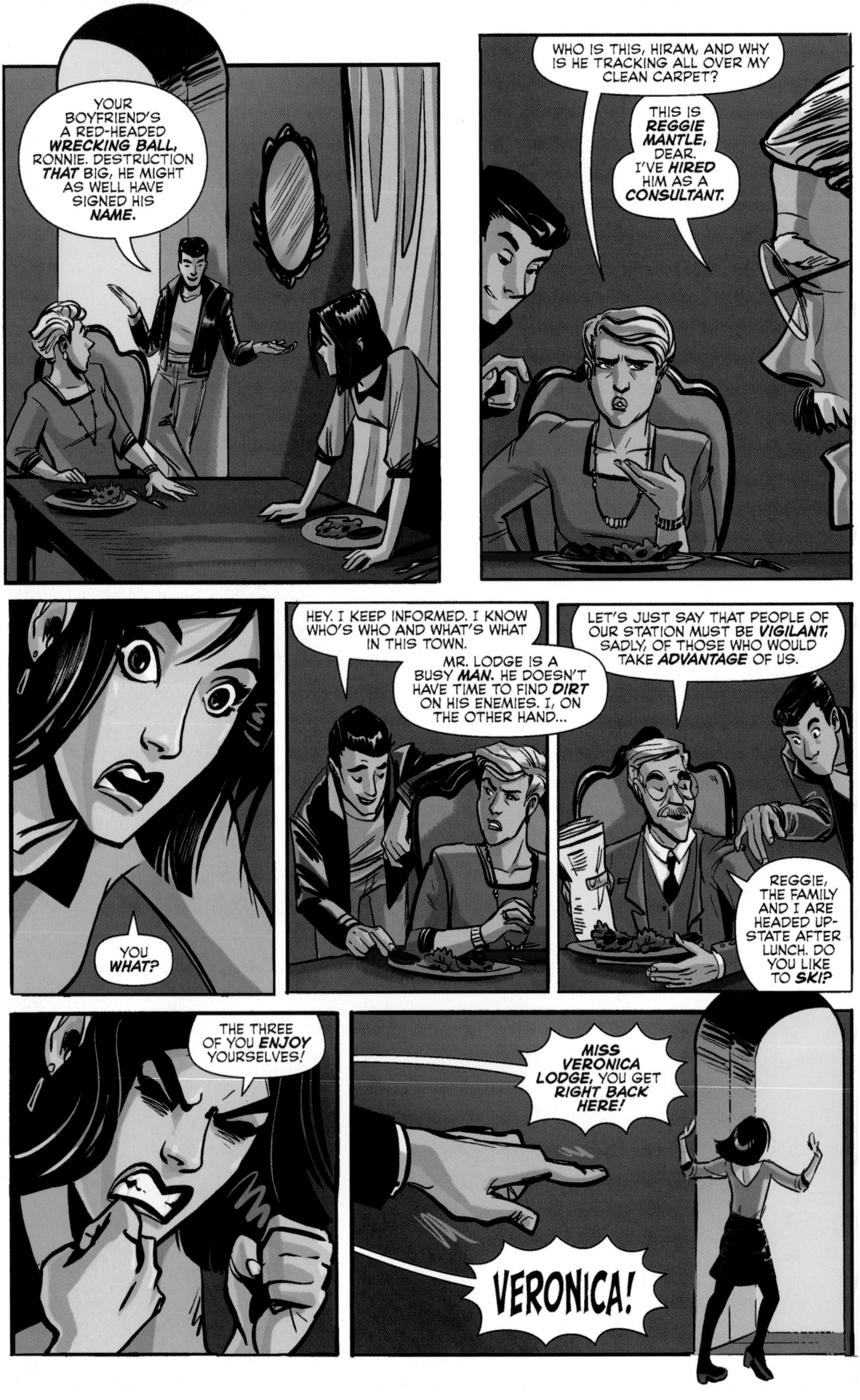
YOUR BOYFRIEND'S A RED-HEADED WRECKING BALL, RONNIE. DESTRUCTION THAT BIG, HE MIGHT AS WELL HAVE SIGNED HIS NAME.
WHO IS THIS, HIRAM, AND WHY IS HE TRACKING ALL OVER MY CLEAN CARPET?
THIS IS REGGIE MANTLE, DEAR. I'VE HIRED HIM AS A CONSULTANT.
YOU WHAT?
HEY. I KEEP INFORMED. I KNOW WHO'S WHO AND WHAT'S WHAT IN THIS TOWN.
MR. LODGE IS A BUSY MAN. HE DOESN'T HAVE TIME TO FIND DIRT ON HIS ENEMIES. I, ON THE OTHER HAND...
LET'S JUST SAY THAT PEOPLE OF OUR STATION MUST BE VIGILANT, SADLY, OF THOSE WHO WOULD TAKE ADVANTAGE OF US.
REGGIE, THE FAMILY AND I ARE HEADED UP-STATE AFTER LUNCH. DO YOU LIKE TO SKI?
THE THREE OF YOU ENJOY YOURSELVES!
MISS VERONICA LODGE, YOU GET RIGHT BACK HERE!
VERONICA!

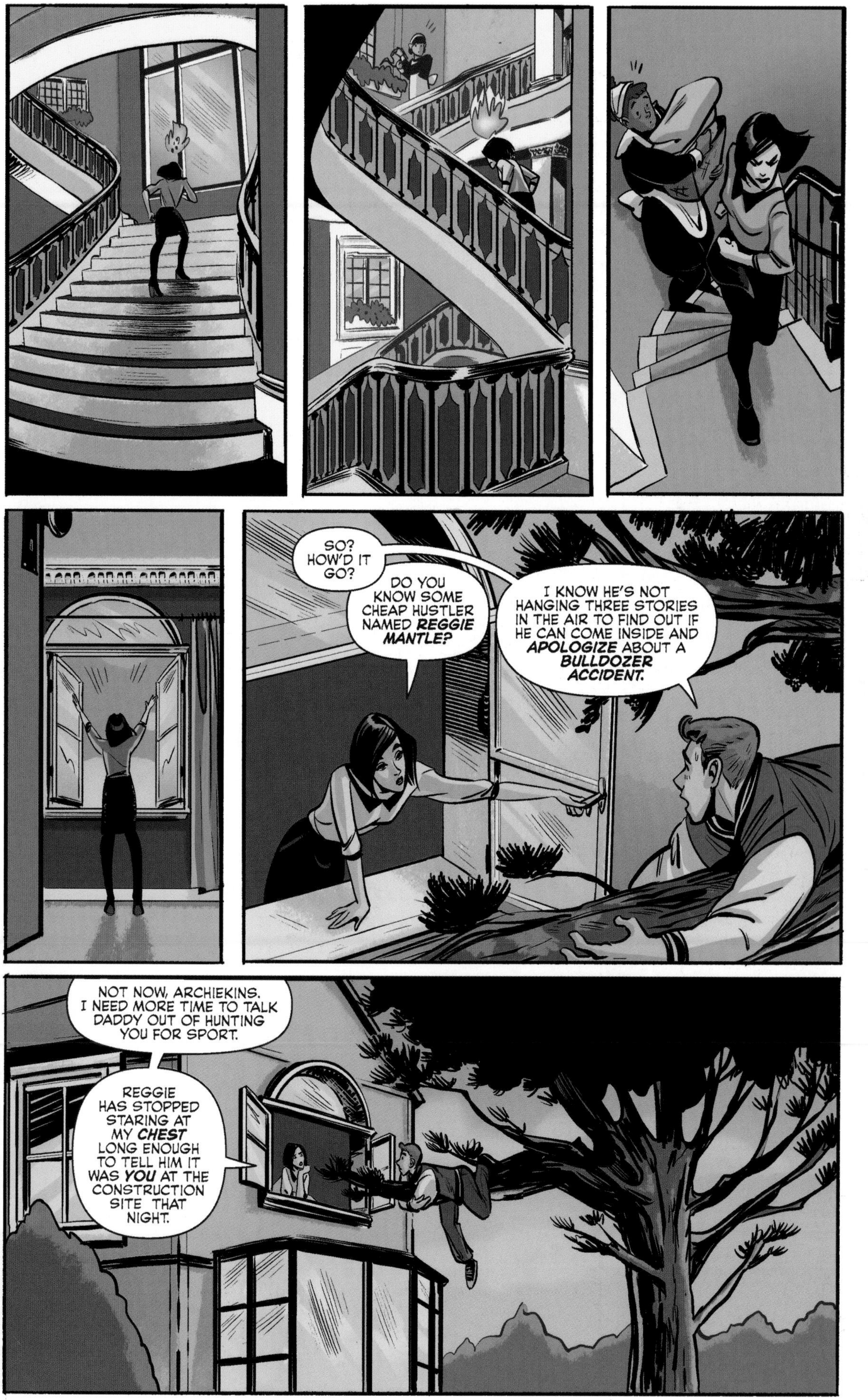
SO? HOW'D IT GO?
DO YOU KNOW SOME CHEAP HUSTLER NAMED REGGIE MANTLE?
I KNOW HE'S NOT HANGING THREE STORIES IN THE AIR TO FIND OUT IF HE CAN COME INSIDE AND APOLOGIZE ABOUT A BULLDOZER ACCIDENT.
NOT NOW, ARCHIEKINS. I NEED MORE TIME TO TALK DADDY OUT OF HUNTING YOU FOR SPORT.
REGGIE HAS STOPPED STARING AT MY CHEST LONG ENOUGH TO TELL HIM IT WAS YOU AT THE CONSTRUCTION SITE THAT NIGHT.

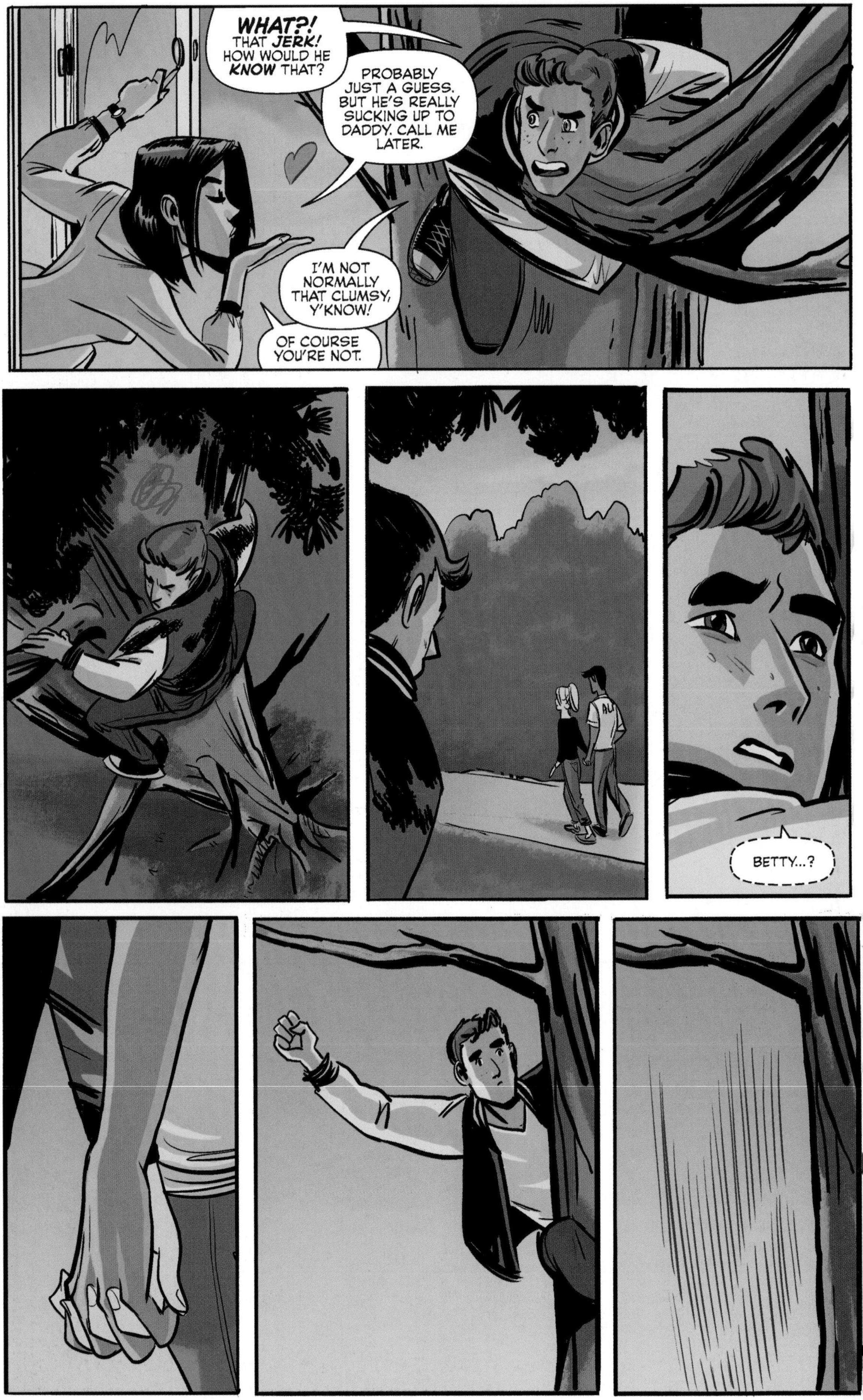

WHAT?! THAT JERK! HOW WOULD HE KNOW THAT?
PROBABLY JUST A GUESS. BUT HE'S REALLY SUCKING UP TO DADDY. CALL ME LATER.
I'M NOT NORMALLY THAT CLUMSY, Y'KNOW!
OF COURSE YOU'RE NOT.
BETTY...?

CHAPTER TWO: SACRED TRUST

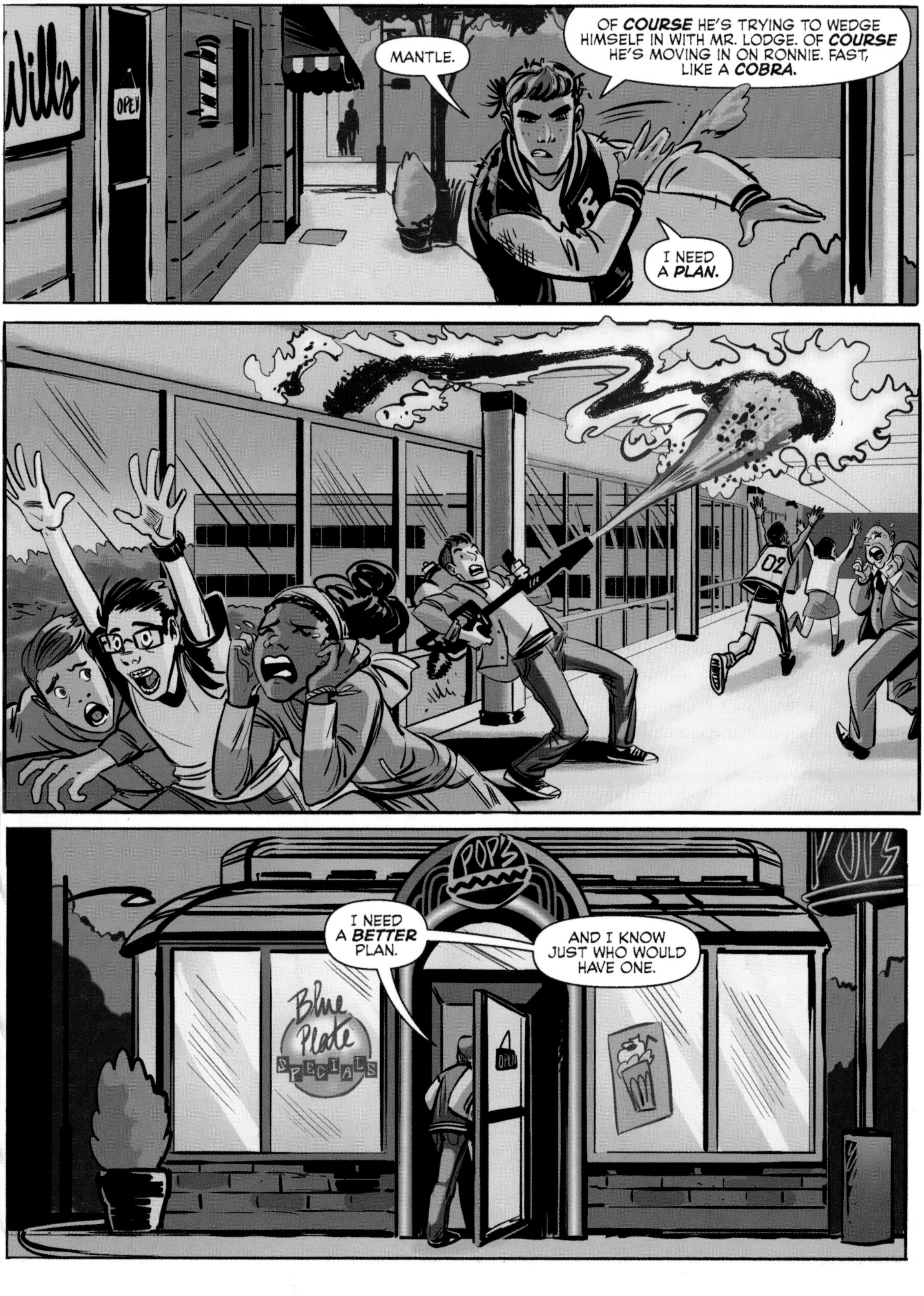
OPEN
MANTLE.
OF COURSE HE'S TRYING TO WEDGE HIMSELF IN WITH MR. LODGE. OF COURSE HE'S MOVING IN ON RONNIE. FAST, LIKE A COBRA.
I NEED A PLAN.
02
POP'S
I NEED A BETTER PLAN.
AND I KNOW JUST WHO WOULD HAVE ONE.
Blue Plate Specials
OPEN

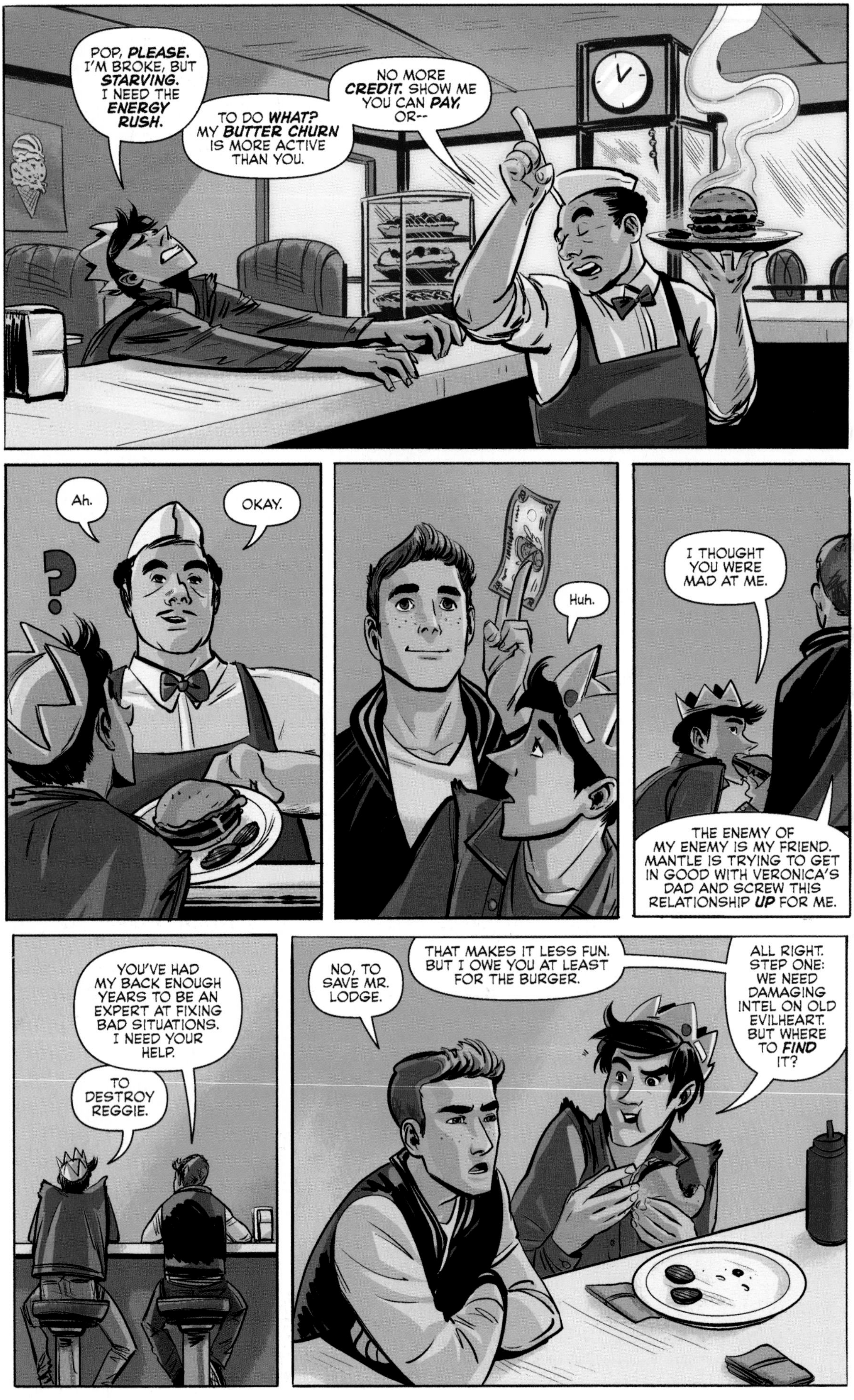
POP, PLEASE. I'M BROKE, BUT STARVING. I NEED THE ENERGY RUSH.
TO DO WHAT? MY BUTTER CHURN IS MORE ACTIVE THAN YOU.
NO MORE CREDIT. SHOW ME YOU CAN PAY, OR--
Ah.
OKAY.
?
Huh.
I THOUGHT YOU WERE MAD AT ME.
THE ENEMY OF MY ENEMY IS MY FRIEND. MANTLE IS TRYING TO GET IN GOOD WITH VERONICA'S DAD AND SCREW THIS RELATIONSHIP UP FOR ME.
YOU'VE HAD MY BACK ENOUGH YEARS TO BE AN EXPERT AT FIXING BAD SITUATIONS. I NEED YOUR HELP.
TO DESTROY REGGIE.
NO, TO SAVE MR. LODGE.
THAT MAKES IT LESS FUN. BUT I OWE YOU AT LEAST FOR THE BURGER.
ALL RIGHT. STEP ONE: WE NEED DAMAGING INTEL ON OLD EVILHEART. BUT WHERE TO FIND IT?

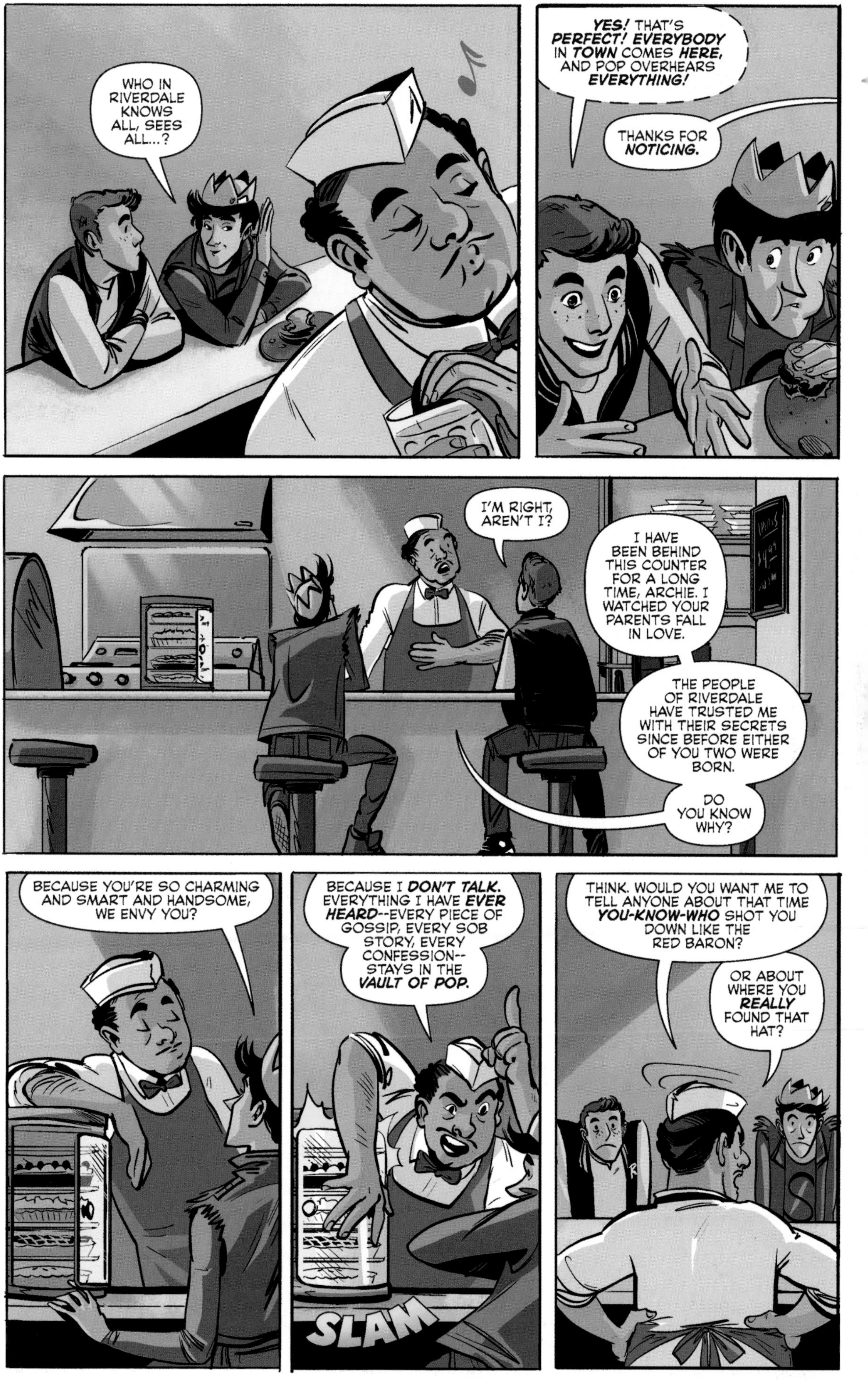
WHO IN RIVERDALE KNOWS ALL, SEES ALL...?
YES! THAT'S PERFECT! EVERYBODY IN TOWN COMES HERE, AND POP OVERHEARS EVERYTHING!
THANKS FOR NOTICING.
I'M RIGHT, AREN'T I?
I HAVE BEEN BEHIND THIS COUNTER FOR A LONG TIME, ARCHIE. I WATCHED YOUR PARENTS FALL IN LOVE.
THE PEOPLE OF RIVERDALE HAVE TRUSTED ME WITH THEIR SECRETS SINCE BEFORE EITHER OF YOU TWO WERE BORN.
DO YOU KNOW WHY?
BECAUSE YOU'RE SO CHARMING AND SMART AND HANDSOME, WE ENVY YOU?
BECAUSE I DON'T TALK. EVERYTHING I HAVE EVER HEARD--EVERY PIECE OF GOSSIP, EVERY SOB STORY, EVERY CONFESSION--STAYS IN THE VAULT OF POP.
SLAM
THINK. WOULD YOU WANT ME TO TELL ANYONE ABOUT THAT TIME YOU-KNOW-WHO SHOT YOU DOWN LIKE THE RED BARON?
OR ABOUT WHERE YOU REALLY FOUND THAT HAT?

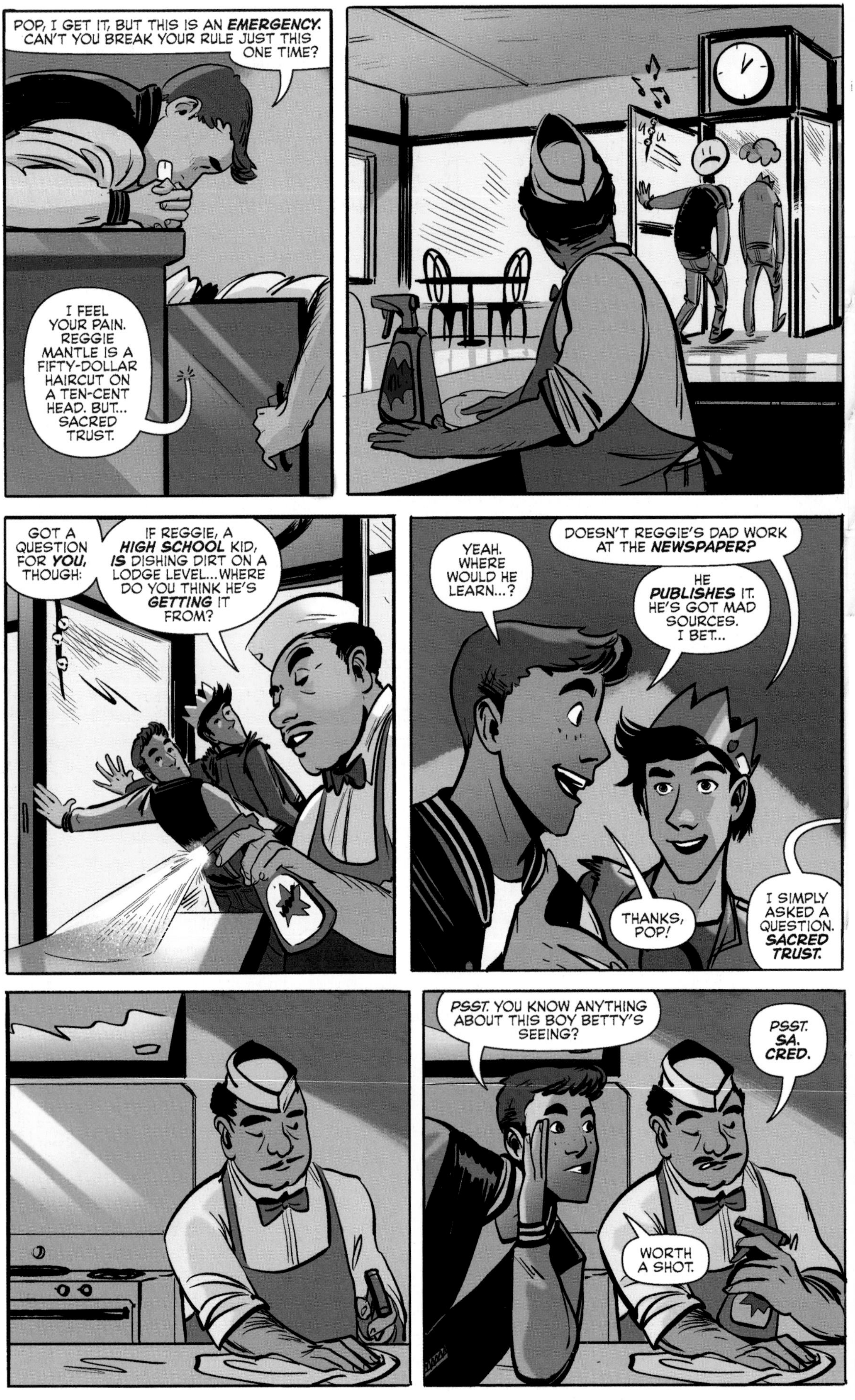
POP, I GET IT, BUT THIS IS AN *EMERGENCY.* CAN'T YOU BREAK YOUR RULE JUST THIS ONE TIME?
I FEEL YOUR PAIN. REGGIE MANTLE IS A FIFTY-DOLLAR HAIRCUT ON A TEN-CENT HEAD. BUT... SACRED TRUST.
GOT A QUESTION FOR *YOU,* THOUGH:
IF REGGIE, A *HIGH SCHOOL* KID, *IS* DISHING DIRT ON A LODGE LEVEL...WHERE DO YOU THINK HE'S *GETTING* IT FROM?
DOESN'T REGGIE'S DAD WORK AT THE *NEWSPAPER?*
YEAH. WHERE WOULD HE LEARN...?
HE *PUBLISHES* IT. HE'S GOT MAD SOURCES. I BET...
THANKS, POP!
I SIMPLY ASKED A QUESTION. *SACRED TRUST.*
PSST. YOU KNOW ANYTHING ABOUT THIS BOY BETTY'S SEEING?
PSST. SA. CRED.
WORTH A SHOT.

CHAPTER THREE: STOP THE PRESSES

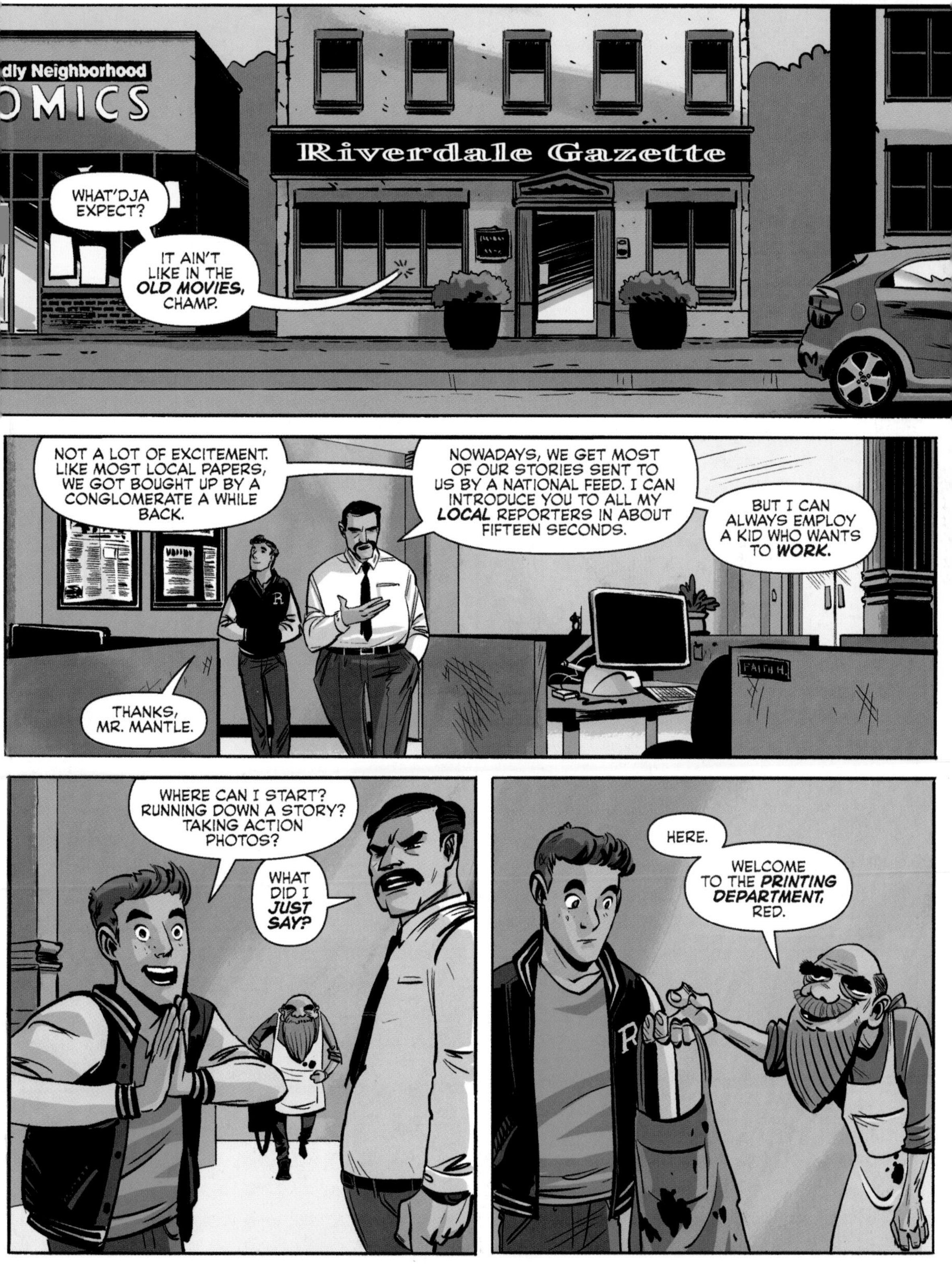

dly Neighborhood
OMICS
Riverdale Gazette
WHAT'DJA EXPECT?
IT AIN'T LIKE IN THE *OLD MOVIES,* CHAMP.
NOT A LOT OF EXCITEMENT. LIKE MOST LOCAL PAPERS, WE GOT BOUGHT UP BY A CONGLOMERATE A WHILE BACK.
NOWADAYS, WE GET MOST OF OUR STORIES SENT TO US BY A NATIONAL FEED. I CAN INTRODUCE YOU TO ALL MY *LOCAL* REPORTERS IN ABOUT FIFTEEN SECONDS.
BUT I CAN ALWAYS EMPLOY A KID WHO WANTS TO *WORK.*
FAITH
THANKS, MR. MANTLE.
WHERE CAN I START? RUNNING DOWN A STORY? TAKING ACTION PHOTOS?
WHAT DID I *JUST SAY?*
HERE.
WELCOME TO THE *PRINTING DEPARTMENT,* RED.

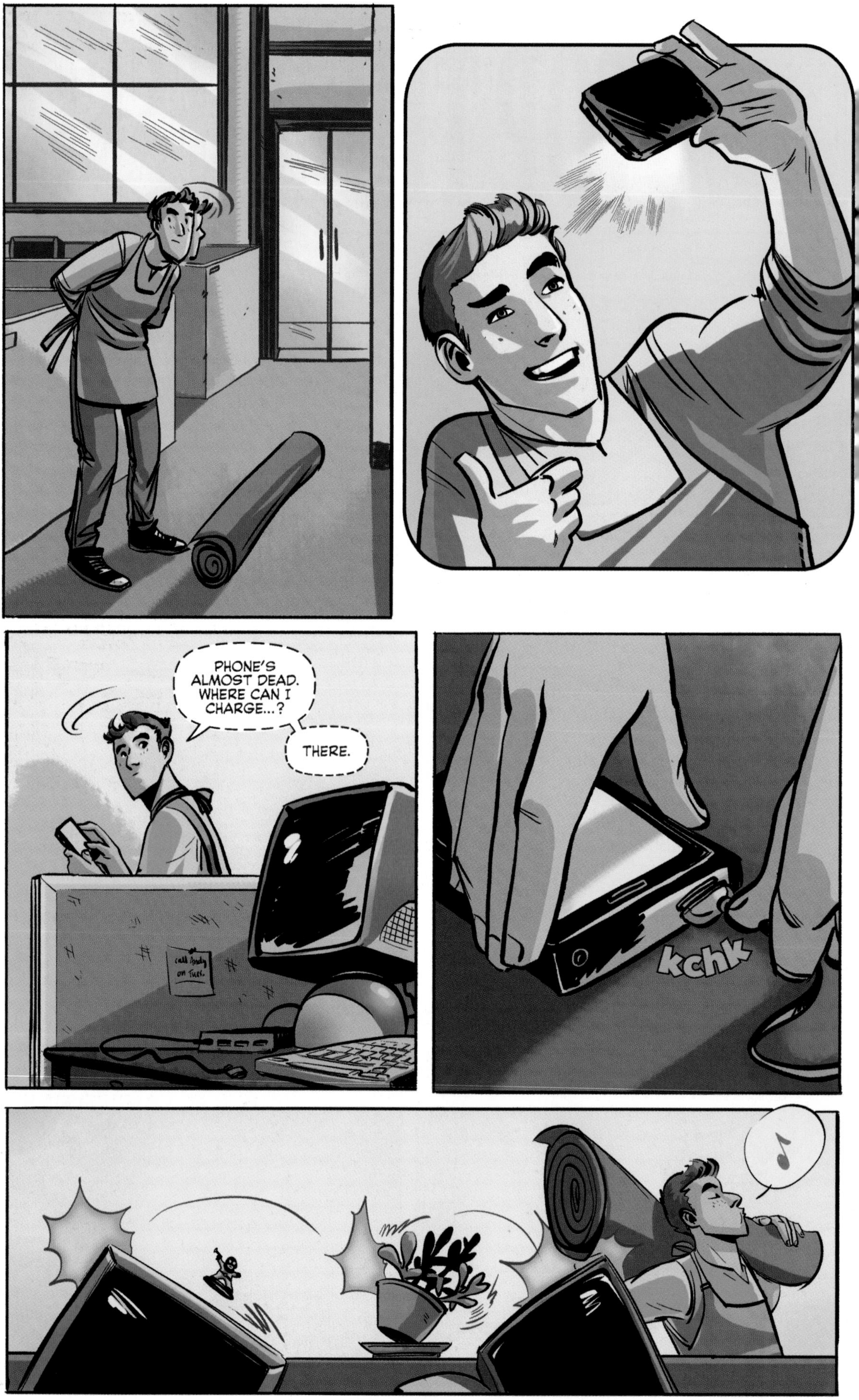
PHONE'S ALMOST DEAD. WHERE CAN I CHARGE...?
THERE.
call Andy on Tues.
kchk

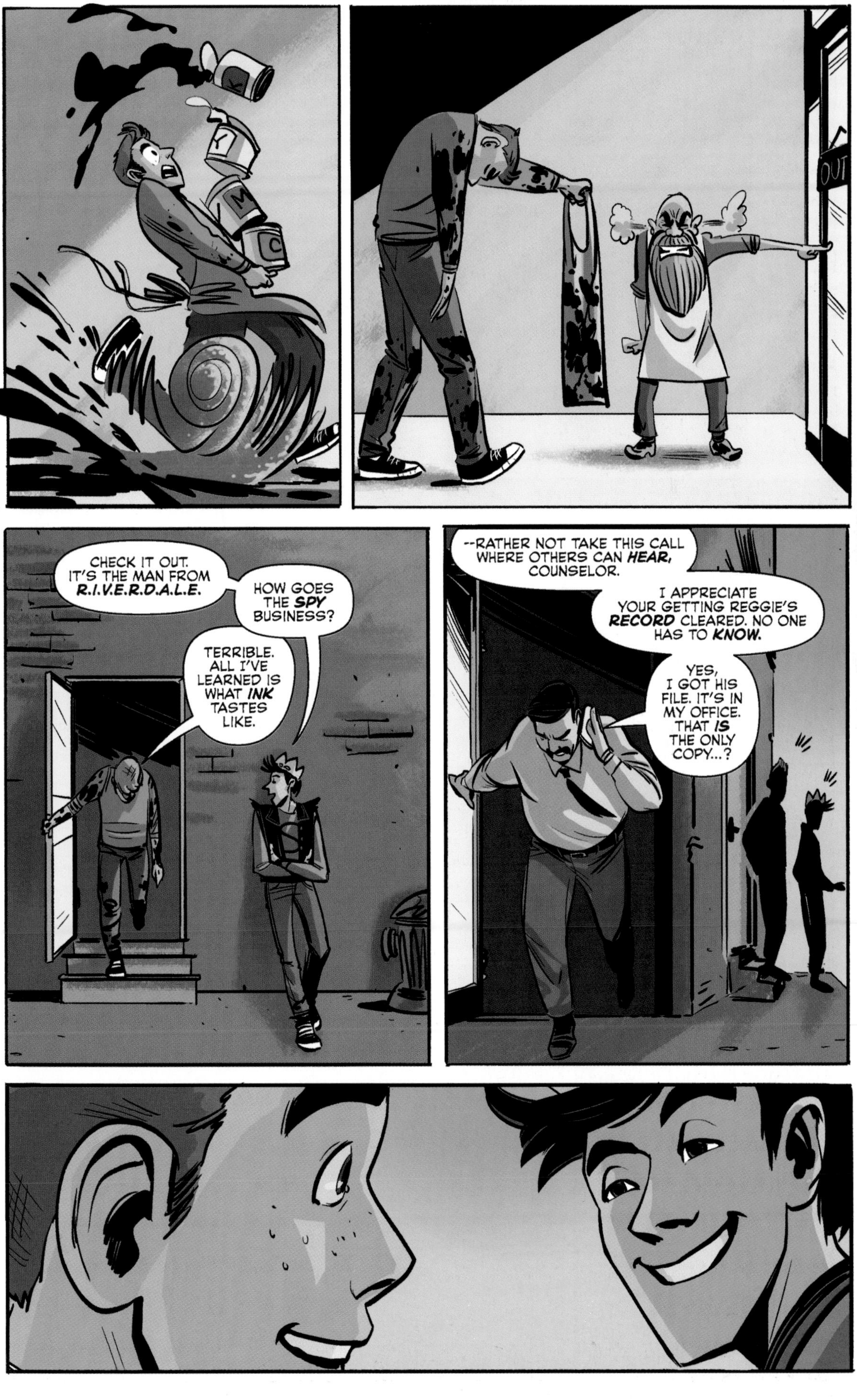
OUT
CHECK IT OUT. IT'S THE MAN FROM R.I.V.E.R.D.A.L.E.
HOW GOES THE SPY BUSINESS?
TERRIBLE. ALL I'VE LEARNED IS WHAT INK TASTES LIKE.
--RATHER NOT TAKE THIS CALL WHERE OTHERS CAN HEAR, COUNSELOR.
I APPRECIATE YOUR GETTING REGGIE'S RECORD CLEARED. NO ONE HAS TO KNOW.
YES, I GOT HIS FILE. IT'S IN MY OFFICE. THAT IS THE ONLY COPY...?

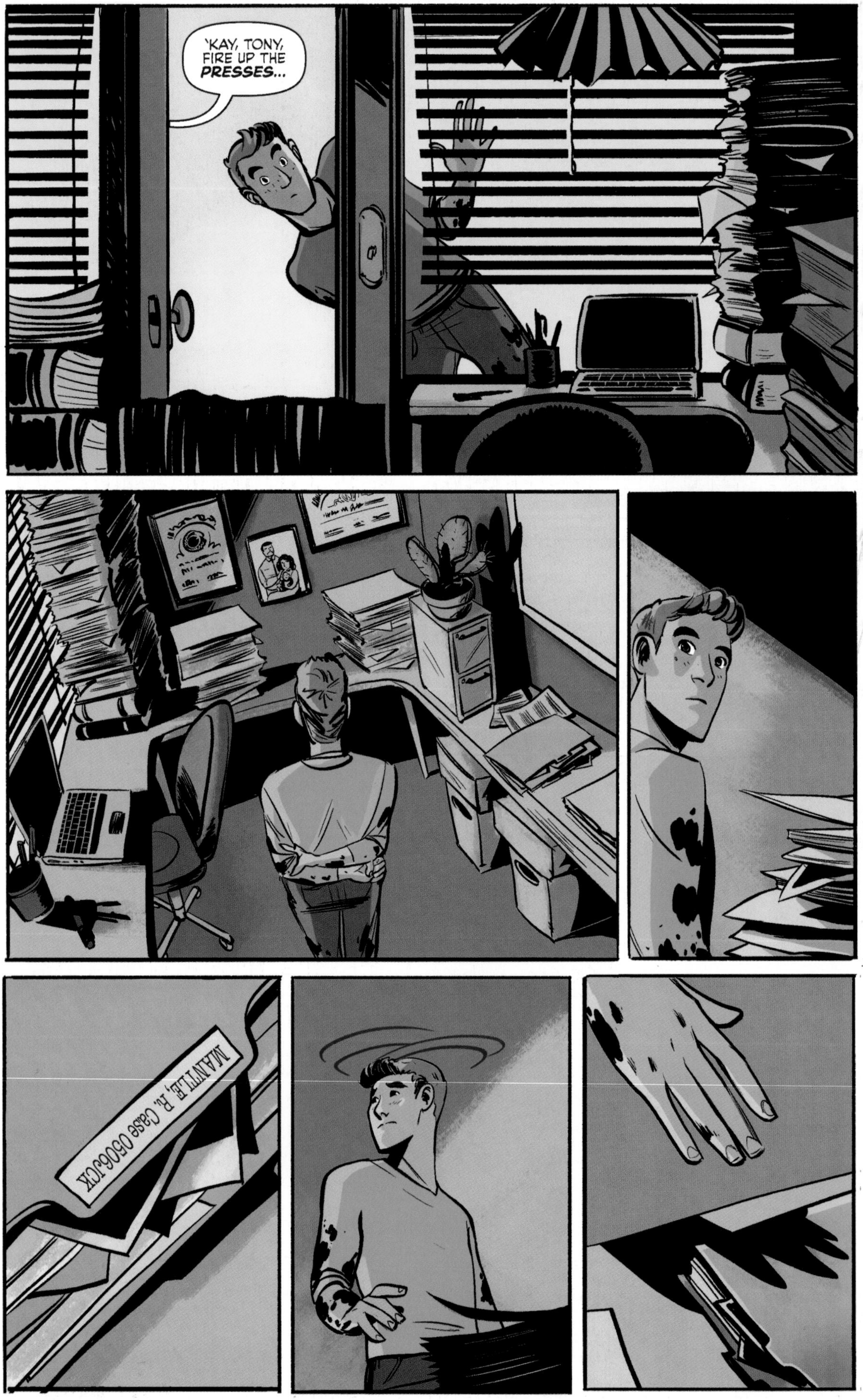

'KAY, TONY, FIRE UP THE *PRESSES*...
MANTLE, R. Case 0506JCK

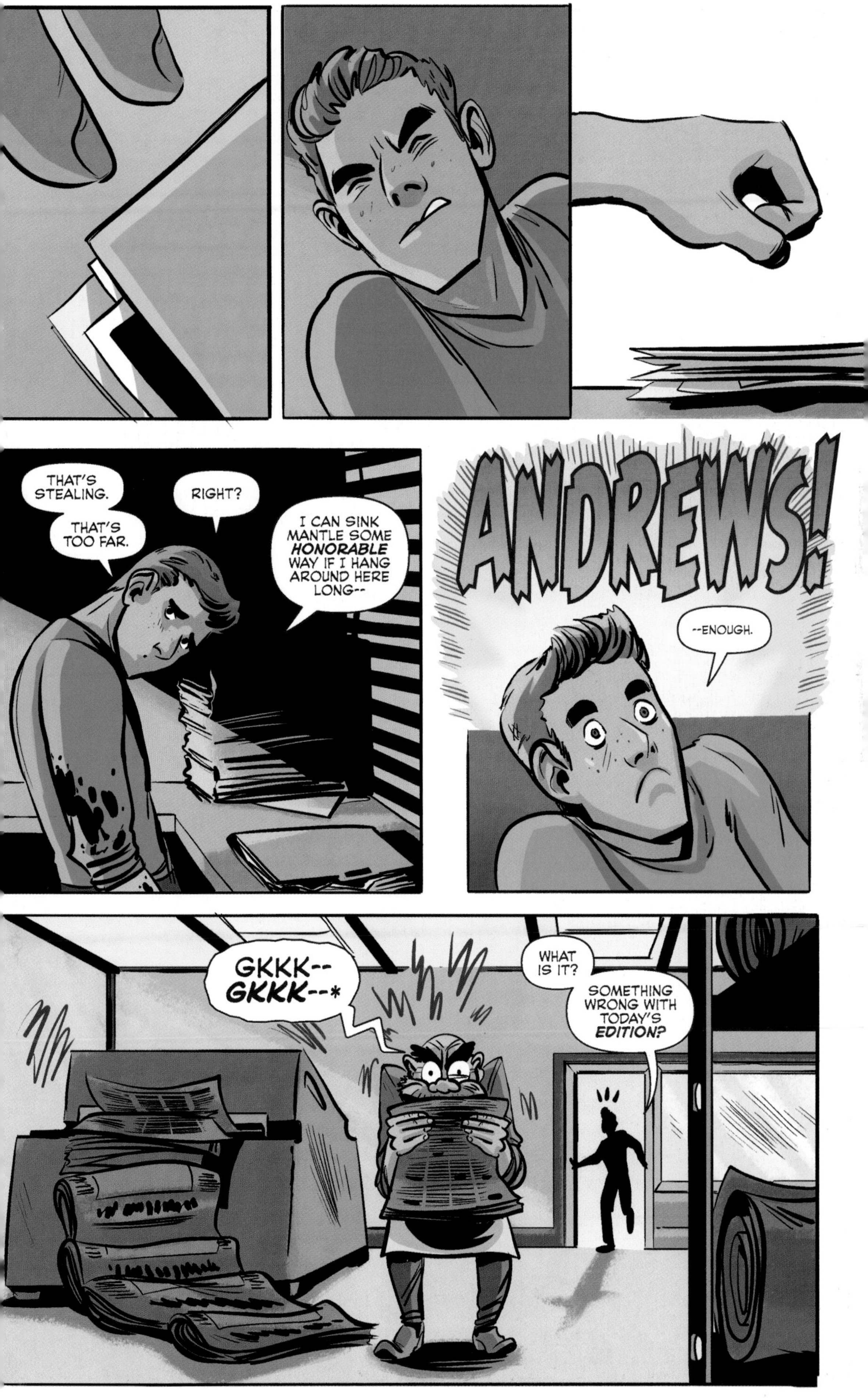
THAT'S STEALING.
RIGHT?
THAT'S TOO FAR.
I CAN SINK MANTLE SOME **HONORABLE** WAY IF I HANG AROUND HERE LONG--
ANDREWS!
--ENOUGH.
GKKK-- **GKKK--***
WHAT IS IT?
SOMETHING WRONG WITH TODAY'S **EDITION?**

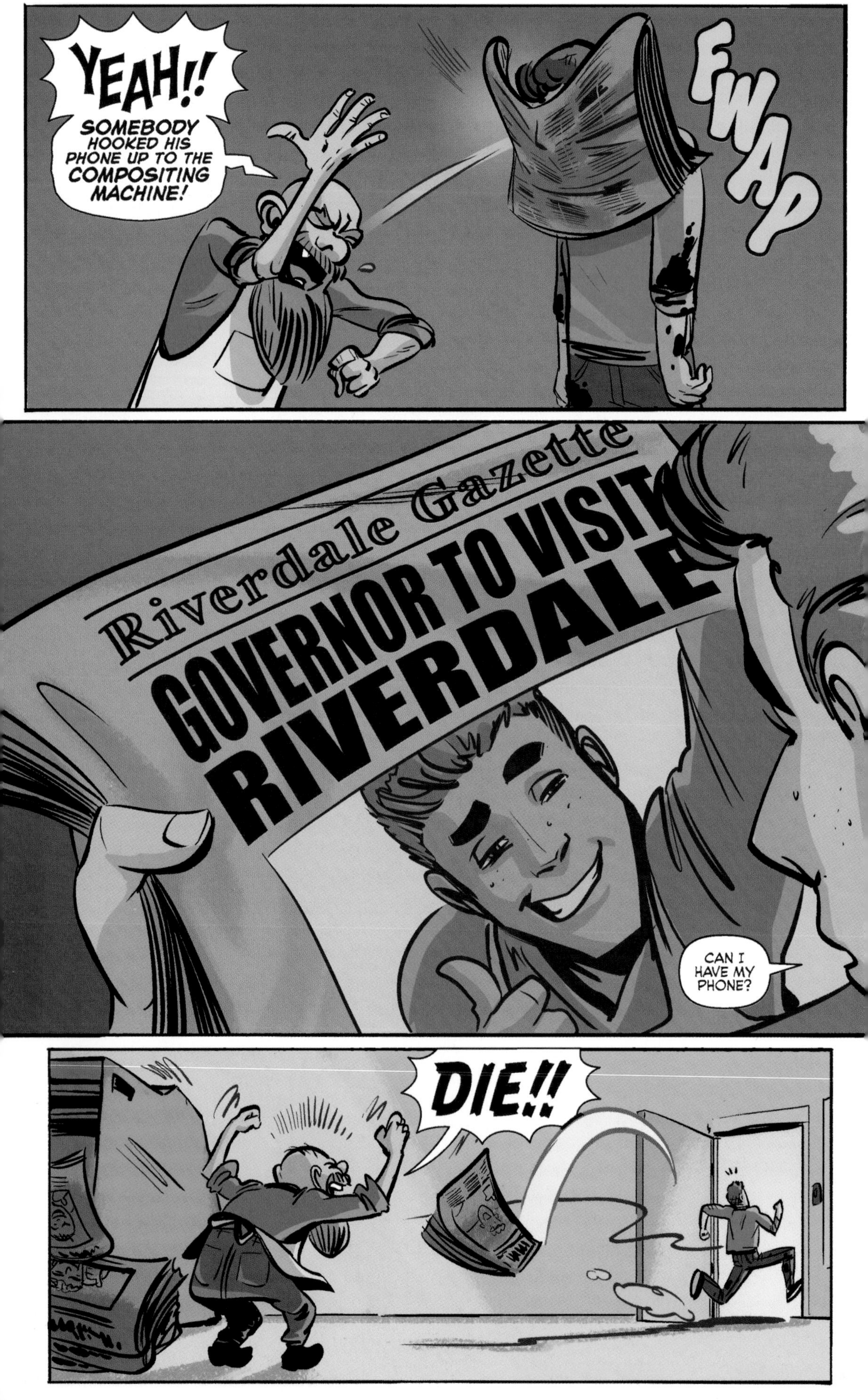
YEAH!!
SOMEBODY HOOKED HIS PHONE UP TO THE COMPOSITING MACHINE!
FWAP
Riverdale Gazette
GOVERNOR TO VISIT RIVERDALE
CAN I HAVE MY PHONE?
DIE!!

CHAPTER FOUR: Since When Do You Call Me "Richard"?

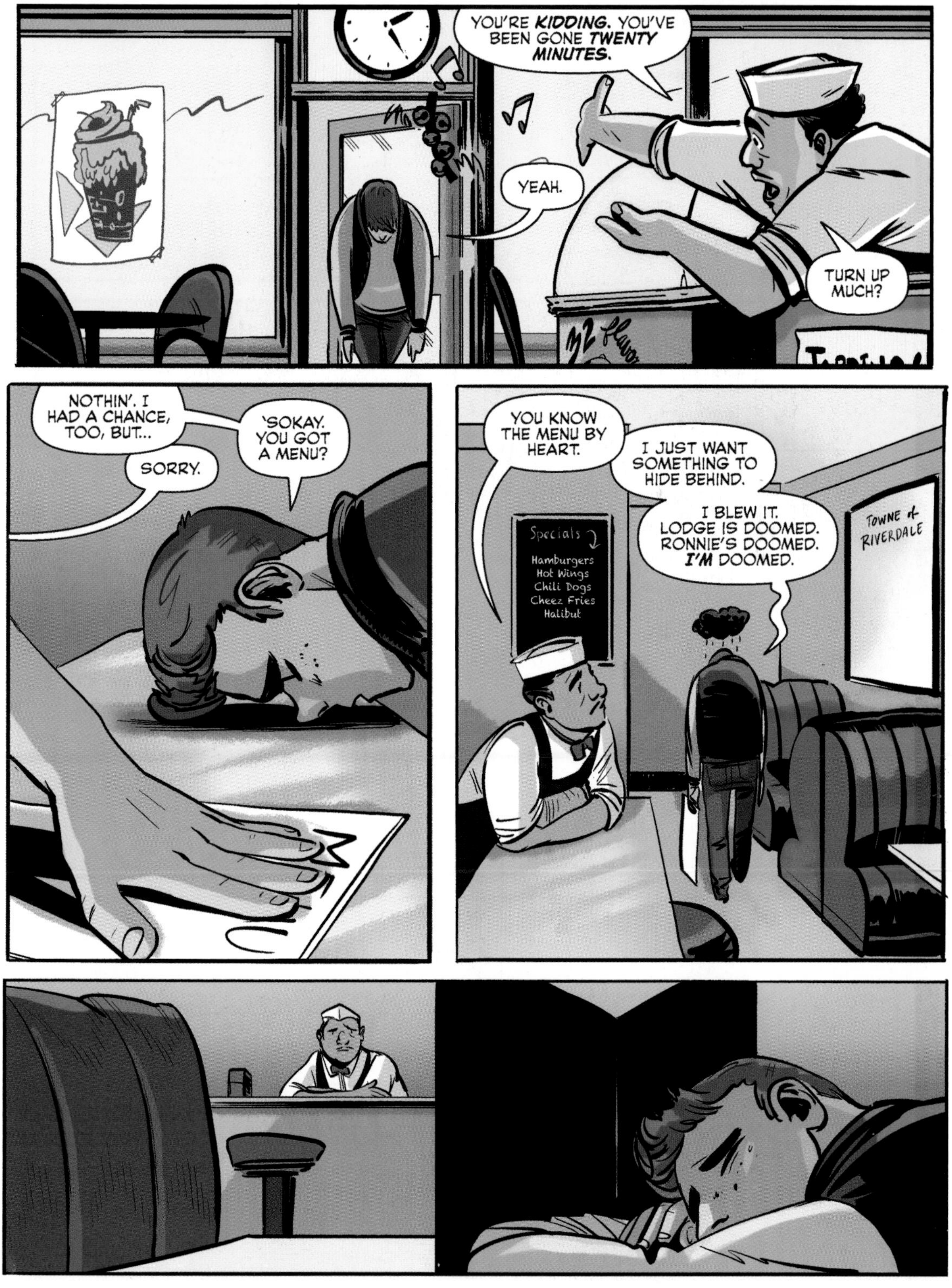
YOU'RE *KIDDING*. YOU'VE BEEN GONE *TWENTY MINUTES*.
YEAH.
TURN UP MUCH?
NOTHIN'. I HAD A CHANCE, TOO, BUT...
SORRY.
'SOKAY. YOU GOT A MENU?
YOU KNOW THE MENU BY HEART.
Specials
Hamburgers
Hot Wings
Chili Dogs
Cheez Fries
Halibut
I JUST WANT SOMETHING TO HIDE BEHIND.
I BLEW IT. LODGE IS DOOMED. RONNIE'S DOOMED. *I'M* DOOMED.
TOWNE of RIVERDALE

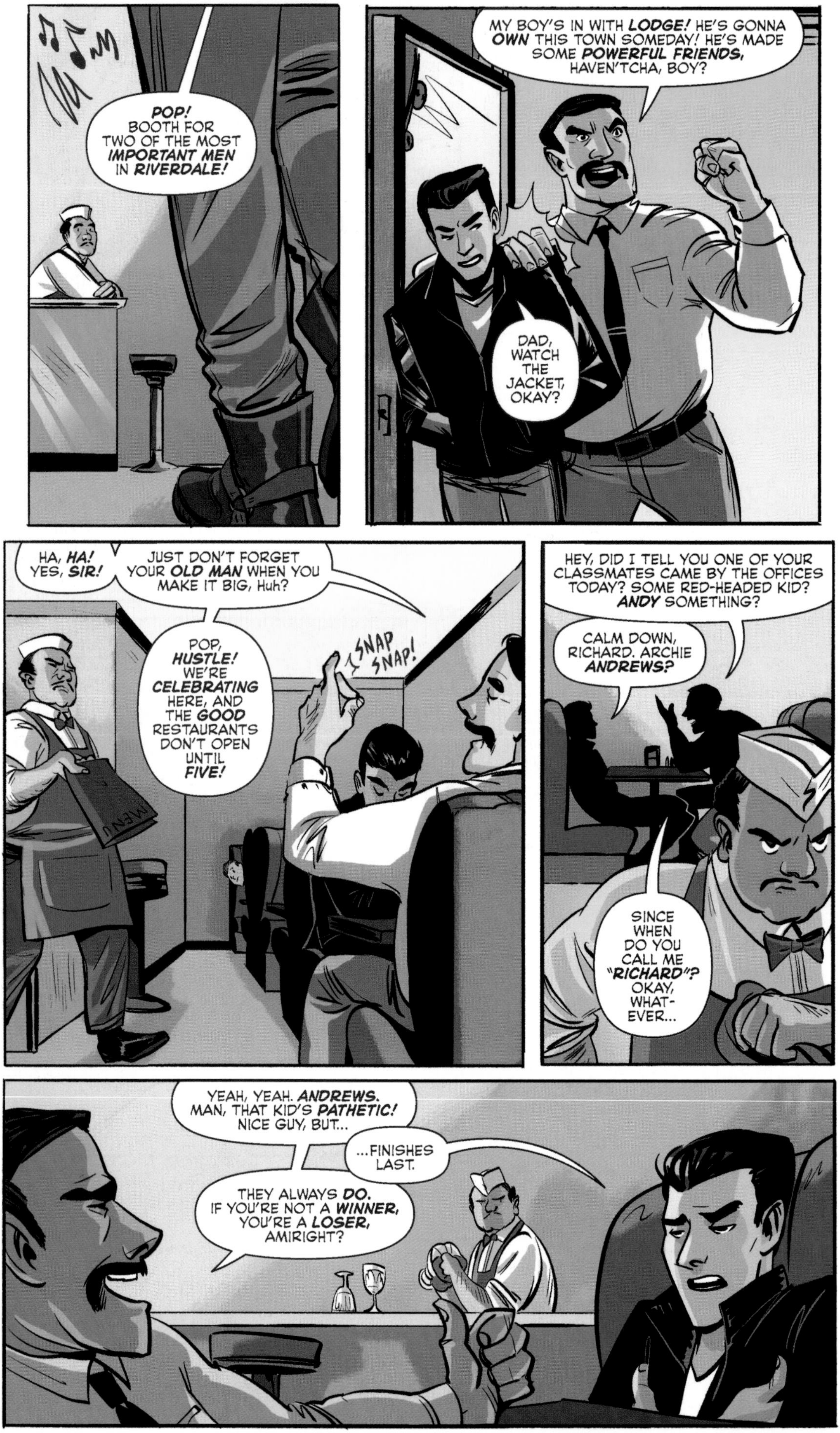

POP! BOOTH FOR TWO OF THE MOST IMPORTANT MEN IN RIVERDALE!
MY BOY'S IN WITH LODGE! HE'S GONNA OWN THIS TOWN SOMEDAY! HE'S MADE SOME POWERFUL FRIENDS, HAVEN'TCHA, BOY?
DAD, WATCH THE JACKET, OKAY?
HA, HA! YES, SIR!
JUST DON'T FORGET YOUR OLD MAN WHEN YOU MAKE IT BIG, Huh?
POP, HUSTLE! WE'RE CELEBRATING HERE, AND THE GOOD RESTAURANTS DON'T OPEN UNTIL FIVE!
SNAP SNAP!
MENU
HEY, DID I TELL YOU ONE OF YOUR CLASSMATES CAME BY THE OFFICES TODAY? SOME RED-HEADED KID? ANDY SOMETHING?
CALM DOWN, RICHARD. ARCHIE ANDREWS?
SINCE WHEN DO YOU CALL ME "RICHARD"? OKAY, WHAT-EVER...
YEAH, YEAH. ANDREWS. MAN, THAT KID'S PATHETIC! NICE GUY, BUT...
...FINISHES LAST.
THEY ALWAYS DO. IF YOU'RE NOT A WINNER, YOU'RE A LOSER, AMIRIGHT?

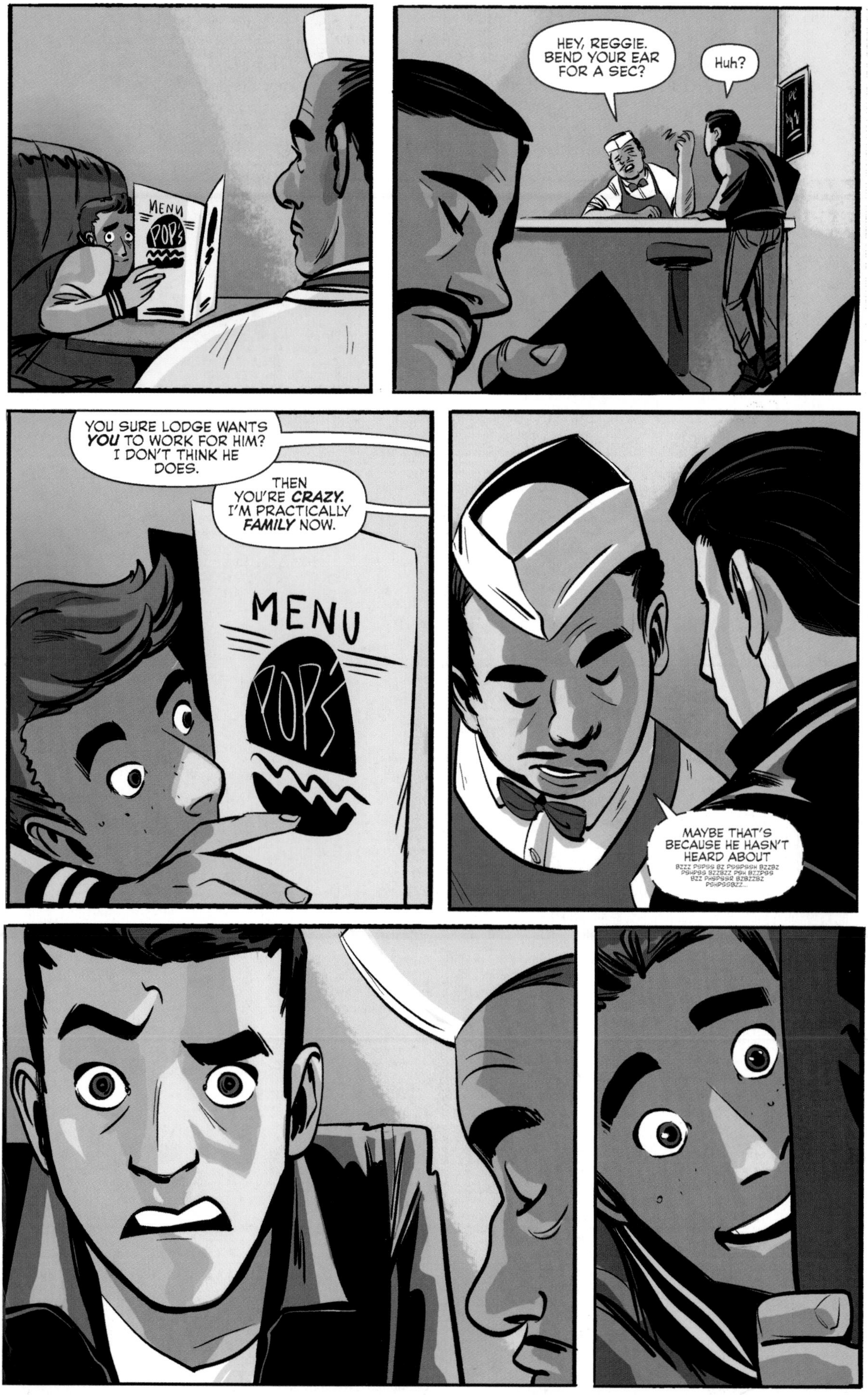
HEY, REGGIE. BEND YOUR EAR FOR A SEC?
Huh?
YOU SURE LODGE WANTS *YOU* TO WORK FOR HIM? I DON'T THINK HE DOES.
THEN YOU'RE *CRAZY.* I'M PRACTICALLY *FAMILY* NOW.
MENU POP'S
MAYBE THAT'S BECAUSE HE HASN'T HEARD ABOUT BZZZ PSPSS BZ PSSPSSH BZZBZ PSHPSS BZZBZZ PSH BZZPSS BZZ PHSPSSR BZBZZBZ PSHPSSBZZ...

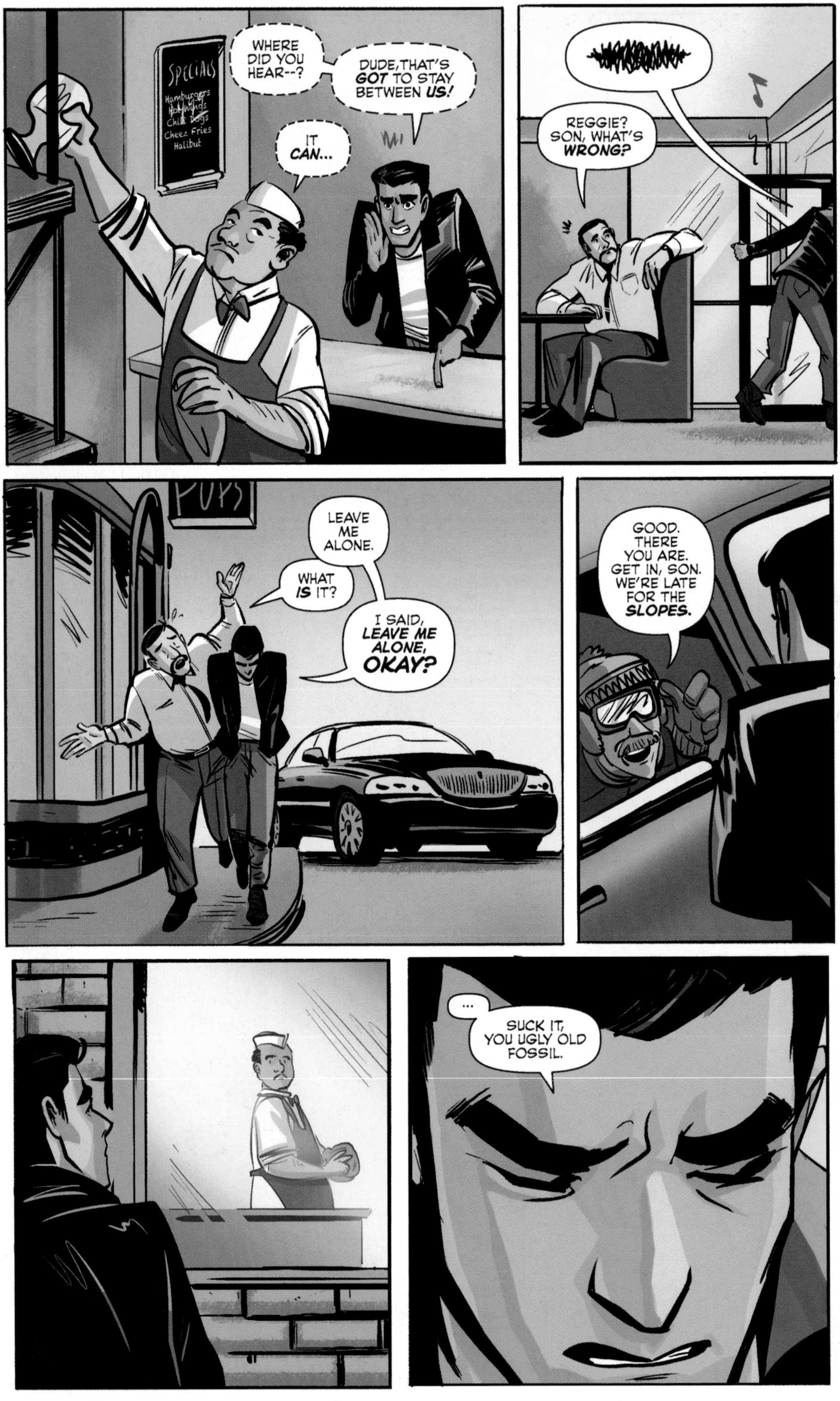
SPECIALS
Hamburgers
Hot Wings
Chili Dogs
Cheez Fries
Halibut
WHERE DID YOU HEAR--?
DUDE, THAT'S **GOT** TO STAY BETWEEN **US!**
IT **CAN...**
REGGIE? SON, WHAT'S **WRONG?**
POPS
LEAVE ME ALONE.
WHAT **IS** IT?
I SAID, **LEAVE ME ALONE, OKAY?**
GOOD. THERE YOU ARE. GET IN, SON. WE'RE LATE FOR THE **SLOPES.**
...
SUCK IT, YOU UGLY OLD FOSSIL.

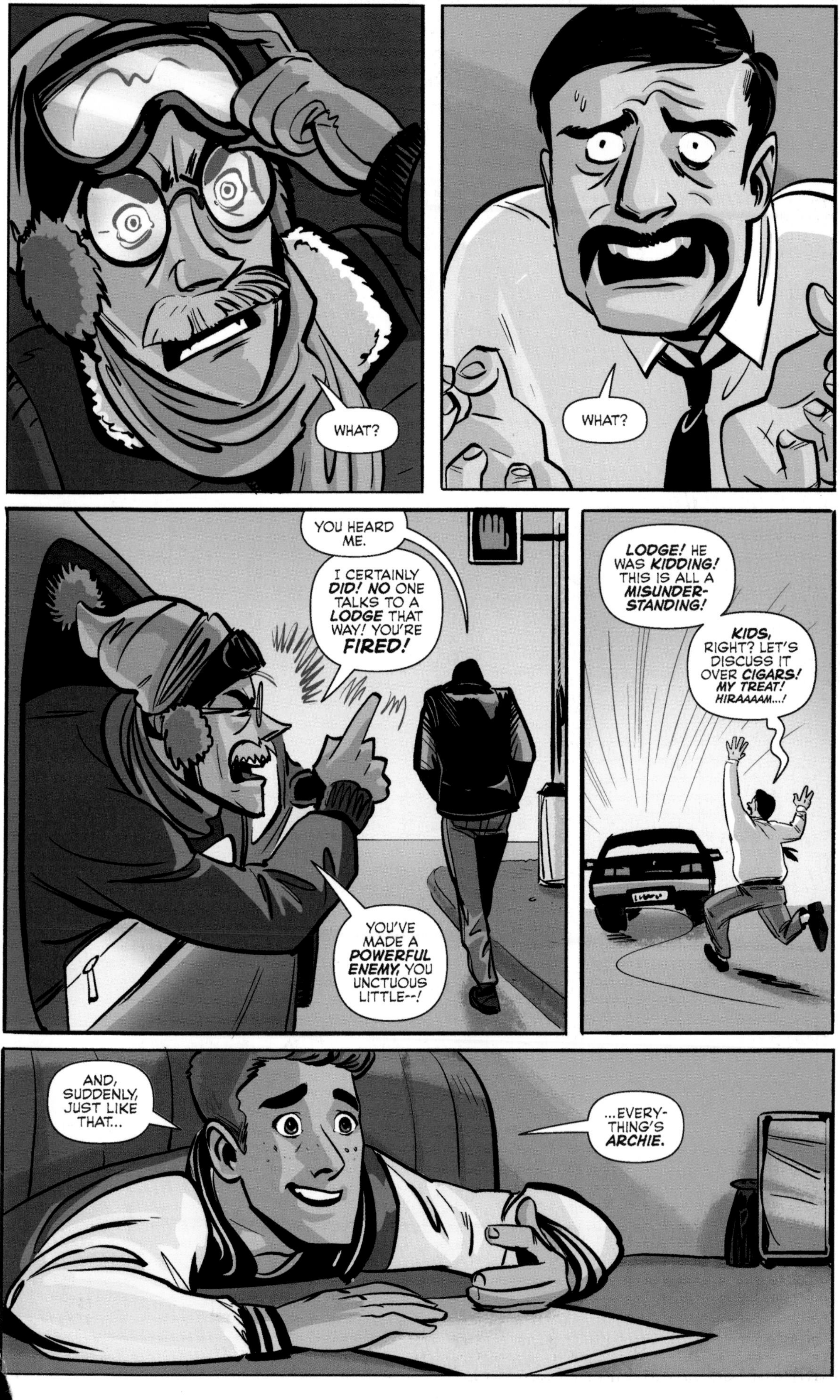
WHAT?
WHAT?
YOU HEARD ME.
I CERTAINLY DID! NO ONE TALKS TO A LODGE THAT WAY! YOU'RE FIRED!
YOU'VE MADE A POWERFUL ENEMY, YOU UNCTUOUS LITTLE--!
LODGE! HE WAS KIDDING! THIS IS ALL A MISUNDERSTANDING!
KIDS, RIGHT? LET'S DISCUSS IT OVER CIGARS! MY TREAT! HIRAAAAM...!
AND, SUDDENLY, JUST LIKE THAT...
...EVERYTHING'S ARCHIE.

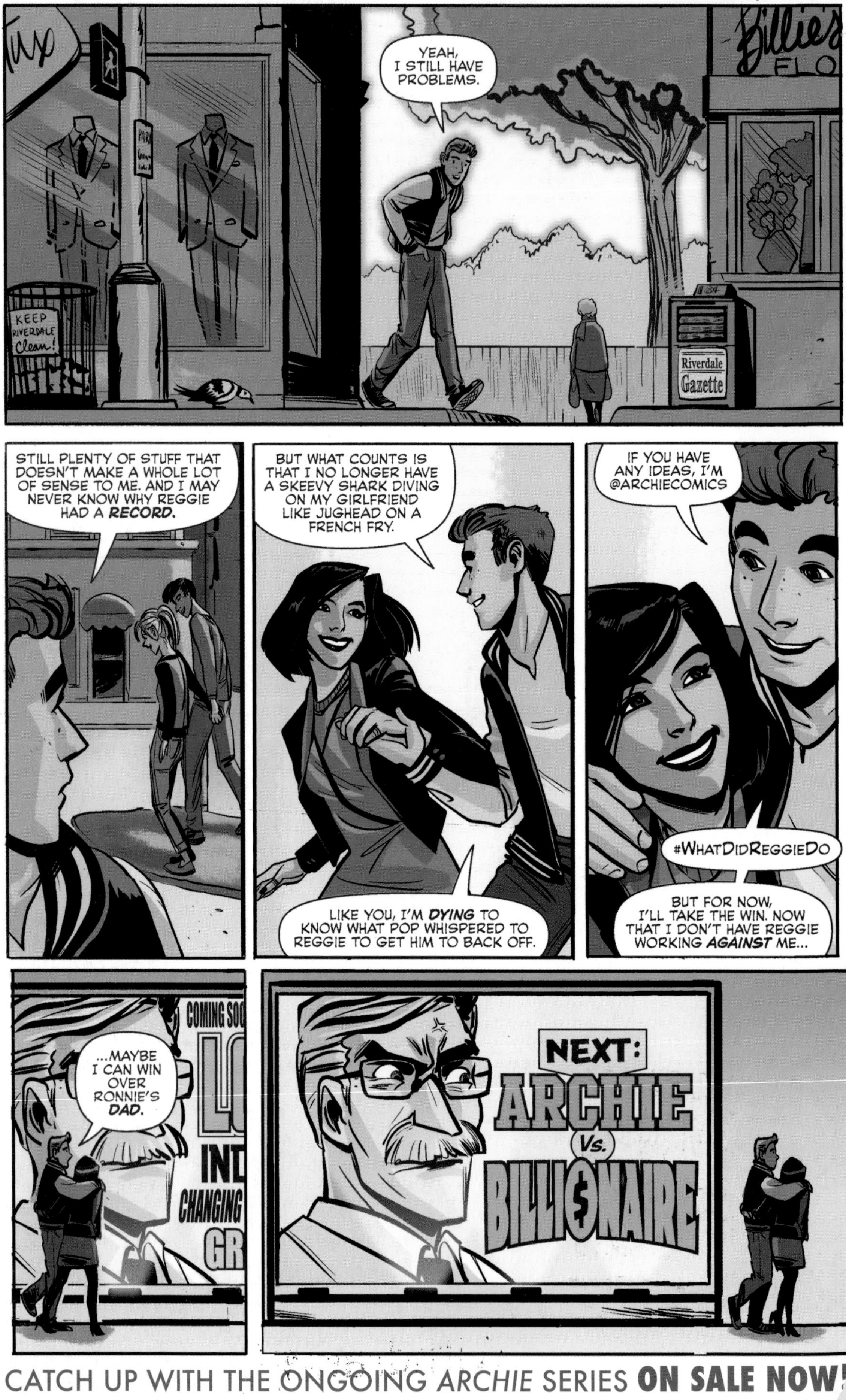
Tux
KEEP RIVERDALE Clean!
YEAH, I STILL HAVE PROBLEMS.
Riverdale Gazette
STILL PLENTY OF STUFF THAT DOESN'T MAKE A WHOLE LOT OF SENSE TO ME. AND I MAY NEVER KNOW WHY REGGIE HAD A RECORD.
BUT WHAT COUNTS IS THAT I NO LONGER HAVE A SKEEVY SHARK DIVING ON MY GIRLFRIEND LIKE JUGHEAD ON A FRENCH FRY.
LIKE YOU, I'M DYING TO KNOW WHAT POP WHISPERED TO REGGIE TO GET HIM TO BACK OFF.
IF YOU HAVE ANY IDEAS, I'M @ARCHIECOMICS
#WHATDIDREGGIEDO
BUT FOR NOW, I'LL TAKE THE WIN. NOW THAT I DON'T HAVE REGGIE WORKING AGAINST ME...
...MAYBE I CAN WIN OVER RONNIE'S DAD.
NEXT: ARCHIE Vs. BILLIONAIRE

CATCH UP WITH THE ONGOING *ARCHIE* SERIES **ON SALE NOW!**